Non-Aligned Movement Summits

New Approaches to International History

Series Editor: Thomas W. Zeiler, Professor of American Diplomatic History, University of Colorado, Boulder, USA

Series Editorial Board:
Anthony Adamthwaite, University of California at Berkeley (USA)
Kathleen Burk, University College London (UK)
Louis Clerc, University of Turku (Finland)
Petra Goedde, Temple University (USA)
Francine McKenzie, University of Western Ontario (Canada)
Lien-Hang Nguyen, University of Kentucky (USA)
Jason Parker, Texas A&M University (USA)
Glenda Sluga, University of Sydney (Australia)

New Approaches to International History covers international history during the modern period and across the globe. The series incorporates new developments in the field, such as the cultural turn and transnationalism, as well as the classical high politics of state-centric policymaking and diplomatic relations. Written with upper-level undergraduate and postgraduate students in mind, texts in the series provide an accessible overview of international diplomatic and transnational issues, events and actors.

Published:

Militarization and the American Century, David Fitzgerald (2022)
American-Iranian Dialogues, ed. Matthew K. Shannon (2021)
America's Road to Empire, Piero Gleijeses (2021)
Global War, Global Catastrophe, Maartje Abbenhuis and Ismee Tames (2021)
The International LGBT Rights Movement, Laura Belmonte (2021)
Globalizing the U.S. Presidency, ed. Cyrus Schayegh (2020)
Public Opinion and Twentieth-Century Diplomacy, Daniel Hucker (2020)
Canada and the World since 1867, Asa McKercher (2019)
Europe's Cold War Relations, eds Federico Romero, Kiran Klaus Patel and Ulrich Krotz (2019)
Scandinavia and the Great Powers in the First World War, Michael Jonas (2019)
The First Age of Industrial Globalization, Maartje Abbenhuis and Gordon Morrell (2019)
International Development, Corinna Unger (2018)
Women and Gender in International History, Karen Garner (2018)
The Environment and International History, Scott Kaufman (2018)
International Cooperation in the Early 20th Century, Daniel Gorman (2017)
Latin American Nationalism, James F. Siekmeier (2017)
The History of United States Cultural Diplomacy, Michael L. Krenn (2017)
The United Nations in International History, Amy Sayward (2017)
Decolonization and the Cold War, eds Leslie James and Elisabeth Leake (2015)
Cold War Summits, Chris Tudda (2015)

Forthcoming:

Reconstructing the Postwar World, Francine McKenzie
Activism Across Borders since 1870, Daniel Laqua
The Left and the International Arena, eds Mathieu Fulla and Michele Di Donato
American Sport in International History, Daniel DuBois
Climate Change and International History, Ruth Morgan
The Fear of Chinese Power, Jeffrey Crean
An International History of US Immigration, Benjamin Montoya
China and the United States since 1949, Elizabeth Ingleson
From World War to Cold War, Andrew N. Buchanan

Non-Aligned Movement Summits

A History

Jovan Čavoški

BLOOMSBURY ACADEMIC
LONDON • NEW YORK • OXFORD • NEW DELHI • SYDNEY

BLOOMSBURY ACADEMIC
Bloomsbury Publishing Plc
50 Bedford Square, London, WC1B 3DP, UK
1385 Broadway, New York, NY 10018, USA
29 Earlsfort Terrace, Dublin 2, Ireland

BLOOMSBURY, BLOOMSBURY ACADEMIC and the Diana logo are
trademarks of Bloomsbury Publishing Plc

First published in Great Britain 2022
This paperback edition published 2024

Copyright © Jovan Čavoški, 2022

Jovan Čavoški has asserted his right under the Copyright,
Designs and Patents Act, 1988, to be identified as Author of this work.

For legal purposes the Acknowledgements on pp. x–xi constitute an
extension of this copyright page.

Series design by Catherine Wood
Cover image: Belgrade First Conference of the 24 Non-Aligned Nations.
LE TELLIER Philippe/Getty

All rights reserved. No part of this publication may be reproduced or transmitted
in any form or by any means, electronic or mechanical, including photocopying,
recording, or any information storage or retrieval system, without prior
permission in writing from the publishers.

Bloomsbury Publishing Plc does not have any control over, or responsibility for,
any third-party websites referred to or in this book. All internet addresses given
in this book were correct at the time of going to press. The author and publisher
regret any inconvenience caused if addresses have changed or sites have ceased
to exist, but can accept no responsibility for any such changes.

A catalogue record for this book is available from the British Library.

Library of Congress Cataloging-in-Publication Data
Names: Čavoški, Jovan, 1981- author.
Title: Non-aligned movement summits : a history / Jovan Cavoški.
Description: First Edition. | New York : Bloomsbury Academic, 2022. |
Series: New Approaches to International History | Includes bibliographical references and
index. | Contents: Introduction –The Historical Meaning of Non-Alignment – Setting the
Stage: the 1961 Belgrade Conference – "Afro-Asianism" vs. Non-Alignment: The 1964
Cairo Conference–Taking a New Turn: The 1970 Lusaka Conference –Third World Strikes Back:
The 1973 Algiers Conference – Searching for a New Order: The 1976 Colombo Conference –
For the Soul of the NAM: The 1979 Havana Conference – Conclusion – Epilogue.
Identifiers: LCCN 2021054365 (print) | LCCN 2021054366 (ebook) | ISBN 9781350032095
(Hardback) | ISBN 9781350228061 (Paperback) | ISBN 9781350032118 (PDF) |
ISBN 9781350032101 (ePub)
Subjects: LCSH: Nonalignment–Congresses–History. | World politics–20th century.
Classification: LCC JZ1313.3 .C39 2022 (print) | LCC JZ1313.3 (ebook) |
DDC 327.09171/6–dc23/eng/20220124
LC record available at https://lccn.loc.gov/2021054365
LC ebook record available at https://lccn.loc.gov/2021054366

ISBN:	HB:	978-1-3500-3209-5
	PB:	978-1-3502-2806-1
	ePDF:	978-1-3500-3211-8
	eBook:	978-1-3500-3210-1

Series: New Approaches to International History

Typeset by Integra Software Services Pvt. Ltd.

To find out more about our authors and books visit www.bloomsbury.com
and sign up for our newsletters.

To my Mother and the memory of my Father

Contents

List of Figures	viii
Series Editor's Preface	ix
Acknowledgements	x
Introduction	1
1 The Historical Meaning of Non-Alignment	13
2 Setting the Stage: the 1961 Belgrade Conference	39
3 'Afro-Asianism' vs. Non-Alignment: the 1964 Cairo Conference	71
4 Taking a New Turn: the 1970 Lusaka Conference	99
5 The Third World Strikes Back: the 1973 Algiers Conference	129
6 Searching for a New Order: the 1976 Colombo Conference	159
7 For the Soul of the NAM: the 1979 Havana Conference	191
Epilogue: 'A House Divided Against Itself'	229
Conclusion	255
Bibliography	263
Index	279

Figures

1. Heads of delegations on the First Non-Aligned Movement Summit, Belgrade, 5 September 1961. © Museum of Yugoslavia — 58
2. Opening ceremony of the Second Summit of the Non-Aligned Movement, Cairo, 5 October 1964. © Museum of Yugoslavia — 87
3. Third Summit of the Non-Aligned Movement, Lusaka, 8 September 1970. © Museum of Yugoslavia — 119
4. Fourth Summit of the Non-Aligned Movement: closing plenary session, Algiers, 9 September 1973. © Museum of Yugoslavia — 148
5. Fifth Summit of the Non-Aligned Movement: President Tito's speech on plenary session, Colombo, 17 August 1976. © Museum of Yugoslavia — 182
6. Sixth Summit of the Non-Aligned Movement: President Tito's speech on general debate, Havana, 4 September 1979. © Museum of Yugoslavia — 219

Series Editor's Preface

New Approaches to International History takes the entire world as its stage for exploring the history of diplomacy, broadly conceived theoretically and thematically, and writ large across the span of the globe, during the modern period. This series goes beyond the single goal of explaining encounters in the world. Our aspiration is that these books provide both an introduction for researchers new to a topic, and supplemental and essential reading in classrooms. Thus, *New Approaches* serves a dual purpose that is unique from other large-scale treatments of international history; it applies to scholarly agendas and pedagogy. In addition, it does so against the backdrop of a century of enormous change, conflict and progress that informed global history but also continues to reflect on our own times.

The series offers the old and new diplomatic history to address a range of topics that shaped the twentieth century. Engaging in international history (including but not especially focusing on global or world history), these books will appeal to a range of scholars and teachers situated in the humanities and social sciences, including those in history, international relations, cultural studies, politics and economics. We have in mind scholars, both novice and veteran, who require an entrée into a topic, trend or technique that can benefit their own research or education into a new field of study by crossing boundaries in a variety of ways.

By its broad and inclusive coverage, *New Approaches to International History* is also unique because it makes accessible to students current research, methodology and themes. Incorporating cutting-edge scholarship that reflects trends in international history, as well as addressing the classical high politics of state-centric policymaking and diplomatic relations, these books are designed to bring alive the myriad of approaches for digestion by advanced undergraduates and graduate students. In preparation for the *New Approaches* series, Bloomsbury surveyed courses and faculties around the world to gauge interest and reveal core themes of relevance for their classroom use. The polling yielded a host of topics, from war and peace to the environment; from empire to economic integration; and from migration to nuclear arms. The effort proved that there is a much-needed place for studies that connect scholars and students alike to international history, and books that are especially relevant to the teaching missions of faculty around the world.

We hope readers find this series to be appealing, challenging and thought-provoking. Whether the history is viewed through older or newer lenses, *New Approaches to International History* allows students to peer into the modern period's complex relations among nations, people and events to draw their own conclusions about the tumultuous, interconnected past.

Thomas Zeiler, University of Colorado Boulder, USA

Acknowledgements

This book is the product of almost fifteen years of intensive studies and extensive archival research undertaken around the world, primarily dedicated to the history of the Cold War in the Third World and the history of global non-alignment. This long-term project, which has not ended with this publication, has taken me to four different continents, thus enabling me to meet along the way many renowned experts and other people who have become not only my collaborators in this academic endeavour but a strong source of friendly support for future personal and professional undertakings.

First of all, this book would not have been possible if my good friend Robert Rakove had not recommended my name to Bloomsbury Press as being the right person to write a new history of the NAM, and my heartfelt gratitude goes out to him. His selfless recommendation was immediately endorsed by Thomas Zeiler, editor of the *New Approaches to International History* book series, and I thank Tom for being so forbearing in providing me with this precious opportunity. However, it was my editor Maddie Holder who really pushed this project through, and I thank her for being an understanding, encouraging and patient collaborator in this protracted work. I also extend my sincere gratitude to the anonymous reviewers who offered their valuable and substantial advice which was accepted with an open mind. Naturally, I am solely responsible for the outlook and contents of this book, as well as for any of its mistakes.

I would also like to name some people who have been the prime 'culprits' for me becoming a historian of the Cold War and non-alignment. Many of them have also become my very good friends over the past twenty years or so, and their own ground-breaking research, as well as their utmost positive bearing towards me, stand at the very origins of my own studies. First of all, I would like to mention three names – Ljubodrag Dimić, Odd Arne Westad and Niu Jun – all of whom I consider as my professional fathers, helping me better comprehend the history of Yugoslavia, the Cold War, China, the Third World etc., and also opening many doors for me along the way, always offering their precious advice, as well as their dedicated support. I thank all three of them for being both at the beginning of my academic career and also seeing its recent scholarly results.

Besides these three scholars, I would also like to mention the name of Lorenz Lüthi who has not only become a close friend, like the men above, but also a source of intellectual inspiration and stimulus for good scholarship on non-alignment, with both of us influencing each other's studies on this topic over the past decade. He initially read this entire manuscript, and provided me with clear insight, continuous encouragement and critical advice that fundamentally shaped the way this book has finally turned out. Another great support in both my private and professional lives has been my best friend, Aleksandar Životić, who has been like a brother to me and also a close collaborator in all things relating to Yugoslavia and the Cold War.

Acknowledgements

I would also like to mention some of the names of other good friends and dear colleagues who have, in their own specific ways, influenced me, my studies in general and the book at hand. I am profoundly grateful to all of them: Roham Alvandi, Etee Bahadur, Madhu Bhalla, Mile Bjelajac, Dragan Bogetić, Gregg Brazinsky, Jeffrey James Byrne, Dai Chaowu, Chaw Chaw Sein, Kenton Clymer, Duško Dimitrijević, Jürgen Dinkel, Andrey Edemsky, Enrico Fardella, Frank Gerits, Piero Gleijeses, Amit Das Gupta, James Hershberg, Andreas Hilger, Darwis Khudori, Mark Kramer, Charles Kraus, Li Danhui, Ma Xipu, Surjit Mansingh, Louie Milojević, Srđan Mićić, Nataša Mišković, Swapna Kona Nayudu, Sue Onslow, Christian Ostermann, Radosav Pušić, Sergey Radchenko, Mira Radojević, Mahesh Rangarajan, Karthika Sasikumar, Bernd Schaefer, Shen Zhihua, Zvonimir Stopić and many others – thank you all for everything!

My gratitude also goes out to my very good friends who were great hosts during my extended stays in the US and India, demonstrating their utmost level of tolerance for me and my research – Judy and Joel Havemann (Joel will be sorely missed) and Jasjit Mansingh.

Different stages of this research have been supported by different institutions over the past fifteen years: the Ministry of Education, Science, and Technological Development of the Republic of Serbia which funded projects at my home institution – the Institute for Recent History of Serbia; the Scholarship Council of the PRC Government which funded my research in China, as well as my PhD studies at Peking University; the 'Dongfang lishi xuehui' foundation that funded some of my archival research in Myanmar, Russia and the US; the Indian Council for Cultural Relations fellowship that enabled me to become a visiting scholar at Delhi University; the Myanmar Ministry of Foreign Affairs and Ministry of Education that supported my stay as a visiting scholar at Yangon University; the most recent one from the Science Fund of the Republic of Serbia that funds a two-year project on the history of Yugoslavia's non-alignment, PROMIS (#6062589, YEH). I thank all these institutions for their support in making all this research possible.

I would also like to express my profound gratitude to the staff at the following institutions for extending their warm welcome to me or my collaborators: Archives of Yugoslavia, Diplomatic Archives of the Serbian Foreign Ministry, Chinese Foreign Ministry Archives, National Archives of India, Nehru Memorial Museum and Library, National Archives and Records Administration (College Park), The UK National Archives, Archives of the Russian Foreign Ministry, Russian State Archive for Contemporary History, State Archive of the Russian Federation, National Archives of Myanmar, Myanmar Ministry of Foreign Affairs Archives, Political Archives of the Office for Foreign Affairs of Germany, Woodrow Wilson Center, Peking University, East China Normal University, Delhi University, Yangon University, George Washington University, Russian Academy of Sciences, High Institute for International Relations (Havana), etc.

Finally, I dedicate this book to my mother Svetlana and the memory of my late father Dušan who left us prematurely more than a quarter of a century ago. By taking me unscathed through all challenges of life, continuously demonstrating her selfless sacrifice and parental love, my mother holds the sole responsibility in making me the man and historian I have become. I thank her for all that from the bottom of my heart. As for my late father, I know he would have been very proud of me and I hope that, in some way, he also cherishes with us this moment of joy.

Introduction

Non-Aligned Movement Summits follows the destiny of one of the major transcending historical phenomena of the Cold War, the Non-Aligned Movement (NAM), an international organization that envelopes most of the postcolonial and non-bloc world. It is the largest gathering of nations after the United Nations (UN), which still exists officially today (currently boasting 120 members), though with a significantly diminished global capacity and influence. However, it becomes readily apparent that this entire historical process ranging from the late 1950s to mid-1980s, covering the period of the NAM's origins, emergence, evolution and gradual decline, is primarily observed from the standpoint of its major summits and other relevant non-aligned meetings, key gatherings where crucial decisions pertaining to the fate of the movement itself and the future of the non-bloc world in general were discussed, shaped and made. It is true that the NAM was not the only organization aspiring to structurally encompass the entire so-called Third World or the Global South; many other organizational competitors also rose and fell during the same period, but the movement was and has remained, together with the Group 77 (G77), the only survivor of the tumultuous decades of the Cold War.[1] In essence, the NAM initially started as a byproduct of the East–West conflict throughout the 1960s and it had henceforth transformed itself into one of the chief protagonists of the North–South conflict during the heyday of the 1970s and the first half of the 1980s.

As was the case with the great powers, summits – a term coined by Winston Churchill in 1950 – became the chief expression of some of the dominant features in the relations between the major actors on both global and regional levels. These were events that represented the culmination of all previous efforts to reach certain conclusions and strike certain deals on a wider and longer-term scale, gather new information and size up opposition numbers; despite some of these events sometimes also producing dubious effects or experiencing contradictory results. These were also particularly solemn occasions where solutions for global problems were often sought, though not always achieved, while, occasionally, new ruptures in relations between these different agents of change were also rediscovered, as were new points of convergence for different protagonists.[2] In the recent historiography there is a rising trend to dedicate more attention to the substance and importance of summits, especially to those taking place between the great powers, and thus trying to re-evaluate them as turning points of international history, taking into consideration both their advantages and disadvantages, immediate and long-term impact.³ Conversely, *Non-Aligned Movement Summits* also tackles issues of the general history of the original non-aligned group and the subsequent NAM, while still elaborating on and analysing them through the framework of all these crucial gatherings, and thus primarily trying to reconstruct all corresponding processes, events and personalities that left a permanent imprint on them. However, this book does not offer a general history of the movement, particularly not an institutional history; nor is it a general history of the Third World during the Cold War, or ever aspires to become one. Its main purpose is to produce, ultimately, a highly revised factual history of the NAM's main events during the Cold War decades, something largely lacking in international historiography until today. In many ways, this book is inspired by Chris Tudda's book published in the same series, which, by using newly available archival sources, strives to reconstruct the context, relevance, meaning and consequences of some of the major summits occurring between the great powers during the Cold War years. This book also tries to follow the same logic with respect to the NAM.

Third World internationalism and multilateralism, also closely related to the aspirations of some countries outside Asia, Africa and Latin America, had a decisive impact on the shaping of the consciousness and self-awareness of all non-aligned nations in their continuous attempts to set off the fundamental restructuring of the political and economic world order, acting both through the NAM and other similar organizations characteristic of that period.⁴ In many ways, unlike the great power summits, in the NAM's case, summitry was the primary form through which its global presence and relevance were ultimately expressed; it was a focal point for all participants to make their relative weight in international affairs more accurately perceived and measured, a place where their opinions, demands and grievances could be heard worldwide, which then reverberated throughout the UN. It was these summits, as well as the NAM's active presence in New York, that ultimately made this organization an international force of solidarity and action to be seriously reckoned with. These specific political events largely occupied international headlines during those years, also capturing the attention of the major international players, and thus having a formative effect on the perception and understanding of the movement's position in world affairs.⁵ In fact, these summits can be divided into two distinctive clusters: 1) summits before the movement officially came into being – those that took place on an irregular, ad hoc basis, representing an amorphous group of different countries individually pursing non-bloc foreign policies; and 2) summits occurring when the NAM had already become a proper international institution marked by clearly defined and codified membership criteria, agenda, structure, procedure, responsibility, code of conduct, internal discipline, etc.

Non-Aligned Movement Summits is not just a factual history of particular non-aligned summits, since these were crucial but not singular events decisively steering the movement's history. In fact, these were gatherings which lasted only for a couple of days, where certain fundamental documents related to the movement's global role were finally adopted and then presented to the world. However, these summits were essentially just the tip of the iceberg – only the visible part of the major undercurrents that influenced the institutional outlook and strategic direction of the movement, while all major decisions passed at these central events had been previously scrupulously discussed and determined during the many official and unofficial interactions which took place in the background among many member states.[6] The main goal of *Non-Aligned Movement Summits* is generally to reconstruct and readdress the importance of all the events and processes leading up to these summits, since they were essentially the ones determining the character and outcome of the NAM's common strategy, and thus revealing the movement not as a sole byproduct of an era but as one of its more important protagonists. There were earlier attempts to deal with this topic in a similar way, but many relevant historical sources were not available to the authors at the time. The time has now come to offer a new study that will put the relevant events in the history of the NAM into a more detailed and tangible historical perspective, in particular discovering the many behind-the-scenes events largely shaping the movement's internal dynamics.[7]

Each of the NAM summits elaborated in this book were closely related to some of the major events and crises occurring between the two blocs, between the great powers and some non-aligned countries or between non-aligned countries themselves, which, conversely, provided opportunities to non-bloc actors, with varied success, to try to influence global events and steer international developments. This served to demonstrate to both superpowers that these nations were, nonetheless, independent, equal and respected participants in international affairs, active contributors to some of the major changes occurring during those years, irrespective of their actual size and strength.[8] As we have seen, the NAM summits were an obvious international platform for the non-bloc and developing world to symbolically state its claim and propose some of the corresponding global solutions for different outstanding issues. Therefore, *Non-Aligned Movement Summits* will concentrate on the first seven NAM summits, from Belgrade in 1961 until New Delhi in 1983, where all major decisions were taken and when the global influence of the group or movement was at its apex. Events leading up to the Belgrade summit – like the Bandung Conference, which ushered in an era of Third World summitry and anti-colonial sentiments on a wider scale, although it was one of its avatars rather than a direct precursor to the NAM, as well as the latter half of the 1980s when the NAM was undergoing a serious identity crisis – will also be briefly covered in this book.

In fact, this work is on the trail of new theoretical projections, providing diversification and hybridization of current studies, which gives much more credit to the non-bloc and Third World agents, gradually analysing the Cold War both from its centre, as well as from its so-called periphery, and challenging the customary paradigm present in the world historiography until the early 2000s that the history of this period was definitively and exclusively decided between the two superpowers and the two blocs standing by their side.[9] Non-bloc actors, as we will see here and in other related studies published in recent years, were as active and sometimes almost as influential as some of the major players of the post-1945 period. Nevertheless, this kind of influence and proactive capacity often depended on specific international circumstances, basic features of the Cold War system and diplomatic astuteness of these nations, rather than the real economic or military might they possessed. If we want to understand the rationale of non-aligned and Third World politics during the decades at stake, we need to observe that part of the world primarily from its own standpoint, from the angle of its own struggles, hopes, reservations, achievements and disappointments. Consequently, *Non-Aligned Movement Summits* tends to observe the Cold War from the viewpoint of major non-bloc and Third World actors – it is more about the impact the world outside the blocs had on the Cold War in general than just the effect superpower rivalry had on that region. This study also tries to walk in the footsteps of some recent magisterial studies, such as the ones written by Odd Arne Westad, Lorenz M. Lüthi, Vijay Prashad, Matthew Connelly, Robert Rakove, Jeffrey James Byrne, Guy Laron, Giuliano Garavini, Paul Chamberlin and others, thus completely altering our perceptions of the influence the Third World and specific countries representing it had on the evolution and transformation of the world order.[10] In many ways, Westad's book on the global Cold War, not only with its fresh and far-reaching concepts but also its extensive documentary base, served as the chief inspiration for my choice to study this topic. As a result, *Non-Aligned Movement Summits* also scrutinizes some of the policies and tangible responses to superpower projections primarily through the lens of the NAM's most important gatherings and the corresponding effect their substantial deliberations and immediate decisions had on the world at large.

When attempting to tackle the historiography of the NAM and the non-aligned world in general, it becomes apparent that many earlier studies relied mostly upon publicly available materials, declarations and resolutions from summits and similar gatherings and the speeches of its leaders, and thus regularly portrayed the history of the movement in bright, often superficial tones, as a relentless and undisturbed march towards global glory and unopposed relevance, without taking into consideration the ups and downs, twists and turns, and factional infighting that often characterized this movement as something with a much more complex history than had been previously believed. In fact, the lack of necessary documentary sources prevented many authors from seriously dissecting the internal history of global non-alignment and the movement itself, which led to a serious deficiency in many of the studies published during the 1960s, 1970s, 1980s and beyond.

Nevertheless, some studies published during the early years often concentrated on the origins and the initial phase of development of the non-aligned group, when the movement as a coherent organization was still in its infancy, and the presence of some of the great historical personalities of the non-bloc world, like Tito, Nehru, Nasser, Sukarno, Nkrumah, Bandaranaike, Haile Selassie and others, guaranteed a touch of glamour and relevance to some of the research dealing with either individual non-aligned countries or this group as a whole. Many of these studies were written by people who had exclusive access to either primary sources or historical witnesses from that epoch, which, in many ways, substituted for the lack of a more general declassification of archival materials at that time. Consequently, this, in many ways, largely makes them still relevant until the present day, with works by G. H. Jansen, Alvin Z. Rubinstein, David Kimche, W. Scott Thompson, B. R. Nanda and others corroborating such claims.[11]

However, the history of the NAM during the 1970s and 1980s, the apex of movement's international role and its global influence, was only partially covered by some less-recent studies published consecutively from the mid-1970s to the early 2000s. Problems with the availability of relevant archival sources was even more acute during this period, since there was almost no temporal distance between the analysed events and these authors, and none of them enjoyed the exclusive access to the decision-makers that the previous generation of authors had. Therefore, theoretical deliberations, associated with some widely known events in the NAM's history, largely dominated the academic discourse during those years. Nevertheless, without these specific studies it would have been quite impossible to have the bulk of the international literature on non-alignment which still possesses a certain degree of academic relevance today. Studies written by authors such as Bojana Tadić, Ranko Petković, Peter Willetts, Richard L. Jackson, M. S. Rajan, A. W. Singham, K. P. Mishra, S. B. Jain, Renu Srivastava, Roy Allison, Momir Stojković and others stand as clear testament to that.[12] Furthermore, the tangible contribution of the older scholarship on non-alignment, especially in its initial period, was the plethora of quite innovative and profound theoretical studies dealing with the essential character and practice of this foreign policy doctrine, thus setting the contemplative foundations of all subsequent deliberations. This literature has become somewhat mandatory for any new research on non-alignment. Theoretical books written by authors such as Leo Mates, Cecil V. Crabb, Peter Lyon, Lawrence W. Martin, Ranko Petković and others remain classics in this respect.[13]

Over the past fifteen years, or even more in some cases, studies of global non-alignment and the NAM, as well as the Cold War in the Third World in general, have been on the rise, becoming one of the hot topics of international scholarship.[14] Different aspects of the history of non-alignment have been interpreted on a number of different levels, especially through specific case studies, which some of the recently published volumes, edited by authors like Sandra Bott, Lorenz M. Lüthi, Nataša Mišković and their colleagues, clearly demonstrate, thus producing a substantial impact on the expansion and diversification of the recent studies on global non-alignment.[15] Nevertheless, the majority of these recent individual works, becoming increasingly based on new archival research around the world, have been either dedicated to the analysis of respective policies of non-aligned countries or their specific relationships with the great powers, with countries like India, Yugoslavia, Indonesia, Ghana, Cambodia, Algeria or Cuba figuring prominently. In addition to some of the works previously mentioned – those standing at the origins of this new academic turn towards Third World research from its own perspective – there are other important authors standing shoulder to shoulder with them, such as H. W. Brands, Srinath Raghavan, Robert McMahon, Piero Gleijeses, David Engerman, Ragna Boden, Bradley Simpson, Sue Onslow, Rami Ginat, Sergey Mazov, Andreas Hilger, Amit Das Gupta, Salim Yaqub, Jesse Ferris, Ryan Irwin, Mohammed Lakhdar Ghettas, Robert Niebuhr, Dragan Bogetić, Ljubodrag Dimić, Rinna Kullaa, Tvrtko Jakovina, Svetozar Rajak, Aleksandar Životić, Jovan Čavoški and many others, whose works will be referred to throughout this book.[16]

Among the very recent studies on the NAM in general, which in certain parts have influenced the way in which *Non-Aligned Movement Summits* is structured and generally engages with some of the relevant issues, the work of Jürgen Dinkel should be emphasized, whose superb institutional history of the movement, also using some of the internationally declassified archival sources, acts as true supplement to this book's elaboration, making these two studies quite complementary. Dinkel's book largely concentrates on the overarching major topics permeating the NAM's internal functioning and external activity, especially during the 1970s and 1980s, without delving too far into the minute history of concrete events, other than the Bandung and Belgrade Conferences in a more general way; unlike the present study which makes these concrete events the main subject of its analysis, thus providing more flesh on the bones laid down by some of these earlier studies.[17]

In addition, Lüthi's recent studies on non-alignment and 'Afro-Asian Internationalism', which proved to be quite ground-breaking in this respect, especially due to their diverse archival research, are intellectually very close to the line of thinking pursued by this book, primarily since both works were highly influenced by intensive intellectual exchanges and frequent deliberations between their authors.[18] Vijay Prashad's book dealing with different Third World conferences as an analysis unit also served structurally as an inspiration for this study, but, somewhat similar to Dinkel's approach, although less dedicated to the institutional history of the NAM, still focuses on some of the more generalized issues, primarily scrutinizing them through literature rather than archival documents, through the social and cultural lenses of the postcolonial world and its humanitarian position in the international system.[19]

Another relevant book recently published in Serbia by Dragan Bogetić, one of country's pioneers in the historical studies of Yugoslavia's non-alignment, also uses summits and different events in the history of non-alignment as a central topic, but it tends to observe them primarily through an individual Yugoslav perspective, using only a fraction of the sources available in the Serbian archives, predominantly older literature, and no foreign archival sources, and without expanding its analysis beyond 1979. Nonetheless, some of its engagement with the overall issues proves to be quite important for any serious studies of non-alignment and it has its fair share of influence on *Non-Aligned Movement Summits*.[20] Furthermore, a recently published international volume dedicated to the sixty years of the NAM, edited by Duško Dimitrijević and the author of this book, also contributed to a fresh and multidimensional approach to recent non-aligned studies, with a chapter written by this author also serving as a general survey of the NAM's evolution during the Cold War years.[21] Nevertheless, all these key studies significantly fill in the scholarly gap we have been experiencing for quite some time, with the present book joining these commendable efforts with a clear intention to define main trends in the evolution of the NAM, while providing us with many lesser known details about the movement's inner functioning.

Non-Aligned Movement Summits, besides relying upon the above-mentioned relevant international literature, is primarily based on a plethora of newly declassified documents from a number of international archives. The bulk of archival materials utilized here come from the Serbian archives, where documents of the former Yugoslav state and communist party are preserved, since Yugoslavia was not only one of the pioneers of global non-alignment, a country with the decisive role in establishing the NAM, but one also enjoying extraordinary influence and prestige among other non-aligned countries. It was also a country with the most widespread diplomatic network covering the entire non-aligned world, while also being privy to the most intimate details of the inner functioning of this group, each and every time being present at the very core of any relevant decision-making process. Some of the Yugoslav archival materials, especially from the Foreign Ministry Archives which are used heavily here, uncovers many unknown facts and hidden details pertaining to many topics, thus reflecting the complex character of the internal history of the NAM. In addition, Indian archival documents, from a country considered as the cradle of non-alignment and one of only few leading non-aligned nations, are also used extensively throughout this book, together with some Myanmar archival sources on the history of non-alignment and the NAM. These lesser-known materials from the non-aligned world are complemented by a diverse collection of newly declassified documents from the archives of the great powers, namely the US, Britain, China, Russia and Germany, which cover many different events and aspects related to the history of non-alignment during the Cold War years.

Alongside this formal introduction and conclusion, *Non-Aligned Movement Summits* is structured through seven specialized chapters, plus an epilogue. The first chapter is a theoretical elaboration of the historical meaning of global non-alignment and some notions closely related to it, such as what constituted its essence, goals, aspirations and motivations during those decades, what were the major factors decisively shaping its emergence and subsequent evolution, who were its main historical protagonists, what were their inclinations to adopting such a strategy and what kind of intentions they aspired to fulfil in this way. Each of the following seven chapters are dedicated to a specific summit, both those before and after the official establishment of the movement in 1970, with a large part concentrating on explaining tangible historical context and different events leading up to these major gatherings, scrutinizing processes shaping its discourse and main topics and elucidating many of the unknown facts pertaining to the internal dynamics of the non-aligned group and the NAM.

The second chapter concentrates on the 1961 Belgrade Conference, which was the founding place of the non-aligned group and the point of origin for the NAM, even though formally the movement came into being nine years later. This was the time when tensions between the two superpowers were on the rise in places such as Berlin, Cuba, Congo, Laos etc., and the non-bloc states were becoming increasingly worried that this uncontrollable spiral of violence could ultimately escalate into a full-scale nuclear conflict between the two blocs. Therefore, acting upon Yugoslavia's initiative, backed by some other key non-aligned states, such as India, Egypt, Indonesia and Ghana, these nations decided to take part in the conference, each attempting to influence the deteriorating global situation, while also trying to provide their own remedies to different international issues.

The third chapter deals with the 1964 Cairo Conference, a gathering that was motivated more by an internal power struggle within the Third World than by any international events occurring within the relationship between the two blocs at that time. This was a moment when the developing world was being increasingly divided between the two camps of nations, which were, in their own way, following their own path regarding the basic role of all non-bloc actors in world politics. One camp, led by Yugoslavia, India and Egypt, was opting for a more 'universalist' non-aligned foreign policy that was dedicated to a nuanced approach to the superpowers, largely emphasizing balanced foreign policy and socioeconomic development as their priorities. The other camp, represented by Indonesia, Ghana and other radicals leaning towards China, sought a more regionalist Afro-Asian policy, largely inspired by the Bandung spirit, firmly dedicated to the anti-imperialist, anti-colonialist and anti-revisionist struggle with both superpowers and other Third World competitors.

The fourth chapter deals with the issue of how the non-aligned group came out of a severe political crisis that plagued them for five years after the Cairo Conference, when no new major conferences were held and when some of the leading non-aligned nations, like Egypt, underwent profound political crisis, with many other non-aligned leaders also being swept away from the historical scene. Since the superpowers were gradually entering into a phase of détente, countries like Yugoslavia, as well as some other non-bloc nations, were becoming increasingly interested in creating a more durable and viable alternative to bloc divisions, utilizing this new wave of lessening tensions, and thus adapting their approaches to these new tendencies in world politics. This was the time when the movement was formally established as an international organization, together with many of its official bodies, at the 1970 Lusaka Conference, while a tentative decision was also made to hold regular summits every three years, thus confirming again the key principle of the NAM continuity.

The fifth chapter explores how the NAM had become an effective tool of Third World politics through different Algerian initiatives, when all the basic instruments of the movement's functioning and influence-making had been set down, thus ending this process of institutionalization at the 1973 Algiers Conference. This was a time when issues pertaining to the economic position and role of the non-aligned and developing world were being intensively discussed, shaping new ideas for introducing major changes into the international system. This was also the period when some of the radicals were gaining the upper hand inside the NAM, especially among the Arabs, thus trying to steer the general debate towards issues of critical importance for them, particularly on the eve of the new major Arab–Israeli war. This summit was a watershed moment when the collective action of the non-aligned world was already yielding its first effects.

The sixth chapter deals with the new global role the NAM was striving to determine under the conditions of international détente, one that would induce a fundamental restructuring of the world order, especially its economic part, when issues of the socioeconomic stability of the developing world, then facing an organized response of the developed one, were coming to the forefront of international politics. The 1976 Colombo Conference was an obvious attempt staged by the NAM to steer itself away from the limitations still imposed by bloc politics and reinvent its position as a political engine of Third World economic development. This was when the concept of the 'New International Economic Order' (NIEO) was launched into the wider world, setting new demands and criteria for the economic progress of the developing world, especially within the UN mechanism.

The seventh chapter tackles a new round of struggles between the radicals and moderates that was actively taking place inside the NAM. The fall of détente and the success of pro-Soviet revolutions and national-liberation struggles in Asia, Africa and Central America marked the moment when some of the leading NAM members, such as Cuba and Vietnam, attempted to transform this organization into the reserve force of the socialist camp, and thus openly aligning the movement with the USSR. On the other side, there was Yugoslavia, backed by India, Sri Lanka and some other countries, that was strictly against such aspirations, actively advocating a more nuanced and balanced policy towards both superpowers. Alignment with any of the two blocs could have implied an outright dissolution of the NAM, so the 1979 Havana Conference was largely marked by this titanic political struggle between the Cuban and Yugoslav lines to determine the political fate of the movement.

The Epilogue covers the period until the mid-1980s when the NAM entered a time of crisis from which it would never recover until the end of the Cold War. The Soviet invasion of Afghanistan, the Iran–Iraq War and the crisis in Central America and Southern Africa reignited tensions between the superpowers, along with the concurrent expanding divisions between the leading member states of the NAM. All these factors influenced the scope of the global effectiveness of the movement, and thus gradually reduced its international impact. Apart from the 1983 New Delhi Conference, elaborated on here in more detail, none of the other NAM gatherings during that decade produced a major effect on world politics, especially when an era of high-level talks and accommodations between the US and Soviet leaders finally took place after 1985. Political divisions previously triggered in Havana had left the NAM largely unable to cope effectively with the sudden end of the Cold War, thus marking its essential demise from the world stage.

In the conclusion to this book, the results of this entire research are summed up, providing us with some answers regarding the role and place of the NAM during the Cold War era, why it was relevant at one time and facing obvious decline during another, what was its tangible contribution to the emergence of Third World's collective political identity and what kind of influence it still portends to have in the world today.

Notes

1 Jacqueline Anne Braveboy-Wagner, *Institutions of the Global South* (London: Routledge, 2009), 13–54.
2 David H. Dunn (ed.), *Diplomacy at the Highest Level: The Evolution of International Summitry* (London: Macmillan Press, 1996), 3–22, 247–68.
3 David Reynolds, *Summits: Six Meetings that Shaped the Twentieth Century* (New York, NY: Basic Books, 2007); Chris Tudda, *Cold War Summits* (London: Bloomsbury Press, 2015); Kristina Spohr and David Reynolds (eds), *Transcending the Cold War: Summits, Statecraft, and the Dissolution of Bipolarity in Europe 1970–1990* (Oxford: Oxford University Press, 2016).
4 Chris Alden, Sally Morphet and Marco Antonio Vieira, *The South in World Politics* (London: Palgrave Macmillan, 2010), 57–90.
5 K. C. Chaudhary, *Non-Aligned Summitry* (New Delhi: Capital Publishing House, 1988); Peter Lyon, 'Non-Alignment at the Summits: From Belgrade 1961 to Havana 1979 – A Perspective View', *The Indian Journal of Political Science* 41.1 (1980), 132–53.
6 Peter Willetts, *The Non-Aligned Movement: The Origins of a Third World Alliance* (London: Frances Pinter Publishers, 1978).

7 A. W. Singham and Shirley Hune, *Non-Alignment in an Age of Alignments* (London: Zed Books, 1986).
8 Robert A. Mortimer, *The Third World Coalition in International Politics* (Boulder, CO: Westview Press, 1984).
9 Tony Smith, 'New Bottles for New Wine: A Pericentric Framework for the Study of the Cold War', *Diplomatic History* 24.4 (2000), 567–91; Odd Arne Westad, 'The New International History of the Cold War: Three (Possible) Paradigms', *Diplomatic History* 24.4 (2000), 551–65.
10 Odd Arne Westad, *The Global Cold War: Third World Interventions and the Making of Our Times* (Cambridge: Cambridge University Press, 2005); Lorenz M. Lüthi, *Cold Wars: Asia, Middle East, Europe* (Cambridge: Cambridge University Press, 2020); Vijay Prashad, *The Darker Nations: A People's History of the Third World* (New York, NY, and London: The New Press, 2007); Matthew Connelly, *A Diplomatic Revolution: Algeria's Fight for Independence and the Origins of the Post-Cold War Era* (Oxford: Oxford University Press, 2002); Robert B. Rakove, *Kennedy, Johnson, and the Nonaligned World* (Cambridge: Cambridge University Press, 2013); Jeffrey James Byrne, *The Mecca of Revolution: Algeria, Decolonization, and the Third World Order* (Oxford: Oxford University Press, 2016); Guy Laron, *Origins of the Suez Crisis: Postwar Development Diplomacy and the Struggle over Third World Industrialization, 1945–1956* (Washington, DC: Woodrow Wilson Center Press, 2013); Giuliano Garavini, *After Empires: European Integration, Decolonization, and the Challenge from the Global South* (Oxford: Oxford University Press, 2012); Paul T. Chamberlin, *The Cold War's Killing Fields: Rethinking the Long Peace* (New York, NY: Harper Collins, 2018), etc.
11 G. H. Jansen, *Afro-Asia and Nonalignment* (London: Faber and Faber, 1966); Alvin Z. Rubinstein, *Yugoslavia and the Non-Aligned World* (Princeton, NJ: Princeton University Press, 1970); David Kimche, *The Afro-Asian Movement: Ideology and Foreign Policy of the Third World* (Jerusalem: Israel Universities Press, 1973); W. Scott Thompson, *Ghana's Foreign Policy 1957–1966: Diplomacy, Ideology, and the New State* (Princeton, NJ: Princeton University Press, 1969); B. R. Nanda (ed.), *Indian Foreign Policy: The Nehru Years* (New Delhi: Radiant Publishers, 1976); J. W. Burton (ed.), *Nonalignment* (New York, NY: James H. Heineman Inc., 1966); Ljubivoje Aćimović (ed.), *Politika nesvrstanosti u savremenom svetu* (Beograd: IMPP, 1969); Ide Anak Agung Gde Agung, *Twenty Years Indonesian Foreign Policy 1945–1965* (The Hague: Mouton, 1973), etc.
12 Bojana Tadić and Ranko Petković (eds), *Non-Alignment in the Eighties: International Round Table*, Petrovaradin, Yugoslavia, 28–31 August 1981 (Beograd: IMPP, 1982); Ranko Petković, *Nesvrstana Jugoslavija i savremeni svet: spoljna politika Jugoslavije 1945–1985* (Zagreb: Školska knjiga, 1985); Peter Willetts, *The Non-Aligned Movement*; Richard L. Jackson, *The Non-Aligned, the UN and the Superpowers* (New York, NY: Praeger, 1983); M. S. Rajan, *Studies on Nonalignment and the Nonaligned Movement: Theory and Practice* (New Delhi: ABC Publishers, 1986); M. S. Rajan, *Nonalignment and Nonaligned Movement: Retrospect and Prospect* (New Delhi: Vikas Publishing, 1990); A. W. Singham and Shirley Hune, *Non-Alignment in an Age of Alignments*; K. P. Mishra and K. R. Narayanan (eds), *Non-Alignment in Contemporary International Relations* (New Delhi: Vikas Publishers, 1981); K. P. Mishra, *Non-Alignment: Frontiers and Dynamics* (New Delhi: Vikas Publishers, 1982); S. B. Jain, *India's Foreign Policy and Non-Alignment* (New Delhi: Anamika Publishers, 2000); Renu Srivastava, *India and the Nonaligned Summits: Belgrade to Jakarta* (New Delhi: Northern Book

Centre, 1995); Pramila Srivastava (ed.), *Non-Aligned Movement: Extending Frontiers* (New Delhi: Kanishka Publishers, 2001); Roy Allison, *The Soviet Union and the Strategy of Non-Alignment in the Third World* (Cambridge: Cambridge University Press, 1988); Momir Stojković, *Tito, Nehru, Naser: nastanak i razvoj politike i Pokreta nesvrstanosti* (Zaječar: RO Zaječar, 1983); Bahgat Korany, *Social Change, Charisma and International Behaviour: Toward a Theory of Foreign Policy-making in the Third World* (Geneva: IUHHEI, 1976); Leo Mates, *Počelo je u Beogradu… 20 godina nesvrstanosti* (Zagreb: Globus, 1982); U. S. Bajpai (ed.), *Non-Alignment: Perspectives and Prospects* (New Delhi: Lancers Publishers, 1983); D. R. Goyal (ed.), *Non-Aligned Movement: From Belgrade to Harare* (New Delhi: 21st Century Publications, 1986); Assassi Lassasi, *Non-Alignment and Algerian Foreign Policy* (Aldershot: Avebury, 1988); W. M. Karundasa, *Sri Lanka and Non-Alignment: A Study of Foreign Policy from 1948 to 1982* (Dehiwela: Image Lanka Publishers, 1997), etc.

13   Leo Mates, *Nesvrstanost: teorija i savremena praksa* (Beograd: IMPP, 1970); Cecil V. Crabb Jr., *The Elephants and the Grass: A Study of Nonalignment* (New York: Praeger, 1965); Peter Lyon, *Neutralism* (Leicester: Leicester University Press, 1963); Laurence W. Martin (ed.), *Neutralism and Nonalignment: The New States in World Affairs* (New York, NY: Praeger, 1962); Ranko Petković, *Teorijski pojmovi nesvrstanosti* (Beograd: Rad, 1974); Ranko Petković, *Nesvrstanost: nezavisan, vanblokovski i globalni faktor u međunarodnim odnosima* (Zagreb: Školska knjiga, 1981); Robert L. Rothstein, 'Alignment, Nonalignment, and Small Powers: 1945–1965', *International Organization* 20.3 (1966); Nazli Choucri, 'The Nonalignment of Afro-Asian States: Policy, Perception, and Behaviour', *Canadian Journal of Political Science* 2.1 (1969); Bojana Tadić, *Nesvrstanost u teoriji i praksi međunarodnih odnosa* (Beograd: IMPP, 1976); Bojana Tadić, *Osobenosti i dileme nesvrstanosti* (Beograd: Komunist, 1982); Satish Kumar, 'Nonalignment: International Goals and National Interests', *Asian Survey* 23.4 (1983), etc.

14   Robert J. McMahon (ed.), *The Cold War in the Third World* (Oxford: Oxford University Press, 2013).

15   Sandra Bott, Jussi M. Hanhimäki, Janick Marina Schaufelbuehl and Marco Wyss (eds), *Neutrality and Neutralism in the Global Cold War: Between or Within the Blocs?* (London: Routledge, 2016); Lorenz Lüthi (ed.), *The Regional Cold Wars in Europe, East Asia, and the Middle East: Crucial Periods and Turning Points* (Washington, DC, Stanford: Woodrow Wilson Center Press, Stanford University Press, 2015); Nataša Mišković, Harald Fischer-Tine and Nada Boškovska (eds), *The Non-Aligned Movement and the Cold War: Delhi-Bandung-Belgrade* (London: Routledge, 2014).

16   H. W. Brands, *Specter of Neutralism: the United States and the Emergence of the Third World* (New York, NY: Columbia University Press, 1989); Srinath Raghavan, *War and Peace in Modern India: A Strategic History of the Nehru Years* (Ranikhet: Permanent Black, 2010); Robert J. McMahon, *The Cold War on the Periphery: The United States, India and Pakistan* (New York, NY: Columbia University Press, 1994); Piero Gleijeses, *Conflicting Missions: Havana, Washington, and Africa, 1959–1976* (Chapel Hill, NC: The University of North Carolina Press, 2002); David C. Engerman, *The Price of Aid: the Economic Cold War in India* (Cambridge, MA: Harvard University Press, 2018); Ragna Boden, *Die Grenzen der Weltmacht: Sowjetische Indonesienpolitik von Stalin bis Brežnev* (Stuttgart: Franz Steiner Verlag, 2006); Bradley R. Simpson, *Economists with Guns: Authoritarian Development and U.S.-Indonesian Relations, 1960–1968* (Stanford, CA: Stanford University Press, 2008); Sue Onslow (ed.), *Cold War in Southern Africa: White Power, Black Liberation* (London: Routledge, 2009);

Rami Ginat, *Syria and the Doctrine of Arab Neutralism: From Independence to Dependence* (Brighton: Sussex Academic Press, 2005); С. В. Мазов, *Политика СССР в Западной Африке 1956–1964: неизвестные страницы холодной войны* (Москва: Наука, 2008); Andreas Hilger (ed.), *Die Sowjetunion und die Dritte Welt: UdSSR, Staatssozialismus und Antikolonialismus im Kalten Krieg* (Munchen: R. Oldenbourg Verlag, 2009); Andreas Hilger, *Sowjetisch-indische Beziehungen 1941–1966: Imperiale Agenda und nationale Identität in der Ära von Dokolonisierung und Kaltem Krieg* (Köln: Böhlau Verlag, 2018); Amit Das Gupta, *Serving India: A Political Biography of Subimal Dutt, India's Longest Serving Foreign Secretary* (New Delhi: Manohar, 2017); Salim Yaqub, *Containing Arab Nationalism: the Eisenhower Doctrine and the Middle East* (Chapel Hill, NC: The University of North Carolina Press, 2004); Jesse Ferris, *Nasser's Gamble: How Intervention in Yemen Caused the Six-Day War and the Decline of Egyptian Power* (Princeton, NJ: Princeton University Press, 2013); Ryan M. Irwin, *Gordian Knot: Apartheid and the Unmaking of the Liberal World Order* (Oxford: Oxford University Press, 2012); Mohammed Lakhdar Ghettas, *Algeria and the Cold War: International Struggle for Autonomy* (London: I.B. Tauris, 2018); Robert Niebuhr, 'Nonalignment as Yugoslavia's Answer to Bloc Politics', *Journal of Cold War Studies* 13.1 (2011), 146–79; Dragan Bogetić and Ljubodrag Dimić, *Beogradska konferencija nesvrstanih zemalja 1–6. Septembar 1961. Prilog istoriji Trećeg sveta* (Beograd: Zavod za udžbenike, 2012); Rinna Kullaa, *Non-Alignment and Its Origins in Cold War Europe: Yugoslavia, Finland, and the Soviet Challenge* (London: I.B. Tauris, 2012); Tvrtko Jakovina, *Treća strana Hladnog rata* (Zagreb: Fraktura, 2011); Svetozar Rajak, 'No Bargaining Chips, No Spheres of Interest: the Yugoslav Origins of Cold War Non-Alignment', *Journal of Cold War Studies* 16.1 (2014), 146–79; Aleksandar Životić and Jovan Čavoški, 'On the Road to Belgrade: Yugoslavia, Third World Neutrals, and the Evolution of Global Nonalignment, 1954–1961', *Journal of Cold War Studies* 18.4 (2016), 79–97; Aleksandar Životić, *Jugoslavija i Suecka kriza 1956–1957* (Beograd: INIS, 2008); Jovan Čavoški, *Jugoslavija i kinesko-indijski konflikt 1959–1962* (Beograd: INIS, 2009); Jovan Čavoški, *Distant Countries, Closest Allies: Josip Broz, Tito, Jawaharlal Nehru and the Rise of Global Nonalignment* (New Delhi: Nehru Memorial Museum and Library, 2015); Kathryn C. Statler and Andrew L. Johns, *The Eisenhower Administration, the Third World, and the Globalization of the Cold War* (Lanham, MD: Rowman & Littlefield, 2006); Sophie Richardson, *China, Cambodia, and the Five Principles of Peaceful Co-Existence* (New York, NY: Columbia University Press, 2010); Paul T. Chamberlin, *The Global Offensive: the United States, the Palestine Liberation Organisation, and the Making of the Post-Cold War World Order* (Oxford: Oxford University Press, 2012), etc.
17 Jürgen Dinkel, *The Non-Aligned Movement: Genesis, Organization and Politics (1927–1992)* (Leiden: Brill, 2018).
18 Lorenz M. Lüthi, *Cold Wars*, 266–306, 531–5.
19 Vijay Prashad, *The Darker Nations*.
20 Dragan Bogetić, *Nesvrstanost kroz istoriju: od ideje do pokreta* (Beograd: Zavod za udžbenike, 2019).
21 Jovan Čavoški, 'The Evolution of NAM's Role in World Affairs during the Cold War Decades', in *The 60th Anniversary of the Non-Aligned Movement*, Duško Dimitrijević and Jovan Čavoški (eds) (Belgrade: IIPE, 2021), 23–50.

1

The Historical Meaning of Non-Alignment

In order to more firmly grasp the role of different non-aligned summits in the evolutionary process of formation and expansion of the NAM, one needs to better understand what global non-alignment was essentially about, its basic rationale and motives, underlying ideas, immediate historical origins, different regional and conceptual emanations, pioneering influences, as well as its role within the Cold War international order. These features mark non-alignment and the NAM's separate historical paths, compared to other similar phenomena present during those decades.

Non-alignment did not emerge as part of some initial deliberations among different newly liberated or non-bloc nations or through implementation of some preconceived theories or ideas, but rather as an expression of different struggles for political or economic independence and as a distinct response to the emergence of two antagonistic blocs in world affairs. It was the ascendancy of the Cold War and the concurrent downfall of European colonial empires that heralded sweeping geopolitical changes, which had ushered in fundamental political, social and economic transformation that eventually enabled the non-aligned foreign policy orientation to expand globally and gradually evolve.[1] In the words of Indonesian President Ahmed Sukarno at the 1961 Belgrade Conference: 'There was no prior consultation and agreement between us before we adopted our respective policies of non-alignment ... We arrived at this policy inspired by common ideals, prompted by similar circumstances, spurred on by like experiences.'[2]

We can define four general historical preconditions that eventually led to the emergence and evolution of global non-alignment: anti-colonial revolutions which introduced political liberation and independence to a majority of Asian, African and some Latin American countries; economic underdevelopment as a dominant common feature of this diverse group of states, which eventually induced many of them to closely link the freedom of their international action with the overriding priorities of economic modernization; the Cold War bipolar system which constituted the general global framework within which non-alignment could freely operate and interact, while simultaneously advocating the lessening of international tensions and reduction of great power interferences; and finally the establishment of the UN with its broad and egalitarian democratic character which created additional opportunities for non-aligned countries to participate equally in the dialogue with the great powers and present their views and ideas freely through individual or collective actions.[3]

The Essence of Non-Alignment

Non-alignment was a foreign policy strategy that clearly implied diplomatic freedom of action and choice with respect to both the main Cold War contenders – i.e. both blocs and the two superpowers – thus strongly emphasizing opposition to any permanent diplomatic or military identification. Essentially, non-alignment originated from the common desire of many newly independent and non-bloc countries to survive politically and develop economically under the conditions of tense international peace.[4] This concept became an instrument of preservation of one's independence and a further guarantee of freedom of choice, primarily one fully tailored to suit the needs and desires of small and feeble nations, while also providing them with a sense of certainty, predictability and stability in their foreign engagements. Non-alignment was an expression of realistic assessments of the new international equilibrium, granting non-bloc nations with a stable basis for forging dynamic mutual cooperation, irrespective of all their historical, geographical, cultural, religious, political, social, economic and other differences. Therefore, non-alignment had also become a constructive means for launching collective actions of small countries, which individually, due to their many internal constraints, could not achieve much on the world stage.[5]

Global non-alignment was an all in one – a foreign policy orientation, a political doctrine and a worldwide movement (at first just a loose group). From the very beginning, this concept was endowed by an established system of guiding principles, most of them clear to everyone involved although not always rigid in their interpretation. But, at the same time, these principles could not represent something more than just a statement of interest, unless they had been previously firmly wedded to any concerted collective political actions, both institutionalized and ad hoc ones, undertaken by different countries adhering to them.[6]

> The word non-aligned may be differently interpreted but basically it was used ... with the meaning non-aligned with the great powers blocs of the world. Non-aligned has a negative meaning, but if you give it a positive connotation it means nations which object to this lining-up for war purposes – military blocs, military alliances and the like. Therefore, we keep away from this and we want to throw our weight ... in favour of peace, once stressed the Indian Prime Minister Jawaharlal Nehru.[7]

The basic character of non-alignment, therefore, was non-bloc actors' clear and open opposition to any kind of bloc affiliation, resistance to any political subjugation and ideological indoctrination exercised by the great powers, standing up to the surrender of sovereign interests and hard-won independence to any other international actors, while simultaneously pursuing disclosed aspirations of achieving economic emancipation and social modernization.[8] During one debate Nehru stressed:

> What does joining a bloc mean? After all it can only mean one thing: give up your view about a particular question, adopt the other party's view on that question in order to please it and gain its favour. It means that and nothing else as far as I can

see, because if our view is the view of that party, then there is no giving up and we do go with that bloc or country.[9]

This point was also once observed by the Egyptian President Gamal Abdel Nasser while welcoming the Ghanaian leader Kwame Nkrumah in Cairo, stressing the fundamentally unreasonable choice of joining any blocs: 'If we are tied to one of the blocs, we would be a weightless appendage whose word does not have any influence ... An independent policy based on non-alignment and positive neutralism will ... make our countries a great force permitting an independent say. Such a position would be met with respect from all over the world.'[10] In fact, this comprehension of independence and freedom of action, primarily a political one, stood as a cornerstone of any deliberations regarding the current and future role of non-alignment.

However, as staunchly opposed to the very essence of bloc policies, non-alignment had never become a dogma for any country advocating it, since this notion was often subjected to frequent reinterpretations and redefinitions before and throughout the existence of the NAM. Basically, non-alignment was, and remained, a rather pragmatic concept, devoid of any dominant ideological guidelines, not only with respect to its own specific materialization but also in its relationship with the promotion of individual goals. Furthermore, any kind of ideological rigidity would have completely voided non-alignment from this dominant pragmatic feature and have totally subverted its true essence, a tendency that any radicalization drive inside the NAM would ultimately demonstrate.[11] Therefore, as already mentioned, freely pursuing non-bloc foreign policy became a dominant propensity of all non-aligned countries, clearly separating them from any similar concepts or organizations, and presenting itself as a 'quest for distinctive, intellectual expression of independence'.[12]

Since the majority of these countries were either former colonies or had suffered under some kind of great power domination or subjugation, any formal alignment with one of the two blocs was primarily perceived as being fundamentally detrimental to the preservation of their newly acquired freedom and tantamount to a devastating moral defeat. Non-alignment was, in fact, a deliberate attempt, even a far cry, which ultimately 'enabled the powerless to hold a dialogue with the powerful and to try to hold them accountable', irrespective of the ultimate measure of success.[13] In short, we can define non-alignment as a policy strictly based on the goal of preservation of independence, which was generally pursued by countries burdened by an overall sense of insecurity and backwardness, thus often facing the incapacity to strongly and timely react to challenges occurring in their wider surroundings. Sometimes such threats implied a kind of closer alignment with one of the superpowers, as occurred during the late 1970s, thus profoundly affecting the basic direction of non-alignment.[14]

Therefore, global non-alignment also contributed to the rise of the so-called 'zone of autonomy' consisting of subordinated political groups standing between the two dominant blocs, though outside their immediate control, thus enabling lesser powers to assume partial influence over the policies of great powers. Essentially, rivalry between the great powers only increased the amount of influence and pragmatism exercised by small states, above all endowing them with the tentative possibility to defect to the other side of the Cold War division or at least threaten them with this kind of defection.[15] Nevertheless, the emergence of non-alignment would have been quite possible even outside the Cold War framework; as a result, it continues to exist today in the form of the multi-vector policies of many developing countries, since the outstanding differences between the Global North and the Global South go well beyond the very nature of the superpower conflict. As long as these non-bloc nations opted for independent, nuanced and diversified international engagements, while also taking into account these global economic and social contradictions, some version of non-alignment, under any name, could still have become a viable alternative.[16]

Originally, non-alignment was not an isolationist policy or a policy of expediency and opportunities, in spite of its pragmatic character, nor it was a policy of self-righteousness and moral superiority, since it strived to remain morally neutral, regardless of some strong anti-colonial and anti-imperialist sentiments. It did not offer an easy escape from troublesome situations, while many critics outright labelled it as inherently 'immoral' as a means of largely discrediting non-alignment and making it less appealing for other potential followers to step in.[17] In the words of an anonymous Indian author, non-alignment was 'anything but the easiest way out of a dilemma; it often brings the wrath of both power blocs on the non-aligned government; it needs courage and conviction to resist the pressure of bigger and greater powers and follow an independent path'.[18] This line of thinking was also picked up by the Ceylonese (Sri Lanka since 1972) Prime Minister Sirimavo Bandaranaike who once stressed all the perils this kind of foreign policy choice often entailed: the 'path of non-alignment is not an easy one for small developing nations to tread on ... I can say with certainty that non-alignment is not the line of least resistance, but is rather the most difficult, challenging and positive policy of our time.'[19]

Such a daring attempt to assume more control over their own destiny, without irresponsibly surrendering it to the will and decision of any of the great powers, was the hardest foreign policy choice any of the non-bloc countries had to ultimately make. In the words of the Ethiopian Emperor Haile Selassie, being non-aligned essentially implied being 'impartial to judge actions and policies objectively, as we see them either contributing to or detracting from the resolution of the world's problems', which sometimes implied cooperating to that end with either or both sides of the Cold War but never surrendering to them. Nevertheless, according to him, those who 'denounce one side on every major problem or issue, while reserving nothing but praise for the other cannot claim to be non-aligned', especially those countries 'whose policies are shaped for them elsewhere' and who 'wait patiently to be instructed'.[20] Therefore, non-alignment also possessed this 'situationist' streak when the position of individual nations or the movement as a whole often depended on the policies one of the blocs was implementing with respect to specific issues.

If these individual policies were in accordance with the NAM's general goals, the potential for mutual cooperation was increasing, otherwise, the probability of a new conflict erupting between bloc and non-bloc actors was also on the rise. In this respect, relentless confrontation with all blocs never dominated non-alignment or the NAM, in spite of its strong non-bloc character. As was the case with the policy of alignment and great power politics in general, non-alignment was also a down-to-earth concept shorn of all idealism, besides the one publicly proclaimed, clearly driven by the intention of promoting and pursuing one country's national interests but never separately from the general cause of the entire group or against it.[21] Only when individual needs came before the general necessities of the NAM did internal strife, significant paralysis of action and increasing irrelevance come into being, as was the case in the 1980s. As one theoretician of non-alignment once emphasized, 'this was a policy, not a creed, a tactic, even a weapon, but not a gospel, for whatever else gospel may do, they do not establish or preserve independent status'.[22]

Nevertheless, with respect to their immediate foreign policy goals there were still some evident differences between some non-aligned countries, primarily based on their own perception of respective national interests. While, on one hand, countries such as India or Burma considered bloc confrontation to be the greatest peril to world peace, and tried to find the means to neutralize the immediate danger of war, countries such as Egypt or Yugoslavia on the other hand, regarded the Cold War as an opportunity to skilfully manipulate the great power rivalry, thus seeking greater economic assistance and ultimately securing their own independence and freedom of strategic choice. Any lessening of tensions between the two blocs, though desirable, could have also led to a rotten compromise between the great powers, one often implying the redrawing of the spheres of influence, which could have proved detrimental to the interests of many non-aligned countries.[23]

The essence of non-alignment could be described as the continuous struggle against all bloc divisions, for fundamental equality in international relations, promotion of economic development, peace, disarmament and constructive cooperation between all members of the international community, irrespective of the size and strength of each country. This kind of dedication openly implied construction of new norms and regulations for all countries to act upon, the great powers included, thus eventually establishing a new international political and economic order.[24] In the words of a Yugoslav diplomat, 'non-alignment is not merely a synonym for independence nor is it an ephemeral disassociation from blocs, it is a complete doctrine striving to effect essential changes in international relations', one where force would not reign supreme, where peace would be the dominant feature of state interactions, while the powerful and rich would not be the only ones determining the fate of the world.[25]

Factually speaking, non-alignment was propelled by an evident desire to inject new historical and political quality into relations between nations and states, irrespective of their actual size and strength, thus moving the world order away from the age-old matrix where only great powers dominated the landscape and dictated the rules of existence and corresponding behaviour.[26] However, in spite of its palpable anti-colonial and anti-imperialist origins, since without the liberation of so many former colonies there would never have been enough nations to pursue such a course, non-alignment was, unlike any of its regionalist competitors, never a policy chiefly driven by these two concepts as some might claim. Therefore, non-alignment was never predominantly an anti-colonial concept but primarily a postcolonial one, adjusted to the conditions and needs of the post-liberation phase of these nations, without ever neglecting the earlier horrors of colonialism. Any ignorance of such facts often led to attempts at excessive radicalization which ultimately proved detrimental or even catastrophic for individual non-aligned countries or even the entire group.

Taking all this into account, participating countries at the Cairo Preparatory Meeting for the Belgrade Conference, held in June 1961, decided to define criteria that all non-aligned countries should fulfil beforehand in order to be considered authentic members of this group. These criteria were: adherence to the policy of independence based on the principles of active peaceful co-existence between different social or political systems; active support for the national liberation struggle; not becoming a party to multilateral military-political alliances created in the context of the East–West conflict; not becoming party to any bilateral military alliances created in the context of the East–West conflict; non-compliance with the establishment of military bases of great powers on the national territory.[27] It is true that such vague criteria often left room for ambiguity or inconclusiveness, as well as different interpretations. Nonetheless, this was the first serious attempt to lay down norms, clear stipulations of what was essentially needed to be a non-aligned country and what kind of role these countries would exercise at different NAM gatherings. In essence, the basic criteria had not changed throughout the Cold War period, only minor clarifications were introduced during the 1970s, with many non-aligned countries still preserving some kind of political, economic or military links with either of the two blocs, though often outside the framework of the direct East–West conflict.[28]

Neutralism and Non-Alignment

The notions of 'neutralism' and 'non-alignment', although sometimes differing in certain nuances, still represented two faces of the same subject and will be used in this book interchangeably, at least in its initial part, although the term non-alignment will obviously dominate the discourse. Neutralism, although a very popular term during the 1950s and 1960s, was often confused with the legally dissimilar term neutrality, but with time made way for non-alignment as the dominant notion describing independent and non-bloc policies of underdeveloped countries during the Cold War.[29] What largely contributed to the abandonment of the term neutralism from the general political discourse was its perception as a negative, passive, deceitful, less lofty and somewhat opportunistic notion that could not be ultimately reconciled with the basic character of the foreign policy principles and actions pursued by these nations. Since this was a policy primarily dedicated to the preservation of world peace and stability, while concurrently stimulating economic development, in the minds of its advocates non-alignment often represented a positive policy and a positive stance in international affairs, which eventually contributed to the term neutralism's ultimate demise from political discourse (the only exception was 'positive neutralism' advocated by Egypt, in a similar vein to Yugoslavia initially using the terms non-engagement, non-bloc policies or uncommitted countries for its understanding of non-alignment).[30] As one anonymous Indian official once said about differences between non-alignment, on one hand, and neutrality and alignment, on the other: 'Non-alignment differs from both these attitudes in that it does not declare in advance that it will or will not take one side or the other, but that it will judge each question as it arises on its merits, as it sees it, and not necessarily as others see it.'[31]

Central non-aligned leaders often emphasized in their speeches this positive and liberating character of non-alignment as opposed to neutralist bias. Nehru once said: 'India is certainly not neutral and her policy of non-alignment is anything but a neutral policy... One cannot be neutral to right and wrong.'[32] Nkrumah was even more open in his remarks regarding this subject: 'Our policy is not a negative one. Positive neutralism and non-alignment does not mean keeping aloof from burning international issues. On the contrary, it means a positive stand based on our own convictions completely uninfluenced by any of the power blocs.'[33] Sukarno was also quite clear when indicating these fundamental differences between the two notions: 'Non-aligned policy is not a policy of seeking for a neutral position in the case of war. Non-aligned policy is not a policy of neutrality without its own colour ... Non-alignment is an active devotion to the lofty cause of justice and freedom to be free.'[34]

Therefore, non-alignment was not simply a policy of equidistance towards both blocs, which also implied a certain amount of neutrality, but rather a proactive and pragmatic approach to international relations that set the course for non-bloc countries to steer clear of the dominant bloc structures, while trying to chart their own path of development, and thus avoiding any worldwide political isolation. This was, in fact, what gradually pushed neutralism out of the general discourse. However, this did not imply that any of these countries abandoned their non-aligned orientation; on the contrary, it clearly indicated that bloc and non-bloc nations had ultimately managed to find common ground with respect to some key issues, but without making any compromises regarding the fundamental principles that both sides cherished.[35] In fact, non-alignment was a policy which Nehru in one of his speeches described as 'positive', clearly having nothing in common with being neutral: 'We wanted to follow not a merely neutral or negative policy but a positive one ... fundamentally keeping away from other countries and other alignments of powers which normally lead to major conflicts', thus 'trying to maintain a certain friendliness and spirit of cooperation with both the great and the small countries of the world'.[36]

Furthermore, it was the Yugoslav President Josip Broz Tito and Nehru in their Joint Statement, issued in New Delhi on 22 December 1954, who for the first time dealt with this issue in a bilateral and international document: 'The policy of non-alignment adopted and pursued by their respective countries is not "neutrality" or "neutralism" as sometimes alleged; but it is an active, positive, and constructive policy seeking to lead to a collective peace on which alone collective security can really rest.'[37] That is why neutralism or semantically better-suited non-alignment should be observed as continuously evolving concepts, not always being on opposing sides, largely subjected to the same changes occurring inside the general Cold War framework. Some of the general principles to which non-aligned countries adhered, even when observed through a neutralist lens, were: Cold War conditions could be mitigated and perhaps even removed altogether; neutralism or non-alignment was morally justifiable; neutralists had to pursue an independent foreign policy; all forms of colonialism had to be eradicated; foreign aid had to be extended without any strings attached.[38] Adherence to these specific principles created a common bond between so many diverse nations, providing them with a certain amount of structural and conceptual cohesiveness and purposefulness, which ultimately maximized the effect of their joint actions.

The Cold War Framework of Non-Alignment

This newly found self-confidence among so many non-aligned countries, closely wedded to their often audacious and confrontationist stand, however, frequently sparked mistrust among the superpowers regarding their true intentions. This was a tendency once well formulated by Nehru, sensing how such policies were stimulating growing discontent among the blocs, and thus creating a strained relationship between the Cold War system and the credo of non-alignment:

> They think we are undependable, because we cannot be made to vote this way or that way ... When they found out that we acted according to our own will, they did not like it ... They could not quite make out what we were or what we were aiming at ... So they did not like what we did in many instances; nevertheless, they respected us much more, because they realized that we had an independent policy, that we were not going to be dragooned this way or that.[39]

However, as Nehru and other non-aligned leaders believed, their respective nations had a lot to gain from expanding cooperation and exchanges with both sides of the Cold War, therefore confrontation with either or both of the two blocs was out of the question – it could only prove to be catastrophic for these nations, since the elementary national interest and basic necessities demanded that such a realist approach to the Cold War division be sincerely embraced by them, although never reconciling themselves with the long-term existence of any of these blocs and their excessive domination.[40]

This kind of tentative approach provided a boost for the influence non-aligned countries exerted on the superpowers and it eventually contributed to their rising importance inside the system of the bipolar balance of power.[41] As Nehru shrewdly observed in 1954: 'When there is substantial difference in the strength of the two opposing forces, we in Asia, with our limitations, will not be able to influence the issue; but when the two opposing forces are fairly even matched, then it is possible to make our weight felt in the balance.'[42] In fact, practitioners of non-alignment observed the international balance of power as a continuously changing phenomenon, not something static that could be forcefully imposed or bought through extending material aid. Therefore, they strived to maintain a high degree of flexibility, thus being sufficiently agile and fully capable of moving from one side of the Cold War divide to the other, while preserving their independence and realizing their national interests but without ever abandoning the basic tenets of non-alignment.[43]

In short, non-alignment was clearly affected by the global power dynamics, but it also exercised a considerable level of influence over its sensitive operations. This was particularly true regarding the issue of peace, which was considered as being far too important to be left only to the great powers to decide its fate. According to some non-aligned leaders, the great powers had demonstrated both clear insensitivity to the worldwide desire for peace and an outright inability to break the diplomatic deadlock that often kept the world on the brink of a devastating nuclear war.[44] It was this general fear of an all-out war, rather than any concrete peace-making initiatives, that ultimately assisted non-aligned countries in their efforts to pursue effectively such a course in world affairs. Eventually, it was a combination of all these factors that initially stirred the great powers' toleration and respect for these smaller nations, thus facilitating their moderating influences and stimulating general responsiveness to their demands.[45]

In fact, Nehru was quite clear about the peace-making role of the non-bloc area in becoming part of the general dynamics of the Cold War system:

> So far as I am concerned, it does not matter what war takes place, we will not take part in it unless we have to defend ourselves. If I join any of these big groups I lose my identity; I have no identity left, I have no views left. If all the world were to be divided up between these two big blocs what would be the result? The inevitable result would be war. Therefore, every step that takes place in reducing that area in the world which may be called the *unaligned area* is a dangerous step and leads to war.[46]

What the great powers often did not properly understand was that their perception that non-aligned countries were fundamentally for or against them was flawed, without taking into consideration that these nations were only acting out of their own self-interest, and instead of looking on the Cold War as a fundamental battle between good and evil, seeing it as something being far more nuanced and diversified, without any Manichean touch.[47]

In fact, in a time of crisis the space for non-aligned mediation drastically expanded and the possibility of influencing crucial bloc policies largely increased, although with a varying degree of success. This depended primarily on the outright ability of non-aligned countries to present themselves as objective and unbiased mediators or, at least, to effectively stage another kind of collective action, while their activities often had to reflect the general strivings of the world public opinion.[48] These nations had gradually become self-proclaimed moral arbiters of world politics, in spite of their evident military or economic deficiencies, skilfully utilizing the power and impact of the world public opinion on the great powers and inside the UN. This evident trend was once strongly emphasized by the Yugoslav president: 'Our material resources are modest and our possibilities are far from being limitless, but our moral power is immense, and this is of paramount importance today. Not only the peoples of our countries, but also public opinion throughout the world expect much of us.'[49] It was this vague but principled character of cooperation between these countries that eventually enabled them to forge wider unity through an internationally recognized movement.[50]

On the whole, non-alignment was a foreign policy strategy fully adapted to the general Cold War conditions where small powers were often perceived as objects of competition for great power influences, but they were still not direct victims of war and great power confrontation.[51] Psychologically, this was a very attractive orientation, since it reflected deep-seated desires of newly liberated states avoiding any formal commitments to their former rulers, yet having a certain amount of influence over their respective policies. Non-alignment was quite an appealing policy because it accorded unexpected importance and status to those countries that were denied that kind of privilege inside the traditional hierarchical international system.[52] What was especially important for these newly independent states was the inherent potential of non-alignment to provide them with infinitely more opportunities for overcoming their social and economic backwardness and dependence left over by the colonialists, thus seeking new levels of modernization and international recognition.[53]

Economic incentives were also some of the major motives behind the general acceptance and incessant perpetuation of the policy of non-alignment by developing countries. Hence, it would be this socioeconomic position of the Global South that would constitute the backbone of all the key NAM initiatives launched during the 1970s. This also inspired some of these nations to undertake a more proactive role against the general Cold War setting, seeking economic assistance from both sides, but also trying to trigger development through closer cooperation with other developing nations, ultimately creating individual preconditions for potentially setting off a major overhaul of the global economic system.[54] Nevertheless, some people considered that such a potential for 'blackmail' was built into the very foundations of the Cold War system, even though non-aligned countries did not perceive it in this way, since for them this was yet another way to guarantee survival.[55] This was essentially the 'art of maintaining political equilibrium through the diversification of dependence, the balancing of weakness', in short, 'creation of an "alternative" lest the influence of one side or the other become too imposing'.[56]

Taking all this into account, we can define six immediate goals of non-alignment that yielded concrete benefits to its practitioners as part of their evolving position inside the Cold War system:

> non-alignment insures political freedom and independence and contributes to national self-respect and moral integrity; in contrast to alliance membership non-alignment permits freedom of expression and action; non-alignment keeps a small nation from getting involved in larger conflicts of no concern to it; alignment would make local problems more difficult to solve; alliances involve military obligations that divert scarce resources from the urgent necessities of economic development; non-aligned nations are in a position to accept and to bid for economic aid from both sides in the Cold War.

Therefore, non-alignment was a policy largely driven by nationalist sentiments and a strong sense of self-preservation, but it was also an outright response to objective international circumstances of the bipolar world order and not a sole product of those same inherent sensibilities.[57]

Therefore, small powers had to choose whether they wanted to accept all the constraints of the Cold War alignment that permanently and fully limited their freedom of decision or to opt for an independent, international stand that also occasionally implied accepting unavoidable compromises under the pressure of concrete circumstances that were often well outside their grasp.[58] As one author said, non-aligned nations 'both suffer and profit from the existence of the Cold War, but they probably profit more, at least in the short run, than they suffer'.[59] These countries also desperately needed global peace to be maintained in order to fully accomplish their internal and external objectives, while most of them struggled incessantly against the policy of radicalism and further polarization in world affairs, which could have only limited their freedom of action. In fact, non-alignment had introduced the spirit of democratization of international relations, the goal of which was to mitigate contradictions and extremes represented by both blocs and their respective ideologies.

Nevertheless, a resounding majority of non-aligned countries were well aware that formal dissolution of one or both blocs did not immediately 'eliminate the conflict of interests which led to the creation of blocs in the first place, nor [would] nations ... live more free and secure only due to the formal abandonment of military-political pacts'. 'By simply disbanding the military-political bloc organisations international contradictions would not disappear, as would not disappear conflicts stemming from them'. Therefore, their struggle had to be much more comprehensive, ultimately mitigating the circumstances and conditions that bred new great power conflicts or spurred a sudden escalation in international tensions.[60] This kind of tendency also clearly implied that relations between different non-aligned countries were neither ideal nor harmonious, since different kinds of political, sometimes even military, conflicts emerged between them based on their disputed historical experiences, different ideological affinities, foreign policy inclinations, levels of economic development or great power dependence, views on the nature and goals of certain political actions and similar.[61] This would prove to be a serious challenge during the late 1970s and 1980s.

Regionalism and Non-Alignment

Despite officially gaining their statehood and political independence during the three subsequent decades after the end of the Second World War, the majority of Asian and African countries still nurtured a strong sentiment that, both politically and economically, they could once again become subjected to the firm control of different great powers. This kind of inherent, although quite reasonable, fear, on the other hand, stirred a strong sense of insecurity, an apprehension that these nations were still not true masters of their own destiny. Thus, the dominant discourse of nationalism and anti-colonialism had become closely related to the wider tenets of non-alignment, directly projecting its impact on the issues of freedom, security, status or relative power of these postcolonial nations. The overall sensitivity of these actors with respect to all these issues was quite intense and it predominantly shaped their relationship with all great powers.[62]

The successful outcome of their struggle for freedom also filled these nations with a sense of moral superiority and correspondingly boosted their missionary zeal, thus having considerable impact on their choice for non-bloc orientation. Therefore, any kind of alignment was sincerely perceived as going directly against basic aspirations of these actors to be treated as truly independent and equal countries. In their eyes, alignment was frequently associated with the notions of imperialism and colonialism, only triggering additional resentment among them. Since these countries did not possess raw military or economic power to stand up to their larger competitors, nor was it in their interest for any of the great powers to unilaterally dominate the entire international system, many of them eventually came to the conclusion that the role of balancers or mediators between the superpowers would ultimately increase their respective weight in world affairs, thus preventing any external encroachments.⁶³

In fact, many different sorts of contradictions (political, social, ideological, economic, cultural and military) could have created fertile ground for the emergence of an even more serious and profound division which could have substituted bloc antagonisms with a perilous ideological, racial or even North–South confrontation. Many non-aligned leaders were concerned that such radicalization could breed new and more serious conflicts in the future, a clash between 'a bloc of the poor and a bloc of the wealthy, a bloc of the advanced nations and a bloc of the developing nations ... a bloc of whites and a bloc of coloured', as once stressed by Nasser.⁶⁴ Burmese Prime Minister U Nu also admonished his colleagues for any excessive intransigence towards past misdeeds that could have otherwise created a 'tragic division of the world on the basis of colour' that would only hinder the attainment of immediate security and developmental goals of non-aligned countries.⁶⁵ For sure, this would have been an unacceptable outcome that could have only put non-bloc countries on a dangerous collision course with one bloc, even with both of them, with some of these states even being compelled to increase their level of dependence on some great powers.

The notion of non-alignment is often identified with the Third World as a whole or with Afro-Asia as its key component, even though there were countries, like Yugoslavia or some Latin American ones, which could be neither socio-politically identified with the underdeveloped Third World nor considered geographically part of the Afro-Asian region, since the true idea of a non-aligned world stretched well beyond such limited criteria. At the same time, such a regionalist approach largely affected the universal and transcendental character of non-alignment, particularly since it did not see itself as being either in open confrontation with any particular bloc or further upholding the petrification of the existing political and economic divisions in the world.⁶⁶ On the contrary, this was more in line with the so-called concept of 'Afro-Asianism' or 'Afro-Asian Internationalism' which partially identified itself with non-alignment, thus causing some confusion in the historiography, but principally it was coloured by a more regionalist and politically radical approach.⁶⁷ This extreme form of neutralism often evolved into a dangerous 'weapon for the irresponsible and the disaffected', a means to vent out all justified and unjustified grievances and frustrations.⁶⁸ Nevertheless, it was Tito and some others who managed to constructively integrate this notion of wider Afro-Asian solidarity into non-alignment but only as a 'function of political commitments, not of geographic location', thus very much taking away the radical appeal and mitigating confrontationist mood.⁶⁹

Non-alignment, as a postcolonial concept, was a non-bloc foreign policy doctrine to which even countries that were not former colonies also subscribed, regardless of their specific historical experiences. However, states preaching Afro-Asianism, many of them being officially non-aligned, were often using their common colonial background and their shared perception of suffering and exploitation as a rallying point against what they saw as imperialist powers still dominating the world order. This sense of oppression that lasted even after the colonial masters had left and a parallel emphasis on racial closeness and solidarity had become a very strong bondage for the radicals inside the Afro-Asianist group. The world they were inspired to build was 'distinct from and united in the face of "the others"'.⁷⁰ Therefore, unlike its non-aligned counterpart which sought to establish itself as a 'universalist' political doctrine, largely devoid of any divisions, Afro-Asianism was playing up issues of regional or historical proximity, emphasizing geographic, social and racial divisions and the 'North–South' conflict, and thus made itself a more regional phenomenon without universal appeal.⁷¹ Furthermore, Afro-Asianism clearly ignored any open bloc affiliations and did not make any distinctions between nations who belonged to either of the two blocs in Asia and Africa or those who pursued strict non-bloc foreign policies.

As indicated above, the Afro-Asianists ultimately became entrenched inside the political discourse of continuous 'anti-imperialist, anti-colonial struggle' that had become their paramount political goal and *raison d'être*. Paying for the deeds of the past had become more prevalent in order to establish a stable nation for the future. This substantially increased the level of radicalism among its adherents, while violence was often seen as the only answer to these accumulated frustrations and the general sense of injustice. In their eyes, peaceful co-existence and non-alignment were observed as just another tool available to the great powers to foment discord among postcolonial nations, thus merely pacifying their justified grievances, deluding their demands and further blunting the edge of their just struggle.⁷² This kind of ideology saw the role of the Third World through its active struggle with the other two worlds, particularly with the capitalist one, which then ultimately subjected developing nations to a protracted confrontation, without resolving any of the pressing domestic issues or overcoming existing political, social or economic barriers.⁷³

Some authors dubbed this kind of ideological orientation as a particular form of 'radical non-alignment', an obscure undercurrent inside the NAM. Followers of such a streak often advocated rapprochement with one bloc or one great power, mostly socialist ones, frequently portraying them as natural allies, while the Soviet-style communism stood for them as the only viable ideology for the Third World. In many ways, these nations (Cuba, Vietnam, Angola, Ethiopia, Nicaragua, etc.) aspired to project their own experiences with the anti-imperialist struggle onto other NAM members, often portraying the Soviet bloc as a sincere ally in the global struggle for liberation. This kind of approach, which also insisted on the original non-alignment being already obsolete, inadequate and adjusted to the European Cold War (criticism of Yugoslavia), only further undermined the independent and non-ideological role of the NAM. This does not mean that there were no radical forces on the right, different conservative regimes like Saudi Arabia, Suharto's Indonesia, Zaire or similar, however, their penchant for radicalization, although also thought wrongful, was far less dominant or threatening than the leftist one.⁷⁴ Radical challenges like these, as we shall see, often triggered speedy mobilization of 'moderate' forces among the non-aligned, primarily those nations denouncing ideological purity or spirit of confrontation, while simultaneously advocating restraint and pragmatism, without any desire to impose their own line of thinking on others but also refusing to be bullied into submission by any radical minority.

It was one of India's leading diplomats, T. N. Kaul, who described in an internal analysis the outstanding differences between Afro-Asianism and non-alignment, primarily stressing the evident advantages the latter possessed over the former's objective limitations:

> Non-alignment is an ideology that is attracting peoples and countries from all regions of the world and should be further developed irrespective of regional and racial ties which it cuts across. We should also stress not only the negative aspects of non-alignment, which are confined to the military field, but pay more attention to its positive aspects and develop further cooperation with non-aligned countries in the political, economic, cultural and other spheres.[75]

This clearly implied that non-alignment was continuously striving to overcome all regional, racial, ideological, political, economic, social and other divisions that often had a highly negative impact on the basic nature of its constructive international role.

Conversely, some key NAM members, like Algeria and some other African nations, were also active adherents of a line assuming some of the characteristics of both non-alignment and Afro-Asianism, the so-called 'Third Worldism'. This was an ideological orientation that aspired to mesh 'romanticized interpretations of pre-colonial traditions and cultures with the utopianism embodied by Marxism and socialism specifically, and "Western" visions of modernization and development more generally', thus spurring intensive debates about future socioeconomic development, but without succumbing to any of the dominant ideologies in the world or trying to align the NAM with either of the two blocs.[76] 'Third Worldism' was 'a new kind of mass-based politics and new forms of economic or social organisation' that were, as some perceived it, different from the 'failed' recipes of US capitalism or Soviet socialism, thus also becoming part of the rationale for the NAM's struggle for the new world economic order during the 1970s.[77]

India, Yugoslavia and Egypt as the Pillars of Non-Alignment

Non-alignment, however, was never a concept exclusively applied to the policies of Third World states, even though the majority of its proponents came from Asia, Africa and Latin America. In fact, 'Yugoslavia had a formative influence on the character of non-alignment and played an influential role in its gradual institutionalization into the Non-Aligned Movement.'[78] Therefore, while India stood at the very origins of the doctrine, since non-alignment was essentially a direct product of the Asian strivings for decolonization, Yugoslavia, nonetheless, was the country that continuously pushed for the establishment of more permanent forms of mutual cooperation. Unlike many Asian or African countries, Yugoslavia's non-alignment was not a logical result of any anti-colonial struggle but a direct outcome of the inter-bloc policy dynamics of the Cold War, when Belgrade, a former Soviet bloc member, decided to break away from its bloc patron in 1948 and adopt a realist, active and flexible approach to world affairs.

Furthermore, the strength of Yugoslavia's appeal among non-aligned countries stemmed from the fact that it was 'a small country which is vigorously modernizing itself, it provides a model for economic development ... it has followed a policy of non-alignment while obtaining economic aid from both East and West ... and economic and technical aid from Yugoslavia allows them [non-aligned countries] to minimize entanglement with the major blocs'.[79] This kind of approach largely contributed to Tito and Yugoslavia being highly regarded throughout the Third World as genuine adherents and proponents of non-alignment.[80] In short, Yugoslavia sought reduction of Cold War rivalries and broadening of the political base of non-alignment by encompassing a growing number of newly independent countries, irrespective of which continent they originated from or which socioeconomic model they adhered to, as long as this assisted the enhancement of wider international solidarity of all non-bloc actors against the general setting of the Cold War.[81]

Three leading non-aligned countries – India, Yugoslavia and Egypt, and their respective leaders Nehru, Tito and Nasser – theoretically and practically shaped the foundations of global non-alignment, thus galvanizing this entire endeavour which would eventually transform itself into the NAM. However, even though Tito, Nehru and Nasser generally shared similar opposition to blocs and great power domination, both in their respective regions and globally, there were certain differences in their styles and practices of non-alignment, which was logical enough, taking into account the great historical and cultural diversity they all came from.[82] Tito was convinced that in his Indian and Egyptian counterparts he had found leaders who shared the same aspirations and faced similar difficulties as himself, but he also saw in the other two a potent force that could gradually readjust some of the practices of the global system of international relations. The 'big three of non-alignment' proclaimed their sincere dedication to such a policy that implied both non-involvement in any great power blocs and desire for preserving an independent stance in foreign affairs, while putting forward the necessity of peaceful co-existence not merely as an alternative but as an imperative of world politics.[83]

Essentially, Nehru was the primary proponent of the doctrine of non-alignment, while its philosophical foundations could be found both in the general thinking promoted by the Indian National Congress during the struggle for national liberation and in his personal contemplation on the nature of India's future role in world affairs where different great powers would still dominate the international landscape.[84] Furthermore, we should also stress that it was Nehru who initially provided the conceptual and philosophical rationale for non-alignment, endowed it with respectable arguments both at home and abroad, and raised the idea that non-aligned countries were perfectly suited to the role of mediators and moderators between conflicting great powers, as long as they shied away from any formal alignments with them.[85] Nevertheless, a common problem was often apparent for other non-bloc countries in emulating India's authentic path of non-alignment, since no other member shared India's vast territorial and demographic size, as well as its socioeconomic or military potential. In fact, Nehru continuously tried to stay ignorant of any great power rivalries, other than the most immediate regional ones directly affecting India's security, while simultaneously taking a firm neutralist stance with respect to many wider international issues.[86]

In 1946, while in the role of Prime Minister of the Interim Government, Nehru laid down the guiding principles of non-alignment:

> We shall take full part in international conferences as a free nation with our own policy and not merely as a satellite of another nation … We propose, as far as possible, to keep away from the power of politics of groups, aligned against one another, which had led in the past to world wars and which may again lead to disasters on an even vaster scale.[87]

In another speech, Nehru was even blunter in his firm dedication to non-alignment's independent character:

> Now, I am not talking in terms of this bloc or that bloc; I am talking independently of the blocs as they have appeared on the world stage … I do not think that anything could be more injurious to us … than for us to give up the policies that we have pursued … and try to align ourselves with this great power or that and become its camp followers in the hope that some crumbs might fall from their table.[88]

These kind of far-reaching statements provided non-aligned countries with not only practical but also theoretical incentives to boost their overall confidence in their international struggle.

In Tito's view, however, non-alignment was based on the assumption that such a policy existed within the framework of a rapidly changing world in which peace was not a static thing to be bought by freezing the status quo. It was, as he perceived it, an unceasing struggle against the fundamental conditions that bred war, one waged by the larger part of the non-aligned world that was transforming itself into a new potent force of international politics.[89] Nasser, somewhat similar to both his elder patrons, was trying to oppose any regional blocs that provided safe haven for 'imperialist and Zionist' interests in the Middle East and to this end he was fully prepared, more so than Nehru and Tito ever were, to utilize growing contradictions between the two superpowers to further strengthen his footing. For him, Egypt stood at the boundaries of three worlds (Arab, Islamic and African), thus endowing his country with a special mission to fulfil in liberating the Middle East and wider Afro-Asia from any foreign oppression or interference.[90]

These three leaders were also conscious enough to understand that non-bloc countries had neither economic nor military power to effectively undermine the bipolar world order. Nevertheless, they were well aware that the nuances of superpower confrontation and the intricacies of the international system they represented still offered extensive opportunities for the world standing between the blocs to establish itself as an area where the views of the superpowers could be moderated and the suspicions of the non-aligned allayed.[91] An independent, active and constructive approach from non-aligned countries, such as those of Tito, Nehru and Nasser, was the only way these actors could have a tangible influence in international affairs, while gaining corresponding advantages, especially security and economic ones, from such a concrete policy. Therefore, closer political and economic cooperation and coordination between them would only add greater weight to their collective actions.[92]

However, there was another notion also closely related to the cause of non-alignment and what it stood for: peaceful co-existence. Peaceful co-existence was initially put forward by the Soviet leader Vladimir Lenin and then picked up by one of his subsequent heirs Nikita Khrushchev to explain the peaceful interaction and competition between the two dominant socio-political international systems, capitalist and socialist, without ever being substantially expanded into the Third World.[93] Yet it was the implementation of the so-called Five Principles of Peaceful Co-Existence, *Panchsheel* (mutual respect for each other's sovereignty and territorial integrity, mutual non-aggression, mutual non-interference into each other's internal affairs, equality and mutual benefit, peaceful co-existence), that not only had a formative influence on the foreign policies of different Asian nations, primarily China, India and Burma, but also a decisive impact on the evolution of global non-alignment as a whole, thus providing new substance to this specific concept of peaceful co-existence.[94]

Yugoslavia was one of the first non-Asian nations that fully embraced these principles not only as a means of boosting its international prestige but also as a tool to further recalibrate its position in world affairs. Tito started promoting his own brand officially dubbed as 'active peaceful co-existence', which found its way into his first joint statement with Nehru, which also dealt with the various causes of tensions and conflicts in the world, and therefore going well beyond just bilateral relations, as the classical notion of peaceful co-existence often implied. According to Tito, this kind of active cooperation between all countries, bloc and non-bloc, should be primarily based on mutual equality and understanding as firm guarantees of any success. Therefore, the immediate outcome of all these joint efforts should be gradual elimination of all international divisions which bred political, economic, social and other causes of war.[95] Essentially, this concept was the basic negation of the divisive Cold War politics, observing peaceful co-existence much wider than just two blocs, while concurrently considering them as the principal obstacle to the worldwide promotion of peace and cooperation.[96]

Non-Alignment as a Third Bloc?

Whenever we discuss global non-alignment, it is inevitable that we stumble upon the story of a 'third force' or a 'third bloc'. In fact, such proclamations served more as a way of discrediting the policy of non-alignment as being fundamentally not too dissimilar from the one represented by the other two blocs. This kind of approach was very close to Alfred Sauvy's original definition of the Third World not only as a grouping connected by similar historical destiny and general underdevelopment, but also as an interest group motivated to become a 'third force' in world politics, since 'like the Third Estate, it has been ignored and despised and it too wants to be something'.[97] The concept of a 'third force' came to prominence with the emergence of the Asian Socialist Conference (ASC), another regional organization representing countries standing between the two blocs in the early 1950s. Nevertheless, adherents of this 'third force' inside the ASC were still strongly opposed to any mention of a 'third bloc', considering their concept more as a rallying cry for Asian nations to strengthen their bilateral ties and expand political and economic cooperation but short of establishing anything resembling a well-disciplined bloc.[98]

As for Yugoslavia, Tito never publicly promoted such an idea, since he was well aware that all non-aligned nations were economically and militarily too feeble to confront even one bloc, not to mention both of them. Nevertheless, he was still conscious enough to recognize that these nations held certain political cards in their hands, especially in the domain of strategic position or direct control over raw materials, which could then be used effectively in their dealings with the great powers through some kind of concerted action but one falling short of any 'third bloc'. In 1952, while meeting Indian socialists, Tito strongly indicated that he was

> of an opinion that the formal establishment of the Third Bloc would not be expedient for the time being and it would be better to continue to work on rapprochement and coordination in the UN on many issues that are of common interest. Otherwise, we could have both of them, i.e. both blocs, against us and that could only harm us.[99]

This line was picked up by Nasser at the Belgrade Conference, who also stated his firm opposition to similar ideas: 'We live in a world suffering from the strife between two blocs and we cannot imagine that a third bloc should enter the arena and increase the tension of this strife instead of easing it.'[100] In fact, it was during Tito's first visit to India and Burma in 1954–5 that both he and Nehru openly denounced any intention of setting up a 'third bloc' as it was in open contradiction with the very essence of non-alignment.

Furthermore, both Tito and Nasser were fully aware that Nehru was firmly against the idea of a 'third bloc'. He considered it as something that 'has no relation to reality' and 'it would be a wrong step, amounting to ourselves coming into the arena of power politics'. Nehru pointed out that none of these non-aligned countries possessed modern weapons or robust economies that could make any 'third bloc' feasible:

> Sometimes it is suggested … that the small countries should band themselves together. If that implies what has been called a Third Force, it is a contradiction in terms because numbers do not create force. They may create moral pressures but not a force. It will not make the slightest difference to the great military powers of today if the military weak countries band themselves together.[101]

Still, Nehru considered that there was more than enough space to create something he dubbed as 'a third way which takes the best from all existing systems … and seeks to create something suited to one's own history and philosophy', thus implying closer interaction between the non-aligned countries in the UN so as to create more public pressure on the great powers.[102]

However, Nehru still advocated the idea of a 'zone of peace' which was supposed to envelop all nations that opposed war, those that spoke against all bloc divisions and who were striving to end all conflicts or curb them to a certain region. According to him, these nations were primarily advocating closer cooperation between all relevant international factors but without creating anything resembling an organized group.[103]

Furthermore, he was trying to offer a way out of this awkward situation related to the idea of a 'third bloc' by promoting substantially different forms of cooperation concerning the fundamental issues of war and peace:

> Mention has been made of a 'third force' ... It would be absurd for a number of countries in Asia to come together and call themselves a third force or a third power in a military sense ... Instead of calling it a third force or a third bloc, it can be called a third area, an area which ... does not want war, works for peace in a positive way and believes in cooperation ... Those countries, who do not want to align themselves with either of the two powerful blocs and who are willing to work for the cause of peace, should by all means come together.[104]

This kind of elaboration made a serious impact on the thinking around this issue, also laying down some of the theoretical groundwork for the subsequent establishment of the NAM.

Thus, as we have seen, none of the crucial members of the non-aligned group ever seriously conspired to set up a 'third bloc' within the Cold War system, in spite of constant accusations levelled by different great powers of the NAM ultimately becoming just another bloc. The non-aligned did not possess political, economic or military means to establish a 'third bloc', there were no dominant powers inside this group that could establish themselves as hegemons, a bloc-like unity of mind and action was incomprehensible to the non-aligned, since they insisted on voluntary participation and individuality, and, finally, this was ideologically, politically, socially, economically, militarily and culturally such a diverse group that it was almost impossible for them to set up anything resembling a bloc-disciplined organization. However, the diversity of views inside this group were further stimulated by its influential members as another sign of its inherent democratic character and strength through diversity.[105]

Yet, respective foreign policies of non-aligned nations urged countries of similar aspirations to establish constructive means for closer cooperation and coordination with respect to certain outstanding issues. In the words of a high-ranking Yugoslav official:

> The uncommitted countries are not a bloc of powers. First of all, they have no power. Not only do they not want to, but they cannot build up a third bloc ... But, in attempting to influence the course of world affairs, the uncommitted do represent *a group*; their representatives get together from time to time, and there is a permanent cooperation between them.[106]

Non-alignment and its most active proponents were conscious enough of what kind of danger emulating a bloc eventually implied; therefore, these nations never aspired to establish themselves as a 'third bloc'. Nevertheless, they did strive to 'foster relations of solidarity among all those who have engaged towards the same end, with determination and perseverance for the necessary overcoming of geopolitical balances, for the traditional authentic democratization of international relations'.[107]

Even though establishing a 'third bloc' was out of the question, the majority of non-aligned countries still acted in a rather rigid fashion inside the UN where they eventually constituted a sounding majority, often voting almost unanimously, and thus triggering accusations from the great powers that they were behaving almost as a well-disciplined bloc.[108] The UN bodies became a place where representatives of non-aligned countries could frequently meet and inform each other of all important international issues, thus gradually becoming the most proficient and proactive group in the sphere of tabling resolutions, launching joint initiatives, organizing discussions on the issues of peace, poverty, equality, disarmament, etc., especially in the General Assembly (GA) and sometimes in the Security Council (SC) too.[109] In all these cases, high levels of voting cohesion were reached, even though sometimes accompanied by a varying level of efficiency and frequently depending on the regional inclinations of certain NAM members.[110] In fact, the greatest success of the NAM inside the UN was the full completion of the process of decolonization by 1990, even though in the field of reducing poverty and bridging the North–South gap results were not that promising.

Conclusion

Historically speaking, global non-alignment had come to prominence as a more comprehensive alternative to the great power system of military-political alliances. For a plethora of non-bloc nations this entire system of blocs and strategic alliances seemed detrimental to their established national interests and unsuitable for the specific historical situation they were experiencing. With time, non-aligned countries had become recognized as 'useful catalysts in reducing international tension and in promoting peace', thus strengthening the previously unseen level of their international visibility, while also boosting their flexibility in dealing with different expressions of alignment in international affairs.[111] Essentially, non-alignment had 'crystalized into an independent, impartial and positive force that did not believe that alliances were inevitable and indispensable for national security'. Therefore, the non-aligned believed that in a world dominated by two mutually antagonistic power blocs, they should make positive contributions towards the lessening of tensions so as to finally ensure a more protracted world peace and increased global security.[112]

Perhaps the best definition of non-alignment, encompassing everything previously discussed, was provided by the Political Declaration adopted at the 1970 Lusaka Conference, when the NAM was formally established:

> The policy of non-alignment has emerged from the determination of independent countries to safeguard their national independence and the legitimate rights of their peoples. The growth of non-alignment into a broad international movement cutting across racial, regional and other barriers, is an integral part of significant changes in the structure of the entire international community. It is the result of the world anti-colonial revolution and the emergence of a large number of newly liberated countries, which, opting for an independent political orientation and development, have refused to accept the replacement of centuries-old forms of subordination by new ones. At the root of these changes lies the ever more clearly

expressed aspiration of member-nations for freedom, independence and equality, and their determination to resist all forms of oppression and exploitation. This has been the substance and meaning of our strivings and actions.[113]

To conclude, what the majority of non-bloc states aspired to achieve was the idea that global non-alignment should decisively break away from any regional limitations (Afro-Asia) or classical political clichés (anti-imperialism, anti-colonialism, anti-revisionism) and set up its own global agenda based on universally acceptable principles (freedom, peace, security, racial, political and social equality, disarmament, economic development) that would finally facilitate the strong link between different non-bloc states and the social systems they represented at the level of the entire international community. Only through this kind of 'universalist' approach would non-aligned states be able to establish stronger bonds between themselves, open a new page in the political dialogue with the great powers and create a more stable political, economic and social surrounding for the phase following political independence – a phase of economic reconstruction and modernization. This point largely reflected Nehru's old statement that policies of great powers directed at granting or withholding aid or technological know-how, while simultaneously manipulating prices of their finished products or keeping low prices of raw materials, posed far greater danger in the long run to the existence of postcolonial nations than any overt military aggression could ever have had.[114]

With time, as we shall see, underdevelopment would become the greatest factor undermining and discrediting non-alignment, what it stood for and what its ultimate goals were. This was all part of an increasing trend inside the NAM that its member states dedicated more attention to regional issues, considering them to have more direct influence on their particular interests, and thus often ignoring more general and major ones. However, it was these comprehensive issues, such as security and development, that had a far more profound and protracted impact on their future.[115] Therefore, the oft-mentioned struggle against colonialism and imperialism was a just and necessary precondition for the emergence of the non-aligned world as we know it. But this was not the only struggle they had to wage to become ultimately stable and modern societies. This proved to be an even bigger challenge to the NAM's unhindered evolution, since it involved overcoming many of the fundamental political, economic and social divisions in the world. Primarily resolving the issue of unequal economic development, one always closely related to the continued independent existence of the world between the blocs, had ultimately become one of the central inspirations and goals of non-alignment, thus putting the NAM at the very centre of a much wider and still relevant North–South relationship.[116] This was the centrepiece of the NAM's presence in world affairs during its 1970s heyday.

Notes

1 Mark Atwood Lawrence, 'The Rise and Fall of Nonalignment', in *The Cold War in the Third World*, 141–2.
2 *Conference of Heads of State or Government of Non-Aligned Countries, Belgrade, September, 1–6, 1961* (Belgrade: GOY, 1964), 25–6.

3   Bojana Tadić, *Nesvrstanost u teoriji i praksi međunarodnih odnosa*, 50–70.
4   Cecil V. Crabb, Jr., *The Elephants and the Grass*, 10–13.
5   S. B. Jain, *India's Foreign Policy and Non-Alignment*, 8–14.
6   Ranko Petković, *Teorijski pojmovi nesvrstanosti*, 18–23.
7   *Conference of Heads of State or Government of Non-Aligned Countries*, 108.
8   Myanmar Ministry of Foreign Affairs (MMFA), 'Non-Alignment Movement', Research Division, 1978.
9   *Jawaharlal Nehru's Speeches: September 1946–May 1949* (New Delhi: GOI, 1958), 220–1.
10 Bahgat Korany, *Social Change, Charisma and International Behaviour*, 103.
11 Leo Mates, *Nesvrstanost: teorija i saveremena praksa*, 78–80.
12 Peter Lyon, *Neutralism*, 72–3.
13 Vijay Prashad, *The Darker Nations*, xv–xix.
14 Mohammed Ayoob, 'The Third World in the System of States: Acute Schizophrenia or Growing Pains?', *International Studies Quarterly* 33.1 (1989), 71–5.
15 John Lewis Gaddis, 'On Starting All over Again: A Naïve Approach to the Study of the Cold War', in *Reviewing the Cold War: Approaches, Interpretations, Theory*, Odd Arne Westad (ed.) (London: Frank Cass, 2001), 31–2.
16 'Pregled diskusije: mesto i uloga nesvrstanosti u savremenom svetu', in *Politika nesvrstanosti u savremenom svetu*, Ljubivoje Aćimović (ed.) (Beograd: IMPP, 1969), 24–5.
17 M. S. Rajan, *Nonalignment and Nonaligned Movement*, 10–11.
18 'Kautilya', 'The Philosophy of Non-Alignment', in *India 1962: Annual Review* (London: Information Service of India, 1962), 8.
19 M. S. Rajan, *Non-Alignment: India and the Future* (Mysore: Mysore University Press, 1970), 13.
20 *Conference of Heads of State or Government of Non-Aligned Countries*, 86.
21 S. B. Jain, *India's Foreign Policy and Non-Alignment*, 12.
22 G. H. Jansen, *Afro-Asia and Non-Alignment*, 402.
23 David Kimche, *The Afro-Asian Movement*, 22–3.
24 'Pregled diskusije: mesto i uloga nesvrstanosti u savremenom svetu', in *Politika nesvrstanosti u savremenom svetu*, 54–5.
25 Dimče Belovski, 'Development of Relations between the Great Powers and Bloc Groupings and Repercussions on the Position and Actions of the Non-Aligned Countries', in *Non-Alignment in the Eighties*, 36.
26 Bojana Tadić, *Nesvrstanost u teoriji i praksi međunarodnih odnosa*, 20–1.
27 Arhiv Jugoslavije (AJ), 837, Cabinet of the President of the Republic (KPR), I-4-a, 'Report on the Cairo Preparatory Meeting', June 1961.
28 Richard L. Jackson, *The Non-Aligned, the UN and the Superpowers*, 43–4.
29 The National Archives (TNA), Foreign Office (FO) 371/161211, 'Neutralism', 30 January 1961.
30 National Archives of India (NAI), Ministry of External Affairs (MEA), HI/102 (12)/80, 'Difference between neutrality and non-alignment', 20 May 1980.
31 'Kautilya', 'The Philosophy of Non-Alignment', 7.
32 Cecil V. Crabb, Jr., *The Elephants and the Grass*, 7.
33 Kwesi Armah, *Peace without Power: Ghana's Foreign Policy 1957–1966* (Accra: Ghana Universities Press, 2004), 142.
34 *Conference of Heads of State or Government of Non-Aligned Countries*, 27.
35 Ranko Petković, *Teorijski pojmovi nesvrstanosti*, 72–5.

36 Jawaharlal Nehru's Speeches 1949–1953 (New Delhi: GOI, 1954), 221.
37 AJ, 837, KPR, I-2, 'Joint Statement, 22 December 1954'.
38 Peter Lyon, Neutralism, 62.
39 Jawaharlal Nehru, India's Foreign Policy, 25.
40 B. R. Nanda (ed.), Indian Foreign Policy, 134–5.
41 Aleš Bebler, 'Non-Alignment and the Theory of Equidistance', Review of International Affairs 12 (1961), 1–2.
42 Corall Bell, 'Non-Alignment and the Power Balance', in Components of Defense Policy, Davis B. Bobrow (ed.) (Chicago, IL: Rand McNally & Co., 1965), 69.
43 Samir N. Anabtawi, 'Neutralists and Neutralism', The Journal of Politics 27.2 (1965), 358–9.
44 Cecil V. Crabb, Jr., The Elephants and the Grass, 80.
45 Ali A. Mazrui, On Heroes and Uhuru-Worship: Essays on Independent Africa (London: Longmans, 1974), 203.
46 George McTurnan Kahin (ed.), The Asian-African Conference (Ithaca, NY: Cornell University Press, 1956), 66.
47 J. W. Burton, 'Introduction to Nonalignment', in Nonalignment, J. W. Burton (ed.), 16–17.
48 Bimla Prasad, 'Opšte iskustvo i perspektive nesvrstanosti', in Politika nesvrstanosti u savremenom svetu, 109.
49 The Conference of Heads of State or Government of Non-Aligned Countries, 168–9.
50 Leo Mates, Nesvrstanost, 236–7.
51 Robert L. Rothstein. 'Alignment, Non-Alignment, and Small Powers, 1945–1965', 404–5.
52 Charles Burton Marshall, 'On Understanding the Unaligned', in Neutralism and Nonalignment, 28.
53 Leo Mates, Nesvrstanost, 178–80.
54 Bimla Prasad, 'Opšte iskustvo i perspektive nesvrstanosti', 110–11.
55 Margaret Legum, 'Africa and Nonalignment', in Nonalignment, 57–8.
56 Robert C. Good, 'State-Building as a Determinant of Foreign Policy in the New States', in Neutralism and Nonalignment, 11.
57 Ernest V. Lefever, 'Nehru, Nasser, and Nkrumah on Neutralism', in ibid., 95, 116.
58 Leo Mates, Nesvrstanost, 113–14.
59 Ernest V. Lefever, 'Nehru, Nasser, and Nkrumah on Neutralism', 117.
60 Edvard Kardelj, Istorijski koreni nesvrstavanja (Beograd: Komunist, 1975), 37.
61 Ranko Petković, Teorijski pojmovi nesvrstanosti, 220–8.
62 TNA, FO 371/161211, 'Neutralism', 30 January 1961.
63 Declassified Documents Reference System (DDRS), CK3100320338, 'Neutralism in the Northeast Asia Area', 1955.
64 Khalid E. Babaa, Cecil V. Crabb Jr., 'Non-Alignment as a Diplomatic and Ideological Credo', 10.
65 The Conference of Heads of State or Government of Non-Aligned Countries, 70.
66 Ranko Petković, Nesvrstanost, 61–4.
67 David Kimche, The Afro-Asian Movement, 144–67.
68 TNA, FO 371/161211, 'Neutralism', 30 January 1961.
69 Robert A. Mortimer. The Third World Coalition in International Politics, 11–12.
70 S. Neil MacFarlane, Superpower Rivalry and Third World Radicalism: The Idea of National Liberation (Baltimore, MD: The Johns Hopkins University Press, 1985), 82–3.

71 Ranko Petković, *Nesvrstanost*, 67–8.
72 Frantz Fanon, *The Wretched of the Earth* (London: Penguin, 2001), 63–5.
73 Edvard Kardelj, *Istorijski koreni nesvrstavanja*, 7–8.
74 Ranko Petković, *Nesvrstanost*, 80–90.
75 Nehrul Memorial Museum and Library (NMML), T. N. Kaul Collection, I-III Instalments, Subject File (SF) 15, 'T.N. Kaul to M.J. Desai', 18 December 1962.
76 Mark T. Berger, 'After the Third World? History, Destiny and Fate of Third Worldism', *Third World Quarterly* 25.1 (2004), 11.
77 Robert Malley, *The Call from Algeria: Third Worldism, Revolution, and the Turn to Islam* (Berkeley, CA: University of California Press, 1996), 88.
78 Roy Allison, *The Soviet Union and the Strategy of Non-Alignment in the Third World*, 4.
79 'Outlook for Yugoslavia – NIE 15-61', May 23 1961 in *Yugoslavia – From National Communism to National Collapse: US Intelligence Community Estimative Products on Yugoslavia, 1948–1990* (Washington, DC: National Intelligence Council, 2006), 264.
80 Cecil V. Crabb, Jr., *The Elephants and the Grass*, 70.
81 Alvin Z. Rubinstein, *Yugoslavia and the Non-Aligned World*, 281.
82 Momir Stojković, *Tito, Nehru, Naser: nastanak i razvoj politike i Pokreta nesvrstanosti* (Zaječar: RO Zaječar, 1983), 49–72.
83 Mohamed Heikal, *The Cairo Documents* (New York, NY: Doubleday & Company, 1973), 251–99.
84 T. A. Keenleyside, 'Prelude to Power: the Meaning of Non-Alignment before Indian Independence', *Pacific Affairs* 53.3 (1980), 464–82; Amit Das Gupta, 'India and Non-Alignment – Formative Years', in *The 60th Anniversary of the Non-Aligned Movement*, 96–104.
85 Rami Ginat, *Syria and the Doctrine of Arab Neutralism*, 8–11.
86 B. R. Nanda (ed.), *Indian Foreign Policy*, 180–3.
87 Jawaharlal Nehru, *India's Foreign Policy: Selected Speeches, September 1946–April 1961* (New Delhi: GOI, 1961), 2.
88 *Jawaharlal Nehru's Speeches: September 1946–May 1949*, 214.
89 Jovan Čavoški, 'Between Great Powers and Third World Neutralists: Yugoslavia and the Belgrade Conference of the Nonaligned Movement 1961', in *The Non-Aligned Movement and the Cold War*, 187–8.
90 Jovan Čavoški, 'Constructing Nasser's Neutralism: Egypt and the Rise of Nonalignment in the Middle East', in *The Regional Cold Wars in Europe, East Asia, and the Middle East*, 89–90.
91 Alvin Z. Rubinstein, *Yugoslavia and the Non-Aligned World*, 113, 116.
92 M. S. Rajan, *Nonalignment and Nonaligned Movement*, 17–21.
93 Nikita S. Khrushchev, 'On Peaceful Co-Existence', *Foreign Affairs* 38.1 (1959), 3–6.
94 *Pancha Shila: Its Meaning and History: A Documentary Study* (New Delhi: Lok Sabha Secretariat, 1955).
95 Ranko Petković, *Nesvrstana Jugoslavija i savremeni svet*, 25.
96 Leo Mates, *Koegzistencija* (Zagreb: Školska knjiga, 1974), 12–21.
97 B. R. Tomlinson, 'What was the Third World?', *Journal of Contemporary History* 38.2 (2003), 309.
98 Kyaw Zaw Win, 'The 1953 Asian Socialist Conference in Rangoon: Precursor to the Bandung Conference', in *Bandung 1955: Little Histories*, Derek McDougall and Antonia Finnane (eds) (Caulfield: Monsah University Press, 2010), 43–55; Jovan Čavoški, 'Ideološki prijatelj iz daleka: Jugoslavija i Azijska socijalistička konferencija', *Istorija 20. veka* 1 (2019), 139–60.

99 Diplomatic Archives of the Serbian Foreign Ministry (DAMSPS), Political Archives (PA), 1952, folder (f) 35, document 410760, 'Tito-SPI talks, 29 May 1952'.
100 *Conference of Heads of State or Government of Nonaligned Countries*, 45.
101 Jawaharlal Nehru, *India's Foreign Policy*, 77–8.
102 David Kimche, *The Afro-Asian Movement*, 24.
103 S. B. Jain, *India's Foreign Policy and Non-Alignment*, 86–7.
104 *Jawaharlal Nehru's Speeches 1949–1953*, 325–6.
105 TNA, FO 371/161211, 'Neutralism', 30 January 1961.
106 Marko Nikezić, 'Why Uncommitted Countries Hold that They Are Not Neutral?', *The Annals of the American Academy of Political and Social Science* 336 (1961), 81.
107 Lazhari Cheriet, 'Alternative to the Bipolarization', in *Non-Alignment in the Eighties*, 46–7.
108 A. W. Singham and Shirley Hune, *Non-Alignment in an Age of Alignments*, 27–30.
109 Peter Willetts, *The Non-Aligned Movement*, 96–8, 102–9.
110 Richard L. Jackson, *The Non-Aligned, the UN and the Superpowers*, 103–5.
111 NAI, MEA, HI/12(1)/72, 'The evolution of the concept of non-alignment', 8 October 1971.
112 MMFA, 'Non-Alignment Movement', Research Division, 1978.
113 *Documents of the Gatherings of the Non-Aligned Countries*, 1 (Beograd: IMPP, 1989), 44.
114 NAI, MEA, HI/102(28)/76, 'Role of non-alignment', 22 April 1976.
115 'Pregled diskusije: mesto i uloga nesvrstanosti u savremenom svetu', in *Politika nesvrstanosti u savremenom svetu*, 38–9.
116 NAI, MEA, HI/12(1)/72, 'Cooperation among non-aligned countries', 11 October 1971.

2

Setting the Stage: the 1961 Belgrade Conference

Until today, international historiography has often had conflicting views about when and where the NAM was truly established, what was the very first major international event where non-alignment was officially proclaimed as a foreign policy credo and whether that gathering was also the point of departure for the movement or came about only later on, especially when one is referring to different Afro-Asian regionalist initiatives preceding the summit in Belgrade. These fundamental issues need to be treated in advance as part of a protracted evolution of global non-alignment.

The 1961 Belgrade Conference, formally the very first summit of non-aligned countries, as well as the point of origin of the NAM but not its true birthplace, represents a major international event, a defining moment and a conceptual watershed in the history of the non-bloc, Third World and developing countries during the early Cold War years. Together with the earlier Asian-African Conference held in the Indonesian town of Bandung in April 1955, a gathering of a similar though not identical format, this summit in Belgrade stands tall as one of two major international events shaping the collective postcolonial and non-bloc identity, thus largely determining the guiding principles, political outlook and international presence of countries standing between the blocs during 1950s and early 1960s.

However, when one discusses the link between the Bandung Conference and the history of global non-alignment, in the international literature a straight line often exists between this gathering and the one in Belgrade, often portraying the preceding Afro-Asian event as a precursor to the global history of the NAM.[1] However, it is only in more recent literature that some of this earlier comprehension has been largely discarded, with this misplaced historical analogy between Bandung and Belgrade becoming less clear and far more complex.[2] Essentially, the Belgrade Conference was largely motivated by ideas, principles and aspirations somewhat different, although not fundamentally, from the ones dominating the Bandung discourse. The NAM was not founded in either of these two places, both envisaged as one-time events; however, the movement's entire subsequent history had much more to do with the summit in the Yugoslav capital than with the one in Indonesia, particularly with respect to the ideas, principles, motivations and format of such events.[3]

In fact, it was the Belgrade Conference that eventually pushed the non-aligned agenda out of the exclusive orbit of anti-colonial and anti-imperialist sentiments and strict 'regionalist' adherence, and set it on a path largely transcending historical, political, social, economic, cultural and other boundaries on four different continents. In this way, this summit was laying down foundations of a more 'universalist' programme largely dedicated to international peace and security and economic and developmental issues which were paramount to the stability and prosperity of non-bloc nations, and thus proving these crucial issues were far more conducive to successfully pushing back against any potential neo-colonialist and imperialist resurgence than any calls for an armed struggle set by Bandung.

The NAM's Afro-Asian Predecessors

Anti-colonialism and anti-imperialism were indeed the initial driving forces behind any collectivist impulses that eventually led to the convening of the first Asian-African Conference.[4] However, that gathering was not the first attempt at establishing something resembling a permanent regional organization through convening a summit of colonial or postcolonial nations. The end of the Second World War, and the subsequent initiation of the process of decolonization in Asia, again triggered initiatives of promoting regional solidarity and cooperation. This was especially true since at that time, besides India, none of these nations could gain their voice inside the newly established UN. Therefore, Nehru, then head of the Indian Interim Government, was already contemplating setting up a permanent anti-colonial and anti-imperialist 'Asian alternative' to the existing international system.[5] It is very interesting to note that this was the only time when Nehru was quite open-minded towards establishing a permanent international organization, something not characteristic of him during either the Bandung or Belgrade conferences.[6]

When the Asian Relations Conference (ARC) finally convened in New Delhi in March–April 1947, with 231 delegates and observers from twenty-eight different Asian nations attending (including Egypt and eight Soviet Asian republics), many of them still colonies, it was evident that Nehru's ideas about Asia's special position in the world would naturally create an undercurrent for all discussions, largely defining the conference agenda around major issues like decolonization, economic development, etc.[7] Even though he could not openly advocate India's non-alignment, Nehru still pointed out that great power blocs evidently stood in the way of materializing aspirations of Asian nations. Therefore, he issued a call to not allow Asia to become once again a mere peon of the great powers, although cooperation with all international factors on an equal and independent basis should be actively pursued, with some delegates even daringly proposing the establishment of a bloc of neutral Asian nations.[8] This was the very first time that such a bold idea was openly tabled, with the non-bloc option gaining early, although timid and reluctant, recognition.

Despite these lofty ideals being proclaimed, this conference also demonstrated, as was the case with Bandung, that common geography or shared colonial suffering were not enough to bridge individual differences, resolve bilateral conflicts or facilitate reaching common political standing. Therefore, disputes between Chiang Kai-Shek's Nationalist Chinese and Indian delegates over Tibet or between Jewish and Arab delegates over Palestine clearly indicated that such troublesome issues could always disrupt any constructive efforts at hammering out wider unity. Even when the Chinese proposal for setting up a permanent Asian organization was readily endorsed by the majority, no definite moves were ever made in the aftermath.[9] Even when twelve Asian and two African countries (Egypt and Ethiopia), plus Australia, met in New Delhi in January 1949 to formally discuss ending the colonial conflict in Indonesia and extending international recognition to that nation, Nehru's proposal for a permanent Asian organization was left unresponded to by other participants.[10] Perhaps the inglorious ending of his brainchild made the Indian prime minister even more sceptical to any similar future undertakings.

Irrespective of this obvious setback, a new framework for non-bloc cooperation was being gradually established, one that would also encompass Yugoslavia. This new framework was set inside the UN where initially an Arab-Asian, later on an expanded Afro-Asian, group was informally put together, dealing with pressing international issues, and thus becoming a kind of mediator in the global matters of war and peace, while also trying to mitigate rising contradictions between the two blocs. Essentially, this group was a revolt staged by small UN members in response to the blatant attempts of different great powers continuously compelling them to vote in a certain way.[11] This informal Arab/Afro-Asian group served as an immediate predecessor to the more potent non-aligned voting bloc in the future.

In fact, it was the Korean War (1950-3) more than any other event that stimulated a sudden rise in the international consciousness and national solidarity among newly liberated Asian and African nations, also bringing Yugoslavia to their flock, thus shaping the UN into their most important political arena. This tragic conflict also served as a linchpin interconnecting globally dispersed non-bloc factors, having almost no mutual contact before or beyond the UN, and transforming them from a separate number of individual initiatives into a more or less organized collective undertaking. This was, indeed, the stellar moment of the Afro-Asian group, irrespective of its few diplomatic achievements. However, with their increasing numbers and proactive position inside the UN, these newly liberated or non-bloc nations still managed to be taken seriously whenever certain multilateral actions were being pursued.[12]

During the initial phase of the war, India, Yugoslavia and Egypt were all non-permanent members of the UNSC, thus providing their respective ambassadors with a precious opportunity to set up a preliminary mechanism for exchanges, consultations and coordination of action between the three nations. Even though New Delhi, Belgrade and Cairo did not always see eye to eye on all issues pertaining to this conflict, getting to know each other's specific positions better largely contributed to their spirit of mutual understanding.[13] India, as an obvious leader, often shadowed by Yugoslavia and Egypt, was highly active on a number of occasions in investing efforts into finding a negotiated solution to the war. This was particularly true after the Chinese intervention in October 1950, as well as throughout the war, although without yielding considerable results due to the staunch opposition of the great powers.[14]

Despite its lacklustre effect, the Afro-Asian group plus Yugoslavia still succeeded in influencing all key UN deliberations without exercising any common ideology, political or military association or any linguistic, cultural or social similarity binding them together. However, what already served as a strong bond between all of these nations was an evident lack of engagement with any of the two blocs, as well as their preference towards pursuing independent policies. Therefore, this was an initial attempt at mobilizing a significant part of the UN, while also serving as a means of directly reaching out to the world public opinion which sympathized with their grievances and identified with their aspirations. Nevertheless, Indian officials were convinced that outright opposition to Western interference as well as shared colonial sufferings should not be the only foundations for cooperation among so many diverse nations, therefore, other common denominators also needed to be addressed.[15]

Unlike India, countries like Egypt, Syria and Indonesia were quite eager to further strengthen the cooperation between Asia and Africa, particularly against colonialist presence or increasing bloc penetration. Indonesia was the first to officially raise the proposal of convening such a regional gathering in August 1953.[16] As would be the case in the future, Nehru initially called out for laying down strict participation criteria which would make a clear distinction between the countries advocating 'independent policy of trying to avoid war' and those becoming members of blocs or military alliances or just drawing closer to them. In this way, he was openly indicating that not geographical adherence but non-bloc commitment should be the ultimate criterion for vetting any multilateral initiatives.[17] This would eventually be the key difference between the non-aligned and Afro-Asian models of organizing the Third World.

Since the international situation was becoming more relaxed after Stalin's death and the end of the Korean War, with the great powers getting ready to convene a conference in Geneva in April 1954 that would deal with Korea and the crumbling French rule in Indochina, prime ministers of five Asian nations (India, Indonesia, Ceylon, Burma and Pakistan) decided to organize a regional conference in Colombo that same month. Essentially, an exclusive Asian political discourse of the past was now being actively merged into a wider Afro-Asian multilateral format.[18] However, what truly marked the importance of the Colombo Powers was their unhidden ability, despite many individual disagreements, to speak in one voice when referring to pressing regional and international issues, while resistance to outside involvement in Asian affairs was becoming more potent, vociferous and organized, regardless of not always achieving such straightforward results.

In fact, the Colombo Conference was a reaction to the more aggressive external interference which, in the mind of five participants, constituted the main political contradiction in the world, with India, Indonesia and Burma perceiving the Western bloc as the greater threat, and Ceylon and Pakistan holding similar views about China and the USSR.[19] Even though none of the prime ministers was able to fully push through their individual agendas vis-à-vis both blocs, with Nehru and the host John Kotelawala holding sternly opposite views, all participants still managed to find common ground on a number of major topics, like decolonization, racism, nuclear disarmament and economic cooperation.[20] In the end, Indonesian Prime Minister Ali Sastroamidjojo raised again the issue of cooperation between the Asian and African countries outside the UN format, proposing a regional conference to be held in the near future, despite Nehru still holding onto his old reservations.[21]

Nevertheless, recent positive exchanges between the leaders of India, Burma and China, as well as formation of the US-led Southeast Asia Treaty Organisation (SEATO) and Central Treaty Organisation (CENTO) by early 1955, eventually compelled Nehru to give a green light to convening an Afro-Asian conference, one that would not observe regional issues separately from the relationships they all shared with Europe and America.[22] When the Colombo Five met again in the Indonesian town of Bogor at the end of December 1954, the conference agenda was far less controversial and it was mainly dedicated to the issue of conference participation. Nehru and U Nu professed their opinion that the new conference should act in favour of the further expansion of the 'zone of peace'.[23] The most controversial issues of this gathering were Chinese and Israeli participation, thus stirring a heated debate, with China eventually being invited to attend, while Israel was left out due to the possibility of an Arab boycott. Finally, it was decided to invite twenty-five countries to the Asian-African Conference (for example, both Vietnams but not both Koreas) plus the Colombo Five, while the final conference agenda encompassed a number of political and economic issues promoted by India (colonialism, racism, world peace and political, economic, social, cultural cooperation).[24]

The Bandung Conference was, in many ways, a defining moment in the history of the Third World, albeit one without an aftermath. By bringing together twenty-nine Asian and African countries (the Central African Federation decided to opt out) with such a diverse political, social and historical background, this gathering aspired to shape a new kind of postcolonial solidarity, one that would be based on the similarity of past reminiscences and the proximity of future ambitions, thus gradually ushering in a new era where, as aspired by some, the new centre of world civilization would ultimately transcend from the West to the vast areas of Asia and Africa.[25] Standing on a moral high ground, armed only with large numbers of its population and objective historical grievances, Afro-Asia sincerely hoped that this new trend in world politics would eventually become a substitute for political divisions of the Cold War and an impetus for overcoming evident inequality between the world's rich and poor.[26] However, all these objective obstacles proved to be much more resilient to any formal proclamations of racial or regional solidarity.

As for the non-aligned countries present at Bandung, they did not aim to create anything resembling 'any separate political, economic or cultural blocs', nor did they aspire to impose on other participants their respective policies as the valid ones. These nations did not abandon their foreign policy credo, however, their primary aim was to demonstrate to the world that negotiations and agreements between ideologically incompatible countries were still possible, while the role of Afro-Asia was to 'set the world a moral and practical example' for reaching meaningful settlements.[27] Nehru and U Nu were particularly active in this respect, trying to mediate between opposing factions edging closer to either of the two blocs. However, as time progressed, attacks against the non-aligned participants intensified, while non-alignment and peaceful co-existence were openly denounced by some attendees. Nehru vehemently opposed such views but he also had to sacrifice some of his principles to forge minimal consensus.[28] Such developments were, nonetheless, a clear signal to Nehru, U Nu and Nasser that this kind of conference format was not an appropriate one for non-aligned countries to effectively pursue their specific objectives.

If the Bandung Conference could not produce a lasting effect on world affairs, except in the wider imagination, for different participating countries it did serve as a springboard for establishing themselves as influential members of the wider Afro-Asian community. For China, this gathering was yet another step in the promotion of its policy of peaceful co-existence as a means of rebranding Beijing's image among its neighbours, leapfrogging US containment policy, as well as trying to diplomatically roll back colonialism and Western bloc presence in the region. Premier Zhou Enlai masterfully fulfilled his role in Bandung, often overshadowing Nehru himself, gaining widespread recognition and admiration, building new bridges, sending out messages of reconciliation, but also skilfully avoiding traps laid to foment discord between China and other participants.[29] On the other hand, this was also a transformative moment for Nasser who had undergone speedy evolution from a timid national leader to one of the major pioneers and advocates of non-alignment in the world, thus also considerably boosting his self-confidence.[30]

Nevertheless, when one deals with some of the long-term achievements of the Bandung Conference, the most significant result of this gathering was the proclamation of the famous ten principles that clearly spoke for racial and national equality, cooperation, respect for sovereignty, territorial integrity, basic human rights, UN Charter and the principle of non-interference, thus also profoundly influencing the subsequent non-aligned agenda in this respect. However, all blocs were not fully denounced and participation in them was largely ignored, except in the widest possible sense. This was the case since almost half of the attending delegations were bloc members themselves.[31] This event also did not refer to the issue of reforming the international political and economic system, one that would better suit the interests of postcolonial nations. Such an oversight, in the long run, also became one of Bandung's major conceptual deficiencies, since it had not offered a meaningful alternative.[32] However, another of Bandung's tangible achievements was the moral effect it produced where for the very first time representatives of the previously colonized countries vociferously proclaimed their refusal to take orders from their former rulers, while at the same time demonstrating their outright ability to constructively and responsibly discuss any major international issues and offer corresponding solutions.[33]

Essentially, elements such as a poorly defined geographical framework and its clear regional isolationism, indiscriminate presence of both aligned and non-aligned countries alike, lack of any coherent principles, outside the ten general ones, as well as divisive political ideas about the oppressed Asian-African majority and privileged 'white' minority in world affairs, all posed limitations on the potential global and long-term effect of this event.[34] Even though borderlines between these two concepts, Afro-Asianism and non-alignment, would sometimes get blurred from the vantage point of today's imagination, the latter, nonetheless, remained a specific political phenomenon that enjoyed its sovereign existence inside this diffuse regional notion of Afro-Asia, largely thanks to the fact that it was not generated by any regional, historical or racial exclusiveness. Not all Afro-Asian nations were non-aligned, while some European and Latin American nations did belong to this emerging group. Hence, these two tangible notions ultimately experienced different evolutionary paths and destinies, while Bandung was their only significant point of convergence, above all as a harbinger of Third World summitry.[35]

Building-up the Non-Aligned Impetus

Without an immediate follow-up to Bandung, non-alignment needed a strong push from outside Afro-Asia. Yugoslavia, as a European country, was naturally not invited to Indonesia, which then triggered serious deliberations in Belgrade about the perils of having a regionally closed group that did not have non-bloc criteria as its main filter for participation.[36] Therefore, the Yugoslav ambassador was instructed to convey to Nehru that 'a need [existed] to launch wide, constructive actions, not only in Asia, but also in the world in general, that could practically curb the pretensions of leading powers to impose solutions ... along the rigid lines of bloc divisions'. It was also suggested that an event similar to Bandung had to be organized in the future, but one which would 'encompass countries of Europe, America'.[37] This was a subtle way to declare that non-alignment generally surpassed any narrow geographical division, that it sought inspiration from the principles of peaceful co-existence, while actively advocating bloc non-adherence and global equidistance, and also dedicating more attention to the issues of international security and economic development. In the words of one author, 'more than any other country, Yugoslavia helped to make of Bandung a prologue to political action rather than a footnote to futility'.[38]

The initial step in this direction was the first tripartite meeting between the leaders of Yugoslavia, India and Egypt on the Brioni Isles in mid-July 1956, an event without any immediate aftermath, but still a harbinger of future winds. Although this meeting suffered from minor misunderstandings marked by Nehru's lingering reservations, Nasser's excessive eagerness and Tito's clear desire to strike a sensitive balance between his guests, nonetheless, this event brought closer the official stance of these three nations on many international issues, creating an image, even a flawed one, of strong unity. It was then ascertained that peace could not be achieved through bloc divisions, but it should be based on the promotion of active peaceful co-existence and advocacy of collective security, which would eventually result in the expansion of the area of peace and cooperation. In this way, a new mechanism for the exchange of views between the three leaders was ultimately established, thus creating the proactive core of the non-aligned group, if not practically then at least in everyone else's perception. This concept was soon endorsed by Sukarno and the ruler of Cambodia Prince Norodom Sihanouk during their subsequent visits to Yugoslavia, thus spreading the 'Brioni spirit' around the Third World.[39]

In a certain manner, this event also somewhat paved the way for the Belgrade Conference, primarily by laying down the agenda that would dominate the non-aligned discourse for years to come, a mix of anti-colonial, security and economic issues, a kind of 'Third World's Yalta', if not in reality, than in its legendary character.[40] This meeting also served as an indirect encouragement for Nasser to nationalize the Suez Canal upon his return from Yugoslavia, even though both Tito and Nehru were totally unaware of such a drastic decision brewing in his mind. However, on the eve of, during and in the aftermath of the Suez Crisis in October–November 1956, the three non-aligned countries closely coordinated their diplomatic activities in the UN, enjoying full backing from both superpowers aspiring, each for its own reasons, to undermine the tripartite British–French–Israeli aggression against Egypt and openly side with the Third World. In the end, through joint efforts of the US, Soviet and non-aligned representatives a diplomatic solution was obtained that largely stabilized and expanded Nasser's international authority.[41]

However, by the end of the 1950s, all leading non-aligned countries were also locked in a conflict with the socialist camp, as their relationship with the Western bloc soared in Southeast Asia, the Middle East and Africa.[42] Since early 1958, Yugoslavia was under a fierce ideological attack from the socialist camp as a revisionist state, while also being accused of leading the Third World astray from both Moscow's and Beijing's projections and trying to set up a 'third bloc' under its guidance.[43] However, throughout 1959, Indonesia was engaged in a political conflict with China over the status of the Chinese minority in that country, while Egypt was acting under mounting pressure from the USSR and China over Nasser's anti-communist and pan-Arab policies that also included attempts at expanding the newly established United Arab Republic (UAR) of Egypt and Syria into Iraq and elsewhere.[44] Finally, the unresolved border conflict between India and China erupted into armed combat in August and October 1959, after the local situation had been steadily deteriorating over a period of months following the unsuccessful rebellion against the Chinese rule in Tibet and the flight of the Tibetan spiritual leader Dalai Lama into India in March.[45]

Such a complex international situation triggered a new round of discussions related to the issue of closer political cooperation between leading non-aligned countries. At the end of 1957, Tito had already entertained the idea of convening a conference of non-aligned nations that would deal with the issues of nuclear disarmament, East–West relations and the lessening of international tensions. He tried to solicit Nehru's support for such an endeavour, but apart from reaching a general understanding, he could not gain his Indian counterpart's backing for such a proposal.[46] Since Cairo, due to outside pressures, was quite ready to stand behind Tito's initiative, in May 1959, UAR diplomats were trying to feel the pulse whether a new tripartite meeting could be summoned.[47] Nevertheless, Nehru was still firmly against Tito's, Nasser's and Sukarno's proposal for a new non-aligned conference that could be interpreted as an act of defiance directed against both Sino–Soviet encroachments, as well as Western interference. The initial idea was to convene such a gathering on the eve of the great powers summit in Paris in May 1960, but to no avail.[48] This kind of a negative trend only served to convince Tito and Nasser that any such initiatives had to be undertaken solely by the two of them, since, in any case, Nehru would be eventually compelled to join in.

As for the dormant Afro-Asian concept, in October 1958 Ceylonese Prime Minister Solomon Bandaranaike proposed to hold a regional economic conference, but nothing came out of this initiative either.[49] Even Nasser's idea of convening a separate Afro-Asian conference which could be then used to issue an invitation to China to moderate its policies with respect to India and Indonesia was immediately rejected by Nehru who considered his conflict with Beijing as a strictly bilateral issue. According to him, any multilateral meetings of this kind could have only further aggravated the escalating situation in Sino–Indian relations.⁵⁰ In addition, Africa had been already pursuing its own means of launching different multilateral initiatives, with a pan-Africanist undertone, whereas ideas about increased regional integration, struggles against colonialism and racism dominated their agenda irrespective of developments on other continents (conferences of African nations in Accra in 1958 and Tunisia in 1960).⁵¹

The Initiative of the Five

However, with the onset of the 1960s, the non-aligned world was confronted with a deteriorating security situation between the major world powers, above all in places like Berlin, where a direct clash was quite possible; Congo, where an unsuccessful attempt at decolonization left that country to tear itself apart through internal factionalism and aggressive foreign interference; Laos, where colliding Cold War interests were undermining the very existence of a neutralist nation; Algeria, where the bloody struggle against the French colonial rule continued unremittingly for six years, serving as a point of convergence for the entire Third World; and Cuba, where the US clandestine involvement against the newly established Fidel Castro regime acted as a harbinger of the more serious confrontation in 1962. Moreover, the collapse of the Paris Summit due to the U2 incident, when the Soviets shot down an American spy plane over their territory, truly sounded alarms that relations between the two blocs were on an accelerating downward spiral.⁵² This kind of tense international situation soon triggered demands for launching a concerted action of leading non-aligned countries. The forthcoming 15th UNGA session seemed as an adequate place for these nations to publicly state their claims.

It was in June 1960 that Nkrumah called for a meeting of 'uncommitted and non-nuclear' countries where a 'non-nuclear third force' would be established.⁵³ The fact that Cyprus and sixteen West and Central African nations gained their independence that same year seemed an auspicious sign that a number of non-bloc nations had been on the rise. Since Khrushchev insisted on the implementation of controversial UN reform along the lines of his 'troika' proposal (three UN General Secretaries from the capitalist, socialist and Third World countries), worldwide attendance seemed the right moment to come forth with new non-aligned initiatives.⁵⁴ In fact, it was this UN gathering that provided leaders like Tito, Nehru, Nasser, Sukarno and Nkrumah with a valuable opportunity to launch constructive proposals for the resolution of pressing world issues, while also renewing their appeal to both Soviet and American leaders to resume their direct dialogue. This joint initiative was dubbed by the press as the dawn of a 'neutralist or third bloc' in the UN.⁵⁵ Facing such a mounting challenge, both Tito and Nasser decided to closely coordinate their activities in New York, particularly when it came to the issues of ending colonialism and setting up a new mechanism for global disarmament talks. The two also reached a consensus that the Soviet UN reform proposal should be strongly rejected, while they were also trying to woo Nehru, waiting for his final decision regarding the joint initiative.⁵⁶

Circles in the East, especially in China, were concerned that Tito would use this venue to exercise his harmful influence on some non-aligned leaders, especially African ones.⁵⁷ Despite widespread pressure, Yugoslavia stood firmly behind any concerted action to assist in setting off a new round of constructive dialogue between the superpowers that could ultimately diffuse world tensions. Nasser was quite ready to invest his entire authority to unblock the UN, even without engaging Nehru, but Tito was still quite optimistic about the prospects for Indian participation.[58] Nevertheless, Nehru continually raised doubts over the feasibility of any joint actions concerning the mediation between the conflicting parties, except, perhaps, in the case of colonialism and disarmament. He often stated that India's low-key individual action with the superpowers could ultimately trigger a more positive effect than any proposed collective endeavours, while simultaneously gaining some good will on both sides of the Cold War spectrum.[59]

However, both Tito and Nasser made a decision to act in a coordinated fashion with Sukarno and Nkrumah, with an overarching goal of 'putting down this conflagration' between Washington and Moscow. All preliminary documents were largely drafted by the UAR and Yugoslav diplomats, often assisted by their Indonesian and Ghanaian counterparts. Still, gravity of the international situation ultimately compelled leaders of all five non-aligned countries, India included, to close their ranks when formulating and submitting this joint appeal as a new UNGA resolution. This decision was finally adopted during the meeting of the five leaders on 29 September inside the premises of the Yugoslav UN mission. In fact, it was the evident failure of the expected British mediation effort, one which the Indian side had initially endorsed, that eventually forced Nehru's hand to stand together with Tito, Nasser, Sukarno and Nkrumah.[60] Conversely, during Tito's earlier meeting with US President Dwight Eisenhower, it seemed that the Americans would also back up non-aligned mediation efforts, though soon enough they would rescind on their positive attitude.[61]

However, as a means of avoiding any international criticism of being uncooperative, Western diplomats decided to render this non-aligned initiative largely ineffective by submitting a number of amendments that aimed to water down the resolution's contents, blunting its edge, and thus compelling the five leaders to eventually withdraw the proposed text. Regardless of the fact that this document initially received the relative majority of votes in the UNGA (forty-one votes for, thirty-seven against and seventeen abstentions), it could still not proceed, since both blocs were clearly reluctant to endorse it or accept any of its subsequent recommendations. This state of affairs clearly demonstrated that there was no point insisting on a mediation which could not be henceforth implemented.[62] Contrary to the general mood, this was still a significant moral victory for the non-bloc countries, since both sides of the Cold War were compelled to listen to their grievances and take their objections into serious consideration, if not now, then definitely in the near future.

Essentially, this episode revealed that non-aligned nations were quite capable of assuming the role of responsible mediators in matters of peace and security, thus inciting some of them to start seriously believing that conditions for convening the first conference of non-aligned nations were ripe enough. In one of his statements, Tito declared: 'I remain convinced that … non-aligned forces are becoming more numerous, unified, and aware of the dangers threatening mankind … They have become a factor great powers must take into account.'⁶³ This indicated that the destiny of mankind should not be left in the hands of few great powers but it should become a responsibility of the entire world. Perhaps this kind of positive mood ultimately opened doors for the greatest contribution of this UNGA session – adoption of the 'Declaration on the Granting of Independence to Colonial Countries and Peoples' in December 1960 – thus ultimately setting the political and legal stage for the total elimination of colonialism on a worldwide scale.⁶⁴

A Further Boost to the Non-Aligned Conference

Regardless of the unfortunate outcome of the events in New York, Tito personally experienced a lack of good will among different non-aligned leaders in order to forge an extensive political front. As a means to further feel the pulse of Afro-Asia, in February 1961, he set off on a two-month voyage to several countries in West and North Africa (Ghana, Togo, Liberia, Guinea, Mali, Morocco, Tunisia and the UAR). This was an outright attempt at triggering a new round of comprehensive exchanges of views with key African and Arab leaders, ultimately aimed at dissecting the world situation and gradually diffusing international tensions.⁶⁵ Some of these leaders were pioneers of non-alignment in Africa, while others were openly leaning to the side of the West, with many of them already divided into two major groupings: the more radical and anti-Western Casablanca Group and the more moderate and pro-Western Monrovia Group.⁶⁶

However, this visit to Africa came under the closest scrutiny of the great powers. US officials were growing suspicious of Yugoslavia's efforts among underdeveloped nations, particularly in Africa, since they saw Tito's voyage as a means of exporting his brand of socialism that could, together with his non-aligned foreign policy, eventually become harmful to Western interests.⁶⁷ Although Moscow largely remained silent on the results of Tito's visit to Africa, it was obvious that the Soviets held very negative views about it, considering that the main goal of this long visit was to actively struggle with the socialist camp for political and economic influence in Africa.⁶⁸ Furthermore, the Chinese side was even more concerned about the immediate results of Tito's activities on the continent, since Beijing was certain of his third bloc conspiracy under the guise of anti-colonialism. Leaders in Beijing primarily observed these visits as a result of Tito's pertinent ability at forging good personal ties with local leaders and making them trust his views and ideas.⁶⁹

Nevertheless, what really inspired Tito to undertake such a voyage was his idea of organizing a non-aligned summit, on the eve of the 16th UNGA session, where all these prominent leaders could discuss without any inhibition issues like preservation of peace, ending colonialism, disarmament, nuclear test ban, a new international role for the UN etc., and thus ultimately striking out a wider international consensus. Afterwards, this joint stance could be presented to both superpowers as a unified resolution, a clear voice of one-third of humanity and almost half of UN membership, not just of five non-aligned countries as had been the case in the previous year. This was considered a last-ditch attempt by the 'consciousness of mankind' to break the dangerous deadlock that had engulfed the international organization, reminding everyone of the sinister pre-Second World War events. Initially, it was only Tito and Nasser who overtly opted for this new initiative. Other leaders, like Sukarno, were seriously reconsidering a second Bandung, while others, like Nehru, were still not quite eager to sponsor any collective undertakings.[70]

Therefore, while Nasser was still probing India and Indonesia, Tito, during his talks with Nkrumah, made an open suggestion that a conference of non-aligned countries should be organized in the near future, preferably in Cairo, while Ghana should also participate as one of the chief sponsors. The Ghanaian leader was quite eager to consider this idea, but was still not ready to publicly endorse it.[71] In the meantime, while Tito was travelling around West Africa, Nehru and Nasser briefly met in Cairo in order to exchange views on a number of issues, including this new conference proposal, but, as expected, Nehru considered this idea as both premature and unnecessary, though he did not reject it altogether. In his mind, any non-aligned conference could not only reveal inherent differences between so many diverse participants but its complex character could also hinder any meaningful dialogue between the blocs. Nevertheless, it was clear that there was still enough room for both Cairo and Belgrade to eventually win over Nehru's favour.[72] Nevertheless, behind the scenes Nasser also started promoting a new non-aligned conference, even if India would not ultimately take part in it, thus demonstrating the depth of his frustrations with Nehru.[73]

Sukarno eagerly picked up the non-aligned conference proposal and started promoting it as a prelude to his new Afro-Asian meeting envisaged by him as Third World's central event. Therefore, Indonesian diplomacy started pushing for a two-track approach regarding these two opposing meetings, which eventually caused extensive confusion with Jakarta's true intentions. Sukarno's initial plan was to hold a non-aligned conference in Europe which would then deal with some critical colonial issues (Algeria and West Irian), while this new Afro-Asian conference would finally act as a prelude to the next UNGA session. In this respect, Indonesia enjoyed China's full backing, since Beijing's goal was to forestall any dominant Indian or Yugoslav influence among Afro-Asian nations.[74] Nevertheless, as well as Tito, Nasser and Nehru, Nkrumah was also dead-set against another Afro-Asian conference, since, in his words, 'it would be very hard to gather aligned and non-aligned countries together, while reaching constructive decisions'.[75]

Confronted with Nehru's implacability and Sukarno's active push for an Afro-Asian meeting, one where Yugoslavia would not be included, Tito decided to actively advocate for a non-aligned conference with all his African hosts. During his talks with the Moroccan King Hassan II, Tito called out for a conference that might 'assist the recovery of the UN, so they [non-aligned countries] could play a positive role in the future ... and correspondingly develop joint action in the UN', thus avoiding any previous disunity. King Hassan eagerly accepted Tito's idea and further elaborated on Morocco's commitment to such an action as a means of confronting the predatory influence of all great powers: 'Underdeveloped and uncommitted countries should help each other not only through bilateral cooperation but on a multilateral basis. Therefore, I concur with your opinion about the conference of uncommitted countries ... in order to reconsider all possibilities for cooperation and reach concrete conclusions'. The king dubbed the non-aligned foreign policy as a 'policy of reason and not folly'.[76]

However, there were also other leaders who were not so eager about such prospects, often putting more stress on issues that spurred divisions among non-aligned countries, those conducive to their isolationism and economic dependence. Such were the views of the Tunisian President Habib Bourgiba who was close to the West and had a weak relationship with Nasser. Tito, nonetheless, still attempted to stress to his Tunisian counterpart that 'through joint action and with everything else we possess, we can do a lot ... while the great powers would have to take into account the [opinion of] uncommitted countries, thus reconsidering their own position'. In his response, Bourgiba expressed his profound doubts over the inherent potential of non-bloc nations, portraying them as not being truly non-aligned, but trying only to accommodate their economic interests with either of the two blocs. He also considered that these nations were acting out of their own self-interest only, without any desire to make any joint efforts ultimately successful. Tito could not agree with such a controversial stance.[77] Only when facing overt French aggression over the status of its base in the city of Bizerte in July, did Bourgiba finally decide to join the preparations for the Belgrade Conference.

Essentially, what galvanized Tito's and Nasser's initiative was Nkrumah's sudden decision to publicly endorse the non-aligned summit which had, as he reiterated, far more prospects for achieving a successful outcome than any Afro-Asian conferences ever could. Therefore, when Tito finally met Nasser both leaders agreed to hold a broad conference of all non-aligned nations, 'since [the] position of these countries holds considerable weight in international relations'. The two leaders also reached the consensus that a comprehensive preparatory meeting should be held beforehand. In addition, both Tito and Nasser concluded that Nehru's initiative to jointly condemn the US-sponsored Bay of Pigs invasion of Cuba should be now utilized to increase positive pressure on India to finally stand behind the Yugoslav–UAR conference proposal that would address all international crisis hotspots not just isolated ones. They were convinced that, when preparations eventually started, Nehru would be more eager to participate than to abstain.[78] Both leaders finally agreed to dispatch a separate letter to the heads of state of twenty-one non-aligned countries, including the representatives of the Provisional Government of Algeria still in the midst of national-liberation struggle, inviting all of them to the preparatory meeting in Cairo and explaining the basic character and criteria of the future event (affirmation of the principles of independence and equality, non-use of force in international relations, lessening of international tensions, resolution of international issues through negotiations, disarmament talks, etc.).[79]

Soon enough, Sukarno joined in as the third sponsor; however, during his interactions with Chinese diplomats, he stressed that the conference of non-aligned countries should never serve as a substitute for a new Afro-Asian meeting, clearly indicating that he had never abandoned his original plan.[80] As for Nehru, a clear willingness of many countries to participate in the forthcoming preparatory meeting ultimately forced his hand to become the last of the co-sponsors. However, the Indian side also demanded the laying down of strict criteria for participation, with any future conference agenda being drafted well in advance, thus strongly insisting on the expansion of the list of invitees and forestalling any unexpected demands for a third bloc. In this way, New Delhi aspired to further discourage any radicals from ever trying to hijack the proceedings.[81] Officials in both Belgrade and Cairo were conscious that India would not allow for the forthcoming conference to be directed against any of the two blocs, but it was still quite significant that Nehru had finally decided to come on board.[82]

The Cairo Preparatory Meeting

The decision to organize a preparatory meeting as a prelude to a broader conference of non-aligned countries exercised diverse impact on the great powers. Officially, Moscow remained unaware of the future format of this gathering, but the Soviets were quite agitated by the fact that Tito and Nasser were leading the way and not Sukarno, a leader much more inclined to their and Chinese views. This only induced the USSR to actively strive to 'unmask Western conspiracy', while simultaneously promoting through Cuba or Indonesia 'the anti-imperialist and anti-colonial character of this meeting'.[83] Nevertheless, some Soviet diplomats stationed in New Delhi overtly suggested that Yugoslavia should exercise a more proactive role in 'moving India out of passive neutralism and forcing it to join any constructive actions', thus indicating that certain conceptual changes were already taking place in Moscow.[84]

As for the US, Washington opted for a 'friendly and relaxed' attitude towards the proposed event, advising some friendly neutrals to attend, while supporting India's specific position as a firm guarantee that pro-Soviet radicals would not take over this meeting or eventually try to set up a neutralist bloc with a pro-communist tilt.[85] This was very much in accordance with the overall policy of the new Kennedy administration of active engagement with the non-aligned world.[86] Therefore, responding to the criticism pronounced by the US ambassador George Kennan that some participants would demonstrate strong anti-Western bias, the Yugoslav Foreign Secretary Koča Popović stressed that any position assumed by the future conference would not be based on the preferences someone had with respect to the East–West conflict but 'on the fact that these are current issues on which we need to assume a stance'.[87] As for the British officials, London was still seeking common ground with the majority of future participants, trying not to stress what kept the two sides apart but rather what could bring them closer together to avoid rapprochement between these nations and the Soviet bloc.[88]

The Chinese leadership was convinced that Yugoslavia had launched a new campaign to set up a third bloc with Belgrade standing at its helm, thus strengthening a joint axis with India against China. As a result, Beijing decided to stage a direct propaganda attack against Yugoslavia, also unmasking Indian duplicity, while struggling against Tito's and Nehru's intentions to dominate this new non-aligned conference, often using a proxy in Jakarta to that end.[89] In late May, Chinese officials approached Indonesian diplomats with a request for China to attend the forthcoming non-aligned event, since without its presence 'this conference would be just another attempt at splitting Asian nations'.[90] Some time later, the Chinese also pointed out to their UAR counterparts that this conference represented 'a split in the united front of peace-loving forces'.[91] Nevertheless, Chinese participation was out of the question not only for Yugoslavia and India, but also for the UAR.

The preparatory meeting in Cairo on 5–12 June was not only dedicated to organizational matters (twenty countries were present). Since it was convened at the level of foreign ministers or their deputies, it was also used to establish a minimal consensus between different participants on all relevant points, without emphasizing any local or mutually divisive issues. The primary contribution of this meeting was the laying down of the groundwork for the future conference, defining the official agenda with respect to central issues (anti-colonialism, non-interference, peaceful co-existence, racial equality, disarmament, role of the UN, economic development, etc.). In addition, regardless of Cuban and Guinean protests over the future venue, but with strong backing from both Indonesia and the UAR, it was decided to hold this summit in Belgrade in early September. Cuba even wanted to quit the meeting and cancel its future participation if its proposal for Havana as the venue were not adopted, but soon enough the Cuban delegation had to stand down in the light of overwhelming pressure mounted by other participants. This was, indeed, a major recognition for Yugoslavia's leading role in the non-aligned world. As a means to offset any future Cuban attempts at sabotage, Yugoslavia actively pursued Brazilian and Mexican participation, while potential Ecuadoran and Bolivian attendance was also being explored and positively encouraged.[92] In the end, the Committee of Ambassadors was established to apply the criteria of non-alignment to all current or prospective invitees, though somewhat flexibly and sometimes with certain bias, as in the case of some pro-Western African nations (Nigeria, Liberia, Senegal), thus preventing them from attending.[93]

However, something else also occurred at this meeting. In Cairo, India 'totally overestimated its strength, respect, influence, and its role [and] demonstrated total lack of knowledge of Afro-Asian problems'. New Delhi was faced with the harsh reality that its dominant position in Afro-Asia was not something preordained or unalterable, but it still had to be decisively fought for.[94] This gathering was marked by a serious confrontation between India, on one side, and Cuba, Ghana, Guinea and Mali, on the other, over the issue of extending invitations to as many non-aligned states as possible. The Indian delegation made an effort to water down the criteria for any future attendance, with Congo's and Algeria's potential participation often acting as a stumbling block (Algeria was then formally accepted as a participant; Congo only later on).[95] In fact, India was confronted with the unpleasant fact that its influence among Afro-Asian countries was dwindling compared to before. As the Yugoslav Foreign Secretariat concluded, China's behind-the-scenes presence was already tangible, while New Delhi 'demonstrated total unfamiliarity with Afro-Asian problems and surprising inability to adjust', thus losing a lot of credibility in the eyes of these nations while pursuing the policy of 'non-engagement towards the non-engaged'.[96]

Although Yugoslavia, unlike India, insisted on the strict and exclusive implementation of the adopted criteria, the Yugoslav officials were, nonetheless, conscious enough that 'India's and Nehru's presence at the Belgrade Conference has positive meaning ... contributing to the prestige and importance of this entire action'. Therefore, Tito decided to talk Nehru into coming to Belgrade, thus insisting on the joint contribution to the future success of this event.[97] Enlisting India's full participation became one of the most difficult tasks for the Yugoslav diplomacy, since until the very last moment it was not clear whether Nehru would personally attend this event, whether he would accept the previously adopted conference agenda and abide by it or whether New Delhi would attempt putting together its own group of supporters at the conference, consisting of countries edging closer to India's stance on certain general issues (Burma, Cambodia, Nepal, Lebanon).[98] In fact, Nehru was convinced that non-aligned countries could not succeed in resolving international problems but they could still stimulate the lessening of tensions around the world.[99]

Challenges Coming from Both Blocs

With Tito and Nasser focusing their attention on placating Nehru's intransigence, less attention was then devoted to the third conference sponsor, Sukarno. Even though preparations for the Belgrade Conference were already well under way, Indonesia did not totally abandon its initiative for a second Bandung. Sukarno only decided, for the time being, to put his weight behind the conference of non-aligned countries, since its success was already guaranteed, while this event would only facilitate smooth organization of the Afro-Asian gathering afterwards.[100] Immediately after the Cairo Preparatory Meeting, Sukarno dispatched one of his leading diplomats to India to continue with Indonesia's lobbying efforts for a second Bandung, proclaiming that Jakarta had already gained 'acceptance from the UAR, Sudan, Ceylon, Burma, China and others'. If India refused to participate, a warning was then issued – Pakistan would eventually assume its place.[101]

Facing dire prospects, China adopted a pragmatic attitude in which it would concentrate on propaganda work to unmask Yugoslavia's 'false anti-imperialist and anti-colonial credentials', but in a way that would also not further alienate other non-aligned countries. Therefore, regardless of certain uneasiness, Mao Zedong personally advised Sukarno during his visit to Beijing in June to attend this summit and actively defend Indonesia's and China's position. During their talks, the Chinese leader praised the fact that countries like Cuba, Guinea and Indonesia would participate, while Sukarno was very critical of Nehru and his views, indicating that Nkrumah, Bandaranaike and Sihanouk were standing on the side of India.[102] When a few days later Sukarno visited Yugoslavia, he conveyed to Tito that China was pretty much against the non-aligned conference, but he also failed to mention that Indonesia was still secretly working with Beijing to convene second Bandung. Nevertheless, Tito then stressed that both countries should exercise a constructive role, making sure that the forthcoming event would not turn into 'a frontal assault against the blocs'.[103]

Yugoslavia was also caught between the US and Soviet conflicting policies over the German question and the status of Berlin, especially after construction of the Berlin Wall was initiated on 13 August. This only complicated Tito's relationship with both superpowers, especially taking into account Yugoslavia's standing reservations regarding German reunification and potential West German rearmament which put Belgrade's position closer to the Soviet line.[104] In order to strike a balance with both blocs, Tito sought to clarify his position during the meeting he had with the US Under-Secretary of State Chester Bowles, but his interlocutor openly expressed his concern that Yugoslavia, due to its evident reservations, could sway some participants closer to the Soviet position on a number of issues. Tito, in response, also conveyed to his guest that the US should radically alter its stance towards colonialism, primarily in Africa, thus gaining more positive points among the nations present in Belgrade.[105]

In fact, in early August, the State Department finally formulated its official position with respect to the Belgrade Conference. It was decided to make an effort to influence its agenda and proceedings by dissuading some friendly countries from travelling to Yugoslavia, while simultaneously encouraging participation by some moderate countries who were dead-set on attending.[106] However, when it became known that Khrushchev had previously sent a personal message to all attendees, the Kennedy administration decided to abandon its 'hands-off' policy by responding in kind, thus actively engaging all participating nations by carefully presenting the US position on a number of issues and expressing greater understanding for their claims. Kennedy was convinced that the Berlin crisis could be utilized to decisively sway the non-aligned public opinion away from the Soviets.[107] Kennan considered that the recent negative developments in the East–West relationship would certainly dominate conference proceedings. Nonetheless, he remained convinced that this summit basically reflected the profound and prevailing mistrust non-aligned nations nurtured towards both blocs.[108]

As for Yugoslavia's relations with the Soviet Union, in June Tito dispatched his Foreign Secretary to Moscow to reach a certain degree of understanding with Khrushchev, but the Soviet leadership only wanted Yugoslavia to influence other participants to eventually endorse Kremlin's position on Berlin. This was out of the question for Tito. At the same time, the Soviets were also counting on some other non-aligned leaders with strong anti-imperialist credentials, above all on Nkrumah, to speak on their behalf, especially since he travelled to Belgrade from a holiday he had previously spent in Crimea in August.[109] It was evident enough that the Soviets felt reassured by the preliminary conference agenda, however, the Yugoslav leadership issued a stern warning to Moscow that anything it sought to potentially gain from this event had to be eventually corroborated by an overt backing of any future non-aligned initiatives, regardless of them being considered pro-Soviet or not.[110]

Nevertheless, Khrushchev still decided to break the self-imposed moratorium on nuclear testing right on the eve of this conference, thus casting a long shadow over Tito's grand international debut. The Yugoslav president was well aware of this hidden intention to take the limelight away from his performance as the summit host. Even though Tito admonished the Soviet ambassador that such an adventurous move could nudge the entire conference in an anti-Soviet direction, he still expressed a certain degree of understanding for the Soviet reasoning behind undertaking such a daring step (continuation of French nuclear tests).[111] In fact, Moscow was also trying to win over Nehru as a means of influencing the positive outcome of the Belgrade Conference, while also rallying India's support for other Soviet initiatives.[112] Nevertheless, Tito's and Nehru's respective performances at the forthcoming gathering would be ultimately appreciated by the Soviets in a very different way.

Many Latin American countries that had initially planned to attend this conference, at least as observers, were being actively dissuaded by the US from travelling, irrespective of the fact that Cuba would be the only participant from that entire region. This kind of policy ultimately resulted in the resignation of the Brazilian President Joanio Quadros, even though his country would eventually participate as an observer (together with

Bolivia and Ecuador). Furthermore, Yugoslavia even lodged a number of protests to the US over its open interference in the Brazilian decision-making process.[113] In this respect, British diplomats stationed in Belgrade worrisomely concluded that such US policies would seriously taint the conference proceedings with a more anti-Western undertone than had been previously expected.[114] Nevertheless, Yugoslavia and India were quite keen on seeing wider presence from different Latin American countries, since they could serve as an active counterweight to Cuban radicalism.[115]

As a result, Yugoslav diplomats in the field were instructed to convey to all conference participants that the main goal of this conference should be 'the lessening of tensions between the East and the West and in the world in general', wedded to a 'realistic and objective, moderate and constructive' approach. A clear consensus must also be reached by all attending leaders so as to avoid this gathering being seen as either leaning towards one of the two blocs or, even worse, resulting in a serious ideological split taking place inside the non-aligned group itself. This was the only way, as perceived in Belgrade, for this summit to be able to proclaim its balanced position to the world, avoiding along the way any militant outbursts. Furthermore, the Yugoslav officials also concluded that issues of economic development and inequality had become the key for reinventing and promoting the role of small nations after the end of decolonization, therefore these significant issues had to stand more prominently on the conference agenda now and in the future.[116]

As for China, driven by an unhidden desire to avoid further alienation from Afro-Asian countries travelling to Belgrade, Zhou Enlai finally dispatched a congratulatory telegram, emphasizing the conference's contribution to the anti-imperialist and anti-colonial struggle. However, this telegram was only addressed to Asian, African and Latin American countries, even though the host country was from Europe. It was evident to everyone that Yugoslavia was again being deliberately ignored by Beijing.[117] In fact, Chinese officials were profoundly displeased that this gathering would be primarily steered by Tito as a host, often backed by Nehru, while this specific duo, in their projections, would strenuously insist on a general position clearly contrary to the fundamental Chinese interests in the Third World.[118]

The First Conference of the Non-Aligned

The Belgrade Conference took place on 1–6 September 1961, with twenty-five full participants and three observers attending, while forty delegations of different national-liberation and leftist movements were present on the sidelines. Even though this was evidently a heterogeneous conference with so many politically, socially and culturally diverse countries coming from four different continents, despite certain differences, an unexpectedly high level of mutual accommodation was eventually achieved. In his opening speech, Tito indicated that this gathering was a direct outcome of a sound effort to mobilize countries who were previously considered objects of great power politics, but were now struggling to become subjects of world affairs. Therefore, he initially insisted on reaching general understanding regarding all crucial issues before closing this conference, leaving only minor ones to bilateral considerations, thus establishing the principle of general consensus as the key manner in which inner workings of the non-aligned group and the subsequent NAM would function in the future.[119]

Issues of colonialism and neo-colonialism, and support for national-liberation struggle initially dominated the speeches presented by the different leaders. For Sukarno, remnants of colonialism and proponents of neo-colonialist policies were triggering the emergence of new divisions between the developed and underdeveloped nations, thus becoming the main contradiction in the world. According to him, any current conflicts and foreign interference were not only stirred by the overt ideological struggle between the two blocs but also fomented by the growing clash between 'foreign interests and new forces' inside the postcolonial world. Therefore, in Sukarno's view, the future would be marked by a final showdown between the 'forces of freedom and justice', agents of change and progress, and the 'old forces of domination', only interested in preserving the old equilibrium. This speech was the harbinger of his concept dealing with the 'new emerging forces' and 'old established forces'. Sukarno's idea to abolish all colonialism in a maximum of two years was strongly backed by a number of leaders, especially the ones from Sudan, Ghana, Morocco, Ceylon, Cuba and Mali. Leaders like Nasser, U Nu, Bourgiba and particularly Nehru were also strong in their condemnation of colonialism and racial discrimination, pointing out the inherent dangers of new means of exploitation encapsulated in neo-colonialism, but they were still concerned that excessive insistence on anti-imperialist struggle could push these nations into a revanchist drive that could ultimately prove quite disastrous for any of them.[120]

These more moderate leaders were generally preoccupied with the deteriorating bloc conflict that could ultimately trigger global catastrophe. They dedicated more attention to the issues of disarmament and multilateral negotiations where growing tensions between great powers could be mitigated, and mutual suspicions potentially avoided. Nehru even gave priority to such a debate, while almost neglecting other issues, such as colonialism and poverty, and thus, together with people like U Nu, largely isolating himself from this debate, and getting into a verbal altercation with Sukarno. For the majority of the conference participants, peaceful co-existence and a constructive role of the UN guaranteed by strong non-aligned presence were the key to achieving success in all these areas, a clear alternative to an all-out war. For others, like Sukarno, such thoughts only corroborated that 'there can be no co-existence between independence, justice on one side and imperialism, colonialism on the other side'. In fact, some participants, like Nasser and Bourgiba, were more involved in criticism of the Soviet resumption of nuclear tests, while the majority of others, like Nehru, Nkrumah and Sihanouk, expressed their deepest regret or remained silent over this matter.[121]

This kind of heated discussion was also supplemented by vociferous demands coming from Sukarno, Nasser, Bandaranaike and Nkrumah to create new mechanisms for closer coordination between all non-aligned nations, particularly inside the UN, but without summoning another summit any time soon. Guinean representatives, on the other hand, insisted on a new gathering taking place after two years, thus creating a new permanent form of interaction. Nehru, however, held opposing views that these countries should only create general conditions for exerting moral-political pressure on the two superpowers in order for them to resume direct talks but he held no illusions about any greater political significance or relative weight of nations currently gathered in Belgrade.[122] As for the Soviet 'troika' proposal, it was again flatly rejected, while a plethora of suggestions aimed at resolving the German question in different ways (two German states, neutralization or reunification) were openly stated by different conference participants, but without reaching any clear consensus and largely contrary to what Tito would state in that respect.[123]

Another significant topic was the issue of growing economic inequality accelerated by the creation of great power economic blocs; therefore, as a proposed remedy, relations between the developed and underdeveloped countries should be based on the promotion of equality and constructive solidarity. This kind of projected positive trend, as stated by many discussants, should be further encouraged through the general control of commodity prices, strict economic planning and accelerated industrialization of the developing world, accompanied by a significant increase in economic aid from the Global North. Some participants saw this proposal as a recipe for overcoming their own backwardness through enhanced economic cooperation between the developing nations themselves, as well as through the eradication of internal deficiencies of every postcolonial society individually, thus ultimately contributing to the immediate suppression of poverty and foreign economic domination.[124] These fresh ideas would eventually become the backbone of the non-aligned economic agenda in the 1970s.

Figure 1 Heads of delegations on the First Non-Aligned Movement Summit, Belgrade, 5 September 1961. © Museum of Yugoslavia.

Naturally, the Yugoslav delegation was one of the most active at the Belgrade Conference, with Tito having separate meetings with a number of participating heads of state or government, as well as with representatives from different national-liberation movements. When it came to the issue of anti-colonial struggle, it was primarily Tito's initiative, backed also by Nkrumah, Sukarno and Nasser, to invite two representatives of the Congo, Prime Minister Cyrille Adoula and his Deputy Antoine Gizenga, allies of the tragically deposed independence leader Patrice Lumumba, to join them in Belgrade. In addition, Yugoslavia and Ghana, closely followed by Afghanistan and Cambodia, also decided to recognize officially the Provisional Government of Algeria.[125] These two ground-breaking decisions fully corroborated Yugoslavia's strong anti-colonial credentials among the other participants. Furthermore, Tito also promised Algerian delegates that he would induce countries like India and Burma to follow in Yugoslavia's footsteps and soon extend their recognition.[126]

Without a doubt, Tito succeeded in assuming central position during the proceedings, leaving a deep but somewhat controversial imprint on the entire event. This was particularly true with his (in)famous speech presented on 3 September. Unlike some other participants, Tito, unexpectedly, demonstrated a rather radical streak on a number of major international issues (Germany, Soviet nuclear testing, colonialism), venting his frustrations against the lack of Western understanding of Yugoslavia's position, as well as criticizing the US's visible attempts to sabotage the organization of this entire event. His actions were considered by the majority of attendees as non-alignment with a strong pro-Soviet tilt, even though this was not his primary intention. When referring to the German question, he used very strong language, openly criticizing Western support for the, as he colourfully phrased it, 'reactionary and fascist circles' in West Germany. At the same time, he also praised the Soviet initiative for the two German states solution as the first serious attempt to constructively resolve this issue. However, the Yugoslav leader still maintained that further militarization of the two blocs in Germany essentially acted as the greatest obstacle to any meaningful solution based on 'peaceful and constructive cooperation', thus openly emphasizing that even a temporary remedy would be better for world peace and stability in general.[127]

As for the Soviet resumption of nuclear tests, unlike some other leaders who were more reserved or critical towards such a move, Tito, regardless of such an open challenge to his authority as the host of this 'peace conference', surprisingly put on display his understanding for the Soviet decision, even accusing France's recent nuclear tests in Sahara as a deliberate provocation triggering Moscow's retaliation. He also used this opportunity to offer a comprehensive solution for disarmament talks by proposing their immediate return under the UN auspices, where all participants, big or small, would enjoy equal and constructive treatment. Tito proposed to set up a multi-phase mechanism where more attention would be dedicated to the resolution of certain crucial issues which demanded worldwide attention, while the ultimate goal of total nuclear disarmament would be left for the future. His initial idea was to introduce a freeze on all military expenditures at the levels recorded in 1960, with an eye on their further downscaling, thus liberating necessary funds to stimulate an increase in economic assistance to underdeveloped countries.[128]

While addressing the necessity of accepting the inevitable character of decolonization, this part of Tito's speech contained a crucial message that economic issues, together with security ones, had become the fulcrum for redefining the role of non-aligned countries inside the international system, gradually moving past the issues of anti-imperialist and anti-colonial struggle. Therefore, he indicated that economic emancipation was a necessary precondition for a comprehensive development of all non-bloc states, while such aid should be rendered by the developed countries and international organizations without any strings attached as a guarantee of creating more stable international surroundings. In parallel, as he stressed, this process had to be accompanied by the strengthening of a multi-faceted economic cooperation between the non-aligned countries themselves, exchanges that would have a trans-regional character and would exist regardless of any current differences between them. To this end, Tito insisted that a world economic conference should be convened in the near future to address seriously all these issues, which would eventually occur in 1964, when the UN Conference on Trade and Development (UNCTAD) was organized.[129]

Essentially, Tito's agenda was to create a guarantee that this summit would eventually become a trigger for a more permanent and organized joint action of all non-aligned countries, without transforming itself into just another bloc of states. His preliminary idea was not to set up a new organization or similar, even though this would eventually lead to the NAM's official emergence in 1970, but to formulate a long-term global strategy for all these non-bloc factors in order to determine their specific place in the existing world order and chart their future activities and evolution, without staging confrontation with either of the two blocs. Therefore, he aspired to gradually move beyond the current political issues and deal with the larger role these countries should exercise inside the Cold War framework, proposing that the two future conferences would act as a major first step in triggering such a daring global overhaul.[130]

However, contrary to Tito, leaders like Nehru were more interested in dealing with the current perilous situation in the world than with long-term trends, focusing on the issues of war and peace, thus promoting direct dialogue between the great powers, while also avoiding overburdening such a sensitive endeavour with excessive individual baggage. Essentially, India was primarily keen on a more low-key diplomacy which did not manifest itself in any widely distributed appeals or declarations. Such leaders were less inclined to devote their attention to some rather hazy issues of the future, tackling so many different countries, while more pressing life or death issues were still at hand. Contrary to Nehru's and Tito's line of thinking, there was also a more radical group being assembled around Sukarno which slowly became bogged down in the issue of anti-imperialist and anti-colonial struggle, not seeing that other political or economic factors had become far more relevant to the future existence of the postcolonial world.[131]

Nevertheless, despite some difficulties related to the behind-the-scenes political haggling, both these approaches finally gained the upper hand through a hard-won compromise. They were used to formulate the final documents of the Belgrade Conference: 'Declaration of the Heads of State or Government of Non-Aligned Countries' which reflected more Yugoslavia's position and the 'Statement on the Danger of War and the Appeal for Peace' which was closer to India's views.[132] The declaration claimed that the issue of peace had become the responsibility of all the nations in the world, not just the two blocs, nuclear catastrophe was not inevitable, while total eradication of colonialism, neo-colonialism, imperialism, arms race and a transition to a more peaceful, egalitarian, stable and just world should be done in a less confrontationist manner but without hesitation. Full acceptance of different political, social and economic systems through peaceful co-existence, as a clear alternative to war and oppression, was a direct precursor to the emergence of a fundamentally different world order. Bridging the gap between the rich and poor nations, while establishing more just trading practices between them, also accompanied by an increase of economic aid, also became highlights of this document. Finally, it was also endorsed by all participants to hand in the 'Appeal for Peace', together with a joint letter, to both Kennedy and Khrushchev by a selected group of non-aligned leaders as an incentive for the two world powers to cease with their sabre rattling and resume their dialogue (Sukarno and Mali's Modibo Keita went to the US, while Nehru and Nkrumah travelled to the USSR).[133]

Conference Aftermath

The Kennedy administration was rather displeased with the course and results of the Belgrade Conference, particularly with its somewhat anti-Western tone, but still Kennedy personally conveyed to both Sukarno and Keita that the US was, nonetheless, ready to continue with its constructive cooperation with all non-aligned countries.[134] However, it was Kennan who sounded the alarm when he heard Tito's speech; his, as he referred to it, blatant endorsement of Soviet arguments on Berlin and nuclear testing, as well as his unsubstantiated criticism of the US.[135] Some Yugoslav officials attempted to explain this as Tito's desire to rhetorically lend a helping hand to Khrushchev, since the Soviet leader was subjected to hard-line pressure over some of his policies, but Kennan was convinced that this sudden change of heart was, indeed, a direct outcome of Soviet meddling, thus signalling, as he perceived it, Yugoslavia's slow drift towards Moscow.[136] Nehru also tried to convince him that it was just 'Tito's instinct to agree with Khrushchev on foreign policy and past accidents and misfortunes in his relations with the West and East Germany', but this could not disperse Kennan's serious doubts over Tito's future course.[137]

Even though Washington wanted to act cautiously to avoid more trouble, the Kennedy administration decided to express its clear dissatisfaction with Yugoslavia's performance, while gradually introducing, mostly through the US Congress, certain punitive measures regarding further technical assistance, the most favoured nation status, and PL 480 wheat sales to Belgrade.[138] However, the US embassy's analysis of the Belgrade Conference was not as negative as one might have expected, though it was still marked by a somewhat condescending attitude. This report reflected the US's position that the most significant outcome of this event was Yugoslavia's success in winning significant favours among Afro-Asian nations through demonstration of a significant capability to successfully organize such a comprehensive event, while simultaneously presenting to its guests different achievements of its socioeconomic system.¹³⁹ Conversely, Kennan's British counterpart ambassador Creswell held more pragmatic views, scrutinizing this event with a less critical eye. He did not consider this summit as being inherently anti-Western, although he was dissatisfied with some 'anti-colonial ranting', so emphasized the moderate success achieved by it, while also expressing his understanding of some of the arguments presented by participants regarding major world problems.¹⁴⁰

As for the Soviets, they were obviously more pleased with the conference results than previously expected. A high-profile member of the CC CPSU Bobodzhan Gafurov was dispatched to Belgrade to closely follow the conference proceedings. His main task was to determine conditions for a fundamental improvement of bilateral relations. According to him, Yugoslavia proved to be a reliable socialist country, edging closer to the USSR on many key issues, while, based on his impressions, Tito exercised a far better performance at the conference than Nehru, Nasser or U Nu ever did.¹⁴¹ Nevertheless, both Nehru and Nkrumah, when meeting the Soviet leadership, remained unmoved and unconvinced by Khrushchev's argumentation over Berlin and his resumption of nuclear tests.¹⁴² Thus, startled by the ferocity of Western reactions, Tito was sure to indicate to the Kremlin that his speech was not the announcement of his return to the socialist camp, but was more inspired by certain similarities between the Yugoslav and Soviet positions on Berlin, colonialism and disarmament. Therefore, in the conference aftermath he publicly invited Khrushchev to cease with all nuclear tests and start negotiations with Kennedy, thus openly demonstrating commitment to Yugoslavia's middle-of-the road political course.¹⁴³

China assessed the Belgrade Conference as a crucial political battleground between the rightist (Yugoslavia, India, UAR), leftist (Cuba, Guinea, Mali) and centrist (Burma, Cambodia, Ceylon) political forces in the Third World, with the former two trying to influence the attitudes of the latter on some of the most important international issues. In general, Tito's role at the conference, his anti-Western speech notwithstanding, was negatively evaluated by Beijing, emphasizing that his goal was to 'fool' both the socialist and Afro-Asian countries, deliberately trying to win the favour of all the international factors.¹⁴⁴ However, China was quite satisfied with Sukarno's performance in Belgrade. Not only that, according to them, he did manage to take over the leading role from Nehru among the Asian leaders but was even more efficient in promoting the anti-imperialist and anti-colonial agenda than Beijing had previously expected.¹⁴⁵

Nevertheless, Sukarno was personally displeased with the conference results, primarily since his views could not garner overwhelming support. Soon enough, Indonesian ambassador to New Delhi emphasized that the Belgrade Conference was useful, but, as he pointed out, there were many more things that only an Afro-Asian gathering would be able to resolve. He even labelled the non-aligned conference as a 'meeting of theoreticians', while the second Bandung would be 'more practical' in its dealings.¹⁴⁶ Indian diplomats accurately observed that 'Sukarno wanted to be in Asia what Tito was in Europe and Nasser was in the Middle East' – one of the regional pillars of global non-alignment.¹⁴⁷ In the words of one of Sukarno's closest associates, his ego could not stand playing second fiddle to Tito, Nasser or particularly to Nehru any longer, so he started opting again for the Afro-Asian conference.¹⁴⁸ These exchanges highlighted that a serious rift between the 'moderates' and the 'radicals' had become almost a permanent companion to non-aligned gatherings.[149]

As a means to counter increased bloc interference, in mid-November, another tripartite meeting was held between Tito, Nehru and Nasser in Cairo. This was a specific moment, since the Egyptian-Syrian state union collapsed right after the Belgrade Conference and Nasser was politically still vulnerable. During the bilateral meeting between Tito and Nasser, both of them stressed that non-aligned countries were experiencing serious pressure from both blocs, especially the Western one, and all these malevolent efforts were intended to finally break up their newly forged unity.[150] However, when Nehru had finally reached Cairo after his visit to the US, he brought discomforting news from Washington that the Kennedy administration was somewhat disappointed with the results of the conference. Tito noted that Moscow was equally disenchanted, but this dual opposition from both superpowers only corroborated the fact that non-aligned states were indeed pursuing an independent foreign policy course. The three leaders eventually agreed to continue with intensive exchanges, while also trying to actively promote the immediate results and spirit of the first non-aligned summit, despite Nehru still being reluctant to clearly define the scope and dynamics of any future cooperation.[151]

Perhaps the most tangible outcome of the Belgrade Conference, as Tito had envisaged, was the initiation of preparations for the world economic conference at the 16th UNGA session (the other one was the establishment of the UN 18 Nations Disarmament Committee in 1962, with eight non-aligned and neutral members). This kind of effort was taken further when thirty-six non-aligned countries (thirty-three full participants and three observers), some of them not even represented in Belgrade the previous year, gathered in Cairo for the Economic Conference of Developing Countries in July 1962.[152] This gathering was summoned on the Yugoslav and UAR initiative, also backed by India, to hammer out a joint position of non-aligned countries regarding the future UN economic conference. In parallel, this event was also trying to set up a working mechanism for gradual reduction of dependence from great power economic blocs, thus achieving a significant degree of economic autonomy based on increased exports, stable balance of payments, economic aid and more intensive economic exchanges between the developing countries themselves, as it had been proposed by Tito in Belgrade.[153]

Nevertheless, while the proposal for establishing a permanent non-aligned economic organization was rejected, conference participants concentrated their attention on the issues of agricultural modernization, industrialization, economic planning, income increase, regulation of commodity prices, easier access to global markets and nationalization of natural resources, eventually reaching consensus on most of them.[154] Unlike the Belgrade Conference, there were far more conciliatory tones present in Cairo with respect to the Western powers, together with less tilting expressed towards the East. Essentially, this event and the successful convening of the UNCTAD almost two years later, regardless of its limited achievements, marked the hesitant beginning of a comprehensive struggle for the radical overhaul of the entire international economic system that would be the highlight of the NAM's performance during the 1970s.[155] In a way, the Belgrade Conference had set the course for the major conceptual changes that would take place by the end of that decade.

Conclusion

As previously discussed, the 1961 Belgrade Conference was not the true birthplace of the NAM but the 'spirit of Belgrade' and the decisions passed at this gathering undoubtedly represented the emergence of an organized global alternative, even a feeble one, to the dominant bloc divisions, irrespective of this event's true scope, immediate results and obvious intentions. The non-aligned world was acquiring its own collective voice in world politics, contrary to the wishes of the superpowers, and this was still the very first political gathering where representatives of four different continents were speaking in a more or less united fashion and tackling major international issues. What these nations considered as potentially the biggest obstacle in the future was the growing necessity to establish some kind of more permanent mechanism for launching a successful collective action.[156] In addition, foundations for key political and economic issues dominating the NAM discourse for another thirty years had also been firmly laid in Belgrade (anti-colonialism and strengthening of international peace and security, development, more just and equitable economic order).

However, even more important was the fact that the Belgrade Conference helped shape the political consciousness of many developing nations, implying that through some kind of collective undertaking, inside and outside the UN, they could gradually strengthen their international position and influence the delicate balance of forces of the Cold War, thus adding more substance to the role and activities of non-bloc actors within this comprehensive global framework. Similar events only served to reiterate the growing awareness of the Third World that it could get out of the colonial quagmire and eventually reinvent its role in international affairs by changing the basic rules of the global political and economic game, but only through acting in a coordinated and organized fashion.[157] Tito even considered that the negative attitude of both blocs to any collective actions of these nations was largely motivated by the fact that its principle justification was essentially directed at 'liquidating bloc reserves, especially in the UN', thus gradually reducing the number of non-bloc members potentially backing any bloc initiatives in the international organization.[158] In any case, it took a lot of effort and political astuteness to render tangible meaning to such a new correlation of forces inside the Cold War equation, while all the leading non-aligned nations, to different extents, had exercised significant impact on the future destiny of this entire foreign policy strategy.

Notes

1 For example Vijay Prashad, *The Darker Nations*, 48–50.
2 Robert Vitalis, 'The Midnight Ride of Kwame Nkrumah and other Fables of Bandung', *Humanity* 4.2 (2013), 261–88; Lorenz M. Lüthi, 'Non-Alignment, 1946–1965: Its Establishment and Struggle against Afro-Asianism', *Humanity* 7.2 (2016), 201–23; Chris Tudda, *Cold War Summits*, 37–66; Jürgen Dinkel, *The Non-Aligned Movement*, 42–83, etc.

3. M. S. Rajan, *Nonalignment and Nonaligned Movement*, 35–6.
4. Mark Philip Bradley, 'Decolonization, the Global South, and the Cold War, 1919–1962', in *The Cambridge History of the Cold War*, 1, Odd Arne Westad and Melvyn Leffler (eds) (Cambridge: Cambridge University Press, 2010), 474–85.
5. Carolien Stolte, 'The Asiatic Hour: New Perspectives on the Asian Relations Conference, New Delhi, 1947', in *The Non-Aligned Movement and the Cold War*, 57–60.
6. *Selected Works of Jawaharlal Nehru (Second Series)* (SWJN), 2 (New Delhi: Jawaharlal Nehru Memorial Fund, 1984), 517–19.
7. G. H. Jansen, *Afro-Asia and Nonalignment*, 54–7.
8. *Asian Relations: Report of the Proceedings and Documentation of the First Asian Relations Conference, New Delhi, March–April 1947* (New Delhi: Asian Relations Organization, 1948), 24–5, 81, 86–7.
9. G. H. Jansen, *Afro-Asia and Nonalignment*, 65–71.
10. Lorenz M. Lüthi, *Cold Wars*, 271–2.
11. David Kimche, *The Afro-Asian Movement*, 37–8.
12. G. H. Jansen, *Afro-Asia and Nonalignment*, 102–13.
13. Dragan Bogetić, *Koreni jugoslovenskog opredeljenja za nesvrstanost* (Beograd: ISI, 1990), 217–18.
14. William Stueck, *The Korean War: An International History* (Princeton, NJ: Princeton University Press, 1995), 140–2, 152–6, 278–80.
15. NAI, MEA, 1871(24)-AWT/53, 'Arab-Asian unity', 17 July 1953.
16. Chinese Foreign Ministry Archives (CFMA), 207-00085-19(1), 'Afro-Asian conference', 4 September 1954.
17. SWJN, 24 (1999), 553–4.
18. Cindy Ewing, 'The Colombo Powers: Crafting Diplomacy in the Third World and Launching Afro-Asia at Bandung', *Cold War History* 19.1 (2019), 1–19.
19. National Archives of Myanmar (NAM), 15/3 (3), File 81, 'Second Meeting, April 28 1954, 2:30pm'.
20. NAM, 15/3 (3), File 81, 'Fourth Meeting, April 29 1954, 3pm'.
21. NAM, 15/3 (3), File 81, 'Sixth Meeting, April 30 1954, 3pm'.
22. SWJN, 27 (2000), 107–10.
23. NAI, MEA, 1(44) AAC/55, 'First Session, December 28 1954'.
24. NAI, MEA, 1(44) AAC/55, 'Second Session, December 29 1954'.
25. G. H. Jansen, *Afro-Asia and Nonalignment*, 191–223.
26. Richard Wright, *The Color Curtain* (New York, NY: Banner Books, 1994), 135–40.
27. DDRS, CK3100053279, 'Results of the Bandung Conference', 27 April 1955.
28. Sarvepalli Gopal, *Jawaharlal Nehru: A Biography*, 2 (Cambridge: Harvard University Press, 1979), 239–41.
29. Chen Duide, *Zhou Enlai feiwang Wanlong* (Beijing: Jiefangjun wenyi chubanshe, 2005), 174–217.
30. Rami Ginat, *Syria and the Doctrine of Arab Neutralism*, 110–16; Yufeng Mao, 'When Zhou Enlai met Gamal Abdel Nasser', in *Bandung 1955*, 89–107.
31. George McTurnan Kahin (ed.), *The Asian-African Conference*, 84–5.
32. Helen E. S. Nesadurai, 'Bandung and the Political Economy of North-South Relations: Sowing the Seeds for Re-Visioning International Societies', in *Bandung Revisited: The Legacy of the 1955 Asian-African Conference for International Order*, See Seng Tan and Amitav Acharya (eds) (Singapore: NUS Press, 2008), 71–7.

33 Vijay Prashad, *The Darker Nations*, 41; Jürgen Dinkel, *The Non-Aligned Movement*, 78–9.
34 Jovan Čavoški, *Jugoslavija i kinesko-indijski konflikt*, 79–80.
35 NMML, Subimal Dutt Collection, SF 86, 'Asian-African Cooperation', 1955.
36 AJ, 837, KPR, I-4-e, 'Asian-African Conference in Bandung', April 1955.
37 DAMSPS, PA, 1955, f-54, 44673, 'Telegram to India', 9 April 1955.
38 Alvin Z. Rubinstein, *Yugoslavia and the Non-Aligned World*, 64.
39 SWJN, 34 (2005), 297–304.
40 Vijay Prashad, *The Darker Nations*, 95–6.
41 Philip Zelikow and and Ernest May, *Suez Deconstructed: An Interactive Study in Crisis, War, and Peacemaking* (Washington, DC: Brookings Institution Press, 2018), 133–311; Jovan Čavoški, 'Constructing Nasser's Neutralism', in *The Regional Cold Wars in Europe, East Asia, and the Middle East*, 99–102.
42 Audrey R. Kahin and George McT. Kahin, *Subversion as Foreign Policy: The Secret Eisenhower and Dulles Debacle in Indonesia* (New York, NY: The New Press, 1995), 54–74, 99–216; Salim Yaqub, *Containing Arab Nationalism: the Eisenhower Doctrine and the Middle East* (Chapel Hill, NC: The University of North Carolina Press, 2004), 147–267; Elizabeth Schmidt, *Cold War and Decolonization in Guinea, 1946–1958* (Athens: Ohio University Press, 2007), 125–79.
43 Jovan Čavoški, *Jugoslavija i kinesko-indijski konflikt*, 115–56.
44 Taomo Zhou, *Migration in the Time of Revolution: China, Indonesia, and the Cold War* (Ithaca, NY: Cornell University Press, 2019), 115–31; Rami Ginat, *Syria and the Doctrine of Arab Neutralism*, 198–213.
45 Sarvepalli Gopal, *Jawaharlal Nehru*, 3, 78–83, 88–104, 133–40.
46 AJ, 837, KPR, I-1/366, 'Tito to Nehru', 16 December 1957.
47 DAMSPS, PA, 1959, f-37, 413975, 'Telegram from India', 21 May 1959.
48 NMML, Subimal Dutt Collection, SF 39, 'S.Dutt instruction', 14 December 1959.
49 Russian State Archive for Contemporary History (RGANI), fond (f) 5, opis' (op) 30, document (d) 306, listy (l) 224-226, 'Afro-Asian economic conference', 21 February 1959.
50 NAI, MEA, 21-A(2)-WANA, 'S.Dutt to R.K. Nehru', 16 December 1959.
51 Frank Gerits, 'When the Bull Elephants Fight: Kwame Nkrumah, Non-Alignment, and Pan-Africanism as an Interventionist Ideology in the Global Cold War, 1957–1966', *The International History Review* 37.5 (2015), 955–7.
52 Lise Namikas, *Battleground Africa: Cold War in the Congo, 1960–1965* (Washington, DC, Stanford: Woodrow Wilson Center Press, Stanford University Press, 2013), 62–95; Aleksandr Fursenko and Timothy Naftali, *Khrushchev's Cold War: the Inside Story of an American Adversary* (New York, NY: W.W. Norton, 2006), 185–213, 263–91, 295–306, 323–37, 342–66; Matthew Connelly, *A Diplomatic Revolution*, 119–41, 194–212, 215–48.
53 Anirudha Das Gupta and A. S. Shahid, 'Ghana's Non-Alignment under Kwame Nkrumah', in *Non-Alignment*, 401.
54 Ilya Gaiduk, 'New York, 1960: Die Sowjetunion und die dekolonialisierte Welt auf der Funfzehnten Sitzung der UN-Vollversammlung', in *Die Sowjetunion und die Dritte Welt*, 107–15.
55 AJ, 837, KPR, I-2/12, 'Overview of the U.S. press, 24-28 September 1960'.
56 AJ, 837, KPR, I-2/12, 'Tito-Nasser talks, 25 September 1960'.
57 CFMA, 109-02207-01(1), 'Tito's attendance of the UNGA', 18 September 1960.

58 AJ, 837, KPR, I-2/12, 'Tito-Nasser talks, 25 September 1960'.
59 AJ, 837, KPR, I-2/12, 'Tito-Nehru talks, 28 September 1960'.
60 AJ, 837, KPR, I-2/12, 'Report on the trip to UN, 13 October 1960'.
61 AJ, 837, KPR, I-2/12, 'Tito-Eisenhower talks, 23 September 1960'.
62 DAMSPS, PA, 1960, f-140, 426134, 'Telegram from UN', 6 October 1960.
63 Josip Broz Tito, *Govori i članci* 16 (1962), 70.
64 Bojana Tadić, *Nesvrstanost u teoriji i praksi međunarodnih odnosa*, 257–61.
65 AJ, 837, KPR, I-2/13, 'Tito's report on his visit to West and North Africa, 29 April 1961'.
66 Colin Legum, *Pan-Africanism: A Short Political Guide* (New York, NY: Praeger, 1965), 48–59.
67 National Archives and Records Administration (NARA), Record Group (RG 59), Central Decimal Files (CDF), 1960-63, box 1375, 668.00/4-2661, 'Yugoslav policy in underdeveloped countries', 26 April 1961.
68 Archives of the Russian Foreign Ministry (AVPRF), f. 144, op. 22, p. 54, d. 24, l. 27–33, 'Tito's visit to Morocco', 29 April 1961.
69 CFMA, 108-00771-02, 'Tito's trip to West and North Africa', 22 April 1961.
70 DAMSPS, PA, 1961, f-116, 45196, 'Telegram from India', 17 March 1961.
71 AJ, 837, KPR, I-2/13, 'Tito-Nkrumah talks, 11 March 1961'.
72 DAMSPS, PA, 1961, f-116, 49399, 'Telegram from UAR', 27 March 1961.
73 DAMSPS, PA, 1961, f-116, 410170, 'Telegram from UAR', 3 April 1961.
74 CFMA, 105-01044-01, 'Indonesia plans convening second Afro-Asian conference', 11 May 1961.
75 DAMSPS, PA, 1961, f-116, 411113, 'Telegram from Ghana', 12 April 1961.
76 AJ, 837, KPR, I-2/13, 'Tito-Hasan II talks, 5 April 1961'.
77 AJ, 837, KPR, I-2/13, 'Tito-Bourgiba talks, 11 April 1961'.
78 AJ, 837, KPR, I-2/13, 'Tito-Nasser talks, 20 April 1961'.
79 AJ, 837, KPR, I-2/13, 'Tito-Nasser letter, 26 April 1961'.
80 CFMA, 109-03037-01, 'Soviet position on the non-aligned conference', 9 May 1961.
81 DAMSPS, PA, f-116, 413744, 'Telegram from India', 30 April 1961.
82 DAMSPS, PA, f-116, 416838, 'Telegram from India', 28 April 1961.
83 CFMA, 109-03037-01, 'Soviet position on the non-aligned conference', 5 June 1961.
84 DAMSPS, PA, f-116, 416236, 'Telegram from India', 22 May 1961.
85 NARA, RG 59, CDF, 1960-63, box 732, 396.1-BE/7-1461, 'State Department's position regarding forthcoming non-aligned meeting in Belgrade', 14 July 1961.
86 Robert B. Rakove, *Kennedy, Johnson, and the Nonaligned World*, 31–6.
87 Dragan Bogetić, Ljubodrag Dimić, *Beogradska konferencija nesvrstanih zemalja*, 157.
88 TNA, FO 371/161211, 'Neutralism', 30 January 1961.
89 CFMA, 109-02356-01, 'Instructions regarding the non-aligned summit', 26 May 1961.
90 DAMSPS, PA, f-116, 417391, 'Telegram from China', 25 May 1961.
91 DAMSPS, PA, 1961, f-117, 419571, 'Telegram from China', 20 June 1961.
92 AJ, 837, KPR, I-4-a, 'Report on the Cairo preparatory meeting'.
93 G.H. Jansen, *Afro-Asia and Non-Alignment*, 287–8.
94 DAMSPS, PA, f-117, 420359, 'Telegram from India', 24 June 1961.
95 NAI, MEA, CON/27/61-AFR I, 'Some aspects of the preparatory meeting'.
96 DAMSPS, PA, 1961, f-117, 420359, 'Analysis of India's stance at the preparatory meeting', 24 June 1961.
97 DAMSPS, PA, f-117, 422060, 'Foreign Secretariat's telegram', 17 July 1961.
98 DAMSPS, PA, f-117, 424796, 'Telegram from India', 12 August 1961.

99 TNA, FO 371/161214, 'Telegram to Lebanon', 11 July 1961.
100 CFMA, 109-02355-01, 'Views on Yugoslavia's plans for a non-aligned conference', 24 May 1961.
101 DAMSPS, PA, 1961, f-119, 419648, 'Telegram from India', 20 June 1961.
102 CFMA, 204-01469-02, 'Mao-Sukarno talks', June 13 1961.
103 AJ, 837, KPR, I-3-a, Indonesia, 'Tito-Sukarno talks, 16 June 1961'.
104 NARA, RG 59, CDF, 1960-63, box 732, 396.1-BE/8-961, 'Telegram from Yugoslavia', 9 August 1961.
105 AJ, 837, KPR, I-3-a, USA, 'Tito-Bowles talks, 30 July 1961'.
106 NARA, RG 59, CDF, 1960-63, box 732, 396.1-BE/8-361, 'Memorandum for the President', 3 August 1961.
107 Robert B. Rakove, 'Two Roads to Belgrade: the United States, Great Britain, and the First Nonaligned Conference', *Cold War History* 14.3 (2014), 346-8.
108 NARA, RG 59, CDF, 1960-63, box 732, 396.1-BE/8-3161, 'Telegram from Yugoslavia', 31 August 1961.
109 W. Scott Thompson, *Ghana's Foreign Policy 1957–1966*, 173-6.
110 DAMSPS, PA, 1961, f-118, 426269, 'Foreign Secretariat's telegram', 28 August 1961.
111 AJ, 837, KPR, I-3-a, USSR, 'Tito-Yepishev talks, 30 August 1961'.
112 AVPRF, f. 90, op. 23, p. 41, d. 17, l. 44-45, 'Role of neutralist countries', 22 August 1961.
113 James G. Hershberg, 'High-Spirited Confusion: Brazil, the 1961 Belgrade Non-Aligned Conference, and the Limits of an "independent" Foreign Policy during the High Cold War', *Cold War History* 7.3 (2007), 373-88.
114 TNA, FO 371/161215, 'Telegram from Yugoslavia', 1 August 1961.
115 NAI, MEA, 76(15)AMS/61, 'Mexico and the conference of non-aligned states', 13 July 1961.
116 DAMSPS, PA, 1961, f-117, 424464, 'Foreign Secretariat's telegram', 10 August 1961.
117 *Zhou Enlai waijiao wenxuan* (Beijing: Zhongyang wenxian chubanshe, 1994), 310.
118 CFMA, 109-02355-01, 'Yugoslavia's plans for a non-aligned conference', 7 August 1961.
119 *Conference of Heads of State or Government of Non-Aligned Countries*, 17-22.
120 AJ, 837, KPR, I-4-a, 'Survey of speeches—first, second, third day'.
121 Ibid.
122 Ibid.
123 Amit Das Gupta, 'The Non-Aligned and the German Question', in *The Non-Aligned Movement and the Cold War*, 151-2.
124 AJ, 837, KPR, I-4-a, 'Survey of speeches – first, second, third day'.
125 AJ, 837, KPR, I-4-a, 'Tito-Nkrumah talks, 30 August 1961'.
126 AJ, 837, KPR, I-4-a, 'Tito-Ben Khedda talks', 2 September 1961.
127 AJ, 837, KPR, I-4-a, 'Tito's speech, 3 September 1961'.
128 Ibid.
129 Ibid.
130 Dragan Bogetić, *Nova strategija spoljne politike Jugoslavije 1956–1961* (Beograd: ISI, 2006), 372-3.
131 DAMSPS, PA, 1961, f-118, 427253, 'Preliminary evaluation of the conference', 11 September 1961.
132 G. H. Jansen, *Afro-Asia and Non-Alignment*, 300-2.
133 Leo Mates, *Počelo je u Beogradu*, 47-52.

134 Robert B. Rakove, *Kennedy, Johnson, and the Nonaligned World*, 80–2.
135 NARA, RG 59, CDF, 1960–63, box 732, 396.1-BE/9-361, 'Telegram from Yugoslavia', 3 September 1961.
136 NARA, RG 59, CDF, 1960–63, box 732, 396.1-BE/9-1361, 'Telegram from Yugoslavia', 14 September 1961.
137 NARA, RG 59, CDF, 1960–63, box 733, 396.1-BE/9-2161, 'Telegram from Yugoslavia', 21 September 1961.
138 Dragan Bogetić, *Jugoslovensko-američki odnosi 1961–1971* (Beograd: ISI, 2012), 41–51.
139 NARA, RG 59, Bureau of Intelligence and Research, Box 2, 396.1/11-1461, 'The Belgrade Conference in retrospect', 14 November 1961.
140 TNA, FO 371/161226, 'Letter from Yugoslavia', 20 September 1961.
141 RGANI, f. 5, op. 30, d. 370, l. 71-72, 'CC CPSU member Gafurov to Khrushchev'.
142 AJ, 837, KPR, I-4-a, 'Nehru and Nkrumah to Tito', 27 September 1961.
143 AJ, 837, KPR, I-3-a, USSR, 'Tito-Yepishev talks, 20 September 1961'.
144 CFMA, 109-02356-01, 'Telegram regarding the non-aligned summit', 2 October 1961.
145 CFMA, 105-01043-02, 'Indonesia's performance at the non-aligned conference', 13 September 1961.
146 DAMSPS, PA, 1961, f-119, 428263, 'Telegram from India', 20 September 1961.
147 DAMSPS, PA, 1961, f-119, 435600, 'Telegram from Tunisia', 24 November 1961.
148 AJ, 837, KPR I-5-b/40-4, 'Talks between Pavlič and Tamsil', 25 November 1962.
149 Ide Anak Agung Gde Agung, *Twenty Years Indonesian Foreign Policy*, 340–2.
150 AJ, 837, KPR, I-2/14, 'Tito-Nasser talks, 18 November 1961'.
151 AJ, 837, KPR, I-2/14, 'Tito, Nehru, Nasser talks, 19 November 1961'.
152 G. H. Jansen, *Afro-Asia and Non-Alignment*, 313–14; Lorenz M. Lüthi, *Cold Wars*, 296–7.
153 AJ, 837, KPR, I-4-a/3, 'Economic conference of non-aligned countries, 9–18 July 1962'.
154 TNA, FO 371/166989, 'Conference on the problems of economic development, 9–18 July 1962'.
155 Jürgen Dinkel, *The Non-Aligned Movement*, 110–11; Sara Lorenzini, *Global Development: A Cold War History* (Princeton, NJ: Princeton University Press, 2019), 96–103.
156 DAMSPS, PA, 1961, f-118, 427253, 'Evaluation of the conference', 11 September 1961.
157 Vijay Prashad, *The Darker Nations*, 101–4.
158 AJ, 507, CC LCY, III/86, 'CC LCY Executive Committee session, 13 October 1961'.

3

'Afro-Asianism' vs. Non-Alignment: the 1964 Cairo Conference

Since the NAM was not formally established in Belgrade, this evident lack of a firm organizational framework had left enough space for different radical interpretations to arise, thus gradually setting the stage for the first serious conceptual rift among the non-aligned nations. This kind of a profound identity crisis almost triggered a total dissolution of the non-aligned group or its soon-to-be substitution by a competing Afro-Asian format. In addition to the East–West conflict which consistently threatened non-bloc countries, this chapter will also reveal how the South–South conflict could sometimes pose an even greater threat to their future.

The 1964 Cairo Conference was a significant event in the evolution of the non-aligned group on its road towards the NAM. Like its immediate predecessor in Belgrade, this gathering was also envisaged as an ad hoc event summoned to deal with the new political, economic, social and security challenges the non-aligned world was then facing. As the Cold War between the two blocs was receding after the Cuban Missile Crisis in October 1962, both superpowers were now investing additional efforts into introducing more stability and predictability into their current and future engagements. The non-aligned group no longer seemed as unified, inspired, dynamic or proactive in promoting their specific agenda, somewhat losing its general focus on action and willingness to act. Dark clouds had descended upon the non-aligned group as it was entering a serious internal crisis which could have easily ended its collective presence on the world stage.

With some non-aligned countries experiencing external interference, these nations were increasingly opting for a more militant approach to dealing with foreign influences, thus hoping that such policies would further boost their security and in parallel assist them in rectifying any past injustices. It had become evident during the Belgrade Conference that the non-aligned group was being increasingly divided between the 'moderate' and 'radical' members: between countries advocating restraint, realism and balance in their external activities, considering the universal ideas of world peace, security and economic progress as paramount (India, Yugoslavia, UAR, Ceylon, Ethiopia and others), and those (Indonesia, Mali, Ghana, Guinea and others) pursuing belligerent policies of an inter-regional crusade against imperialism, colonialism, neo-colonialism, exploitation and domination of a few great powers, especially Western ones, thus transforming galvanized Afro-Asia into the centre stage of world politics. In fact, this moderate group enjoyed more understanding from both Washington and Moscow at that time, since the alternative proved to be even worse for both of them, while countries such as China extended its full support to the radical group as part of its own internal and external radicalization drive.

This entire division quickly evolved into an overt political competition between the two ideological models (Afro-Asianism and non-alignment) and the two conference formats (Bandung and Belgrade), with both sides vociferously proclaiming to be speaking in the name of the wider community standing between the two blocs. This was especially true for the duo India–Yugoslavia and Indonesia–China, since they both stood at the forefront of each group and victory of the opposite camp could have served as a crushing defeat for the other, thus effectively rendering one side incapable of exercising any meaningful role in the future destiny of the Third World.[1] Therefore, the Cairo Conference proved to be the first serious identity crisis the non-aligned group experienced, one that would produce a protracted negative effect on its functioning in the late 1960s.

Superpowers Engage the Third World

Soon after the Belgrade Conference, the Cold War had started to undergo significant changes that would gradually lead to a superpower détente by the end of that decade. Since both Washington and Moscow were confronted with the possibility of a nuclear war over Cuba, a tacit understanding was reached between them that any kind of excessive adventurism should be avoided at any cost.[2] After almost a decade of mutual sabre rattling over a number of crisis hot-spots around the world, both superpowers came to the realistic conclusion that direct collision was out of the question, primarily because of their relationships in Europe, while their competition in the Third World would not be allowed to escalate again beyond the point of no return.[3] The most visible outcome of this new spirit of superpower accommodation was the conclusion of the Limited Nuclear Test Ban Treaty (LNTBT) in August 1963. However, conclusion of this treaty was inspired more by the Soviet and American fears over China soon obtaining nuclear weapons than by any additional concerns for global security.[4] Naturally, this was good news for the world in general but still not entirely favourable for many non-aligned countries still facing individual pressure from the blocs. Consequently, issues of local or regional security were gaining prominence on the non-aligned agenda.

Another global factor that also profoundly influenced the non-aligned political course at that time was the ideological and political split between China and the Soviet Union. The origins of such a process could be initially located in China's internal political struggle over the future course of socialist development, as well as in growing ideological contradictions between Beijing and Moscow in interpreting the very tenets of socialism or peaceful co-existence. In this context, Yugoslavia, due to its specific socialist system and constructive relationship with the West, was heavily criticized by China for allegedly influencing the Soviets in surrendering to similar revisionist impulses. However, in time, this kind of disagreement, wedded together to ideological purism promoted by both sides, led to an intensive political and ideological struggle for leadership both among other communist parties and the wider world, thus finally destroying overall socialist unity and significantly altering the general dynamics of the global Cold War.[5]

Furthermore, since Beijing could not gain a serious foothold among European communists, except with Albania, it was the Third World that had become the main arena for the Sino-Soviet competition. It was this ideological appeal of Maoism – its radicalism, voluntarism, sheer size, fighting spirit, as well as its uncompromising and rigid character – that drew some Afro-Asian leaders to toe Beijing's line, while also demonstrating their open discontent with the Soviet policy of gradual accommodation with the West. These leaders, like Sukarno or Nkrumah, perceived their disenchantment as part of a rising global movement that was meant to exact rightful revenge on the global forces of oppression and domination, while also triggering an overhaul of the international system. Another manifestation of such a radical course would be an attempt at organizing the second Afro-Asian conference which went against not only the further existence of the non-aligned group but also significantly undermined Soviet interests in the Third World.[6]

This was also a time when Western attempts at turning the tide of decolonization eventually led to the escalation of conflicts between the US and its allies and some non-aligned countries. From the perspective of Third World leaders, superpower interference into Asian, African and Latin American affairs was evidently on the rise, thus directly undermining independence or freedom of choice for their respective nations.[7] The case of the Congo proved to be quite edifying since its struggle for total decolonization was basically left unfinished, foreign involvement was on the rise, while externally sponsored separatism had become an integral part of internal politics. Negative sentiments were also apparent with respect to the failed attempts to finalize the liberation of the Portuguese colonies in Africa, particularly since Washington put its strategic interests above calls for ending colonialism.[8] However, ultimate triumph of the Algerian national-liberation struggle in 1962 proved to be a turning point for the political forces in the Third World, indicating that the path of a dedicated armed struggle was the only way of achieving full independence. Algeria had become one of the leading countries in both the non-aligned and Afro-Asianist discourses, with its first president, Ahmed Ben Bella, actively promoting revolutionary struggle while carefully balancing his non-aligned and communist allies in promoting his country's centrality in Third World affairs.[9]

The primacy of Cold War considerations in superpower dealings with non-aligned countries, particularly when interests of bloc members far superseded any of their grievances, logically contributed to the rise of militant and radical sentiments. Nkrumah, Sukarno and to some extent Nasser served as good examples of how the mishandling of the non-aligned world could stir far more trouble than initially trying to reign in ambitions through a certain degree of flexibility and understanding. The negative fallout from the Congo Crisis, where Nkrumah was at the forefront of all African efforts for mediation, together with his rising pan-Africanist ambitions, were bound to put the US and Ghana on a collision course. Concurrently, Ghana's conflict with many of its Western-leaning neighbours, as well as Western powers now actively seeking Nkrumah's overthrow, largely contributed to his increasing isolation and dissatisfaction. Reaching out to the more radical Sino-Indonesian camp seemed a logical outcome at that time.[10]

Nasser's intransigence over Arab–Israeli relations – always with an eye to seeking retribution in the future, together with his expansionist pan-Arab policies of confronting pro-Western Middle Eastern monarchies, like Saudi Arabia, in places such as Yemen – as well as his attempts to expand Egyptian influence deep into Africa, all proved to be serious obstacles on the road of UAR's full reconciliation with the US, Britain or France. In the meantime, he was quite forthright in receiving military and financial assistance from the USSR, crowned by Khrushchev's visit to Cairo in May 1964. Nevertheless, Nasser was much more pragmatic by not engaging himself into direct confrontation with either of the superpowers, nor actively trying to solicit either their aid or tacit approval, while still opting for a more realist non-aligned approach.[11]

Nevertheless, Sukarno proved to be the real maverick, entering into a full-scale confrontation with the West, seeking alliance with China, while also trying to reshape the face of Afro-Asian politics along more confrontationist lines. Ever since the overt Western meddling into Indonesia's affairs started in the late 1950s, Sukarno had opted for an authoritarian style of governance internally, while externally he was relying more heavily upon the socialist camp and its military aid.[12] With the onset of the 1960s, he actively advocated viewing the world separately from the Cold War and bloc/non-bloc paradigm, arguing for a political, social and racial polarization between the anti-imperialist nations of Asia, Africa and Latin America, the so-called 'new emerging forces'. He also actively aspired to overturn the unjust, oppressive and discriminatory international system, and the imperialist, colonialist and neo-colonialist Western powers, the so-called 'old established forces', staunchly defending their old privileges and world hegemony. These ideas fitted perfectly into the radical Afro-Asianist discourse, thus enjoying full endorsement from China which had become Indonesia's closest supporter on the world stage.[13] The situation became dire when, after Britain decided to grant independence to Malaysia in 1963, which also included territories in the island of Borneo, Sukarno perceived this as yet another move directed against Indonesian interests. As a response, he launched the 'Konfrontasi' campaign of a military submission of British and Malaysian forces on the island, while also trying to diplomatically isolate this newly established state, although often reaching very dubious results.[14]

However, it was the Sino-Indian border conflict (October–November 1962) and India's subsequent defeat that marked a clear watershed in the relationship between Afro-Asianism and non-alignment, thus accelerating their definitive political divorce. This was the moment when India's non-alignment came into direct peril, when an unexpected national humiliation triggered a previously unforeseen rapprochement between New Delhi and the Western powers, thus causing alarm in many non-aligned capitals.[15] Both Tito and Nasser were seriously upset with these developments, fully aware that without Indian participation there could never be any global non-alignment. Knowing fully well that Nehru was still a sincere adherent of the doctrine, Yugoslavia and the UAR decided to conduct active behind-the-scenes diplomacy among non-aligned countries, as well as with the two blocs. Both Belgrade and Cairo dispatched different envoys, therefore striving to construct a suitable pretext for Nehru to find a successful formula for balancing his new military commitments to the blocs and his sincere adherence to non-alignment. Yugoslavia then even entertained the idea of convening another Belgrade-type event to mediate this conflict, but the Chinese were resolute against Yugoslav attendance. However, unlike Tito and Nasser, other Afro-Asian leaders, although actively pursuing mediation efforts in Colombo at another ad hoc conference, largely remained cautious, reserved and inactive either in their open backing of India or strong condemnation of China.[16] In time, India's conflict with China and Pakistan would trigger transformation of its non-alignment into a pragmatic and utilitarian policy directed more at promoting national interests while pursuing expediency.[17]

Resumption of the Afro-Asian Initiative

After the modest success of the Belgrade Conference, adherents of the Afro-Asianist concept perceived these new circumstances as an impetus for convening another regionally based gathering, one that could, as they thought, more successfully cope with the issues of imperialism and colonialism. In early July 1962, Sukarno's globe-trotting envoy, Mrs Supeni, reiterated the proposal for convening the second Afro-Asian conference, indicating that thirty nations had already expressed their interest. However, this time she also suggested that Indonesia and China should reconsider extending the conference format to include Latin America, thus transforming the gathering into a tricontinental initiative.[18] In this respect, any ideas about convening another non-aligned conference would have been rendered redundant with the realization of this new Afro–Asian–Latin American framework. Nevertheless, some prominent officials in Jakarta were also well aware that Indonesia did not possess the political capacity to finalize such a global conference due to its many internal contradictions.[19]

Since India did not want to face any further diplomatic isolation, New Delhi reluctantly agreed to attend this potential new Afro-Asian gathering, but Cairo was still very much against such a conference taking place any time soon. Both nations were concerned that many old and new regional rivalries might eventually undermine any promising prospects. Both India and the UAR understood well that the Indonesian initiative was employed, first and foremost, as a direct means for Sukarno to improve his international standing by finding a new arena to demonstrate his international importance, since, in his mind, Tito had taken control over global non-alignment.[20] Nevertheless, when Nehru and Nasser met again in Cairo in early October 1962, they agreed not to attend any future Afro-Asian conferences, pointing out that conditions were still not ripe enough.[21] However, the abrupt break-out of the Sino-Indian border war put all these preparations on a temporary hold, even though Sukarno actively entertained the idea of convening another Colombo Conference in early 1963 as part of his general preparations for a second Bandung.[22]

Nevertheless, in the aftermath of this tragic conflict, India decided to strengthen its committment to intensifying and diversifying its ties with leading non-aligned countries. New Delhi's stature inside the non-aligned group had become one of its top foreign policy priorities in the following years, its previous disinterest and passivity largely becoming a thing of the past.[23] China also made its policy towards Asian, African and Latin American nations the main event, where its influence and revolutionary model were often considered the most suitable for rendering tangible results. In many ways, as Beijing perceived it, China became a spokesman for the poor and the oppressed nations of the world, thus further increasing polarization between the developed and developing worlds, while also trying to drive a wedge between different members of the non-aligned group.[24] Furthermore, China was also trying to utilize Sukarno's old insecurities vis-à-vis Nehru or Tito, openly advising him to supplant his Indian counterpart, and thus finally assuming firm control over Afro-Asian affairs.[25]

Apart from India, the worldwide political recognition for the non-aligned group had also become one of Yugoslavia's external priorities. Even the remote possibility of convening yet another Belgrade-type conference was being seriously considered by the Yugoslav officials as a necessary step in reinvigorating the global role of non-alignment.[26] Tito observed the current world situation as one gradually evolving towards polycentrism, where emerging splits inside both camps were slowly blunting the overwhelming dominance of bipolarity, although not fully suppressing it as the main feature of the Cold War world order. In this kind of situation, as he thought, profound respect for the equality of rights and duties of all nations was quite necessary, thus imposing certain moral and legal obligations on the international community as a whole when dealing with different international issues. In addition, topics such as anti-colonial struggle, economic development, disarmament, etc. were equally important for overall stability, while emphasizing only one of them at the expense of the others would represent a serious failure to fully grasp the complexity of the contemporary world.[27]

During their subsequent meeting in Yugoslavia in May 1963, Tito openly conveyed to Nasser his strong commitment to having another non-aligned conference organized in the near future, primarily as a means of providing a boost to the concept itself, while also closing the ranks between countries advocating it, thus preventing any adversarial concepts from gaining significant foothold. Since Nasser was about to attend the first conference of the Organisation of African Unity (OAU) in Addis Ababa, where African nations were pursuing their own model of integration, Tito bluntly recommended that his proposal be seriously discussed at the forthcoming event. Nasser was quite entertained with this idea, but he still left it for some other time, while Tito did not insist on it again.[28] It seemed as if the non-aligned initiative had lost its momentum during the previous year. As noted by an Egyptian official, the non-aligned group had become rather inactive after Belgrade and it needed a strong push on the side of both UAR and Yugoslavia.[29]

Nevertheless, Indonesia, backed by China and Pakistan, became increasingly keen to convene a new Afro-Asian conference as soon as possible. As for Nasser, the second Bandung was still unacceptable – first of all due to its wider and uncritical representation that could have provided more space to controversy and dispute, indiscriminately putting together both bloc and non-bloc countries, while he also did not want to distance himself from both Tito and Nehru who would not attend such a gathering due to different reasons. At the same time, in his opinion, a new non-aligned conference would still be able to bring together many more African countries than was the case in 1961, which was essentially more in line with Nasser's new African policy than with Sukarno's regional combinations.[30]

Second Belgrade or Second Bandung?

During Bandaranaike's visit to Cairo in October 1963, Nasser followed up on Tito's earlier initiative and he unilaterally raised the issue of a new non-aligned conference where the UAR and Ceylon, together with Yugoslavia, should become new conference sponsors. His main argument in this respect was the obvious lessening of tensions between the two blocs, which was, however, now accompanied by their even greater interference in the emerging conflicts around the non-aligned world. This complex situation, as he saw it, demanded adequate political response on behalf of non-aligned countries and Nasser's preliminary idea was to hold this gathering in September 1964.[31] India immediately claimed such a proposal to be contrary to any Chinese or Indonesian plans. As Nehru suggested, Tito's platform proposed at the 18th UNGA session, one that dealt equally with the issues of colonialism, discrimination and racism, disarmament and economic development, should become the future agenda of this new conference.[32]

However, Beijing and Jakarta were also not sitting by idly. Even before Nasser raised the conference issue, Zhou Enlai urged a visiting Indonesian delegation to step up its efforts for convening a new Afro-Asian summit.[33] In addition, in mid-December 1963 an instruction was dispatched to all Indonesian representatives abroad to raise the issue of an immediate convening of the seventeen-country preparatory committee where issues going beyond just the East–West divide would be deliberated.[34] Nevertheless, since Nasser, Bandaranaike and to some extent Tito proposed their own initiative, China gradually concentrated its efforts along a two-track approach. One track was to continue with the diplomatic efforts of promoting Afro-Asian solidarity, while the other one was the attempt to increase Beijing's imprint on the non-aligned meeting.[35]

Thus, in early November, Zhou Enlai conveyed to the UAR ambassador that China was interested in taking part in the new non-aligned conference, since, due to the Sino-Soviet split, Beijing had already become a non-bloc country.[36] This action was mirrored by the Indonesians who were also ready to propose Chinese participation in the non-aligned gathering, considering that the Bandung Conference was essentially a non-aligned meeting where China was also present.[37] Naturally, this position was not shared by India, Yugoslavia or the UAR, even though Ceylon and Algeria were already having second thoughts about China's potential attendance or their own participation in the Afro-Asian meeting.[38] In fact, Indonesia had started to advocate that the second Bandung should take place beforehand in order for it to successfully resolve any contentious bilateral issues, while only afterwards one could proceed with organizing an expanded non-aligned conference dealing with major international problems.

The Indonesians also held the opinion that some bloc nations, such as Pakistan or Iran, should not be discriminated from participating in either of these two gatherings.[39]

Since the destiny of the two conferences remained uncertain, China decided to launch an attempt at swaying most of Africa in Beijing's favour. In mid-December 1963, Zhou Enlai set off on his seminal voyage to fourteen African and Asian nations plus Albania. In the final report from this trip, it was clear that one of its dominant goals was to foil an elaborate conspiracy being forged between the Soviets, Yugoslavs and Indians to organize a non-aligned conference instead of an Afro-Asian one, while Zhou was also dedicated to winning over as many African countries as possible for the Sino-Indonesian initiative.[40] Since Pakistani leader Ayub Khan managed to persuade a reluctant Bandaranaike to stand behind the Sino-Indonesian proposal, China also had high hopes that the majority of African countries would also eagerly back the Afro-Asian bid.[41] However, Beijing was also preparing a back-up plan – Sihanouk's proposal to ultimately set up an organization of Asian unity, an Asian counterpart of the OAU, while Sukarno's long-standing idea about convening a conference of the 'new emerging forces' was also being considered as another response to a non-aligned summit.[42]

During Zhou's second meeting with Nasser, the Egyptian leader highlighted his preference for the non-aligned conference, since relations between non-aligned countries were much closer than relations between bloc and non-bloc nations of the Bandung model. He also added that the non-aligned conference would only deal with outstanding international issues, without raising any of the contentious bilateral issues. Secondly, Nasser also stressed that the new non-aligned conference would be held within a much wider format, bringing together not only Afro-Asian but also European and Latin American countries.[43] In his later response, Zhou explained why China chose to go along with Sukarno's initiative. First of all, China was still an aligned country, contrary to earlier claims, thus Beijing could not participate in any non-aligned meetings. He also emphasized that Bandung had been organized six years before Belgrade, therefore the second Afro-Asian conference should also be held before the second non-aligned summit.[44] Nasser then stressed that non-alignment enjoyed a much broader basis for reaching a meaningful consensus among so many actors on so many different issues which this regionalist framework could never do, thus leaving Zhou without any new arguments to raise.[45]

When he arrived in Algeria afterwards, Zhou expected to find his hosts more eager to attend the second Bandung. During his talks with Ben Bella, he expressed his endorsement for the Afro-Asian conference, indicating that China harboured profound doubts about the essential character of the non-aligned summit, particularly if India raised the border issue when China was not present at that event.[46] The Chinese Premier emphasized that the Bandung model offered far greater opportunities for economic cooperation between Afro-Asian countries, as well as for the struggle against neo-colonialism, but Ben Bella, nonetheless, rejected the whole idea as being premature and he stood firmly by his earlier decision to back the new non-aligned initiative.[47] During visits to Morocco and Tunisia, the Chinese delegation discovered that these two countries were also rather keen on attending the non-aligned conference, considering the Afro-Asian one unnecessary.[48] In fact, Bourgiba even warned Zhou that an armed conflict with world imperialism, often argued by Beijing, would not guarantee a clear victory for the socialist countries, while Chinese incessant criticism of Yugoslavia and the USSR could not bring them any additional points in Africa.[49]

Since visits to the UAR, Algeria, Morocco and Tunisia proved to be disappointing in this respect, Zhou Enlai decided to put his hopes on the forthcoming visits to Ghana, Guinea and Mali. Ghana was very much sceptical about the prospects of the new non-aligned conference, tacitly indicating that some countries, like India, were not non-aligned any longer, while Nkrumah extended his strong support to the Afro-Asian competitor.[50] Since the new Afro-Asian conference was mentioned publicly in the joint Sino-Ghanaian communiqué, this sounded the alarm in both Belgrade and New Delhi that this new initiative could receive wider endorsement in West Africa after suffering diplomatic failures in the North.[51] Irrespective of these developments, Ghanaian officials nonetheless indicated privately that they did not see the two conferences as being competitive but complementary.[52]

As for his visit to Mali, Zhou went to great strides to win over his hosts by advocating peaceful co-existence and also openly endorsing the non-aligned conference, thus somewhat modifying his entire approach. Keita raised the issue of Mali's non-aligned orientation, but he also gave his formal backing to the second Bandung. Nevertheless, Malian officials indicated to their guests that their main focus was on the continuous struggle against imperialism and colonialism, while only 'revisionists', like Yugoslavia, insisted on issues like peace, co-existence and disarmament, since they were of no immediate benefit to such struggle.[53] Contrary to some expectations, the visit to Guinea did not yield any substantial results, since Sekou Toure clearly stressed that he would not attend any future non-aligned conferences, but he was also strongly opposed to organizing any Afro-Asian gatherings.[54]

Since only a few countries, such as Ghana, Mali, Sudan and Somalia, openly proclaimed their desire to attend the Afro-Asian conference, on his return Zhou Enlai also paid visits to Ceylon, Burma and Pakistan. It was already evident to Zhou that the majority of the Third World countries had largely decided to put their bid behind the non-aligned initiative.[55] His visit to Burma was also not very successful in this respect either, since the country's new ruler, Ne Win, refused to take part in any of the two conflicting conferences.[56] Meanwhile, in Ceylon serious misunderstandings had also surfaced. Even though Zhou publicly declared that these two conferences were not mutually exclusive, nevertheless, he did emphasize that their goals were essentially different. Contrary to that, Bandaranaike insisted that the non-aligned conference must be also mentioned in the joint communiqué in order for Ceylon to officially extend its support for the Chinese initiative too.[57] Eventually, it was only Pakistan and Indonesia that firmly and decisively stood by China on this matter.[58]

As soon as Zhou's voyage ended, Indonesia became very active in its lobbying efforts, directly proclaiming that it was pointless even convening the non-aligned conference.[59] In fact, as one Indonesian official said, when the Belgrade Conference took place Europe was at the centre of Cold War competition and non-aligned countries were able to offer their contribution to the general reduction of tensions, but now this confrontation had transited to Asia and Africa and the towering issue had become a struggle against imperialism and neo-colonialism. This was an area, they thought, where the Afro-Asian conference had much more to say than the non-aligned one ever could.⁶⁰ As a means of subverting competitors, rumours were also being actively spread by Beijing and Jakarta that a non-aligned conference was merely a last-ditch initiative of Yugoslavia and India, essentially a lost cause, since the two countries had basically ceased to be anti-imperialist.⁶¹

Parallel Lives of the Two Initiatives

In spite of all these tensions, some countries were also looking for a compromise, often proposing that the non-aligned conference should take place in 1964, while the Afro-Asian one should be convened early the following year. This was especially true of Algeria which actively argued for overcoming artificially imposed divisions and mutual exclusiveness between the two conferences, implying that the second Bandung was a mere regional extension of its more 'universalist' non-aligned counterpart.⁶² Moreover, ideas were also circulated to officially name this meeting the 'conference for progress and peace' or 'conference for promotion of international cooperation', thus shelving the title non-aligned due to being too narrowly identified with the superpower conflict. In this way, as some thought, the comprehensive character of the non-aligned meeting would ultimately render the Afro-Asian conference a belated one. Nevertheless, India stood staunchly against such proposals, considering terms such as non-alignment or Yugoslavia's non-engagement as quite sufficient and to the point.⁶³

Nevertheless, it was the UAR that insisted on the immediate diplomatic action that would bring about the earlier realization of the non-aligned preparatory meeting. However, as a means of getting out of this conceptual stalemate, Yugoslavia submitted a proposal that implied the widest possible representation at the preparatory meeting, together with an agenda that would deal equally with the anti-colonial, anti-racial, peace, disarmament and economic issues, which would then enable the non-aligned meeting to cover all bases. This new initiative, it seemed, was very close to Nehru's original idea about extended representation in Belgrade, one that had caused so much dissent then and which had not been endorsed by Yugoslavia. But times had changed.⁶⁴ The Indian side also intended to use the future gathering to stage a public re-examination of the meaning and role of the policy of non-alignment, because events taking place since 1961 had caused some confusion about the doctrine's true aim and character, often substituting it with the passive features of neutrality.⁶⁵ Besides, Yugoslavia also wanted to use the success of the future preparatory meeting to mobilize non-aligned nations for the forthcoming UNCTAD conference, thus generating wider positive energy for that crucial event.⁶⁶

In many ways, if the Bandung-type conference occurred first, this would give rise to many controversies and many participants would afterwards consider the idea of convening another non-aligned meeting a moot point.⁶⁷ Therefore, Yugoslav and Indian officials, also tacitly backed by Cairo, agreed that a broader participation should be pursued, while two preparatory meetings should be held – one at the ambassadorial level in Cairo or elsewhere to chart tangible steps concerning the conference agenda, while also making the preliminary list of attendees, and the other at the level of foreign ministers somewhere else, possibly in New Delhi, since the non-aligned initiative needed a further boost in Asia.[68] Eventually, it was agreed to organize a preparatory meeting in Colombo, but Bandaranaike was adamant against having another similar meeting at the level of foreign ministers later on. This caused a certain degree of confusion among other conference sponsors.[69]

In mid-February 1964, invitations to attend the meeting in the Ceylonese capital the following month were sent out to all participants of the Belgrade Conference. While some countries immediately agreed, others such as Indonesia, Ghana, Mali and Guinea remained silent.[70] In early March, as a means of off-setting this negative trend, a high-level Yugoslav delegation was dispatched to Ghana to influence Nkrumah to officially endorse this new conference. They were largely successful in this act, irrespective of his standing reservations.[71] In addition, the same delegation also paid a visit to Guinea and they managed to influence Toure into agreeing to dispatch his representatives to Colombo.[72] As for Keita, Ben Bella personally went to Bamako to talk to him; however, in spite of Algerian good will, Malian delegation would not travel to Colombo and it would come to the Cairo Conference only at the very last minute.[73] In this case, Zhou Enlai's visit bore some fruit, as was the case with Burma. Concurrently, India was actively lobbying to induce Latin American attendance of the preparatory meeting, thus reducing Cuba's potentially harmful influence. The logic behind India's activity was very similar to Yugoslavia's right before Belgrade.[74]

As a response, Indonesians dispatched Mrs Supeni to Colombo, but her main task was to clarify to other participants why the Afro-Asian conference was far more necessary than the non-aligned one. Before her departure she indicated that Indonesia appreciated the recent official endorsement of the Afro-Asian conference by Ben Bella and Tito in their joint communiqué, but she still suggested that the second Bandung should take place in Cairo right before the non-aligned conference, while the two events should be organized in the shortest possible period of time.[75] Therefore, countries such as Yugoslavia, India, the UAR and Ceylon had reached the consensus that at the forthcoming preparatory meeting they should establish clear but loose criteria that would encompass as many potential non-aligned participants as possible, while it was also agreed that the Afro-Asian conference should not be either publicly denounced or openly endorsed. In fact, it should be stressed by all attendees that its potential failure would also influence the destiny of the non-aligned conference, thus silencing any vociferous opposition from Indonesia and others.[76] Everything was arranged in advance so as to guarantee the Colombo preparatory meeting ultimately being successful, even if moderately.

When this event finally transpired, Bandaranaike admonished attending delegations against staging attempts at sabotaging this meeting or watering down the principles of non-alignment.[77] As suspected, Indonesian representatives already came prepared to propagate the second Bandung as an event aimed at discrediting imperialism, while the new non-aligned conference they labelled as a weak face-saving attempt to salvage the imperialists and their damaged reputation.[78] In spite of these outbursts, hosts backed by the Yugoslav, Indian and UAR delegations had managed to steer the general discussion in a constructive manner by advocating for peaceful co-existence and economic development as some of the key preconditions to realizing the specific interests of non-aligned countries. They also promoted the spirit of anti-imperialist and anti-colonial struggle, a subject close to the hearts of Indonesians and their allies, but only as an integral part of the general struggle for peace, equality and development in international relations. The only concession made to the Indonesians was the inclusion of the formulation 'new emerging forces' into the final document, but more as a second name for the national-liberation movements in the colonies than as a substitute for non-aligned countries.[79]

Eventually, the preparatory meeting did manage to put together an extensive list of potential participants by somewhat relaxing the participation criteria, particularly stressing the attendance of the many newly liberated African countries that had officially accepted non-alignment as their foreign policy credo at the earlier OAU summit. This was a clear way to gain wider support, even if it sometimes meant sacrificing quality to quantity, thus finally outbidding the second Bandung. The future conference agenda was also generally defined.[80] In addition, a permanent preparatory committee of ten ambassadors had been set up in Cairo dealing with all technical and organizational issues, particularly exploring possibilities for inviting many more countries to attend.[81] This was proposed by Yugoslavia as a means of avoiding another ministerial meeting in the coming months that could have otherwise given rise to some new dissent, especially between Ceylon and India. In general, Yugoslav and Indian delegates were content with the outcome of the preparatory meeting and with the prospects of definitely having a non-aligned meeting in Cairo in early October, well before the second Bandung taking place.[82] Since Nasser also conveyed to the Indonesians that he would host two more summits in Cairo during that summer, an African one and an Arab one, it was evident that there was no possibility to squeeze in an Afro-Asian conference any time soon.[83]

Parallel Offensives of the Two Initiatives

In the light of these new developments, Chinese officials were seriously disturbed by the results of Yugoslavia's and India's diplomatic offensive. According to them, this joint conspiracy also enjoyed significant UAR backing, as well as Soviet propaganda support.[84] In this respect, Deng Xiaoping conveyed to the Indonesian ambassador that the new non-aligned conference should not distract China and Indonesia from pursuing their own goals, since that gathering would not discuss seriously any crucial issues, like the anti-imperialist and anti-colonial struggle, support for the national-liberation movements, anti-American opposition, etc.[85] Something similar was reiterated by Zhou Enlai, when he indicated that the Afro-Asian conference should be organized even after the non-aligned one took place, since these two gatherings were, in many ways, essentially different. This was quite a different stance from the one Zhou presented during his tour of Africa.[86]

Soon afterwards, Indonesian Foreign Minister Subandrio sent out invitations for the Afro-Asian preparatory meeting in Jakarta in April 1964.[87] Right from the start, the Indonesians had tried to manipulate the list of participants, making it more Jakarta-friendly, so even China was initially excluded from it so as to avoid any unnecessary controversies. Nevertheless, Zhou Enlai soon stressed that the Chinese high-level delegation would also be present at this event as an incentive for some African nations to attend.[88] As a result, two conflicting groups had come to prominence at this preparatory meeting, one was the China–Indonesia–Pakistan group, while the other one was the India–Ceylon group, occasionally backed by UAR delegates, with both sides bickering about the future conference agenda. In fact, the presence of many delegates previously travelling to Colombo had ensured that the Jakarta meeting would not go against any of the decisions adopted there. Ultimately, it was decided to hold the Afro-Asian conference in Africa the following year, probably in Algiers.[89] Nevertheless, Indonesia was quite upset that the new non-aligned conference would steal the limelight from its brainchild. As stated by Sukarno, any excessive insistence on peaceful co-existence, primarily seen as a rapprochement between Washington and Moscow, could have basically undermined the underlining purpose of both these conferences, making their subsequent anti-imperialist proclamations quite pointless.[90]

On the eve of the Cairo Conference, Yugoslavia decided to strengthen its bargaining position by dispatching its Deputy Foreign Secretary Mišo Pavićević to a number of Asian non-aligned countries in order to level out certain controversies before the summit took place.[91] During his talks in Jakarta, the Yugoslav special envoy surprisingly managed to reach a high level of understanding with both Sukarno and Subandrio soliciting their constructive approach to the conference proceedings, without raising any of the contentious issues. In India, in spite of Nehru's sudden death in May, Pavićević managed to achieve full consensus on all the important issues and the two countries had agreed to undertake a concerted effort to guarantee the conference's successful outcome. Both sides, with Ceylon's consent, also came to the conclusion that emphasis should be put on equal treatment of peaceful co-existence and anti-colonialism, as well as on making clear distinctions between the practices of forging necessary economic ties with former colonial rulers and the notion of neo-colonialism as a new form of exploitation.[92] During the visit to Cambodia, Sihanouk pointed out to his Yugoslav guest that the only reason he had decided to travel to Cairo was due to his personal friendship with Tito, otherwise he would have stayed out.[93] This highlighted that Yugoslavia succeeded in achieving more or less total unanimity of views with some Asian nations.

By September 1964, the non-aligned conference had largely managed to outbid its Afro-Asian competitor. Not only would this gathering be organized months before the other one, but even on the topic of the conference agenda it had succeeded in enveloping all the crucial issues that had direct impact on the present and future affairs of the Third World. Alongside issues such as peaceful co-existence, disarmament and economic development which the Afro-Asianists considered part of the non-aligned political discourse, this event would also tackle other important topics like neo-colonialism, racial discrimination, inequality and great power interventionism, which others considered as characteristic of the agenda of the Afro-Asian conference. Yugoslavia also refrained from arguing equidistance towards both blocs, intending to deal seriously with any outstanding issues, even if this involved openly criticizing one or both superpowers.[94] In this respect, Belgrade enjoyed positive though reserved backing from the US which, unlike in 1961, considered the forthcoming event a place where further radicalization of the Third World could be largely forestalled.⁹⁵

Therefore, in an instruction dispatched to all Yugoslav embassies, the Foreign Secretariat indicated that the main goal of the non-aligned conference should be promotion of the struggle against all manifestations of subjugation, interference and inequalities, like neo-colonialism and economic underdevelopment, by principally advocating peaceful co-existence and arguing for more intensive political and economic exchanges between the developing countries themselves as a necessary precondition of a successful anti-imperialist and anti-colonial struggle. Yugoslavia also proposed new codification of the principles of co-existence that would serve as a precursor to any future collective actions.⁹⁶ In a confidential note delivered to the Cuban ambassador in Belgrade, it was professed that the outright purpose of the forthcoming summit should be full integration of the results of the policy of co-existence with the interests of struggle for equality and total liberation of nations, with any bilateral conflicts being pushed to the sidelines, and thus preventing them from subverting the general course of the conference.⁹⁷

Nevertheless, the Indonesians were preparing for a fierce diplomatic battle over the issue of 'new emerging forces', struggle against imperialism and criticism of Yugoslavia's and India's overall performance before and during this event.⁹⁸ However, some delegations from African countries still gave preference to peaceful co-existence as the guiding principle in their struggle against imperialism and colonialism. They were very much against the radical agenda promoted by Indonesia, Mali and others, since such an approach, as they perceived it, could have triggered more bilateral conflicts, instead of successfully resolving any contentious issues. Therefore, as viewed by many, the emphasis should be primarily on the issue of closer mutual cooperation, since exclusive insistence on a continuous anti-imperialist struggle could have undermined long-term unity of non-aligned nations.⁹⁹ However, one victory was already scored by the Afro-Asianist camp when during his October visit to Beijing Sihanouk suddenly decided not to attend the Cairo Conference, regardless of his earlier promises to both Tito and Nasser. Everybody suspected that China had much to do with this shocking decision.¹⁰⁰

It was already evident that two dominant groups of participants would come to the forefront during the Cairo Conference. The first group would gather around Yugoslavia, India, Ceylon and the host UAR, insisting on issues like peaceful co-existence and economic cooperation, although not discerning any other topics, while the other group headed by Indonesia, Ghana, Mali and potentially Guinea would concentrate its efforts on promoting the concept of decisive anti-imperialist and anti-colonial struggle.¹⁰¹ Before the conference even started, it was obvious that Yugoslavia and the hosts would exercise the leading role, closely followed by the Indian delegation led by the new Prime Minister Lal Bahadur Shastri. The importance of the Yugoslav mediation was already evident when a number of prominent guests from India, Tunisia, Ethiopia and other countries had come to Belgrade to seek a unified position at the forthcoming event beforehand.¹⁰² Even Sukarno had asked for reception with Tito before the conference opening, but as this was technically impossible to organize, the Yugoslav president managed only to receive the Indonesian vice-foreign minister.

Tito then stressed to his guest that any open rift between the participants should be avoided, since otherwise that would be tantamount to lending a helping hand to the enemies of non-alignment.[103]

On the eve of the Cairo Conference, UAR officials emphasized that, due to the strong possibility that the radicals, particularly Indonesians, could still try to hijack the conference proceedings, Yugoslavia, India and the hosts should tread carefully and do their utmost to influence other participants into assuming a constructive posture, moving beyond just the perceived role of non-aligned countries as mediators between the superpowers, while laying more stress on the independent role these nations should exercise in international relations.[104] There were also serious internal doubts regarding Cuban participation, since India, Yugoslavia and the UAR were still harbouring suspicions about Havana's true non-bloc adherence and its overt intentions of talking on Moscow's behalf at the summit. However, acting upon Soviet advice the Cubans decided to surrender any standing reservations and take an active part in this event, thus temporarily mending fences with Tito. Beijing also tried to influence Cuba not to show up in Cairo but without any success.[105]

These underlying tendencies were quite evident at the ministerial meeting held in Cairo on 1–4 October, when an alteration had been successfully introduced into the previously agreed conference agenda by the Indonesian, Malian and Guinean delegations. This change implied that the struggle against imperialism, colonialism and neo-colonialism should hold primacy in any deliberations over peaceful co-existence. However, this unplanned concession was also balanced by the other group when formulation of 'new emerging forces' was totally dropped from the summit agenda.[106] This ministerial meeting also made a decision regarding Moise Tshombe's potential participation as the Congo's representative, formally requesting President Kasavubu to attend the summit in person or dispatch someone else. Tshombe, who aided the former Belgian colonialists and Western mercenaries during and after the decolonization struggle, stood as an ominous symbol of neo-colonialism for the majority of participants, especially African ones. When Tshombe eventually did arrive at Cairo, he was arrested by the local authorities, placed under house arrest and eventually expelled.[107]

The Cairo Conference

The Cairo Conference finally took place on 5–10 October 1964. The greatest success of this gathering was its ability to gather in one place so many state representatives – fifty-seven of them, more than twice that of Belgrade three years before (forty-seven full participants and ten observers, as well as ten guest delegations from the national-liberation movements). The outright majority of participants were largely preoccupied with current world events, with many of them warmly greeting the lessening of tensions between the blocs. However, some countries, like Yugoslavia, still considered that such a positive process should gradually encompass the entire world and it should also be applied not only to the relationships between the great powers themselves but also to their respective policies vis-à-vis small and underdeveloped non-bloc countries.[108]

As expressed in Nasser's opening speech, non-alignment did not evolve into a pure negation of international alignments but it had become a clear affirmation of an independently proclaimed stance in world politics. Therefore, non-aligned nations decided to intensify their diplomatic activities inside the UN to ultimately hold a general conference on disarmament, as well as to diligently work on instilling new dynamism into the recently established UNCTAD mechanism by holding the developed countries accountable for the present situation in the world economic system, while also promoting the easy access of developing countries to the markets and technologies of developed ones.[109] This summit also endorsed the Yugoslav initiative to extend a formal recommendation to the UNGA to adopt the 'Declaration on the Principles of Peaceful Co-Existence', thus making a contribution to the process of codification of these principles as part of international law.[110]

During the general debate, Tito's conceptual conflict with Sukarno became the hallmark of all the divisions plaguing this event and the non-aligned world in general. These two leaders had very tense public and private altercations about the ideas of 'new emerging forces', peaceful co-existence, Chinese policies, future role of non-alignment, etc. Tito regarded the lessening of tensions in the world as a positive signal which could ultimately trigger a fundamental realignment of international forces, one also accompanied by creation of new practices in international relations, thus putting the non-aligned world at the centre of any future global negotiations as another independent political factor. Sukarno, on the other hand, held views that this new international situation was just another rotten compromise between the superpowers made largely at the expense of the postcolonial world which had become the prime target of their aggressive policies. Therefore, he believed that peaceful co-existence was a concept that could be only implemented between the great powers and not between them and feeble newly independent nations, since the great powers would never allow them to freely choose their own path of development. Sukarno also claimed that non-alignment had already become obsolete, just a past phase in the evolution of 'new emerging forces'.[111]

However, in his response Tito openly accused his Indonesian counterpart of deliberately distorting the very concept of peaceful co-existence, which, according to him, was an all-encompassing phenomenon acting as a source of all crucial demands and essential needs of non-aligned countries, a clear and viable alternative to war and discrimination, a necessary precondition to any successful struggle for freedom and equality. It was not just another guarantee of a status quo as Sukarno had claimed. In Tito's words, calls for radical solutions were the shortest path to another armed conflict that could wipe out the entire non-aligned world, but he was also very critical of the great powers themselves, especially how they often interpreted peaceful co-existence in a selective and discriminatory fashion, however and whenever it suited them.[112] The majority of other participants decided not to take sides in this heated debate, although many of them tacitly agreed with Tito's stance. Nevertheless, Sukarno's message did succeed in gaining some hearts and minds, though only Toure and Keita openly backed his agenda.[113] It was evident that both Tito and Nasser lacked Nehru's strong presence to more effectively push together against these radical ambitions.[114]

Figure 2 Opening ceremony of the Second Summit of the Non-Aligned Movement, Cairo, 5 October 1964. © Museum of Yugoslavia.

During their private meetings, Tito openly admonished Sukarno for his policies which would eventually descend into a debacle if not altered any time soon. According to the Yugoslav president, peace was an essential precondition to resolving other outstanding issues, since nothing could be accomplished during wartime. Economic development was crucial as a countermeasure against the rise of neo-colonialism, he pointed out, but this could not be achieved by continuously attacking the same countries that non-aligned countries aspired to cooperate with. Struggle against colonialism was a multifaceted endeavour, not just a military one, and it needed a comprehensive response. Therefore, such a struggle should not be confronted with the struggle for peace, but they needed to back each other up. Sukarno eventually went on the defensive, formally accepting some of Tito's argument, but essentially he did not change his mind.[115] As acknowledged by different observers, Tito and Sukarno's conceptual rift had already become an insurmountable one.[116]

In a private conversation with Bandaranaike, Tito clarified that Sukarno's concept of 'new emerging forces' was not just another substitute for non-alignment, but implied a clear division of the world into two new competing blocs revolving around the issues of racial and class confrontation, which was a very dangerous line of thinking indeed.[117] Nevertheless, Yugoslav officials considered that the Cairo Conference had become a good indicator for Indonesians to appreciate how isolated Jakarta had become in this respect, thus directly inducing Sukarno's potential gradual return to the flock of fully dedicated non-aligned nations where he had initially belonged.[118] However, when withdrawing his country from the UN in January 1965, Sukarno clearly indicated to Tito that he well understood Yugoslavia's reasons for pursuing peaceful co-existence and non-alignment, since Belgrade was not under any direct imperialist threat, but Indonesia, as well as many other Afro-Asian nations, were experiencing an imperialist and neo-colonialist backlash, therefore they had to opt for an armed struggle as a means of survival.[119]

In other issues, the Indian proposal to dispatch a mission to Beijing to demand China not detonate its first atomic device was flatly rejected by the majority, as well as Shastri's idea for all participants to join the LNTBT. Conversely, his proposal for a non-violent resolution of conflicts, without mentioning the border ones, did enter the final document. Furthermore, the Indian delegation did succeed in giving more prominence to the issue of South–South economic cooperation.[120] Even Cuba was very pleased with the outcome of this event, emphasizing specifically Yugoslavia's constructive role which had ultimately assisted the Cubans to successfully present some of their own proposals regarding the presence of foreign bases on its soil.[121] Fundamentally, the lesson both Yugoslavia and India had derived from this summit was that the majority of African nations still attributed far greater importance to the issues of imperialism, colonialism and neo-colonialism than expected, since foreign interference and colonialism were still life-or-death issues for many of them. Therefore, for many Africans the concept of peaceful co-existence had become firmly wedded to the successful completion of decolonization.[122]

In fact, the moderates had managed to largely steer the summit's course, making only minor compromises with the radical group. Even the final declaration was tailored in such a way that it was a true offspring of the documents previously adopted in Belgrade, now only enriched by a more prominent mentioning of imperialism, colonialism and neo-colonialism as primary sources of international tensions and conflicts.[123] During the conference proceedings, a shadow of uncertainty was hovering over the UAR, Yugoslav, the Indian and Ceylonese delegations that the final document would ultimately become far too general, extensive and overwhelmed by marginal issues, thus blurring its main purpose and the wider effect it was supposed to produce. Therefore, they decided to set up a drafting committee expanded by Indonesian, Guinean and Ghanaian representatives, which ultimately succeeded in putting together a concise and clear document, the 'Program for Peace and International Cooperation'. In this document a new definition of the principles of peaceful co-existence was proclaimed, limiting them to a list of nine comprehensive principles, but now encompassing not only the original Five Principles and eight out of the ten Bandung principles but also adding some new content, while also providing more substance and clarity to the old ones. This document, however, still suffered from some of the weaknesses related to achieving compromised solutions from sometimes irreconcilable positions.[124]

Nevertheless, the Cairo Conference did succeed in forging a more or less general consensus on all crucial international issues. What was even more important, was that this event also created a direct link between the two clusters of dominant issues: one related to non-alignment, peace, economic development and the lessening of international tensions, while the other actively argued for anti-colonial and anti-imperialist struggle. Furthermore, economic development still did not possess enough capacity to transform itself into a potent force for forging wider unity among non-aligned countries as envisaged by India and Yugoslavia, while anti-imperialist and anti-colonial struggle proved to be an insufficient remedy for successfully mitigating divisions and resolving conflicts between these nations as argued by the Indonesians.[125] However, in this way, each and every participant was able to identify at least one issue closely related to their respective national policies, thus providing a stimulus for mitigating any local or regional divisions that could have affected the overall spirit of cooperation. The majority of African countries, and some Arab ones too, were successful in skilfully balancing the necessity to forcefully advocate peaceful co-existence and economic development and the obvious imperative to continue with the struggle against all manifestations of colonialism and racism. Therefore, the final declaration in Cairo was an outright expression of general striving for setting up a fundamentally different international system that would gradually become more attuned to the needs of the developing world.[126]

The non-aligned agenda promoted at this summit ultimately succeeded in emphasizing the next stage of the political evolution of the non-aligned group, beyond but not without the primordial issues of anti-imperialism and anti-colonialism. Some authors have called this specific compromise solution a reluctant merger between Afro-Asianism and non-alignment, a return to a pre-Belgrade stage, observing this both as an unprincipled concession and a pragmatic necessity.[127] The evident desire to prop up wider conference attendance so as to establish a strong counterweight to the assertive aspirations of the competitive group eventually led some UAR diplomats to make certain accusations, mainly laid at Yugoslavia's doorstep: 'Yugoslavia is willing to pretend that countries are nonaligned if they claim they are, in the expectation that in the future the country may become truly nonaligned. This may merit as a long-term proposition, but it is scarcely designed to ensure the success of a particular conference.'[128] This kind of statement clearly highlighted the inherent disgruntlement of some African and Arab representatives over the ideological wrestling taking place between the European and Asian wings of non-alignment that significantly affected group's cohesiveness.

The only thing that was not properly addressed in Cairo, which the UAR and Ceylonese delegations often advocated before and after this event, was a widely present, although not publicly proclaimed, intention to ultimately set up a permanent organization encompassing all non-bloc countries. This proposal was ignored by the majority of participants, Yugoslavia included, with many of them primarily driven by fears that such a controversial idea could ultimately endanger the successful outcome of the entire summit. Already plagued by some incidents, raising again the idea of a 'third bloc' could have seriously undermined a hard-won consensus, while also overshadowing many other far pressing issues. Nevertheless, it was still agreed at this conference that non-aligned nations should occasionally hold joint consultations, while also, from time to time, organizing meetings of foreign ministers during the UNGA sessions.[129]

Conference Aftermath

As compared to other great powers who were generally satisfied with the results of the Cairo Conference, China demonstrated a more heightened interest in this gathering. This was primarily due to the fact that many participants had previously decided to openly endorse the LNTBT, which Beijing stridently opposed, while the unresolved Sino-Indian border issue could have been raised by some of them. Consequently, Chinese leaders undertook a very cautious approach to this summit, putting a lot of faith in Sukarno's political astuteness.[130] In an internal analysis the Chinese Foreign Ministry considered Tito's performance in Cairo as his diplomatic defeat, since he, they stressed, could not successfully further his own agenda. The Chinese side was highly critical of Tito's attempts to isolate the so-called leftists at this event, while openly joining hands with the Indians in condemning Beijing's ongoing nuclear activities and its specific position with respect to the border conflict. In fact, the Yugoslav president was portrayed by Beijing as an 'imperialist running dog' who would never dare to openly criticize the US and endanger the economic assistance he had been receiving from Washington.[131]

In general, the Chinese observed the Cairo Conference as a moderate success, considering that Indonesia and its allies had ultimately managed to outmanoeuvre Tito's, Shastri's and Nasser's proposals. Nevertheless, the fact that this conference had taken place well before the Afro-Asian one was still not highly appreciated in Beijing.[132] Furthermore, as a means to influence the summit's outcome, China successfully detonated its first atomic device only a few days after the summit's closure, thus somewhat repeating Khrushchev's act on the eve of the Belgrade Conference with the resumption of nuclear tests. Almost as an act of defiance to both superpowers, China stirred great admiration among many Third World nations, thus openly symbolizing the ultimate achievement of technological equality with the developed world.[133] Therefore, Beijing was convinced that major international trends proved to be very conducive to the future success of the Afro-Asian conference, an event that could decisively shape the face of a new global anti-imperialist and anti-revisionist united front.[134]

Nevertheless, another event also marked the aftermath of the Cairo Conference. It was Khrushchev's sudden removal from office by Leonid Brezhnev. In fact, Moscow was quite content with the outcome of the summit, while the Soviets observed with approval the rise of Nasser's influence as compared to Tito's and Shastri's weakened positions.[135] Sudden changes in the Kremlin raised particular concern with Tito and Nasser that Moscow could now try to mend bridges with Beijing at the expense of non-aligned countries, resulting in the Soviet Union's reduced involvement in the Third World. Nasser was especially distressed that a possible Soviet withdrawal of any assistance could be imminent, thus seriously hampering his regional ambitions. However, it soon became clear that no significant changes in the Soviet policy towards Yugoslavia, UAR, India, China or the Third World would occur any time soon. Both Tito and Nasser were rather relieved with these prospects, since they could still somewhat count on the Soviets in their ongoing attempts to counter any Chinese encroachments into future non-aligned activities.[136]

From the very start it was evident that the second Bandung was bound to face unplanned troubles. Not only had it been outmanoeuvred by the Cairo Conference in many different ways, but some of the crucial participants were already having second thoughts. During the non-aligned summit Ben Bella confided in the Yugoslav delegation that he could not bear any more pressure created by the Sino-Soviet dispute, so he decided to ask for postponement of the entire event for at least three months but even better until November 1965.[137] Even though the Chinese were not ready to accept this solution, soon enough they were forced to change their mind and cave in to Algerian demands, postponing the second Bandung until June 1965.[138] Indonesia's withdrawal from the UN in January that same year, and its aggressive advocacy of the 'new emerging forces' concept, together with China's increasing internal and external radicalization had all started to reflect upon the feasibility of conference preparations. The entire initiative had been slowly losing momentum, which was already clear during the poorly organized 10th anniversary celebration of the Bandung Conference in April 1965.[139]

In fact, escalation of the Vietnam War with the initiation of the 'Rolling Thunder' bombing campaign of North Vietnam in March 1965, together with the increasing US ground troops involvement, seemed an opportune moment for non-aligned countries to use the positive effect of the Cairo Conference for launching a joint mediation effort.[140] Following Tito's invitation, representatives of fifteen non-aligned nations met in Belgrade in mid-March to issue a joint appeal (Indonesia abstained). Although Yugoslavia submitted a draft that clearly stressed 'condemnation of U.S. aggression', some attendees refused to sign in, but when this formulation was deleted, Cuba and Mali withdrew their signatures. Nevertheless, four other nations soon joined (Kenya, Tanzania, Uganda and Nepal), and the document became internationally known as the 'Appeal of 17 Non-Aligned Nations' (Sudan joined later on as the eighteenth signatory). However, both Vietnams immediately rejected this initiative, while the Johnson administration decided to skilfully manipulate this appeal to insist on negotiations without any preconditions, thus discerning the North Vietnamese demands for the prior cessation of hostilities.[141] China then used this event to launch a frenzied propaganda campaign against Yugoslavia for deliberately assisting US imperialists.[142] In the aftermath, there were also other attempts staged by non-aligned countries, like Mali, India and Ghana, to initiate mediation of this escalating conflict but also without yielding any concrete results.[143]

However, in the latter part of 1965, tectonic changes had rocked the very foundations of the Third World, triggering a comprehensive realignment of forces. At first, due to a protracted factional infighting in the Algerian leadership, in mid-June Ben Bella was suddenly overthrown by his Defence Minister Houari Boumedienne, thus effectively ending the intense revolutionary phase in that country's foreign policy.[144] Sukarno's extreme proximity to Beijing and the Communist Party of Indonesia (PKI), and his overambitious foreign policy, eventually induced the rapid rapprochement between the army leadership and different rightist political groups. Being aware that Sukarno could seek a compromise with these opposing forces, on 30 September local communists launched an unsuccessful coup aimed at eliminating the army leadership, thus triggering the army's counter-coup that eventually ended in the total destruction of the

PKI. The extent of China's role in these events still remains unclear, but, nonetheless, this episode marked a tragic end to the Sino-Indonesian axis. As for the leading non-aligned countries, they rapidly adapted to the new reality of General Suharto's rule, in spite of Sukarno formally remaining president until 1967.[145] A similar fate also befell Nkrumah during his visit to China and North Vietnam in February 1966, when he was also overthrown in a pro-Western military coup and forced to live in exile in Guinea until his untimely death in 1972.[146]

The two coups staged in Algeria and Indonesia signalled the end of the entire Second Bandung initiative which was finally abandoned by China and the rest of Afro-Asia in November 1965.[147] Even though such an outcome was an outright victory for non-alignment, these sweeping changes could not produce a wider positive effect. Except for Tito, Selassie, Sihanouk and Bandaranaike, an entire array of major historical figures, including the recently deceased Nehru, who led their respective countries towards full independence and international prominence, while also shaping the initial destiny of global non-alignment, had unexpectedly departed from the historical scene leaving behind them a mixed historical legacy to their often less-than-formidable heirs. Their sometimes controversial legacies were still marked by many positive achievements in the areas of nation-building, boosting national self-esteem and nurturing the nation's spirit of resistance, thus providing a new set of rallying points to their often fragmented societies.[148]

Conclusion

As we have seen, Second Bandung, unlike Second Belgrade in the form of the Cairo Conference, eventually never took place and the Afro-Asian Movement, as a competitor to the future NAM, aimed at a similar target group, though with a somewhat different set of principles and goals, eventually became a phenomenon that never was, just a footnote to history and a forgotten episode. By creating a tentative compromise between the two ideological and conference models, above all through emphasizing some of the elements of anti-imperialism and anti-colonialism, the Cairo summit had managed to reinvent itself beyond the immediate constraints imposed by the more militant states comprising parts of the non-aligned world.

However, this entire struggle between the two conference models, often resembling a zero-sum game, had largely drained the vitality from the non-aligned group, also shifting its initial focus and blurring its fundamental purpose, thus frequently paralysing its functioning on a more regular and organized basis, while also stirring additional disagreements among its diverse membership. This was, indeed, a Pyrrhic victory for this group from which it barely survived. Such tragic developments eventually compelled this loose community of nations from four different continents to attempt to redefine its role on the international scene, but still without reaping any tangible success, thus only longing for an already belated diplomatic breakthrough. Events pertaining to the failed Vietnam War mediation clearly stressed these obvious deficiencies, serving as an ominous reminder of how much work still had to be invested into finally transforming this entire group into a more relevant and permanent political factor in world affairs. The time for a new round marked by comprehensive collective action had still not come but, nonetheless, it was still implacably drawing near and only a new threat of an existential crisis, one from which the non-aligned could not have recuperated again, would ultimately propel these nations into a frantic search for a new cause and altered framework of existence.

Notes

1 Lorenz M. Lüthi, *Cold Wars*, 298–9.
2 Aleksandr Fursenko and Timothy Naftali, *Khrushchev's Cold War*, 438–528; James Hershberg, 'The Cuban Missile Crisis', in *The Cambridge History of the Cold War*, 2, 65–87.
3 Melvyn P. Leffler, *For the Soul of Mankind: The United States, the Soviet Union, and the Cold War* (New York, NY: Hill and Wang, 2007), 182–233.
4 Lorenz M. Lüthi, *Cold Wars*, 296–7, 345–7; Rohan Mukherjee, 'Nuclear Ambiguity and International Status: India in the Eighteen-Nation Committee on Disarmament, 1962-1969', in *India and the Cold War*, Manu Bhagavan (ed.) (Chapel Hill, NC: The University of North Carolina Press, 2019), 137–42.
5 Lorenz M. Lüthi, *The Sino-Soviet Split: Cold War in the Communist World* (Princeton, NJ: Princeton University Press, 2008), 219–85; Sergey Radchenko, *Two Suns in the Heavens: The Sino-Soviet Struggle for Supremacy, 1962-1967* (Washington DC, Stanford: Woodrow Wilson Center Press, Stanford University Press, 2009), 56–117.
6 Jeremy Friedman, *Shadow Cold War: The Sino-Soviet Competition for the Third World* (Chapel Hill, NC: The University of North Carolina Press, 2015), 101–47; Li Qianyu, *Cong Wanlong dao Aerjier: Zhongguo yu liu ci YaFei guoji huiyi* (Beijing: Shijie zhishi chubanshe, 2016), 167–207.
7 Odd Arne Westad, *The Global Cold War*, 131–52, 180–90.
8 Lise Namikas, *Battleground Africa*, 160–222; Robert B. Rakove, *Kennedy, Johnson, and the Nonaligned World*, 121–7.
9 Jeffrey James Byrne, *The Mecca of Revolution*, 113–229; Assassi Lassassi, *Non-Alignment and Algerian Foreign Policy*, 82–7, 147–54.
10 W. Scott Thompson, *Ghana's Foreign Policy*, 271–413; Kwesi Armah, *Ghana's Foreign Policy*, 145–84.
11 Malcolm H. Kerr, *The Arab Cold War: Gamal Abd al Nasir and His Rivals, 1958-1970* (Oxford: Oxford University Press, 1971), 27–125; Jesse Ferris, *Nasser's Gamble*, 70–261.
12 Bradley R. Simpson, *Economists with Guns*, 62–112.
13 Ide Anak Agung Gde Agung, *Twenty Years Indonesian Foreign Policy*, 415–42; Taomo Zhou, *Migration in the Time of Revolution*, 132–51; Jovan Čavoški, 'On the Road to the Coup: Indonesia between the Nonaligned and China', in *1965 – Indonesia and the World*, Bernd Schaefer and Baskara T. Wardaya (eds) (Jakarta: Gramedia Publishers, 2013), 66–74.
14 Matthew Jones, *Conflict and Confrontation in South East Asia 1961-1965: Britain, the United States, Indonesia, and the Creation of Malaysia* (Cambridge: Cambridge University Press, 2002), 98–232.

15 Srinath Raghavan, *War and Peace in Modern India*, 267–310; Tanvi Madan, *Fateful Triangle: How China Shaped U.S.-India Relations during the Cold War* (Washington, DC: Brookings Institution Press, 2020), 141–67.
16 Jovan Čavoški, 'Saving Non-Alignment: Diplomatic Efforts of Major Non-Aligned Countries and the Sino-Indian Border Conflict', in *The Sino-Indian War of 1962: New Perspectives*, Lorenz Lüthi and Amit Das Gupta (eds) (London: Routledge, 2017), 160–78; G. H. Jansen, *Afro-Asia and Non-Alignment*, 331–49.
17 M. S. Rajan, 'India and World Politics in the Post-Nehru Era', *International Journal* 24.1 (1968–9), 146.
18 CFMA, 105-01789-02, 'Mrs. Supeni-Chinese ambassador talks', 2 July 1962.
19 DAMSPS, PA, 1962, f-105, 431593, 'Preparations for the second AA conference', 21 September 1962.
20 DAMSPS, PA, 1962, f-105, 429379, 'Recent activities concerning the second AA conference', 11 September 1962.
21 CFMA, 105-01789-01, 'Pushing North Korea, Mongolia, North Vietnam to convene the second AA conference', 19 October 1962.
22 DAMSPS, PA, 1963, f-65, 41293, 'Telegram from China', 7 January 1963.
23 AJ, 837, KPR, I-5-b, India, 'Foreign Secretariat's debate on India, 14 May 1964'.
24 AJ, 507, CC LCY, IX, 60/II-134, 'Chinese activities in Asia, Africa and Latin America', 31 May 1963.
25 Taomo Zhou, *Migration in the Time of Revolution*, 147.
26 G. H. Jansen, *Afro-Asia and Non-Alignment*, 367–8.
27 Josip Broz Tito, *Govori i članci*, 18 (1966), 426–37.
28 AJ, 837, KPR, I-3-a, UAR, 'Tito-Nasser talks, 13 May 1963'.
29 DAMSPS, PA, 1963, f-111, 433760, 'Telegram from UAR', 16 October 1963.
30 G. H. Jansen, *Afro-Asia and Non-Alignment*, 365–6.
31 DAMSPS, PA, 1963, f-111, 434971, 'Telegram from UAR', 26 October 1963.
32 DAMSPS, PA, 1963, f-111, 438824, 'Telegram from India', 1 December 1963.
33 DAMSPS, PA, 1963, f-111, 433382, 'Telegram from China', 8 October 1963.
34 DAMSPS, PA, 1964, f-173, 4695, 'Telegram from UN', 6 January 1964.
35 DAMSPS, PA, 1963, f-111, 439177, 'Foreign Secretariat's telegram', 5 December 1963.
36 DAMSPS, PA, 1963, f-111, 435922, 'Telegram from China', 3 November 1963.
37 DAMSPS, PA, 1963, f-111, 437284, 'Telegram from UAR', 15 November 1963.
38 DAMSPS, PA, 1963, f-111, 440651, 'Telegram from Algeria', 17 December 1963.
39 DAMSPS, PA, 1964, f-173, 4841, 'Talks between Nikezić and Asmaoen', 7 January 1964.
40 CFMA, 203-00495-01, 'Report on the visit to 14 countries', 27 May 1964.
41 DAMSPS, PA, 1964, f-173, 44122, 'Telegram from UAR', 3 January 1964.
42 DAMSPS, PA, 1963, f-65, 441262, 'Telegram from UAR', 23 December 1963.
43 CFMA, 107-01027-06, 'Zhou Enlai-Nasser second meeting', 17 December 1963.
44 CFMA, 107-01027-07, 'Zhou Enlai-Nasser third meeting', 19 December 1963.
45 DAMSPS, PA, 1963, f-111, 441938, 'Telegram from UAR', 29 December 1963.
46 CFMA, 203-00614-06, 'Zhou Enlai-Ben Bella fourth meeting', 26 December 1963.
47 DAMSPS, PA, 1964, f-111, 4272, 'Telegram from Algeria', 30 December 1963.
48 CFMA, 203-00620-03, 'Premier's visit to Tunisia', 10 January 1964.
49 AVPRF, f. 144, op. 25, p. 58, d. 7, l. 121–126, 'Conversation between the Soviet and Tunisian ambassadors', 22 October 1964.
50 CFMA, 203-00400-02, 'Visit to Ghana', 15 January 1964.

51 DAMSPS, PA, 1964, f-111, 42150, 'Foreign Secretariat's telegram', 17 January 1964.
52 DAMSPS, PA, 1964, f-56, 43503, 'Telegram from Ghana', 29 January 1964.
53 CFMA, 203-00625-02, 'Chen Yi-Malian Foreign Minister talks', 17 January 1964.
54 CFMA, 203-00402-02, 'Visit to Guinea', 27 January 1964.
55 DAMSPS, PA, 1964, f-111, 47776, 'Telegram from China', 5 March 1964.
56 CFMA, 203-00642-02, 'Zhou Enlai-Ne Win talks', 17 February 1964.
57 DAMSPS, PA, 1964, f-111, 49037, 'Telegram from Ceylon', 11 March 1964.
58 CFMA, 203-00634-01, 'Premier's visit to Pakistan', 11 March 1964.
59 NARA, RG 59, Central Foreign Policy Files (CFPF), 1964–66, box 1830, POL 8, 'Conflicting proposals for non-aligned and Afro-Asian conferences', 9 January 1964.
60 DAMSPS, PA, 1964, f-178, 411783, 'Telegram from Indonesia', 26 March 1964.
61 DAMSPS, PA, 1964, f-173, 41510, 'Foreign Secretariat's telegram', 15 January 1964.
62 DAMSPS, PA, 1964, f-174, 413585, 'Telegram from Algeria', 20 February 1964.
63 NARA, RG 59, CFPF, 1964–66, box 1830, POL 8, 'Telegram from Hong Kong', 13 March 1964.
64 NARA, RG 59, CFPF, 1964–66, box 1830, POL 8, 'Telegram from Ceylon', 19 February 1964.
65 DAMSPS, PA, 1964, f-173, 412598, 'Telegram from UAR', 12 February 1964.
66 DAMSPS, PA, 1964, f-173, 42306, 'Telegram from UN', 18 January 1964.
67 NARA, RG 59, CFFF, 1964–66, box 1830, POL 8, 'Telegram from Yugoslavia', 14 February 1964.
68 DAMSPS, PA, 1964, f-173, 44060, 'Talks with the Indian Foreign Minister', 5 February 1964.
69 DAMSPS, PA, 1964, f-173, 44712, 'Telegram from UAR', 8 February 1964.
70 DAMSPS, PA, 1964, f-173, 48079, 'Telegram from UAR', 14 March 1964.
71 NARA, RG 59, CFPF, 1964–66, box 1830, POL 8, 'Ghana and the non-aligned conference', 12 March 1964.
72 AVPRF, f. 144, op. 25, p. 59, d. 19, l. 21–25, 'Visit of the Yugoslav delegation to Guinea', 17 April 1964.
73 DAMSPS, PA, 1964, f-173, 46331, 'Telegram from Algeria', 29 February 1964.
74 NAI, MEA, 118(78)/WII/64, 'Non-Alignment and Latin America', February 1964.
75 DAMSPS, PA, 1964, f-173, 49445, 'Telegram from Indonesia', 19 March 1964.
76 DAMSPS, PA, 1964, f-174, 412985, 'Foreign Secretariat's telegram', 14 March 1964.
77 NARA, RG 59, CFPF, 1964–66, box 1830, POL 8, 'Telegram from Ceylon', 25 March 1964.
78 NAI, MEA, 118(78)/WII/64, 'Report on the Colombo preparatory meeting', March 1964.
79 AJ, 837, KPR, I-4-ε/4, 'Report on the Colombo preparatory meeting, 23–29 March 1964'.
80 NARA, RG 59, CFPF, 1964–66, box 1830, POL 8, 'Preparatory non-aligned meeting', 7 April 1964.
81 DAMSPS, PA, 1964, f-174, 420778, 'Foreign Secretariat's telegram', 15 May 1964.
82 NARA, RG 59, CFPF, 1964–66, box 1830, POL 8, 'Telegram from Yugoslavia', 10 April 1964.
83 G. H. Jansen, *Afro-Asia and Non-Alignment*, 374–5.
84 CFMA, 109-02792-03, 'Conspiracy of the Tito Clique', 2 April 1964.
85 CFMA, 105-01869-07, 'Deng Xiaoping-Indonesian ambassador talks', 12 March 1964.
86 CFMA, 105-01869-06, 'Zhou Enlai-Indonesian ambassador talks', 19 March 1964.

87 NAI, 118(78)/WII/64, 'Subandrio to Nehru', 7 March 1964.
88 DAMSPS, PA, 1964, f-178, 416280, 'Telegram from China', 9 April 1964.
89 NAI, 118(78)/WII/64, 'Report on the preparatory meeting in Jakarta', April 1964.
90 DAMSPS, PA, 1964, f-175, 428819, 'Telegram from Indonesia', 7 July 1964.
91 NARA, RG 59, CFPF, 1964–66, box 1829, POL 8, 'Telegram from Yugoslavia', 6 August 1964.
92 NARA, RG 59, CFPF, 1964–66, box 1829, POL 8, 'Second Non-Aligned Conference', 15 August 1964.
93 DAMSPS, PA, 1964, f-174, 432078, 'Foreign Secretariat's telegram', 7 August 1964.
94 NARA, RG 59, CFPF, 1964–66, box 1829, POL 8, 'Telegram from Yugoslavia', 24 September 1964.
95 DAMSPS, PA, 1964, f-176, 439177, 'Telegram from U.S.', 2 October 1964.
96 DAMSPS, PA, 1964, f-175, 435888, 'Foreign Secretariat's telegram', 13 September 1964.
97 AVPRF, f. 0104, op. 20, p. 127, d. 8, l. 70–72, 'Note handed over by the Foreign Secretariat to the Cuban ambassador', 3 October 1964.
98 NARA, RG 59, CFPF, 1964–66, box 1829, POL 8, 'Telegram from Indonesia', 21 September 1964.
99 DAMSPS, PA, 1964, f-176, 438259, 'Telegram from Sudan', 24 September 1964.
100 CFMA, 113-00404-04, 'Cambodia and the Second Non-Aligned Conference', 16 October 1964.
101 NARA, RG 59, CFPF, 1964–66, box 1829, POL 8, 'Telegram from UAR', 8 October 1964.
102 AVPRF, f. 144, op. 25, p. 58, d. 7, l. 114–120, 'Puzanov-Hernandez talks', 22 September 1964.
103 AJ, 837, KPR, I-3-a, Indonesia, 'Tito-Suwito meeting, 26 September 1964'.
104 DAMSPS, PA, 1964, f-176, 439035, 'Telegram from UAR', 29 September 1964.
105 AVPRF, f. 0104, op. 20, p. 127, d. 8, l. 77–79, 'Cuba's policy towards non-aligned countries'.
106 AJ, 837, KPR, I-4-a/5, 'Conference bulletin no. 5', 4 October 1964.
107 AJ, 837, KPR, I-4-a/5, 'Conference bulletin no. 6', 5 October 1964.
108 AJ, 837, KPR, I-4-a/5, 'Speeches of heads of delegations'.
109 Ibid.
110 AJ, 837, KPR, I-4-a/5, 'Codification of the principles of peaceful co-existence'.
111 AJ, 837, KPR, I-4-a/5, 'Sukarno's speech'.
112 AJ, 837, KPR, I-4-a/5, 'Tito's speech'.
113 NARA, RG 59, CFPF, 1964–66, box 1829, POL 8, 'Telegram from Tanzania', 15 October 1964.
114 Ide Anak Agung Gde Agung, *Twenty Years Indonesian Foreign Policy*, 350–1.
115 AJ, 507, CC LCY, III/104, 'Tito's report on the Cairo Conference, 28 October 1964'.
116 NARA, RG 59, Bureau of Intelligence and Research, Bandung I&II, box 1, 'Telegram from UAR', 6 October 1964.
117 AJ, 837, KPR, I-4-a/5, 'Tito-Bandaranaike talks', 9 October 1964.
118 DAMSPS, PA, 1964, f-176, 442723, 'Foreign Secretariat's telegram', 14 November 1964.
119 AJ, 837, KPR, I-1/438, 'Sukarno to Tito', 19 January 1965.
120 NAI, MEA, FIII/102/33/81, 'Non-Aligned Summit Conferences, 1961–1979'.
121 AVPRF, f. 0104, op. 20, p. 127, d. 8, l. 80–83, 'Cuba's position', 8 December 1964.

122 NARA, RG 59, CFPF, 1964–66, box 1829, POL 8, 'Telegram from Yugoslavia', 2 November 1964.
123 NARA, RG 59, CFPF, 1964–66, box 1829, POL 8, 'Telegram from UAR', 16 October 1964.
124 AJ, 837, KPR, I-4-a/5, 'Final report on the Second Conference of Non-Aligned Countries'.
125 NARA, RG 59, CFPF, 1964–66, box 1829, POL 8, 'U.S. assessment of the Second Conference of Non-Aligned Nations', 23 October 1964.
126 DAMSPS, PA, 1964, f-176, 442723, 'Foreign Secretariat's telegram', 30 October 1964.
127 G. H. Jansen, *Afro-Asia and Non-Alignment*, 384, 391–2.
128 Alvin Z. Rubinstein, *Yugoslavia and the Non-Aligned World*, 247–8.
129 NARA, RG 59, CFPF, 1964–66, box 1829, POL 8, 'State Department's telegram', 7 November 1964.
130 DAMSPS, PA, 1964, f-176, 438567, 'Telegram from China', 26 September 1964.
131 CFMA, 109-02792-03, 'Yugoslavia and the Second Non-Aligned Conference', 20 October 1964.
132 CFMA, 109-02792-03, 'China and the Second Non-Aligned Conference', 27 October 1964.
133 CFMA, 107-00835-03, 'Reactions on atomic bomb explosion', 16 October 1964.
134 CFMA, 107-00932-05, 'Second Non-Aligned Conference', 1 November 1964.
135 Political Archive of the Office for Foreign Affairs of Germany (PAAA), A17440, 'Talks on the Cairo Conference', 2 November 1964.
136 А. Н. Артизов, В.П. Наумов и др. (ред.), *Никита Хрущев 1964: стенограммы пленума ЦК КПСС и другие документы* (Москва: МФД, 2007), 357–62.
137 NARA, RG 59, CFPF, 1964–66, box 1829, POL 8, 'Telegram from Yugoslavia', 15 October 1964.
138 CFMA, 107-00932-02, 'Visit of the Algerian special envoy', 20 December 1964.
139 DAMSPS, PA, 1965, f-136, 416041, 'Telegram from Indonesia', 30 April 1965.
140 John Prados, *Vietnam: The History of an Unwinnable War, 1945–1975* (Lawrence, KS: University Press of Kansas, 2009), 62–102; Brian VanDeMark, *Road to Disaster: A New History of America's Descent into Vietnam* (New York, NY: Custom House, 2018), 203–93.
141 DAMSPS, top secret, 1965, f-1, 52, 'Latest developments concerning Vietnam', March 1965.
142 CFMA, 109-02949-01, 'Yugoslavia's conspiracy concerning the 17 nations appeal', March 1965.
143 Robert B. Rakove, 'The Rise and Fall of Non-Aligned Mediation, 1961–6', *The International History Review* 37.5 (2015), 1005–7.
144 William B. Quandt, *Revolution and Political Leadership: Algeria, 1954–1968* (Cambridge, MA: MIT Press, 1969), 204–43.
145 Taomo Zhou, *Migration in the Time of Revolution*, 152–70; Bradley R. Simpson, *Economists with Guns*, 171–206; Jovan Čavoški, 'On the Road to the Coup', 75–81.
146 June Milne, *Kwame Nkrumah: A Biography* (London: Panaf Books, 1999), 151–88.
147 Li Qianyu, *Cong Wanlong dao Aerjier*, 208–31.
148 Fouad Ajami, 'The Fate of Nonalignment', *Foreign Affairs* 59.2 (1980), 367–9.

4

Taking a New Turn: the 1970 Lusaka Conference

With major changes already taking place in the world by the end of the 1960s, the non-aligned group had to rediscover its new meaning and rationale for existence beyond just the security and ideological issues dominating the discourse of the 1950s and the 1960s. This kind of fundamental soul-searching also implied extricating the entire group from a quagmire left by the last summit, providing it with a new purpose closely related to the future existence of postcolonial societies, while also redefining the group's mode of existence through establishing more permanent forms of collective organization.

Essentially, the 1970 Lusaka Conference was a defining moment in the history of the non-aligned group when this conceptually loose and formally undefined framework for action, primarily represented by the two ad hoc summits of 1961 and 1964, had finally transformed itself into a fully fledged international organization – the NAM, with its clearly defined set of principles and ideas, concrete programme of future activities and permanence in both institutional existence and summit continuity. However, this gathering came at the very end of a profound organizational and conceptual crisis when, five years after the Cairo summit, there were no new multilateral events of this sort, while any new initiatives were largely left unanswered by the majority of non-aligned countries. In many ways, this troublesome and turbulent transitional period was marked by total diplomatic paralysis, leaving a strong impression with the great powers that non-alignment was becoming increasingly irrelevant.

Facing such a complex situation, Yugoslavia and some other influential non-aligned countries had decided to undertake a number of diplomatic initiatives that could regalvanize this group, close the ranks, primarily with the aim of reinventing the meaning and role of non-alignment, while setting up a more permanent mechanism for cooperation that could transform all non-bloc factors into a more relevant and widespread international movement ready to set off a constructive dialogue with the great powers on a number of key issues. Despite many ups and downs, as we shall see in this chapter, Yugoslavia and its allies had managed to reignite the spirit of cooperation and collective action that had finally led to the NAM's official emergence as the central spokesperson for the developing world, one standing at the crossroads of rising demands for liberation, autonomy and prosperity. Issues of economic development and modernization, revolving around the ideas of propelling a major overhaul of the international system, would ultimately become the focal point of the NAM's activities on the world stage throughout the 1970s.

Between Interventionism and the Emerging Détente

The adverse impact of the intensive competition between the Afro-Asian and non-aligned conference models had left the majority of the Third World in disarray, with many non-bloc countries lacking excessive energy or guiding thought for organizing a new major gathering that would be capable of coping with the rapidly deteriorating situation. Fundamental changes were taking place among the core Third World nations, suddenly sweeping away from the international scene some of the key non-aligned leaders that had marked the previous twenty years of postcolonial history, ultimately substituting them with their more authoritarian and less ideological successors.[1] For many non-aligned countries it seemed as if the forces of imperialism and neo-colonialism were on a relentless march marked by new military interventionism, active foreign interference and expanding economic domination. Prospects seemed very dark for the non-aligned, while the so-called postwar 'long peace' proved to be neither long nor peaceful for many.[2]

However, with a growing spirit of mutual accommodation, both superpowers were becoming more ready to impose bloc divisions and spheres of influence as a permanent treat of international relations, thus gaining additional guarantees for the geopolitical gains they acquired after 1945. This process also entailed propping up global stability between the two sides, while also incessantly trying to control the UN by avoiding embracing small and medium countries as equal participants in the decision-making process concerning major international issues. Such strategic topics, like peace, security and development, would largely remain the exclusive domain of the superpowers and the object of their direct negotiations, even though non-aligned countries would incessantly strive to somewhat turn the tables in their favour. The example of the conclusion of the Nuclear Non-Proliferation Treaty in July 1968, which only cemented the nuclear monopoly of a handful of great powers, seemed quite edifying in unmasking these emerging inequalities, even though the threat of nuclear war was concurrently receding.[3] Many of these tendencies would remain the same during the superpower détente, thus having a major impact on how the NAM played out its own policies in the future.

However, while the Cold War was undergoing gradual stabilization in Europe and between the superpowers, both Washington and Moscow were, nonetheless, pursuing proactive Third World policies aimed at moulding postcolonial societies according to their own image and, as they perceived it, propelling them into their own brand of modernity by introducing sweeping political, economic, social, cultural and other changes. However, this call to proselytize proved to be a far greater challenge for the proponents of the US modernization theory or Soviet socialist transformation than each of them expected. Modernization and development did not always mean the same thing for the superpowers and those standing at the other end of such policies.[4] In many ways, the Third World also began to fight back, either with arms in their hands or by sharpening their political tools and slowly seeking strength in growing numbers.

In fact, by the mid-1960s superpower détente was slowly in the making and probably would have materialized even before the end of that decade save for the Vietnam War. Each superpower had its own reasons for engagement, ranging from preserving most of

Southeast Asia within the US sphere of influence to the intensive Sino-Soviet competition over North Vietnam where each communist giant tried to demonstrate its unwavering support as a means of offsetting each other's gains in the Third World. With time, the US became painfully aware of its power limitations, therefore pursuing accommodation with the USSR as a means of preserving some of its global stature. Nevertheless, the chaos of the Cultural Revolution in China and defeat of its primary allies in Afro-Asia led to the rapid reduction of Beijing's Third World involvement, except in some marginal revolutionary groups, while China also insisted that Hanoi should refuse any peace negotiations and continue with its dedicated struggle.[5] As for the North Vietnamese, they were becoming masters in manipulating these parallel geopolitical competitions, while resourcefully pursuing their goal of national unity and liberation. The evident progress of Vietnam's uncompromising stance and the devastating psychological effect left by the Tet Offensive on the US gradually led to the opening of peace negotiations in Paris in 1968. In parallel, the formation of the Provisional Revolutionary Government of South Vietnam (PRGSV) in 1969, a North Vietnamese proxy representing rebel forces in the South, acted as an extended diplomatic hand that firmly connected the Vietnamese struggle with the non-aligned world.[6]

Nevertheless, the greatest challenge to non-alignment came in the Middle East, directly undermining its active core, somewhat similar to what had befallen India in 1962. Nasser's regional policies were already overburdened with his parallel struggle against Israel and his Arab adversaries. While some, such as Saudi Arabia or Jordan, were interested in reining in his ambitions by leaning to the side of the West, others, like Syria, headed by the radical leftist Baath Party, overtly challenged Nasser's leadership credentials by highlighting his diminished revolutionary spirit. Mutual armed provocations between Syria and Israel contributed to the rapid deterioration of the situation in 1966–7, thus forcing Nasser to act more resolutely.[7] However, after making a gross miscalculation of Israeli intentions and capabilities, also threatening Tel Aviv's security and well-being by closing the Straits of Tiran, Nasser triggered an Israeli pre-emptive strike on 5 June 1967 that in a matter of few days totally annihilated joint military forces of the UAR, Jordan and Syria, bringing about Israeli occupation of the West Bank, Gaza Strip, Sinai Peninsula and the Golan Heights. The Six-Day War proved to be an overwhelming catastrophe for Nasser personally, undermining the very foundations of his domestic and foreign power.[8]

Furthermore, this regional conflict quickly escalated into a Cold War confrontation with the two blocs largely aligning firmly behind one or the other side, with both belligerents seeking security in closer association with the superpowers. The Johnson administration, although officially seeking ceasefire in the UN, essentially adopted a policy of openly supporting Israel with expanding arms deliveries, while demanding Tel Aviv's flexibility over any future peace agreement.[9] Therefore, facing such daunting odds, Nasser opted for a 'natural alliance' with the Soviet Union, thus forging a defence and economic arrangements which indicated a close Cold War alignment. This kind of sudden foreign policy shift initially implied massive arms transfers from the Soviet bloc to the UAR and other Arab states, as well as extension of crucial economic aid.[10]

Eventually, at the Arab League (AL) summit in Khartoum in August 1967, attending delegations managed to adopt the policy of 'The Three No's' – no recognition of, no negotiations with and no peace for Israel – clearly indicating that the war option was still on the table. The situation would remain tense in the UAR for years, particularly with the eruption of the so-called War of Attrition in March 1969, marked by intensive armed skirmishes along the Suez Canal for the following eighteen months, which demonstrated Nasser's growing desperation with both superpowers unable to force Israel's hand to grant necessary concessions. Nevertheless, he was ready to negotiate with either of them to achieve some kind of a peaceful solution that would guarantee withdrawal from the occupied territories. If that failed, increased Soviet military presence in Egypt still served as a powerful deterrent.[11] In essence, following all these events, the UAR's commitment to non-alignment and its initiatives would be dictated by its immediate national interests and security challenges.

However, in the latter half of the 1960s, newly liberated African states were gaining prominence following an evolving historical shift on that continent where West African nations, spearheading the initial decolonization drive, were being rapidly supplanted by their Eastern and Southern African counterparts, particularly Tanzania and Zambia, who had already taken over the role of central players. This was particularly true when the focus of African liberation struggle descended on Southern Africa to these so-called 'frontline states' facing the last remnants of colonialism and racism on the continent in Angola, Mozambique, South Rhodesia, South Africa and Namibia. Furthermore, during these years Tanzania and Zambia were receiving most of the political or economic scrutiny from the great powers and non-aligned states alike. Therefore, hosting the third non-aligned summit in the Zambian capital Lusaka stood as a clear signal of not only the greater weight carried by African states inside the NAM but also the more significant presence of Eastern and Southern African nations in formulating the new non-aligned agenda for the 1970s.[12]

However, while non-alignment was still recuperating from all these internal fractures, during 1968 the entire world was merged into a revolutionary situation, a real generational upheaval, where in both blocs emerging social forces from the margins violently expressed their dissatisfaction, particularly venting their frustrations against the established elites and the way they were managing Cold War contradictions. A clash between these opposing social poles most violently manifested in the shape of rallies staged against the Vietnam War across the US, riots in Paris that eventually led to De Gaulle's resignation, as well as in the form of 'Prague Spring', an attempt at internally and peacefully reforming the socialist system, which eventually resulted in the invasion of the five Warsaw Pact countries.[13] This obvious demonstration of weakness by both superpowers in running their own blocs eventually created favourable conditions for initiating the superpower détente that would serve as the grand historical background against which the most active phase of the NAM's transformation would take place.[14]

Recuperating From the Afro-Asianist Challenge

As discussed in the previous chapter, the 1964 Cairo Conference had left a bitter aftertaste of many profound divisions, thus creating a strong impression that non-alignment was undergoing a serious internal crisis and the right amount of externally applied pressure, as perceived by some, would cause it to definitely crumble and disappear from the historical scene. Some critics even considered that decisions made at this summit were out of touch with the new harsh reality then plaguing the Third World, thus eventually dissipating the non-aligned group's ability to adequately react or assume a proactive stance accordingly. Nevertheless, new initiatives for reinvigorating this club of non-bloc nations and transforming it into a more potent and viable mechanism for collective action were still on the table, accompanied by an increasing focus on the issues of foreign non-interference and economic development.[15]

Therefore, any proposal for convening a new non-aligned meeting was still being largely decided between the pioneers – Yugoslavia, India and the UAR – sometimes resulting in growing discontent among other members of the group claiming that these three nations had somewhat monopolized the leadership role.[16] Furthermore, in January 1966, Cuba, together with some other Third World radicals, attempted to establish a new organization in place of a now almost defunct AAPSO. This would be, as Castro envisaged, a more comprehensive institution, the so-called 'Tricontinental', one also encompassing Latin America, and with an official seat in Havana. However, this attempt to partially supplant the non-aligned group with a competing superregional format largely failed due to the Sino-Soviet and Sino-Cuban contradictions present at that event, which seriously hampered the organization's already bleak future.[17]

The sudden downfall of Nkrumah, just a few months after the tragic events in Indonesia, sounded the alarm among African nations that neo-colonialism was on the march again. These developments had triggered an idea, largely promoted by the UAR, that convening a new non-aligned conference was now more than necessary. In spite of Nasser's efforts, the majority of potential African participants labelled this proposal as being both premature and not well thought-out, while India was also reluctant to attend due to its sensitive relationship with both superpowers after its recent war with Pakistan in August–September 1965.[18] Unfortunately, Yugoslavia's initiative of discussing African issues at this new gathering proposed by Nasser, one that would eventually usher in a new non-aligned summit, was effectively torpedoed by some countries from that continent which were more prone to regionalist than 'universalist' responses to such local challenges, preferably under the OAU auspices.[19]

However, in March 1966, UAR officials made a tentative probe for the forthcoming Tito–Nasser meeting being expanded into a tripartite one with the new Indian Prime Minister Indira Gandhi also attending.[20] This idea was soon picked up by the Indians who considered that direct consultations between the three leaders would be the most meaningful way to demonstrate to the world that the policy of non-alignment was not in crisis.[21] This was especially important for Indira Gandhi who, after Shastri's recent death during Soviet-mediated peace talks with Pakistan in Tashkent, was facing an escalating internal political and economic upheaval, one which also brought about restrictions in US economic aid.[22] Therefore, when Tito and Nasser finally met in Alexandria in April, they both concluded that new activism on their behalf was necessary for preserving non-alignment as a global factor of influence, thus basically endorsing the idea of a tripartite meeting in New Delhi.[23] Yugoslavia was also contemplating encouraging Indonesia to attend as the fourth member, thus propping up Sukarno's fledgling position in his final showdown with the generals, but this idea was rejected outright by the other two participants.[24] Eventually it was agreed to hold this meeting in the Indian capital in late October.

As the US diplomats concluded, this entire initiative was, in a way, Tito's personal attempt to forestall the dissolution of the non-aligned group by reinvigorating its active core of the three key nations, thus demonstrating to other members that the entire concept was still very much 'vital, effective, and of value'.[25] In fact, Yugoslav officials were well aware that the non-aligned world was not undergoing dissolution but differentiation where an exclusive and small group of radical nations was being established again, one considering non-alignment as a mere tool in their continuous struggle against imperialism and colonialism. Conversely, the regionalist drive of some nations, for example, Arab and African, was having a negative impact on the cohesiveness and universal character of non-alignment. Some participants of the Belgrade and Cairo Conferences were also increasingly subscribing to one or the other bloc agenda, while some other countries were being transformed into non-alignment's cautious proponents, despite some of them either being formal bloc members, edging closer to one of the two blocs, or being formally neutral (Romania, Iran, Pakistan, Japan, Sweden, Austria, etc.).[26]

When the three non-aligned leaders finally met in New Delhi on 20–5 October 1966, they were conscious that the eyes of the entire non-aligned world were on them, with some harsh critics, such as Algeria or Cambodia, actively arguing for an expanded meeting beyond this tripartite format.[27] Therefore, in his opening address, Tito stressed that these three nations did not intend to speak on behalf of all other non-aligned countries, but that the three leaders aspired to set the pace for any future undertakings by making a tangible and proactive contribution to the continuity of non-alignment.[28] Taking all this into account, while dismissing any formality in their deliberations, the three leaders initiated a free exchange of opinions on all relevant issues, with Gandhi taking lead in presenting Asian affairs, Nasser Middle Eastern and African ones, and Tito concentrating on Europe.

Initially, Gandhi stressed that the international situation had fundamentally changed, since previously 'Europe was at the centre of tensions', but 'now this centre has moved to Asia'. According to her, the Vietnam War was at the very core of all external efforts directed at undermining Asian and world stability. She saw the recent disappearance of strong and progressive Asian and African non-aligned leaders as the central factor in inviting more active foreign interference, coupled with the inherent weakness demonstrated by all these nations. Gandhi, therefore, identified the triangular relationship between the US, USSR and China as the key political factor fundamentally shaping the general situation in Asia and the world, thus also having an adverse impact on the security of non-aligned countries in general.[29] Taking into account that the Washington–Beijing–Moscow strategic triangle was still a few years away from materializing, this was a far-sighted prognosis on Gandhi's behalf.

After hearing her argument, Nasser expressed his position that non-aligned countries had become excessively preoccupied with their own internal problems. He then emphasized that this tripartite meeting should ultimately act as a propellant for any new non-aligned peace initiatives, also exercising its role as a rallying cry for any future conferences of a similar format. However, in Nasser's mind, this would be only possible if the majority of potential future participants had been preliminary vetted for attendance based on the new, more precise criteria.[30] With this proposal, Nasser went beyond what had been set in 1961/4, thus transforming this into a somewhat radical alley of thinking. Tito concurred with this point, proposing that readdressing the non-alignment criteria had to be applied not only to the existing members of the group but to all other countries being in general disagreement with any bloc policies, even if they were formally bloc members themselves. However, Nasser thought this kind of approach unfeasible, while Gandhi also concurred.[31] For the time being, Tito decided to drop this idea altogether.

However, on Nasser's initiative the three leaders also tackled economic issues. They all noticed that the issues of rising indebtedness of developing nations, high interest rates and high prices of industrial goods dictated by the developed world, as well as low prices of raw materials that constituted the bulk of exports of developing countries had all become central to the socioeconomic sustainability of these countries. Nasser pointed out that additional efforts should also be invested into injecting new dynamism into closer economic, technical and scientific cooperation between these three nations, while also stimulating more intensive exchanges, going beyond just trade and encompassing the establishment of joint industrial enterprises that would take part in international trade.[32] However, this specific initiative could not really yield any major results, not only due to the substantial differences in economic systems of India, Yugoslavia and the UAR but primarily due to the difficult general situation Cairo was in after its crushing defeat from Israel.[33]

In spite of the limited scope of its impact, this tripartite meeting indicated that non-alignment was still a factor in world affairs, while only through tangible and coordinated efforts could it stand up to the escalation of armed conflicts, thus realistically applying some of its agenda in the spirit of peaceful co-existence and worldwide cooperation. International reactions to this event were modest (USSR) and somewhat positive (US), with only China holding negative views. This meeting, as observed by organizers, tried to inject new life into the non-aligned group, initially on a trilateral basis, then gradually expanded its cumulative effect to all other nations. In fact, the most important contribution of this meeting, even without having an immediate follow-up, was the return of economic and developmental issues as the central part of the non-aligned discourse, thus acting as a harbinger of substantial deliberations dominating the NAM's agenda a few years later.[34]

Nevertheless, a widespread enthusiasm for this meeting and its results was clearly lacking among other non-aligned countries, with many of them remaining reticent, while others blamed the organizers for assuming a role far exceeding their true credentials.[35] In addition, Algerians also vented their frustrations that economic problems were gaining too much prominence, while with respect to the issue of anti-imperialist struggle in places like Vietnam or similar these three nations could not reach a meaningful consensus beyond just general ideas about the cessation of hostilities or peaceful mediation.[36] As one could see, conceptual divisions were still very much alive within this entire group, thus not only undermining potential new activities but also seriously affecting the purposefulness and focus of its wider role.

Profound Crisis as a Trigger for New Initiatives

However, the 1967 Arab defeat had initiated a major shift in the balance of forces inside the non-aligned group. Essentially, another core non-bloc nation was struck by a sudden catastrophe, affecting the very future of non-alignment. In many ways, this conflict questioned the validity of this foreign policy strategy. As Indian ambassador to Cairo Apa B. Pant once said, 'non-alignment has obviously been the first casualty' of this war, especially due to the subsequent Soviet military involvement with the UAR.[37] Yugoslavia was one of Cairo's most active non-aligned supporters at that time, extending substantial diplomatic, economic and military support. In fact, Tito was trying to direct the collective response of all socialist countries in support of Nasser, while in parallel also attempting diplomatic mediation encompassing a search for a peaceful solution with Israel, mending fences between the Arabs and the Soviets, and covertly re-establishing the political dialogue between Nasser and the US. Even though these attempts were not very successful due to different factors, Tito did succeed in positioning himself as the only non-aligned leader capable of directly talking to all three sides. However, Yugoslavia's rapprochement with Moscow initiated against the setting of the Sino-Soviet conflict was then intensified, which also had serious impact on Belgrade's non-aligned course.[38]

Unlike Yugoslavia, India was not as proactive in its support of Nasser, extending only limited economic assistance, none of it military, dispatching its own envoy to Cairo well after the Yugoslav one, and only acceding to represent UAR interests in Washington after diplomatic relations were broken off. India was primarily concerned with the closure of the Suez Canal which had a serious impact on the rise of prices of food New Delhi was then importing from the US.[39] Nevertheless, both Yugoslavia and India were very active in the UNGA, trying to table different resolutions that could stimulate some kind of a compromised solution, but without achieving any concrete results beyond the UNSC-sponsored Resolution 242 which vaguely demanded withdrawal from occupied territories.[40] Conversely, Nasser had become somewhat disenchanted with non-alignment, believing that a fully fledged military alliance with the Soviets could have saved him from an Israeli attack.[41] This sounded the alarm in both Belgrade and New Delhi that Cairo was slowly drifting away from the non-aligned flock into the wide-open arms of one bloc.

Nevertheless, as a means of reinvigorating non-alignment, Yugoslavia decided to launch a new initiative for a non-aligned conference that would conceptually exceed the limitations of the Cairo Conference, while adjusting the entire doctrine to the new challenges and attacks it was subjected to throughout the Third World. Tito wanted to use his trip to a number of Asian and African nations at the very start of 1968 (Afghanistan, Pakistan, India, Cambodia, Ethiopia and the UAR) as a springboard for presenting his ideas and probing reactions from his hosts. Topics such as the Vietnam War and the Middle Eastern crisis obviously dominated these conversations, but ideas about forging a complex unity and establishing more intensive coordination of activity among non-aligned nations, particularly in the economic sphere, were being actively floated by all interlocutors. This kind of exchange was largely stimulated by intensive diplomatic preparations for the forthcoming second UNCTAD session in New Delhi.[42]

During his talks with Indira Gandhi, Tito pointed out that the policy of non-alignment was being revitalized by different participants, even those who used to be very passive in this respect, therefore conditions for another summit or at least a ministerial meeting were suitable enough. However, as he saw it, the basis for this new gathering should be more extensive, enveloping all countries that sought peace and development, not just the ones present in Belgrade or Cairo. Gandhi generally agreed with this assessment. Haile Selassie expressed a similar reaction – he also expected his guest to dispatch a new call for a conference soon after his return home. As for Nasser, in spite of recent developments, he appreciated Tito's idea of a new non-aligned meeting that would expand its attendance criteria to countries that had not been 'fully emancipated from the blocs' but could still contribute to the cause of peace and development. The complex world situation, according to Tito, had to be observed in a much wider format than from the perspective of an exclusive small group of non-aligned countries only. He also informed Nasser about his meeting with Alexei Kosygin during his visit to India, when the Soviet premier stressed that non-aligned countries should act based on a preconceived programme of action, while Moscow would eventually back them up. Finally, during a press conference in Cairo on 7 February, Tito publicly proclaimed his intention to call for a new non-aligned conference.[43]

Since he managed to obtain the green light from his Asian and African counterparts, on 1 March 1968, Tito decided to send a personal message to thirty-four world leaders, inviting them to join him in this initiative. The majority of the invitees were from the non-aligned group, but some were also perceived as pursuing independent policies, even inside the blocs, therefore they also needed to be addressed (De Gaulle, Pope Paul VI, Ceaușescu, Shah Reza Pahlavi). Some observers even considered that the Yugoslav president aspired to use this conference to take 'hold of the Middle Eastern situation' away from the great powers, thus strengthening non-aligned mediating efforts, while also demonstrating Yugoslavia's distance from the Soviet Union.[44] During his meeting with Brezhnev in April, Tito indicated that the driving force of his initiative was the concept that developing countries should have a larger say in the UN, but, as he reckoned, this could be only achieved by snatching these nations out of the Western economic grip and inciting them to follow a generally agreed line with respect to all crucial international issues.[45] It seemed that this initiative was primarily directed at reducing the influence of both blocs on non-aligned countries in general.

This proposed conference, as the Yugoslavs saw it, would primarily deal with major issues – peace, the struggle against the use of force, pre-emptive and proxy wars, foreign interference and hegemonism – wedded together with the issues of decolonization and eradication of racial discrimination. However, other crucial matters were economic independence, equality between small and big countries, rapid economic development and a more balanced international economic system. This conference, essentially, would form the basis for a joint action in the UN, particularly with respect to the UNCTAD and UNGA sessions, and its success would be guaranteed by the extensive participation of so many different countries.[46] Contentious issues, like Vietnam or the Middle East, except in a general form of opposition to foreign aggression and interference, were largely dropped from the potential conference agenda in order to avoid any controversy, thus achieving greater unity at the future gathering. Yugoslav officials were, nonetheless, convinced that non-aligned countries still lacked the proper organizational capacity to transform their hidden potential into a more concrete action.⁴⁷

As well as sending his personal notes, Tito also decided to dispatch his closest aides on an extensive tour of eleven countries in the East, West and North Africa, while diplomats on the ground in different non-aligned capitals were also holding intensive discussions.⁴⁸ Most of the positive reactions came from the Middle Eastern and African countries. Nasser was the first one to promise his full engagement in the successful realization of this project, thus strengthening his own international position.⁴⁹ Toure also guaranteed his full backing of Tito's proposal aimed at putting together a much wider platform and attendance of this conference.⁵⁰ Bourgiba, however, although basically not against this option, admonished that such a conference had to be seriously prepared in advance, otherwise the failure of such an event could potentially prove catastrophic for the very future of non-alignment.⁵¹

Nevertheless, countries in Eastern and Southern Africa, especially Zambia, were quite eager to take an active part in preparations for such a gathering, advocating a wider platform for discussions, one also tackling specific African issues.⁵² Ethiopia was quite interested in contributing to the successful organization by openly promoting Addis Ababa as a venue for the preparatory meeting, sometimes even probing whether setting up the main event in Ethiopia would also be advisable. Although this largely met strong Arab opposition due to Selassie's close relationship with Israel, many other potential participants agreed with this idea.⁵³ Furthermore, Yugoslavia was also contemplating having New Delhi or Colombo as summit venues, since Asian countries could better provide balance and restraint to the conference proceedings, but this line was still not publicly pursued so as to avoid any counterclaims.⁵⁴

Conversely, some non-aligned countries expressed serious reservations with respect to this Yugoslav initiative. One of these was Algeria, with Houari Boumedienne considering that summoning a new non-aligned conference was not a bad idea per se, but that the potential for its tangible success was rather limited or, even worse, such a gathering could demonstrate the evident weakness of the non-aligned group.⁵⁵ Another country that also held its reservations was, surprisingly, India, whose main concern was with the timing, as well as with Yugoslavia's insistence on the widest possible representation, which could have potentially included Pakistan. In fact, the exclusive character of conference sponsors seemed to officials in New Delhi as if Tito and Nasser were arranging everything between themselves, without consulting others, thus also contributing to India's reluctance.⁵⁶

However, for both Yugoslavia and the UAR, Indian participation was still an imperative. Officials in both Belgrade and Cairo were aware of Indira Gandhi's internal and external difficulties, which ultimately compelled her to act in such a restrained fashion.⁵⁷ In the end, after visits from Yugoslav special envoys and the Ethiopian emperor, the Indian side decided to drop all its standing reservations, except in the case of potential Pakistani participation, above all since Gandhi could not refuse Tito's ideas. The conference agenda, as insisted by the Indians, had to be in strict accordance with the decisions made at the Belgrade and Cairo conferences, without implementing any experiments with expanded attendance.⁵⁸ Nevertheless, Yugoslavia's openness to potential Pakistani participation was a way for Tito to try to facilitate Romania's, Belgrade's closest ally in Eastern Europe, attendance at any future gatherings with a similar format.[59]

Therefore, in order to bypass all these controversies, Yugoslavia made an about-face, emphasizing the participation of all attendees of the Cairo Conference, which also included some Latin American countries which otherwise remained silent. In effect, Tito's earlier position was forcefully modified under India's pressure.[60] However, even though the majority of countries agreed with Addis Ababa acting as the host for a preparatory meeting in July, it appeared that the Ethiopians had become overwhelmed with the responsibility they had to shoulder regarding the success of the entire event, particularly when the host was compelled to walk a tightrope between so many different participants. Concurrently, Ethiopian officials were seriously considering asking for a postponement of the preparatory meeting until 1969.[61] It seemed to different observers that the future of the projected gathering was rather bleak, suffering from postponement malaise right from the start.

Coming out of Paralysis

The intervention of the Warsaw Pact forces in Czechoslovakia in August 1968 acted as a warning signal for Yugoslavia, shedding Tito's illusions and raising his fears of being next in line for the implementation of the 'Brezhnev Doctrine' of limited sovereignty of socialist countries. These unfortunate events brought about a significant cooling of Soviet–Yugoslav relations, thus effectively ending the pro-Soviet tilt in Yugoslavia's non-alignment.[62] Seeing this crisis as both an outright challenge and a possible opportunity to mobilize the non-aligned world behind the agenda of clear opposition to any foreign aggression and interference, Belgrade expected a harsh reaction on behalf of all these nations with respect to such a blatant breach of sovereignty and independence of a small country. Nevertheless, Tito was rather disappointed with the ensuing events, becoming painfully aware that particular national interests of non-aligned nations often outweighed their general cause.[63]

For example, Nasser openly conveyed to the Yugoslav ambassador that he was not interested in endangering his relationship with Moscow, since he was struggling to overturn the occupation of his own country. Therefore, he did not wish to create another platform for pro-Western non-aligned countries to simply smear the Soviets.[64] As for India, even though Indira Gandhi expressed her gravest concerns with these unfortunate events, her country's strained relationship with China and Pakistan required improved security relations with the USSR, therefore New Delhi was not ready to further insist on criticizing Soviet activities.[65] In fact, it was only Yugoslavia, Ethiopia and certain other countries (Tunisia, Zambia, Indonesia, Ceylon) that came out with a strong condemnation of the Soviet bloc, with Addis Ababa even advocating convening a conference of selected non-aligned leaders, preferably in Belgrade, who would deal with the issue of aggression against a sovereign nation. Nevertheless, due to the obvious lack of widespread interest, this entire initiative was left to fade away, while it was ultimately decided to postpone any non-aligned meetings for 1969.[66]

Eventually, when the immediate effect of the events in Czechoslovakia receded, Yugoslav officials, still nurturing hope that the new non-aligned meeting would happen under their watch, decided to further pursue consultations with different non-aligned countries, especially India, Ethiopia and the UAR, but without insisting on a summit taking place any time soon. The only focus should now be a preparatory meeting where a new platform for joint action could be drafted.[67] However, even though Ethiopia was publicly still very much interested in hosting this event, privately Selassie and his aides were slowly losing their interest under such complex international circumstances.[68] Nevertheless, some other countries, such as Algeria, were now becoming even more eager to take an active part in this initiative, internally emphasizing that they needed to move away from being solely reliant on the USSR.[69] Such a sudden turn of events signalled to Yugoslavia that Arab countries were gradually propping up their independent stance by opting again for a non-aligned meeting.[70]

As a means to feel again the pulse of the non-aligned world, in January 1969, Tito dispatched two high-ranking diplomats to the UAR, India, Indonesia, Afghanistan and Ethiopia, to try to mend broken ties, while eventually transforming bilateral contacts into a multilateral joint action. The future summit proposed by Belgrade would primarily discuss the place and role of non-alignment in a rapidly changing world. Postponing this kind of a meeting for another year, as it was concluded by everyone involved, would rapidly render non-alignment as totally ineffective and very much irrelevant. Nevertheless, serious preparations were necessary beforehand so as to further guarantee the event's final success, one that would finally establish more or less permanent bodies of the non-aligned group (secretariat, information centre, annual foreign ministers meetings or similar). Each of the countries involved decided to take action in its own region, thus India took responsibility for Asia, Ethiopia for Africa and Yugoslavia for Europe and Latin America.[71]

However, on India's insistence, it was decided not to hold a preparatory meeting but rather a consultative one, thus giving room to all potential participants to seriously prepare for this new round of deliberations, without creating the impression of being under additional pressure of holding a new summit imminently.[72] As was concluded during a tripartite meeting between the Ethiopian, Indian and Yugoslav special envoys in Addis Ababa in February, it was crucial that this new initiative was not perceived by others as yet another attempt staged by only a handful of countries, thus enabling each potential participant to actively take part in substantially influencing all preparations and subsequent crucial decisions. As well as New Delhi, Belgrade was also considered to host this new meeting, with the Ethiopian capital still figuring as a potential summit venue. Due to firm Indian opposition, future participation was still generally limited to the attendees of the Cairo Conference.[73]

By the end of April 1969, it had become evident that more than thirty countries extended their consent to attend the consultative meeting, while a growing number of them also insisted on holding it in Belgrade. Soon enough, Ethiopia ultimately dropped out as a potential host. Nevertheless, because of the possibility that the June meeting of communist parties in Moscow, largely directed against China in the aftermath of the Sino-Soviet border clashes, could also produce an adverse impact, the Yugoslav leadership understood well that the success of this consultative meeting was essential for revitalizing dormant cooperation between non-aligned countries.⁷⁴ In fact, as suspected by Tito, Moscow was actively working to undermine this event, often accusing Yugoslavia of 'trying to revise the entire concept of non-alignment to the detriment of the USSR'.⁷⁵ Therefore, initially it was agreed to hold the consultative meeting in late May; however, since Ethiopia proved to be rather inactive, Yugoslavia and India were compelled to undertake their own diplomatic action in Africa, thus postponing the entire event until June or July.⁷⁶ However, in the light of Cairo's dependence on Soviet aid, the UAR was becoming increasingly less active in this respect, thus carefully avoiding being seen as the driving force behind this initiative.⁷⁷

Furthermore, the entire Yugoslav diplomatic tactics were largely driven by the concept that this consultative meeting should concentrate its attention on analysing the current international situation, re-evaluating changes taking place in recent years, while using agreed conclusions as a springboard for summoning a preparatory meeting where concrete issues pertaining to the future summit and the joint action plan would be elaborated in more detail. Without previously holding this second gathering, organizing any new summits in the future would ultimately prove to be somewhat pointless.⁷⁸ In some articles published in the Yugoslav press at that time, it was pointed out that besides stimulating economic progress as a shield against neo-colonialist domination, the other chief goal of this gathering should be the necessity to fundamentally change the system dominated by powerful nations and blocs they comprised.⁷⁹

As Tito stressed in some of his speeches, all these activities should demonstrate that the resolution of critical world issues should not be handed over to two or three great powers, while totally ignoring the will and aspirations of billions of people, thus submitting them to the role of passive objects of international relations. Therefore, he proposed that major international issues should be on the future agenda, but unlike in previous cases, the non-aligned should not remain satisfied with only adopting declarations, instead they should also initiate joint actions, especially inside the UN, encompassing all small nations feeling endangered by the assertive policies of great powers. Tito still timidly opted for wider participation, sometimes indicating that not all non-aligned countries were truly independent, while some bloc countries acted in an independent way but he did not insist on that point.⁸⁰ It was this new feature of non-alignment proposed by Tito – 'small countries against the large ones' – that particularly upset the Soviets and spurred their fierce opposition.⁸¹

However, wider participation was still a taboo for the Indians, while Tunisians also stated their opposition, sometimes also intimating that Tito was more interested in the consultative meeting just taking place, irrespective of its concrete contribution and results.⁸² Nevertheless, the greatest degree of reluctance towards holding the consultative meeting was unexpectedly demonstrated again by Algeria. Algiers was not involved in any preparatory work, while it vigorously insisted on the exclusive participation criteria, applying it only to the, as they said, 'most progressive' nations, while also arguing for a postponement of the entire event only after unity had been previously guaranteed. Furthermore, in this respect Algerians also enjoyed Soviet backing, since Moscow did not want to see the non-aligned consultative meeting lashing out against its policies towards Czechoslovakia or China.⁸³ Also induced by the

Soviets, Cuba ultimately decided not to attend the consultative meeting at all, unlike the Algerian delegation that came to Belgrade at the last minute.[84]

Yugoslavia's role as the host of this event had come at the cost of forcing Belgrade into accepting many unwanted compromises with respect to attendance criteria, introducing the discussion on the Middle East, avoiding deliberations on setting up a permanent organization, while also changing the basic character of the gathering by avoiding anything resembling a clash between small and big countries.[85] Nevertheless, without convening this meeting in mid-1969, regardless of its real impact or relevance, non-alignment would have definitely ceased to exist globally, beyond just few isolated countries, since a lot of time had passed since the last summit. During many different consultations, it was eventually decided to invite only the Cairo Conference participants and observers, with relatively few new additions (Malaysia, Singapore, South Yemen, Jamaica and Guyana), but now at the level of special government representatives not ministers. This consultative meeting had two key points on its core agenda: the role of non-alignment under new international conditions and how this could be supplemented by expanding consultations and intensifying cooperation between non-aligned countries themselves.[86] Even though many were not satisfied with the format and purpose of this event, it was still a major success to have so many non-aligned countries in one place after a five-year recess.

Non-Alignment Returns to Belgrade

The Belgrade Consultative Meeting finally took place on 8–12 July 1969, with forty-four countries acting as full participants and seven countries attending as observers, with only the Palestine Liberation Organisation (PLO) eventually joining in, on Algerian insistence, as another full attendee, in spite of being only a national-liberation movement. Algerian representatives also tried to overturn the initial consensus naming Yugoslavia as the standing chairman but other delegations refused to back that up. This kind of tense opening seemed to herald a bad omen, particularly due to Algeria's attempts at filibustering the work on the final communiqué. Up until the very last moment, Algerian representatives strived to impose their radical version of the final document, while also playing on the differences between other delegates. Some observers, nonetheless, considered that Algerian intransigence was primarily inspired by its own rigid anti-imperialist and anti-colonial views, not being part of any Soviet-coordinated action launched against this meeting.[87]

The overwhelming number of delegations, nevertheless, managed to reach a higher degree of understanding concerning some of the crucial issues: the current role of non-alignment in world affairs; overcoming passivity ascribed to the non-aligned group by the great powers; resisting foreign interference into local conflicts; adopting a new platform for joint action that would go beyond just mitigating bloc divisions and enriching it with a new content related to the stabilization and democratization of international relations; rectifying economic relations between the developed and developing nations in favour of a more balanced and egalitarian system; boosting economic exchange between different non-aligned countries; elevating the importance of the UN as a central forum where such initiatives could gain wider recognition and acceptance; support for the anti-colonial and national-liberation struggle in Africa and the Middle East, etc.[88]

However, the key difference in opinion during the general debate rose over the issue of holding the third non-aligned summit, particularly whether prospects were still bright enough to ultimately realize such a concrete goal. The majority of participants – headed by Yugoslavia, Ethiopia, Indonesia, Tanzania and others – tentatively also backed by India, considered that convening another summit was not only a requirement to keep the non-aligned group functional but also a necessity to further strengthen mutual cooperation, while transforming it into a more permanent and organized one. These countries stressed the similarities that made these nations a more cohesive and proactive factor on the world stage. On the other hand, representatives from Algeria, Guinea, Yemen, Senegal, Congo-Brazzaville, etc. thought that favourable conditions for another summit did not yet exist, with some of them also questioning the current relevance of non-alignment, the adequacy of its principles, its lack of revolutionary spirit, spectre of opportunism, as well as the danger of becoming a third bloc. In essence, these delegations based their argument on all the negative factors accumulated during the past five years.[89] However, after a fierce debate, the final communiqué adopted a compromise formula that holding the next summit was desirable, but only after serious preparations had been previously completed.[90]

The other contentious issue at this gathering tackled future participation criteria, i.e. whether the criteria adopted in 1961/4 was still relevant or a new approach was necessary. Many participants (Indonesia, Ghana, Tunisia, Ethiopia, etc.) stood behind Yugoslavia's proposal that all this criteria needed to be readdressed by expanding it to all countries that became independent after 1964, as well as to some former bloc countries pursuing independent policies, allowing some of them to regain part of their lost sovereignty from the blocs. However, due to India's fears of potential Pakistani attendance, this idea was flatly rejected by the Indian delegation, and backed by some other participants (Cyprus, Ceylon, Afghanistan), claiming that such modifications would only signify clear abandonment of the fundamental principles of non-alignment, rendering insignificant the very essence of this term.[91] In the end, it was agreed to continue with the 1961/4 participation criteria, including only OAU members, as well as some other countries with clear non-bloc credentials.[92]

In spite of certain contradictions, the Yugoslav side was satisfied with the preliminary results of this meeting, above all with this re-affirmation of non-alignment by fifty-one countries, where concepts of collective and continuous action, inside and outside the UN, had finally prevailed, contributing to the more permanent character of the entire group. In addition, a tentative consensus over holding a new summit in the near future had also been reached.[93] American observers largely agreed with the Yugoslav assessment, indicating that the mere fact of holding a non-aligned meeting after such a long intermission was a great feat indeed, one generally ascribed to the Yugoslav diplomatic astuteness. According to them, it was very important that these satisfactory results did not cause a serious rift among different participants, while the moderate line towards the blocs was preserved as the key part of the mainstream.[94] However, British analysts considered this meeting as a gathering no one really wanted, except for Tito himself, an initiative not well thought out, largely intended to strengthen Belgrade's respective position vis-à-vis Moscow.[95]

Nevertheless, soon enough Yugoslavia decided to press on with holding another non-aligned gathering at the forthcoming UNGA session as part of discussions for organizing a preparatory meeting next year. Belgrade aspired to achieve this by revitalizing unifying principles, carefully balancing between necessity and overmanagement, while avoiding being seen as using non-alignment only to further Yugoslav national interests.[96] Another goal of this proposal was to harness the momentum generated by the consultative meeting, thus further boosting cooperation in the UN, while additionally promoting the principle of continuity of action. This idea was also supplemented by a corresponding Tanzanian diplomatic offensive to host one of the future non-aligned gatherings.[97] This meeting of fifty-nine non-aligned foreign ministers, more than assembled in Belgrade in July, took place on 27 September 1969 on the occasion of the 24th UNGA session, when it was agreed to hold the preparatory meeting in Dar-es-Salaam in the first half of 1970 (seventy-four countries were initially invited). In this way, Yugoslavia was finally relieved from the ungrateful role of the sole initiator of any new non-aligned activities.[98]

However, despite this preliminary agreement, there were still many uncertainties surrounding the future summit, particularly the ones related to its timing, venue, agenda and participation criteria, as well as whether major issues should also be deliberated at the preparatory meeting or only during the summit.[99] In early 1970, similar to before, Tito went on a month-long journey to a number of East and North African countries (Tanzania, Zambia, Uganda, Ethiopia, Sudan, the UAR and Libya), trying to openly lobby for smooth preparations for the future summit, which, he envisaged, had to be convened before the 25th UNGA session in order to produce a corresponding global effect. The strength of the non-aligned, as concluded by the Yugoslav president, was in their ability to mobilize world opinion behind certain general policies, while the moment was auspicious enough, due to the initiation of détente, to hold the superpowers accountable for some of their actions.[100] This visit clearly demonstrated that African nations were, indeed, gaining prominence inside the non-aligned group.

Preparations for the New Summit

By 1970, the world was undergoing tremendous political, economic and social change initiated by the superpower détente, which we will cover in more detail in the next chapter. Nevertheless, both the great powers and non-aligned countries were already living in an increasingly interdependent world, one driven more by the spirit of cooperation, even a limited one, than confrontation, and one also marked by a fragmented and stratified international security structure but which, nonetheless, further considered, to a certain degree, the interests of all members of the international community, irrespective of their size and strength. In addition, rapid economic development stimulated by huge advancements in science and technology had also become one of the main features of this period. Therefore, unlike in the past, these significant changes served as an outright boost for the non-aligned group to rearrange its global agenda and decisively seek its rightful place, one that depended more on the political acumen and economic pragmatism than just on sheer will to forcefully induce certain changes.[101]

Nevertheless, participation criteria had become one of the key obstacles once again. Indian envoys were actively courting African nations not to allow Pakistani attendance, presenting this as New Delhi's unalterable red line, but Indians were still open to additional negotiations in this respect, though only during the summit rather than beforehand. In essence, the Indian position was that the non-aligned should not adjust their principles to the needs of new participants, but should be sought by them.[102] Furthermore, for completely different reasons, Algerians were also staunchly against expanded participation, limiting it to only twenty or so dedicated nations. The quality, rather than quantity, of participation, as perceived by them, was the only way of securing the strength and cohesion of the entire group.[103] What proved to be especially controversial was the official plea made by the PRGSV for full attendance at future gatherings, a request that triggered a heated debate. Besides that, the US-backed coup against Sihanouk in March 1970 left a huge void with respect to Cambodia's attendance, which now had two governments, one in exile in China with the former ruler in charge and the new one headed by General Lon Nol back home, each of which demanded to be considered the legitimate representative.[104]

On the other hand, issues of the summit host and the summit action plan were also being actively scrutinized. The Arabs were adamant against Addis Ababa as the venue, while Yugoslav diplomats warned that the time and place of the new summit was of the utmost importance for its eventual success, thus an adequate decision had to be adopted soon.[105] The Tanzanian hosts went along with the Algerian position, considering that the preparatory meeting should act like a small summit and not as a mere technical gathering.[106] This ran contrary to Indian and Yugoslav plans that this meeting was purely a technical one, thus leaving any profound deliberations for the summit. However, Belgrade also aspired that this preparatory gathering should determine the political platform of the future conference, with an increased attendance also serving as a means of pushing through any corresponding Yugoslav initiatives.[107] In addition, some Asian non-aligned countries (Indonesia, Singapore, Malaysia, Ceylon, etc.) also held a special meeting in Colombo in March, aspiring to mitigate Arab and African pressures, thus insisting that economic issues should constitute the main discussion point.[108]

The preparatory meeting for the third non-aligned summit finally took place in Dar-es-Salaam on 13–17 April 1970, with fifty-one countries attending as full participants and eight as observers (Burma, Nigeria and Saudi Arabia were not present). In his opening speech, Tanzanian President Julius Nyerere stressed that issues of socioeconomic development should, from now on, dominate the non-aligned agenda, since they also constituted the gravest threat to the future existence of these countries, thus becoming a new expression of his earlier deliberations on the nature and destiny of non-alignment in the context of individual and collective self-reliance. Many of the ideas presented were closely related to his own experimentations with a specific brand of socialism, the so-called 'Ujamaa' or 'familyhood'.[109] Therefore, Nyerere advocated a joint plan of action encompassing a maximum degree of economic self-reliance, but now manifested through fostering intensive and mutually binding economic and technical cooperation between non-aligned countries themselves in many different areas on sub-regional, regional and inter-regional levels. This kind of approach also entailed a reduction in the excessive economic dependence on great powers, while any future foreign aid, as he saw it, should be henceforth provided through multilateral organizations, like the UN, and not only on a bilateral basis, thus preventing any further blackmail on behalf of the blocs.[110]

Nyerere was picking up the ideas previously promoted by Tito, Nehru and Nasser at earlier gatherings that economic component was the key pillar of independence of non-aligned countries, the guarantee of their secure and stable future, thus transforming the dominant discourse from primarily a political one into a more socioeconomic one, but one still closely wedded to different political commitments in the field of security. Thus, all these points eventually entered the final communiqué, clearly indicating that collective self-reliance and mutual cooperation had to be closely intertwined with concomitant changes being introduced into the field of non-discriminatory and non-reciprocal practices, thus formally depriving developed countries from any working mechanisms for suppressing justifiable grievances of developing nations.[111] Initially, to the surprise of many attendees, the Indian delegation was strongly against the inclusion of any economic or developmental issues into the summit agenda, but they were soon forced to accede.[112] In fact, the Western powers were somewhat pleased to see certain divisions emerging at this event, since many of the proposed objectives were assessed by them as being largely unattainable but still anti-Western in their essence.[113]

Despite some general agreeement, technical issues still caused a serious rift. Other than the participation criteria, the PRGSV and Cambodian attendance was also a contentious issue, with many attendees divided over recognizing one or the other government. The PRGSV plea was left to be decided at the summit, while Sihanouk's and Lon Nol's requests were subjected to deliberations conducted by a five-nation sub-committee. Furthermore, countries like Algeria, Cuba and Syria also aspired to having national-liberation movements, above all the PLO, as full participants and not guests, but this idea was also rejected. When it came to the issue of who would host the next summit, there were eventually four candidates: Addis Ababa, New Delhi, Algiers and Lusaka. Despite aggressive Algerian lobbying, it was decided to hold the third non-aligned summit in the Zambian capital in September. Some participants also raised the stipulation of holding summits regularly every four years, shadowed by annual ministerial meetings, but no common ground was ever found in this respect. Finally, the sixteen-nation Standing Committee was also established in order to coordinate preparations for the summit.[114]

The first meeting of the Standing Committee was held in New Delhi on 8–9 June and a consensus was reached to hold the summit on 8–10 September, while the meeting of foreign ministers would be held two days prior to that. The issue of Cambodian representation was also raised by Yugoslavia, but no unanimity could be reached, although Lon Nol's attendance was already out of the question.[115] The second meeting of this body was held in Lusaka on 26–7 July and it largely dealt with the contents of the final documents, with Zambia coordinating the drafting job. A preliminary list of national-liberation movements attending as guests was also put together, with Cambodia's representation still left unresolved. India was adamant against the PRGSV presence, while Yugoslavia strongly promoted it.[116] The third meeting was organized on the eve of the summit, when the final report on all preparatory activities was finally submitted to the ministerial meeting.[117] In parallel, non-aligned representatives in New York held regular deliberations related to drafting documents for the upcoming UNGA session, using as a point of reference decisions previously made by the Standing Committee.[118]

However, the issue of Cambodian representation would become one of the most contentious, with Yugoslavia heading efforts in Asia and Africa to lobby for Sihanouk's attendance, while Indonesia and Malaysia led the way among his opponents.[119] As once confessed by a high-ranking Indonesian diplomat, if Sihanouk had been exiled in Yugoslavia or France and not in China, Jakarta would not have been so firmly against him.[120] However, during the ministerial meeting before the summit, it was finally decided to accord PRGSV representatives with the observer status, Trinidad and Tobago was accepted as a full participant, while neither Sihanouk nor Lon Nol representatives were seated at the summit, although there were significantly more countries voting for the exiled ruler than against (seventeen for, seven against, fifteen abstaining). Still, Sihanouk's representatives saw this as their first significant diplomatic triumph.[121] Nevertheless, Cuban representatives would later criticize such a decision as a 'disgrace', labelling it as a 'strike against the principles of non-alignment'.[122]

As for the Arab countries, Algeria openly demonstrated its discontent for not hosting the next summit, often implying that Zambia was not ready to carry out such a demanding task, while Cairo had started to imply that Nasser, due to different reasons, would not personally attend this event. At that time, he was in Moscow, undergoing medical treatment, while simultaneously holding negotiations with the Soviet leadership over UAR's conflict with Israel.[123] In the end, Nasser opted not to attend Lusaka, dispatching his foreign minister instead, thus inducing other Arab leaders to follow in his footsteps. Another reason for his non-attendance was his personal diplomatic effort to mediate the growing conflict between the PLO and the Jordanian King Hussein which further escalated at the time of the forthcoming summit.[124] However, Belgrade grossly resented Nasser's unexpected decision, suspecting Soviet pressure as the true rationale behind it. In Tito's opinion, this move could have undermined global non-alignment, thus not only affecting the representation of other leaders but also inciting the argument to the superpowers that this kind of policy had largely become unsustainable, disorganized and irrelevant.[125] For the first time, the results of Nasser's decision to seek alignment with the Soviet bloc had produced a direct impact on the fate of the new summit, thus forcing Tito's hand to invest even more diplomatic effort into the Lusaka summit achieving tangible success.[126]

The Lusaka Conference

The Lusaka Conference finally opened on 8 September with Zambian President Kenneth Kaunda's speech in front of fifty-four delegations attending as full participants. In addition to those attendees, there were also ten observers present, mostly from Latin American countries, while the OAU, Austria, Finland and different national-liberation movements were invited as official guests. The conference agenda was divided into five parts, each dedicated to a specific issue, such as peace and security, preservation of independence, economic development and self-reliance, cooperation between non-aligned countries, future of the movement, etc. Nevertheless, this was the very first non-aligned summit that primarily dealt with issues directly affecting non-aligned countries, with major international topics not at the forefront of the current debate. Still, a justifiable fear was evident that the great powers could try to stir an ideological split among the participants.[127]

Unlike fierce deliberations in the political and economic working committees where a five-nation sub-committee was preparing final documents (Algeria, Zambia, India, Indonesia and Yugoslavia), the general debate was largely constructive and avoided unnecessary polemics, with Indochina or the Middle East only occasionally overwhelming the largely tolerant tone of discussion. Since this summit was held in the southern part of the African continent, local issues pertaining to colonialism and racism clearly dominated the landscape. All speakers criticized harshly the inhumane practices of different colonialist and racist regimes, while this newly found dynamism would transform itself into an agreement by all non-aligned countries to sever all political and economic ties with these regimes, thus effectively isolating them in the Third World.[128]

However, participants from the Arab countries were generally preoccupied with the Middle Eastern crisis, insisting on a full Israeli withdrawal from occupied territories, as well as on self-determination for Palestine. However, since these nations were largely represented at the level of foreign ministers, this debate evidently took a backseat among other discussions proving more relevant to other participants. This was obvious when the Arab demand for imposing UN sanctions on Israel was somewhat watered down and modified by other delegations and adopted in a more generalized form.[129] In addition, all speakers advocated for a political solution for Indochina, as well as withdrawal of all foreign troops, while the PRGSV representative Madame Binh, although present as an observer, was also allowed to make a speech during the general debate.[130] However, unlike the two previous summits, European political issues were evidently underrepresented – even the Czechoslovak crisis – thus causing significant frustration among the Yugoslav delegates.[131]

Two other major issues primarily dominated the general debate and the work in the two committees: economic development and economic cooperation between non-aligned countries. This dimension of the summit was largely shaped by Nyerere's ideas previously stated at the preparatory meeting. This new global concept of socioeconomic development, as agreed by many, had to be enriched with the idea of collective self-reliance as a key precondition for any accelerated transformation. This kind of approach could only be obtained through active introduction of many fundamental changes into the economic systems of developing nations individually, inspiring them to constructively and prudently use their vast human and material resources, develop their scientific and technological capacity accordingly, and thus more rapidly bridging the widening gap between the rich and poor in the world. Only through their expanded mutual cooperation, both inside and outside the UN, could gradual evolution of the currently unbalanced and underrepresented world economic system be ultimately achieved.[132]

Figure 3 Third Summit of the Non-Aligned Movement, Lusaka, 8 September 1970. © Museum of Yugoslavia.

Since the role of the UN as the centre stage for non-aligned countries was reiterated, general debate also tackled the issue of their future role and continuity of joint actions, thus finding a new solution which proved to be elusive in the past. Initially, Kaunda proposed the formation of an 'adequate machinery for coordination of non-aligned activities'. This idea was in accordance with the Zambian draft document stipulating regular summits every three to four years, preceded by pre-planned preparatory and ministerial meetings, and guaranteed by the establishment of a permanent secretariat.[133] Other participants, like Tito, Indira Gandhi, the Algerian Foreign Minister Abdelaziz Bouteflika, etc., also called for forging stronger and more permanent bonds as a means of collectively withstanding any external challenges.[134] During his conversation with Gandhi, Selassie, Nyerere and others, Tito stressed that non-alignment should be strongly reaffirmed as a permanent factor in world politics, not just a passing phenomenon, and this should be achieved only through the firmness of its principles, clarity of its vision and continuity of its actions.[135]

Since ideas about creating permanent institutions of the nascent NAM were being floated by other attendees, Tito opted for establishing only permanent technical and not political bodies (i.e. secretariat), making them primarily responsible for the organization of future events. This would then guarantee a certain degree of coordination and continuity, but without being subjected to the potential dictate of a group of countries, potentially radical ones, poised to create something resembling a 'third bloc' by taking control over any permanent political bodies.[136] Therefore, the adopted 'Resolution on the Strengthening of the Role of Non-Aligned Countries' finally authorized Zambia as the coordinator of the Standing Committee to initiate the collective work on preserving continuity and increasing efficiency with respect to implementing current summit decisions and planning the next one. This basically implied creating the first executive bodies of the NAM, thus transforming a loose group into a permanent movement but one still expecting complete institutionalization.[137] Only after Lusaka can we talk about the NAM, not prior to that.

Despite certain disagreements, the two working committees had successfully managed to put together the two most important documents of this summit. The first was the 'Declaration on Peace, Independence, Development, Cooperation, and Democratisation of International Relations', where for the very first time the basic political principles and goals of non-alignment were clearly and scrupulously defined and elaborated, while non-alignment was emphasized as a factor decisively standing up to all encroachments pursued by great powers. The second was the 'Declaration on Non-Alignment and Economic Progress', where the economic dimension of non-alignment dominated for the very first time, stressing the complementary character existing between all developing nations.[138] In addition, fifteen other resolutions and statements dealing with specific international issues (the Middle East, Indochina, Cyprus, UN, decolonization in Africa, racism, disarmament, seabed status, etc.) were also passed.[139] Soon enough, some of the concepts shaped in Lusaka also influenced the adoption of some key documents presented at the 25th UNGA session, such as the 'Declaration on the Friendly Relations between Countries', the 'Declaration on the International Strategy of Development' and the 'Declaration on the Security and Peace', while the UNSC was compelled by concerted non-aligned action to broaden its non-permanent membership from six to ten countries, reflecting more equitable regional distribution.[140]

Conference Aftermath

As for the international reactions to this event, they were less radical or rigid compared to the ones displayed by the great powers in 1961 and 1964, although very much reserved, with the Soviets either maintaining silence or extending a somewhat positive praise for not being put on the same footing as the US.[141] The Americans decided to largely ignore the results of the Lusaka Conference. The White House, as presented by Nixon's National Security Advisor Henry Kissinger, considered this gathering as causing 'hardly a ripple', dear to Tito's heart but 'not very significant', while he described the NAM as lacking 'momentum, purpose, and force'.[142] Even though Tito was convinced that the Lusaka Conference was one of the key factors bringing Nixon to Belgrade only few weeks later, these words of neglect, nonetheless, would come to haunt Kissinger in the UN in the near future.[143] However, the biggest surprise compared to before was China's utmost positive reaction, which particularly emphasized the NAM's continuous struggle against the practices of both superpowers, as well as its consistent support for PRC's legitimate return to the UN.[144]

In essence, at this summit the completion of decolonization and the achievement of economic progress had become the central goals of the NAM, continuity and moderation were the words of the day, self-reliance and collective action were clearly defined as guiding principles, while peaceful co-existence was substituted with the democratization of international relations as a new means of pursuing active struggle against bloc divisions, spheres of influence and political or economic subjugation. Most participants were quite satisfied with the outcome of this gathering, considering that its progressive character and the contents of its final documents were not eclipsed by large attendance, while both leftist and rightist radicalism were temporarily curbed. As for the Arab delegations, they witnessed that even without their leaders this summit could unimpededly function, inducing them not to repeat that mistake again, while some of the bilateral relationships were also improved during this event, indicating that personal contact was often essential for the NAM's successful functioning.[145] As the Yugoslav Foreign Secretary Mirko Tepavac concluded, expectations were 'within limits, closer to optimal than minimal', stimulating positive evolution of views presented by all participants. However, Tito was somewhat dissatisfied that the continuity of action was not sufficiently stressed, still leaving the issue of timing for the next summit unresolved, although not uncertain, while the NAM's universal character and concrete strategy, in his mind, were not elaborated on enough, thus requiring some members to invest more efforts into efficiently resolving and clearly defining all these issues.[146]

Conclusion

One of the greatest contributions of the Lusaka Conference was the laying down of three main principles propelling future non-aligned cooperation – collective self-reliance, joint activities based on the agreed programme of action and using moral and political prestige to mobilize all like-minded forces for a coordinated action – thus also largely shifting the focus of the NAM's rationale from political to economic issues that would mark its proactive stance until the end of that decade.[147] The NAM was, therefore, becoming an agency of the growing North–South conflict, perceiving itself as going well beyond the original East–West division of the world. In fact, strong foundations for more successful collective undertakings of the non-aligned were, therefore, firmly set in Lusaka, thus making this summit a real turning point, in spite of all interested parties still being required to work more assiduously to achieve desirable effects. This was particularly true since the movement was transforming itself from a loose association of non-bloc countries, meeting as and when required, into a more potent organized political force that had to strictly observe permanence and continuity of action.[148]

However, according to some US analysts, this summit also became the 'swan song' of the classical non-alignment previously promoted by Tito, Nehru and Nasser, with Yugoslavia no longer considered the central force behind the emerging movement but rather one of the main actors now shaping the NAM's subsequent destiny.¹⁴⁹ Regardless of such claims, Tito remained one of the most influential and most respected non-aligned leaders until his death, although from Lusaka afterwards he had to act more in a fashion of being first among equals, sharing some of his leadership credentials with others. Perhaps, the greatest loss for the movement was Nasser's untimely death in late September 1970, which left Arab politics in disarray, while placing Tito as the last of the elders of non-alignment trying to defend their common legacy in the face of new challenges. Therefore, compared to a decade before, a further contribution of the Lusaka summit was the emergence of a new active core of global non-alignment in which Egypt would no longer play a central role, Indonesia, Ghana and Guinea were no longer at the forefront of any new initiatives and India and Yugoslavia had to substantially readjust their roles as pioneering states as they were being actively supplanted by the new leading champions of non-alignment during the 1970s – Algeria, Sri Lanka, Cuba, Zambia and Tanzania.

Notes

1 Odd Arne Westad, *The Global Cold War*, 107–8; Lorenz M. Lüthi, *Cold Wars*, 300–2.
2 Michael E. Latham, 'The Cold War in the Third World', in *The Cambridge History of the Cold War*, 2, 260–75.
3 Vojtech Mastny, 'Europe and the Making of Détente', in *The Regional Cold Wars in Europe, East Asia, and the Middle East*, 123–33; Lorenz M. Lüthi, *Cold Wars*, 348–51.
4 Nils Gilman, *Mandarins of the Future: Modernization Theory in Cold War America* (Baltimore, MD: The Johns Hopkins University Press, 2003), 155–240; Oscar Sanchez-Sibony, *Red Globalization: Political Economy of the Soviet Cold War from Stalin to Khrushchev* (Cambridge: Cambridge University Press, 2014), 125–69, 204–44.
5 Brian VanDeMark, *Road to Disaster*, 295–520; Ilya V. Gaiduk, *The Soviet Union and the Vietnam War* (Chicago, IL: Ivan R. Dee, 1996), 57–193; Qiang Zhai, *China and the Vietnam Wars, 1950–1975* (Chapel Hill, NC: The University of North Carolina Press, 2000), 157–79.
6 Lien-Hang T. Nguyen, *Hanoi's War: An International History of the War for Peace in Vietnam* (Chapel Hill, NC: The University of North Carolina Press, 2012), 87–129.
7 Guy Laron, *The Six-Day War: The Breaking of the Middle East* (New Haven, CT: Yale University Press, 2017), 23–85, 227–55; Laura M. James, 'Egypt: Dangerous Illusions', in *The 1967 Arab-Israeli War: Origins and Consequences*, Wm. Roger Louis, Avi Shlaim (eds) (Cambridge: Cambridge University Press, 2012), 56–78.
8 Michael B. Oren, *Six Days of War: June 1967 and the Making of the Modern Middle East* (New York, NY: Ballantine Books, 2002), 61–304; Said Aburish, *Nasser: the Last Arab* (New York, NY: St Martin's Press, 2004), 249–81.
9 William B. Quandt, *Decade of Decisions: American Policy toward the Arab-Israeli Conflict, 1967–1976* (Berkeley, CA: University of California Press, 1977), 37–71; Peter Hahn, 'The Cold War and the Six Day War: US Policy towards the Arab-Israeli Crisis', in *The Cold War in the Middle East: Regional Conflict and the Superpowers, 1967–73*, Nigel J. Ashton (ed.) (London: Routledge, 2007), 16–34.

10 Yaacov Ro'i, 'Soviet Policy toward the Six Day War through the Prism of Moscow's Relations with Egypt and Syria' and Boris Morozov, 'The Outbreak of the June 1967 War in Light of Soviet Documentation', in *The Soviet Union and the June 1967 Six Day War*, Yaacov Ro'i and Boris Morozov (eds) (Washington, DC, Stanford: Woodrow Wilson Center Press, Stanford University Press, 2008), 1–65.
11 Michael Sharnoff, *Nasser's Peace: Egypt's Response to the 1967 War with Israel* (New York, NY: Transaction Publishers, 2017), 95–121; Isabella Ginor and Gideon Remez, *The Soviet-Israeli War 1967–1973: The USSR's Military Intervention in the Egyptian-Israeli Conflict* (Oxford: Oxford University Press, 2017), 53–209.
12 Sue Onslow, 'Tanzania, the Non-Aligned Movement, and Non-Alignment', in *The 60th Anniversary of the Non-Aligned Movement*, 304–17; Andy DeRoche, 'Non-Alignment on the Racial Frontier: Zambia and the USA, 1964–1968', in *Cold War in Southern Africa: White Power, Black Liberation*, Sue Onslow (ed.) (London: Routledge, 2009), 133–46.
13 Mark Kurlansky, *1968: the Year that Rocked the World* (New York, NY: Ballantine Books, 2003); Jeremy Suri, *Power and Protest: Global Revolution and the Rise of Détente* (Cambridge: Harvard University Press, 2003), 164–212.
14 Frank Castigliola, 'US Foreign Policy from Kennedy to Johnson' and Svetlana Savranskaya, William Taubman, 'Soviet Foreign Policy, 1962–1975', in *The Cambridge History of the Cold War*, 2, 125–33, 140–8.
15 DAMSPS, PA, 1966, f-158, 445763, 'Policy of non-alignment', 12 September 1966.
16 AJ, 837, I-4-a/6, 'Telegram from Mali', 7 March 1966.
17 AVPRF, f. 0104, op. 22, p. 135, d. 10, l. 10–25, 'Afro-Asian-Latin American People's Solidarity Organisation', 31 January 1966.
18 NARA, RG 59, CFPF, 1964–1966, box 1825, POL 8, 'Telegram from UAR', 12 March 1966.
19 NARA, RG 59, CFPF, 1964–1966, box 1825, POL 8, 'Telegram from India', 2 April 1966.
20 AJ, 837, I-4-a/6, 'Telegram from UAR', 12 March 1966.
21 AJ, 837, I-4-a/6, 'Telegram from India', 25 April 1966.
22 Priya Chacko, 'Indira Gandhi, the "Long 1970s", and the Cold War', in *India and the Cold War*, 185–8.
23 DAMSPS, PA, 1966, f-158, 441369, 'Note on the tripartite meeting', 11 May 1966.
24 NARA, RG 59, CFPF, 1964–1966, box 1825, POL 8, 'Telegram from Yugoslavia', 9 June 1966.
25 NARA, RG 59, CFPF, 1964–1966, box 1825, POL 8, 'Yugoslav attitude toward little summit', 26 August 1966.
26 DAMSPS, PA, 1966, f-158, 441369, 'Telegram from UN', 21 November 1966.
27 NARA, RG 59, CFPF, 1964–1966, box 1825, POL 8, 'Telegram from India', 17 October 1966.
28 AJ, 837, I-4-a/6, 'Tito's speech', 21 October 1966.
29 AJ, 837, I-4-a/6, 'First session', 21 October 1966.
30 Ibid.
31 AJ, 837, I-4-a/6, 'Session at Rashtrapati Bhavan', 23 October 1966.
32 AJ, 837, I-4-a/6, 'Third session', 22 October 1966.
33 NAI, MEA, WII/162/29/66, 'Joint Communiqué of the tripartite meeting of foreign ministers', 14 December 1966.
34 DAMSPS, PA, 1966, f-158, 436774, 'Foreign Secretariat's telegram', 31 October 1966.

35 NARA, RG 59, CFPF, 1964–1966, box 1825, POL 8, 'Telegram from India', 26 October 1966.
36 AVPRF, f. 144, op. 27, p. 63, d. 7, l. 130–136, 'Conversation between the Soviet and Algerian ambassadors', 26 November 1966.
37 NMML, Apa B. Pant Collection, SF 16, Part 1, 'Letter from UAR', 19 June 1967.
38 Dragan Bogetić and Aleksandar Životić, *Jugoslavija i arapsko-izraelski rat 1967* (Beograd: ISI, 2010), 131–209; Michael Sharnoff, *Nasser's Peace*, 59–61, 121–7.
39 NMML, Apa B. Pant Collection, SF 16, Part 1, 'Letter from UAR', 21 September 1967.
40 Michael Sharnoff, *Nasser's Peace*, 179–93.
41 AJ, 837, KPR, I-3-a, USSR, 'Tito-Podgorny talks', 20 and 24 June 1967.
42 AJ, 837, KPR, I-2/37, 'Tito-Zahir Shah talks, 9 January 1968'; 'Tito-Ayub Khan talks, 11 January 1968'; 'Tito-Sihanouk talks, 21 January 1968'.
43 AJ, 837, KPR, I-2/37, 'Tito-Gandhi talks, 23 January 1968'; 'Tito-Selassie talks, 29 January 1968'; 'Tito-Nasser talks, 5 February 1968'.
44 NARA, RG 59, CFPF, 1967–1969, box 2869, POL 8, 'Telegrams from NATO', 3 April 1968.
45 *Југославија-СССР: сусрети и разговори на највишем нивоу руководилаца Југославије и СССР 1965–1980* (Београд: Архив Југославије, 2016), 306.
46 DAMSPS, PA, 1968, f-144, 48943, 'Foreign Secretariat's telegram', 15 March 1968.
47 NARA, RG 59, CFPF, 1967–1969, box 2869, POL 8, 'Telegrams from Yugoslavia', 5 April and 8 May 1968.
48 TNA, Foreign and Commonwealth Office (FCO) 41/27, 'Tito's diplomatic initiatives', 22 March 1968.
49 DAMSPS, PA, 1968, f-144, 48726, 'Telegram from UAR', 7 March 1968.
50 DAMSPS, PA, 1968, f-144, 411137, 'Telegram from Guinea', 20 March 1968.
51 DAMSPS, PA, 1968, f-144, 410178, 'Telegram from Tunisia', 15 March 1968.
52 DAMSPS, PA, 1968, f-144, 410038, 'Foreign Secretariat's telegram', 10 April 1968.
53 DAMSPS, PA, 1968, f-145, 419694, 'Telegram from Ethiopia', 27 May 1968.
54 NARA, RG 59, CFPF, 1967–1969, box 2869, POL 8, 'Telegram from Yugoslavia', 4 April 1968.
55 DAMSPS, PA, 1968, f-144, 48818, 'Telegram from Algeria', 11 March 1968.
56 DAMSPS, PA, 1968, f-144, 411287, 'Telegram from India', 22 March 1968.
57 DAMSPS, PA, 1968, f-144, 413668, 'Telegram from UAR', 9 April 1968.
58 TNA, FCO 41/27, 'Report from India', 16 May 1968.
59 R. V. R. Chandrasekhara Rao, 'India and Non-Aligned Summitry', *The World Today* 26.9 (1970), 399–400.
60 DAMSPS, PA, 1968, f-145, 418435, 'Foreign Secretariat's telegram', 31 May 1968.
61 DAMSPS, PA, 1968, f-145, 423397, 'Telegram from Ethiopia', 24 June 1968.
62 Ljubodrag Dimić, *Jugoslavija i Hladni rat: ogledi o spoljnoj politici Josipa Broza Tita (1944–1974)* (Beograd: Arhipelag, 2014), 346–62.
63 DAMSPS, PA, 1968, f-146, 431940, 'Foreign Secretariat's telegram', 11 September 1968.
64 AJ, 507, CC LCY, III/136, 'CC LCY Presidium session', 31 October 1968.
65 Swapna Kona Nayudu, ''When Elephant Swallowed the Hedgehog': The Prague Spring and Indo-Soviet Relations', CWIHP Working Paper No. 83 (2017), 12–20.
66 TNA, FCO 28/867, 'Report from Ethiopia', 10 October 1968.
67 DAMSPS, PA, 1969, f-145, 4985, 'Foreign Secretariat's telegram', 16 January 1969.
68 DAMSPS, PA, 1969, f-145, 43734, 'Telegram from Ethiopia', 29 January 1969.
69 DAMSPS, PA, 1969, f-145, 43946, 'Telegram from India', 3 February 1969.

70 NARA, RG 59, CFPF, 1967–1969, box 2869, POL 8, 'Telegram from UN', 3 February 1969.
71 DAMSPS, PA, 1969, f-145, 46348, 'Summary of activities', 24 February 1969.
72 TNA, FCO 28/867, 'Report from India', 31 January 1969.
73 DAMSPS, PA, 1969, f-145, 45464, 'Telegram from Ethiopia', 12 February 1969.
74 DAMSPS, PA, 1969, f-145, 414081, 'Information on the consultative meeting', 21 April 1969.
75 NARA, RG 59, CFPF, 1967–1969, box 2869, POL 8, 'Telegram from Yugoslavia', 11 March 1969.
76 DAMSPS, PA, 1969, f-145, 411694, 'Telegram from Ethiopia', 2 April 1969.
77 DAMSPS, PA, 1969, f-145, 414081, 'Position of Arab countries', 21 April 1969.
78 NARA, RG 59, CFPF, 1967–1969, box 2869, POL 8, 'Telegram from Yugoslavia', 2 April 1969.
79 TNA, FCO 28/867, 'Report from Yugoslavia', 23 May 1969.
80 AJ, 837, KPR, I-4-a/7, 'Tito's speeches', April–May 1969.
81 NARA, RG 59, CFPF, 1967–1969, box 2869, POL 8, 'Telegram from Yugoslavia', 3 May 1969.
82 TNA, FCO 28/867, 'Report from Yugoslavia', 30 April 1969.
83 Assassi Lassassi, *Non-Alignment and Algerian Foreign Policy*, 126; AJ, 837, KPR, I-4-a/7, 'Algeria's stance towards non-aligned activities', 10 June 1969.
84 DAMSPS, PA, 1969, f-146, 419204, 'Telegram from Cuba', 23 May 1969.
85 NARA, RG 59, CFPF, 1967–1969, box 2869, POL 8, 'Telegram from Yugoslavia', 24 June 1969.
86 TNA, FCO 28/868, 'Summit meeting of non-aligned states', 7 July 1969.
87 TNA, FCO 28/868, 'Algeria and the non-aligned meeting', 28 August 1969.
88 *Consultative Meeting of Special Government Representatives of Non-Aligned Countries: Belgrade, July 8–12, 1969* (Beograd: Medjunarodna politika, 1970), 29–168.
89 AJ, 837, KPR, I-4-a/7, 'Bulletin', 9 and 10 July 1969.
90 *Consultative Meeting*, 171–4.
91 AJ, 837, KPR, I-4-a/7, 'Bulletin', 9, 10 and 11 July 1969.
92 *Consultative Meeting*, 171–4.
93 DAMSPS, PA, 1969, f-149, 426060, 'Foreign Secretariat's telegram', 15 July 1969.
94 NARA, RG 59, CFPF, 1967–1969, box 2869, POL 8, 'Belgrade: a qualified success', 15 July 1969.
95 TNA, FCO 28/868, 'Non-aligned consultative meeting', 25 July 1969.
96 NARA, RG 59, CFPF, 1967–1969, box 2869, POL 8, 'Telegram from Yugoslavia', 4 August 1969.
97 DAMSPS, PA, 1969, f-151, 432651, 'Foreign Secretariat's telegram', 11 September 1969.
98 DAMSPS, PA, 1969, f-151, 434957, 'Foreign Secretariat's telegram', 2 October 1969.
99 DAMSPS, PA, 1970, f-237, 41722, 'Foreign Secretariat's telegram', 21 January 1970.
100 AJ, 837, KPR, I-2/44, 'Tito-Kaunda talks, 3 February 1970'; 'Tito-Selassie talks, 10 February 1970'; 'Tito-Qaddafi talks, 26 February 1970'.
101 DAMSPS, PA, 1970, f-237, 417883, 'Consultations for the new non-aligned conference', 16 March 1970.
102 NAI, MEA, WII/128(1)/70, 'MEA report', 31 January 1970.
103 DAMSPS, PA, 1970, f-237, 48022, 'Telegram from Algeria', 27 February 1970.
104 AJ, 837, KPR, I-4-a/8, 'Preparations for the meeting in Tanzania', 4 April 1970.

105 DAMSPS, PA, 1970, f-238, 412703, 'Foreign Secretariat's telegram', 8 April 1970.
106 DAMSPS, PA, 1970, f-237, 48903, 'Telegram from Ethiopia', 5 March 1970.
107 RGANI, f. 5, op. 62, d. 351, l. 84–91, 'Yugoslavia's participation in the preparatory non-aligned meeting', 27 April 1970.
108 NARA, RG 59, CFPF, 1970–1973, box 1965, POL 8, 'Telegram from Ceylon', 25 March 1970.
109 Vijay Gupta, 'Nature and Content of Tanzanian Non-Alignment', in *Non-Alignment*, 391–6; Martin Meredith, *The State of Africa: A History of Fifty Years of Independence* (London: Free Press, 2006), 249–59.
110 *Non-Alignment in the 1970s: Opening Address by J.K. Nyerere* (Dar-es-Salaam: Government Printer, 1970).
111 NAI, MEA, WII/128(1)/70, 'Preparatory meeting of non-aligned countries', 21 April 1970.
112 NARA, RG 59, CFPF, 1970–1973, box 1965, POL 8, 'Telegram from Tanzania', 10 April 1970.
113 TNA, FCO 28/1178, 'Letter from Tanzania', 27 April 1970.
114 NAI, MEA, HI/121/15/70, 'Report on the preparatory meeting', April 1970.
115 NAI, MEA, WII/128(1)/70, 'Report on the first Standing Committee meeting', 12 June 1970.
116 AJ, 837, KPR, I-4-a/9, 'Report on the second Standing Committee meeting', 28 July 1970.
117 AJ, 837, KPR, I-4-a/9, 'Conference bulletin', 6 September 1970.
118 NAI, MEA, WII/128(2)/70, 'Telegram from UN', 3 September 1970.
119 NARA, RG 59, CFPF, 1970–1973, box 1966, POL 8, 'Telegram from Malaysia', 23 July 1970; 'Telegram from Cambodia', 20 August 1970.
120 AJ, 837, KPR, I-4-a/9, 'Conversations between our officials and foreign representatives', 4 September 1970.
121 AJ, 837, KPR, I-4-a/9, 'Conference bulletin', 7 September 1970.
122 AJ, 837, KPR, I-4-a/9, 'Conference bulletin', 10 September 1970.
123 DAMSPS, PA, 1970, f-240, 427119, 'Meeting of the Yugoslav delegation', 16 July 1970; Craig Daigle, *The Limits of Détente: the United States, the Soviet Union, and the Arab-Israeli Conflict, 1969–1973* (New Haven, CT: Yale University Press, 2012), 115–20.
124 Lorenz M. Lüthi, *Cold Wars*, 252–4.
125 DAMSPS, PA, 1970, f-240, 432596, 'Telegram from UAR', 25 August 1970.
126 NARA, RG 59, CFPF, 1970–1973, box 1966, POL 8, 'Telegram from Yugoslavia', 2 September 1970.
127 AJ, 837, KPR, I-4-a/9, 'Report on the third conference of non-aligned nations', 14 September 1970.
128 AJ, 837, KPR, I-4-a/9, 'Conference bulletin', 8, 9 and 10 September 1970.
129 Ibid.
130 AJ, 837, KPR, I-4-a/9, 'Continuation of the general debate', 10 September 1970.
131 AJ, 837, KPR, I-4-a/9, 'Talks with members of the Yugoslav delegation', 10 September 1970.
132 NAI, MEA, HI/121/15/70, 'Declaration on non-alignment and economic progress'.
133 NARA, RG 59, CFPF, 1970–1973, box 1966, POL 8, 'Telegram from Zambia', 7 September 1970.
134 AJ, 837, KPR, I-4-a/9, 'Conference bulletin', 8, 9 and 10 September 1970.

135 AJ, 837, KPR, I-4-a/9, 'Tito-Gandhi talks', 7 September 1970; 'Tito-Selassie talks', 7 September 1970; 'Tito-Nyerere talks', 8 September 1970.
136 AJ, 837, KPR, I-4-a/9, 'Tito's conversation with journalists', 11 September 1970.
137 NAI, MEA, HI/121(1)/72, 'Cooperation among non-aligned countries', 11 October 1971.
138 NAI, MEA, WII/128(2)/70, 'Third non-aligned summit conference', 22 September 1970.
139 NAI, MEA, HI/121/15/70, 'Lusaka Conference final documents'.
140 AJ, 837, KPR, I-4-a/9, 'Program and activities of the non-aligned after Lusaka', 10 February 1971.
141 DAMSPS, PA, 1970, f-242, 435243, 'Telegram from USSR', 18 September 1970.
142 Foreign Relations of the United States (FRUS), 22, Eastern Europe. Eastern Mediterranean, 1969–1972 (Washington: USGPO, 2007), 537, 541.
143 AJ, 837, KPR, I-3-a, USA, 'Nixon's visit', September–October 1970.
144 DAMSPS, PA, 1970, f-242, 434759, 'Foreign Secretariat's telegram', 22 September 1970.
145 AJ, 837, KPR, I-4-a/9, 'Report on the third conference', 14 September 1970.
146 AJ, 837, KPR, I-4-a/9, 'Talks with members of the Yugoslav delegation', 10 September 1970.
147 Antun Vratuša, 'Possibilities for Promoting Mutual Cooperation of Non-Aligned and Other Developing Countries on the Basis of the Principle of Collective Self-Reliance', in *Non-Alignment in the Eighties*, 212.
148 MMFA, 'Non-Alignment Movement', Research Division, 1978.
149 CIA Records Search Tool (CREST), CIA-RDP85T00875R001500020044-2, 'The third nonaligned summit: the swan song of Yugoslav predominance', 30 March 1979.

5

The Third World Strikes Back: the 1973 Algiers Conference

Everything that had been building up related to the non-aligned group and the subsequent NAM, both in its organizational and conceptual sense, finally reached its completion at the 1973 Algiers Conference. As we shall see, this summit and all events surrounding it represented a transformative historical moment when the movement had finally become a fully consolidated and finely tuned tool in the collective struggle of the Global South. At the same time, the movement's membership rapidly expanded by almost half compared to those present at Lusaka, while the NAM essentially readjusted its agenda and found its own purpose for existence and action that went far beyond the issues dominating the earlier stage, like bipolar confrontation or decolonization. In fact, non-alignment finally ceased to exist as a mere verbal formulation of a specific foreign policy practice as had been the case in the past.

Economic and developmental issues expressed in the form of collective self-reliance and closer political and economic integration of the Global South, firmly wedded to the ideas of fundamentally restructuring the international economic and financial system devised at Bretton Woods, had all become the central focus of the NAM's proactive stance which clearly entailed formulating a new strategy of development for the world's underrepresented majority. The main source of inspiration for such changes was the obvious failure of the UNCTAD format of the North–South dialogue and the modest expansion of the spirit of détente into the Third World. At the Algiers Conference the NAM had basically transformed itself into a chief protagonist of the North–South conflict, an outright expression of the more profound existential struggles of one half of humanity, thus creating an institutional precedent that ushered in an epoch characterized by the apex of the movement's influence on the world stage. A clear sign of these new tendencies would be the NIEO concept officially launched at the fourth summit.

Non-Alignment in Détente's Shadow

The global turmoil of 1968 undoubtedly signalled to both Cold War blocs that their respective regimes were facing a deepening crisis of legitimacy among the very masses they often presented as their chief proponents and ardent advocates. These stressful developments only proved to both superpowers that the moment had come to further lessen mutual tensions and give preference to negotiations as the primary tool in mitigating some of the internal and external contradictions they all faced. Therefore, the overall trend towards stabilization of inter-bloc relations in Europe, as well as rising calls for bridging certain aspects of the existing division through expansion of contacts on different levels and in different aspects, served as a significant boost for ultimately launching global détente by 1969–70.[1]

The origins of this process can be primarily traced to Europe where calls for securing new modalities of inter-bloc engagement had been progressively gaining prominence in countries such as France and West Germany. These trends in the West were also mirrored by the two significant Soviet bloc diplomatic initiatives launched respectively in 1966 and 1969 which called for the summoning of a European security conference with the aim of redefining inter-bloc relations. In fact, De Gaulle's independent course within the Western bloc, as well as his personal diplomacy vis-à-vis Moscow, although not achieving any major diplomatic breakthroughs, nonetheless created a favourable atmosphere for further strengthening mutual trust. However, the rise of the West German Social Democrats under the leadership of new Chancellor Willy Brandt heralded a turning point in the West German approach to the Eastern bloc, the so-called *Ostpolitik*. This new foreign policy course implied significant accommodations with bloc adversaries, even East Germany, but never at the expense of overall Western unity, while the use of different political, economic and humanitarian incentives served as a boost for stimulating cooperation over some key security issues. Even though the idea of future German reunification was never denounced by Bonn, it was never precipitated at the expense of current concrete political and economic gains. The conclusion of the non-aggressive West German-Soviet Treaty in August 1970, the September 1971 Four Power agreement on Berlin, as well as the December 1972 Basic Treaty between the two Germanies were clear indicators of Brandt's successful adoption of détente under specific local conditions.[2]

However, despite these European antecedents of détente, this entire process was, nonetheless, primarily represented by the significant lessening of tensions between the two superpowers. Both Washington and Moscow had become painfully aware that a certain degree of intra-bloc polycentrism had to be tolerated, although reluctantly, since the outright ability of both bloc leaders to implacably impose their will on their minor partners had become more difficult or, even worse, could have triggered more profound internal disagreements and conflicts. In essence, the origins of the superpower détente could be primarily found in the basic insecurities demonstrated by both sides in holding together their respective blocs, while concurrently facing increasing limitations imposed on their power projections in the shape of Moscow's intensifying conflict with China or Washington's inability to painlessly extricate itself from Vietnam.[3]

For each superpower, détente represented a somewhat differing set of ultimate goals. For Moscow, it was the symbol of global political and military parity with the other superpower, one guaranteeing not only psychological advantage for the Eastern bloc but also enabling the USSR to gain unfettered access to some of the Western technologies, thus potentially reducing the economic gap between the two sides. Furthermore, détente was also the way in which Moscow sought to extract official Western recognition for the geopolitical gains acquired after 1945, thus finally legitimizing and cementing Soviet domination over Eastern Europe. Yet détente was also a means of diffusing tensions along the Soviet Western flank while waging more intensive confrontation with China. Nevertheless, it was still paramount for Brezhnev to use these negotiations with the Nixon administration to further prop up a prolonged peace between the superpowers. Arms control negotiations brought about the SALT I agreement for the mutual freezing of nuclear arsenals, together with the first Anti-Ballistic Missile Treaty as a central piece of nuclear deterrence, which both still guaranteed mutual destruction but also introduced order and predictability into the general relationship.[4]

As for the Nixon–Kissinger White House duo, détente primarily implied a tacit acknowledgement of the relative decline of US power and a grudging acceptance of the evident rise of multipolarity in world affairs. Unlike its predecessors, the Nixon administration decided to treat the USSR as a normal great power conducting rational foreign policy based on its careful observance of national interests and not as an embodiment of ideological evil. Preventing US–Soviet competition from escalating into a disastrous armed conflict, while in parallel seeking Soviet assistance regarding some regional issues, had all become highlights of the US drive to embrace détente. However, what primarily stood behind this decision to seek changes through increasing bloc interconnectivity and linkage between different issues crucial for the two sides was the overarching plan to solicit both Soviet and Chinese assistance in satisfactorily ending the Vietnam War. The Nixon–Brezhnev summits in May 1972 and June 1973 stood as a clear sign of superpower readiness to accommodate each other in certain areas by recognizing mutual fundamental interests while establishing the basic rules of global engagement.[5]

The final dimension of the superpower détente was the so-called triangular diplomacy between Washington, Beijing and Moscow, where the Nixon administration pursued the line of taking advantage of the deteriorating Sino-Soviet conflict, thus trying to position the US closer to either of the two communist giants than they were to each other. While Moscow was trying to prevent a potential anti-Soviet Sino-US axis from ever materializing, Beijing, frantically engaged in overcoming international isolation, decided to acquiesce with the secret US overtures directed towards a tentative rapprochement. After two years of both overt and clandestine contacts between the two sides, Kissinger's secret visit to Beijing in July 1971 marked the beginning of direct Sino-US dealings that would be crowned with Nixon's official visit to China in February 1972. These high-level exchanges ushered in an era of rapid normalization of bilateral relations short of extending official diplomatic recognition, thus transforming the bipolar Cold War framework into more of a triangular one. In the meantime, the PRC would also return to the UN as a UNSC permanent member instead of Taipei in October 1971, primarily through strenuous diplomatic efforts of many non-aligned countries.[6]

However, compared to the superpower détente, the position of the world outside the blocs was far less rewarding or promising, often facing different attempts at establishing greater bloc control over the processes of Third World emancipation. While the Nixon administration, on the one hand, saw the Third World as a potential impediment to the normal flow of negotiations between the superpowers on more relevant strategic issues, for the Kremlin, on the other, détente was a completely separate process from the imminent continuation of a successful Third World national-liberation struggle. These conflicting perspectives, put aside during the first years of superpower negotiations, would eventually burst open, especially when particular bloc interests clashed with the receding dynamic of détente in places like the Middle East or Southern Africa.[7]

Therefore, many non-aligned countries did not see these positive currents in Europe offering them brighter prospects than at any time before. Furthermore, some of them were even induced either to completely discard the positive meaning of these global changes or passively accept everything as being inevitable, not enjoying any immediate or extensive Third World participation. These were dangerous tendencies for small powers indeed, ones also signalling a potential split inside the NAM over the character of any future joint action aimed at safeguarding the interests of weaker states existing in the 'grey areas' between the blocs.[8] Some leading non-aligned countries, such as Egypt (UAR was changed into the Arab Republic of Egypt in 1972), even argued for charting the NAM's future role against the background of this newly emerging great power triangle, since, as they saw it, such a specific redistribution of power would fundamentally determine the essence of international affairs for years to come.[9]

In fact, deterioration of the overall situation in the Third World also produced an adverse impact on many non-aligned countries, with some of them, such as Egypt, India and Iraq, reaching out to one of the superpowers, in this case the USSR, to establish closer political, military and economic ties through the conclusion of a string of treaties of friendship and cooperation (May 1971, August 1971 and April 1972), all which extended better security guarantees against their respective regional rivals. Something similar was also occurring on the other side of the spectre with countries like Indonesia seeking more military backing from the US or similar. Such decisions produced an ambiguous effect on the role and character of non-alignment in general, with some nations questioning the feasibility of such external arrangements, while also raising questions about how these treaties generally fitted into the bigger picture and what was the essence of a precarious relationship between the particular national interests of member states and the general principles and policies of the NAM.[10]

In many ways, the Vietnam War was the basic propellant for both the US and the USSR to undertake steps towards lessening tensions, which primarily implied for Washington a less humiliating extrication from the conflict, while for Moscow a much-needed ending to a war that introduced so many unnecessary tensions into superpower relations.[11] While the two warring parties were negotiating in Paris without reaching any tangible results, this conflict was, nonetheless, expanding into Cambodia and Laos, producing a devastating effect on these two neutral nations.[12] Frustrated by the results of the Sino-US and US–Soviet rapprochement which could have left them short of total victory, the North Vietnamese leadership opted for a new major offensive during spring–summer 1972 which could have eventually served as a *coup de grâce* in their strategy to finally break the will of another US president. The so-called Easter Offensive was another strategic failure, eventually resulting in much fiercer US bombings of North Vietnam. With both sides painfully discovering the improbability of success on their own terms, peace was finally achieved in Paris in late January 1973, thus ending the US direct military involvement in Indochina.[13]

In addition to the Vietnam War which largely preoccupied the superpower agenda, the Middle East also remained one of the central hotspots where bloc interests not only directly clashed but also produced a serious impact on the NAM's coherence. While the two superpowers were engaged in promoting détente, they were primarily interested in reining in their respective regional allies, and simultaneously forwarding different peace initiatives, like the 'Rogers Plan', which only managed to set up a temporary ceasefire without tackling any final settlement. Nevertheless, the Nixon administration was primarily motivated by a long-term projection of turning the tables on the Soviets by imposing a line on the Arabs that the achievement of concrete gains depended solely on the reduction of their military dependence on Moscow and the enticement of Washington's good will. Yet the USSR was only trying to preserve its significant strategic standing in the region which had been shaken by Egypt's unexpected diplomatic manoeuvring and occasional tilting towards Washington.[14]

However, after Nasser's sudden death, the new Egyptian leader Anwar El Sadat, although paying lip service to his predecessor's policies, was also seeking ways to implement more pragmatic ones that would primarily serve Egyptian national interests, while preventing their misuse by any foreign powers for enhancing their own military presence in the region. In this respect, he had even started secretly signalling to the Nixon administration that US–Egyptian relations were not beyond repair, since, in his mind, Washington was the only power able to push through the Israeli withdrawal from occupied territories, thus also extending tangible security guarantees to Cairo in the future. To this end, Sadat also started tightening his grip on power by removing any pro-Soviet Nasserite elements in the government. This was a significant departure from Nasser's entire foreign policy course, although one still formally pursued in the spirit of non-alignment's equidistance.[15]

Since the Soviets were concerned with Egypt's potential political drift towards the West, they prompted Sadat to conclude the friendship and cooperation treaty, which, in spite of Soviet expectations, only served as another leverage to strengthen his military potential and gain additional diplomatic points. Even expelling thousands of Soviet advisors in July 1972 was also part of Sadat's double game to eventually squeeze out more military assistance from the Soviets, while concurrently signalling to the Americans that he was quite ready for a new diplomatic settlement.[16] However, frustrated by the lack of willingness demonstrated by both superpowers, in early 1973, Sadat finally endorsed the military option, meticulously building up his war coalition until the Algiers Conference. His primary goal was to force a change in the superpower behaviour by aggressively pursuing limited tactical goals, thus creating a dramatic military opening for the final political settlement of the separate Egyptian–Israeli conflict, a hidden intention that was lost to many Arab leaders.[17]

However, while Sadat was pursuing his zig-zag policies, India was strategically entering into a crisis period facing potential conflict along all of its borders. Due to different challenges, India had initiated careful realignment with the USSR which aimed at strengthening New Delhi's security against a potential Sino-Pakistani attack.[18] However, with the eruption of a dramatic humanitarian crisis in East Pakistan

(Bangladesh) in March 1971, the consequence of a prolonged political crisis which then escalated into a violent Pakistani military crackdown marked by massive atrocities, India was quickly overwhelmed by millions of Bengali refugees. In parallel, the Sino-US rapprochement was taking place, largely facilitated by Pakistani mediation, thus stirring fears in New Delhi that a potential Sino-Pakistani–US coalition could be formed. This triggered Indira Gandhi's decision to conclude the friendship and cooperation treaty with the USSR, thus also causing a lot of nervousness in the NAM. In the end, a war broke out in December 1971, one which ended in a swift and devastating Pakistani defeat, resulting in separation and ultimate independence for Bangladesh. Even though this option sounded right from the perspective of India's security interests, a war-induced break up of fellow Asian and Muslim country caused an uproar among some of the NAM members. Eventually, the UNGA voted overwhelmingly, Yugoslavia included, for a resolution criticizing India for such an outcome. Fears from endorsing separatism ultimately compelled many non-aligned countries to vote in such a fashion.[19] Nevertheless, India, unlike Egypt, still managed to remain one of the key NAM countries, carefully balancing its movement obligations and the precarious relationship with Moscow.

However, all these developments had also spurred the movement's leadership reshuffle, one already initiated at Lusaka. While Egypt was preoccupied with its deadly struggle with Israel, Yugoslavia and India, although still being at the very centre of the NAM's decision-making process, were being increasingly overshadowed by Algeria's proactive stance in Third World affairs.[20] In a series of skilfully implemented political moves, Algeria successfully nationalized British, US and, above all, French assets in its oil and gas industries in 1967–71, thus, for better or worse, taking full control over its economy, while also charting new practice for Third World emancipation. Even though Algeria's non-alignment still bragged strong anti-imperialist leanings, Boumedienne's foreign policy, nonetheless, had assumed a more pragmatic and realist posture which assisted him in not only exercising the leading role inside the NAM but also rapidly improving relations with all great powers largely on his own terms.[21]

Promoting NAM Continuity in New York

The period after the Lusaka Conference had a lasting effect on the future of global non-alignment, delving deep into the issues pertaining both to policy formulation, as well as its practices. Ideas about NAM continuity and its further institutionalization had become the driving force behind any new non-aligned initiatives. In fact, without a properly organized collective effort it was quite improbable that these countries would have ever created any kind of substantial leverage for ultimately influencing some of the great powers' policies. Instead, an incoherently established international organization, one without any concrete goals or inherent purpose, clearly implied either the shortest path towards the movement's rapid dissolution or it could generate a turn towards mutually binding agreements between individual NAM members and blocs, thus also heralding a similarly disastrous outcome for the movement. Therefore, it was essential to guarantee successful continuation of the institutionalization process initiated in the

Zambian capital, while simultaneously putting additional efforts into implementing new conceptual clarity in the movement's global agenda.[22]

With major global changes underway, Tanzanian representatives proposed holding a new NAM meeting, one where prominent members could openly discuss certain critical issues taking place after the last summit and eventually determine the prospects for holding the next one in the near future.[23] Tito readily agreed with this proposal after his encounter with Sadat, insisting that any new gatherings, like a consultative meeting or similar, should primarily strive to further propel the NAM's institutional evolution as its main objective, without stirring additional 'polarisation and confrontation' with respect to some controversial regional issues. In a similar vein as before, corresponding messages were then dispatched from Belgrade to a number of non-aligned leaders, with fourteen of them readily endorsing this initiative.[24] India was also interested in convening a consultative meeting imminently, but New Delhi advocated holding it on the eve of the 26th UNGA session, rather than before as it had been devised by the Yugoslavs.[25]

However, some other leading non-aligned countries were also demonstrating disinterest in hosting any new meetings. It seemed to others that the eagerness for promoting non-alignment had significantly receded since 1970. As he told Tito's personal envoy, Kaunda shared Yugoslavia's inclination towards organizing a ministerial meeting, but he planned to convene it only in late 1972, since the next summit, as he had planned earlier, would be held only in 1974. The only thing the Zambians were then ready to reconsider in their agenda was holding a meeting of the Standing Committee in September 1971.[26] However, some other members expressed their dissatisfaction with Kaunda's evident passivity. For example, Algerian officials were keen to organize another summit in 1972, preferably in Algiers, while a meeting of non-aligned foreign ministers could be organized somewhere in Asia in late 1971, potentially in Ceylon, as a way to collectively address the deteriorating situation in both South and Southeast Asia.[27]

Concurrently, this obvious lack of enthusiasm for launching new initiatives also reflected itself upon the NAM's inner workings inside the UN, where non-aligned countries largely restricted their activities to the traditional diplomatic topics. As a response, Yugoslavia called for holding additional meetings of the old Standing Committee, which still coordinated non-aligned presence in the UN bodies dealing with the Middle Eastern crisis, peace-keeping operations, international security and socioeconomic issues.[28] In such an awkward situation, Zambia eventually decided to endorse Yugoslavia's idea of holding a consultative meeting in New York before the next UNGA session in autumn 1971. Issues of electing a new Standing Committee, the state of implementation of the Lusaka summit decisions, preparations for the third UNCTAD session in Chile, as well as the organization of the NAM ministerial meeting in 1972 would be all on the agenda of this gathering.[29]

Nevertheless, not all non-aligned representatives were keen on holding a consultative meeting, while others could not even agree on its date or whether it should be held at the level of experts or foreign ministers. For example, India made its attendance conditional upon the future gathering constructively dealing with the humanitarian crisis in East Pakistan.[30] Therefore, two meetings of the Preparatory

Committee (essentially the old Standing Committee) were held on 19–20 August 1971, attended by thrity-five delegations. It was agreed to open the consultative meeting at the expert level on 16–17 September, while the foreign ministers attending the UNGA session would meet later on as part of the same event. The main goal of this ad hoc consultative meeting would be to reaffirm the importance of the decisions adopted at Lusaka, evaluate their current level of implementation, while also charting a joint action plan.[31]

Therefore, two rounds of consultations were held on 16–20 September in New York, when the Final Communiqué was drafted, while on 30 September foreign ministers finally met to adopt this document and prepare themselves for the UNGA session (forty-six delegations attended as full participants, with six Latin American as observers). The emphasis was on international crisis hotspots and how decisions made at the last NAM summit could eventually assist in their resolution. Also discussed was further intensification of non-aligned cooperation in the UN, supplemented by a corresponding strengthening of its authority against the subversive activities of both blocs (backing the UN Secretary General's proposal for instituting three UNSC vice-chairmen, one from the ranks of the non-aligned, forwarding democratization of the UN where the non-aligned would have expanded presence in different bodies, support for PRC's return to the UN). Finally, a decision was adopted to hold the next ministerial meeting sometime during 1972, well before the 27th UNGA session, thus reconfirming the continuity of the NAM, while the existing Standing Committee would continue observing its previous duties.[32]

Preparations for the Ministerial Meeting in Georgetown

Based on what had been decided in New York, this future ministerial meeting had to formulate a collective response to all central world issues not only by addressing certain universally important principles but also implementing moral and political pressure on all parties engaged in this global dialogue. The main purpose of this event would be levelling certain differences between the NAM members themselves, while creating an adequate political climate guaranteeing the widest possible attendance and increased organizational potential.[33] Furthermore, the NAM was quite ready to embrace détente as a new international reality, but the movement also aspired to continuously insist on making the superpower détente a more universal one, transcending both blocs and encompassing all regions and all members of the international community. The main goal of such a daring strategy would be gradual disruption of the existing global status quo which was, as seen in many NAM capitals, only conserving the present level of inequality between the developed and developing worlds, as well as imposing further limitations on the independence and sovereignty of all non-aligned nations.[34]

It was generally planned to hold three preparatory meetings of the Standing Committee before the ministerial meeting took place. In order to incite wider Latin American attendance, the majority of participants agreed to hold the first preparatory meeting in Georgetown, the capital of a new member Guyana, on 17–20 February 1972. During this event, the agenda of the future meeting was basically defined, while some broader topics were also addressed: implementation of the Lusaka Conference decisions and future cooperation and coordination among non-aligned countries. The ministerial meeting venue was still not decided, since Chile and Lebanon withdrew their earlier applications, while other countries were reluctant to come forward.[35] In addition, many things pertaining to the economic agenda of the future meeting had been also discussed at the G77 meeting in Lima in October–November 1971 as part of preparations for the third UNCTAD session, thus indicating overlapping responsibilities between the two international organizations.[36]

The attendance issue also created certain controversies, since the Indian delegation, though informally, probed for Bangladeshi membership, but this attempt was blocked by Algerian representatives, since by that time only three non-aligned countries officially recognized new authorities in Dhaka (India, Yugoslavia and Senegal). There were also disagreements over the future status of the PLO delegation; however, the AL was accorded with observer status. Any new requests for participation were, therefore, left to be decided at the ministerial meeting, with only Chile becoming a member in the meantime. Moreover, the Zambian delegation also tried to steer the general agenda away from political issues and more towards the economic ones as agreed at the previous summit. Priority to these views was also accorded by the Guyanese Prime Minister L. F. S. Burnham in his opening speech, where he emphasized that non-aligned countries had to overcome economic subjugation through increased control over their own national resources and continuous exchange of ideas and technologies, thus ceasing 'being pawns' and 'falling prey to the blandishments of our enemies masquerading as friends'.[37]

In the meantime, during a meeting of the Standing Committee in New York in early April, it was unanimously agreed to have Georgetown as the venue for the ministerial meeting on 8–12 August 1972.[38] However, the second preparatory meeting in Kuala Lumpur on 23–6 May dedicated its attention to a number of international issues, primarily those related to the superpower détente and its impact on the NAM, the failure of the third UNCTAD session, and also invited non-aligned countries to extend their support to the PRGSV in its efforts to politically regulate the Indochina conflict, as well as to increase their assistance to the PLO and different African national-liberation movements. It was heralded by some delegations (Algeria and Sri Lanka) that the issue of holding the fourth NAM summit in 1973 would also be raised in Georgetown.[39] At this event it was also agreed to hold the third preparatory meeting in Georgetown on 3–5 August, on the eve of the ministerial meeting, together with an informal meeting of all non-aligned ambassadors on 7 August, when the final agenda, procedures and the complete list of participants would be defined.[40]

Unlike the majority of other delegations, Egyptian representatives still believed political issues should dominate the agenda of the forthcoming ministerial meeting, not economic ones as advocated by the Zambians and others. Moreover, Cairo was desperately trying to revive the Egypt–India–Yugoslavia axis as a means of exercising more direct control over any future proceedings, while enlisting additional backing from a number of countries that seemed to be edging closer to the activities of the old 'big three' of non-alignment.[41] Yet Kaunda was disturbed that the NAM had become engulfed again in the empty talk of numerous declarations, therefore, he believed, it was necessary to implement more radical measures that would transform mutual cooperation and corresponding policies into a more effective machinery, one largely reflecting the emerging necessities of all members confronted with a rapidly changing international situation.[42]

What also contributed to such a tense relationship were: the rising US pressure related to the possibility of the PRGSV and Sihanouk delegations attending this meeting as full members; China and North Korea gaining more ground with the non-aligned; demands for South African, Israeli and Portuguese expulsion from the UN were multiplying, as well as those for the restoration of Puerto Rico's legal status; and new ideas for getting the US and Soviet navies out of the Mediterranean were also being strongly advocated.[43] Furthermore, the Soviets were also trying to influence the Cubans to avoid showing up in Georgetown but eventually this scheme did not work, since Havana aspired to occupy a more central role in the NAM. One of the reasons for such insubordination were Cuba's sincere fears that any potential US–Soviet reconciliation could ultimately entail painful concessions made at its expense.[44]

Potential institutionalization of the movement in the direction of setting up a new bloc was largely rejected, although the necessity for establishing a permanent coordinating body was, nonetheless, recognized by the majority of the participants.[45] However, there were some countries, like Sri Lanka, that perceived the current situation in the movement as such that the entire 'non-aligned structure was crumbling', thus preventing the forthcoming meeting from substantially addressing major world issues.[46] In fact, some radical advocates even thought of détente as being primarily a European phenomenon, one bearing no importance to the Third World whatsoever, therefore it should not be addressed by the NAM in any way.[47] Furthermore, serious competition was also triggered between Algiers and Colombo becoming venues of the next summit. However, Algeria enjoyed overwhelming support from many Arab and African countries, which, conversely, stirred discontent among Asian participants considering that the time had finally come for Asia to host another similar summit after Bandung.[48]

The Ministerial Meeting in Georgetown

When the ministerial meeting finally took place in Georgetown in early August, attendance was far greater than at Lusaka (fifty-nine full participants, ten observers and nine guests), with some countries absent (Chad, Equatorial Guinea, Gabon and Togo) and others, again, taking their rightful place as members (Burma, Malawi, Mauritius, Malagasy Republic and Cambodia), and also four new additions (Bahrain, UAE, Chile and the PRGSV). This event was a proper international conference, one also dealing, as well as summit details, with current world issues and the movement's activities in general (the mandate of the Preparatory Committee was renewed until the next summit, while the Economic Committee was also founded and agreed to meet once every two years at a ministerial level). What made the Georgetown Meeting even more important was a number of key documents adopted there, some of them having a long-term impact on the NAM's agenda: the 'Georgetown Declaration', the 'Action

Program for International Economic Cooperation', the 'Statement on the International Security and Disarmament', etc. Moreover, after this event, representatives of the national-liberation movements would be officially invited only as observers, not as guests, as it had been previously the case.⁴⁹

This meeting took the international situation more seriously than any previous non-aligned gatherings. All participants wholeheartedly embraced détente in the 'Georgetown Declaration' as ultimately being to their own advantage, but they also called for its expansion into different regions beyond Europe, encompassing the issues plaguing each and every country in the world, not just the two blocs and a handful of great powers. In this way, the NAM and its members could finally gain an equal footing with their larger partners, thus exercising a more prominent role in the stabilization of world affairs. The non-aligned had also called for establishing zones of peace in different parts of the world as a means of propping up regional stability, development and cooperation, while the international role of the UN, as they advocated, should be further strengthened through holding the great powers accountable whenever they were acting outside its mandate. In order to achieve this goal, it was decided to hold regular annual meetings of foreign ministers in New York on the eve of every UNGA session, with a new Standing Committee also being established to supervise preparations for these events.⁵⁰

However, the greatest contribution of the Georgetown Meeting was in the sphere of economic relations, where for the very first time a serious attempt was made to chart a concrete economic programme that would act as a platform for launching more substantial cooperation between the developing countries in their efforts to increase pressure on the developed world to overturn some of its discriminatory practices.⁵¹ Therefore, ideas and concepts declared in the 'Action Program for International Economic Cooperation', based on the principles of collective self-reliance and strong opposition to neo-colonialism, would become the foundation for corresponding decisions pertaining to the emergence of the NIEO initiative at the Algiers summit. Primarily, this programme followed the line of introducing substantial internal economic and social reforms into each developing country as a precondition for enhancing their mutual cooperation, accelerating development and decreasing their dependence on developed nations. This move would then stimulate adoption of specific measures to ensure the success of collective actions undertaken by these countries: foundation of producer associations for different commodities, guarantee of long-term contracts for supplies of raw materials, coordination of exports to developed countries, economic and financial integration of developing countries, preferential treatment in mutual trade, expanded scientific and technological exchanges, reduction of the impact of multinational corporations on developing nations, etc.⁵²

However, despite all these important features, this meeting would not pass without certain controversies. On Yugoslavia's initiative, it debated the PRGSV participation as a full member of NAM. This proposal was strongly opposed by Indonesia, Malaysia, Singapore, Nepal and Laos, together with some pro-Western African countries, but eventually Sri Lanka's compromise solution of endorsing the PRGSV delegation as a full participant got the sounding majority of votes. Since the primordial non-aligned principle of taking decisions by consensus was thus abandoned, with the majority now outvoting the minority, Indonesian, Malaysian and Laotian foreign ministers staged a walkout in protest.[53] Indonesian and Malaysian officials considered the dispute a serious split occurring inside the NAM's ranks, a dangerous precedent for different insurgency movements in non-aligned countries to be eventually 'legalized' in this way.[54] The consensus issue was also on the table when Asian countries proposed to hold the next summit in Colombo, but Algeria used the overwhelming backing of Arab and African votes to steamroll the opposition. This caused deep resentment among many Asian delegates.[55]

The other controversy was the participation of Sihanouk's delegation, also actively promoted by Yugoslavia and Somalia, which was finally resolved through accepting its attendance by a wide margin, contrary to the decision taken at Lusaka, with some other countries (Singapore, Nepal, Burma, India) openly stating their reservations or worries about the adverse effect this could produce in the UN (Lon Nol's ambassador was still officially seated there). As for Bangladesh's attendance, the final decision, in spite of many sympathies, was postponed due to the strong opposition raised by some Arab countries (Libya, Kuwait, Morocco).[56] As a result, Indian and other Asian delegations were quite disturbed with the way Arab and African representatives had enacted control over the proceedings, while always pushing through their individual agendas, irrespective of positions of others.[57]

Guyanese hosts were also troubled by these controversies casting a long shadow on the entire event and the future of the NAM's unhindered functioning.[58] However, even though such misunderstandings testified that a minority inside the movement could no longer block its inner workings, this also created a dangerous loophole with a determined majority, the Arab–African bloc, loosely interpreting the notion of consensus, attempting to impose controversial decisions on others which could be then interpreted as being either harmful to the NAM's cohesiveness or perilous to the interests of some individual members. However, some Yugoslav analysts considered that a somewhat limited impact of regionalist tendencies, if not allowed to escalate, could eventually prove to be more conducive to the gradual alignment of individual interests of member states with the general goals of the movement, thus further contributing to its unity and cohesiveness.[59]

As for the great powers, the US was quite disturbed with the results of this meeting, considering that the NAM was pushed even further down the anti-American alley, with radical African and Arab delegations now succeeding in their attempt to antagonize moderate Asian participants. What also annoyed the Americans was the NAM's open endorsement of policies inspired by an overt animosity directed against all great powers, which had started to characterize its newly found global activism.[60] Most Western powers, nonetheless, considered that the NAM had critically moved to the left, thus clearly abandoning the policy of equidistance between the two blocs.[61] As for the Soviets, they also expressed their restraint not only due to Sihanouk's diplomatic victory as Beijing's protégé but also due to the excessive radicalization of the NAM, going even beyond Moscow's liking. Furthermore, the NAM's stripping of the UN of its political importance by largely embracing an economic agenda was also problematic for the Kremlin. However, the USSR was also concerned with Yugoslavia's proposal for holding a non-aligned conference on the Mediterranean, also actively backed by Algeria, since any potential neutralization of that region could also seriously affect Soviet interests.[62]

Nevertheless, this ministerial meeting had an ultimately positive outcome, since decisions made at Lusaka were even more clearly defined in Georgetown. Emancipation of some members was further encouraged, the NAM was injected with a new dynamism to act decisively, while its new programme of action was substantially redesigned. This was quite evident when the Standing Committee resumed its work in October, setting up small groups of members that would coordinate activities in different areas. This practice guaranteed the NAM's unhindered functioning at the basic level, while the issue of additional institutionalization was left to be determined in the future.[63] Therefore, countries like Singapore were issuing calls for the redefinition of the role and principles of non-alignment in accordance with the new global realities.[64] Others, like Egypt, aspired to reactivate the movement based on its old political foundations, bringing back some of the strength, cohesiveness and glamour of the early 1960s, when the non-aligned group was, as they perceived, small and exclusive but more effective in addressing crucial security issues.[65]

In fact, it was some Asian countries that were predominantly frustrated with the recent negative experiences. They demanded for procedural matters, like the consensus issue, to be seriously addressed during the next preparatory meeting in Afghanistan. Otherwise, the Asians were also poised to establish their own regional group inside the NAM as a means of preserving their fundamental interests.[66] In this respect, when dealing with certain regional issues, a simplified approach of 'majority prevails over minority' could not be directly applied but serious effort had to be invested in advance by all sides to reconcile many different approaches, especially when some of these issues proved to be crucial for a specific group of nations.[67] As for the Yugoslavs, the solution for this profound dispute was in the formula adopted at Lusaka that only one comprehensive document should be passed, accompanied by a number of more specific ones, thus guaranteeing the broadest possible agreement with respect to essential issues, while allowing a certain degree of differentiation when addressing more individual ones. In this way, none of these decisions could be ever forcefully imposed on any reluctant members, while any vociferous minority would also not be allowed to block other participants from acting upon them.[68]

Preparations for the Fourth Summit

Other than its role to supervise preparations for the Algiers summit, the preparatory meeting in Kabul was also supposed to evaluate the NAM's activities after Georgetown, thus expanding cooperation into new areas, readdressing tasks of economic coordination, while also trying to iron out certain differences still lingering from the last gathering.[69] Asian countries were particularly active in their preparations, organizing frequent mutual exchanges and preparing their delegations to collectively travel to Kabul, while Malaysia and Indonesia were also poised to raise again the consensus issues and firmly tie it to the revision of the acceptance criteria for new NAM members.[70] When the sixteen-nation Preparatory Committee met in the Afghan capital on 13–15 May 1973, the initial intention of the hosts was to discuss only organizational matters, like the summit agenda, acceptance of new members and determining the role of consensus, without delving into any other major issues. However, the Yugoslav delegation insisted that the international situation and the NAM's wider political and economic role should be also tackled, a point which was eventually endorsed by everyone else.[71]

Without stirring much debate, a detailed summit agenda was quickly adopted, in spite of some Indian reservations, together with the agenda of the ministerial meeting immediately preceding the central event. It was also decided to hold the summit in Algiers on 5–8 September (ministerial meeting would be on 2–4 September), with another preparatory meeting convening there at the end of August. On Sri Lanka's insistence, all participants ultimately agreed to clearly state that the fifth NAM summit would be held in Colombo, thus alleviating Asian suspicions about their further marginalization.[72] Yugoslavia also tried to push for setting up a coordinating bureau, but Algeria, India and Zambia opposed this proposal, leaving it to be decided some other time. Moreover, India was adamant that summit documents should only address non-aligned countries, thus surely preventing Pakistan from attending, while countries like Senegal or Morocco argued for the expansion of the NAM agenda to the entire Third World.[73]

When it came to the matter of according new status to certain countries, things did not always go so smoothly (North Korea's request was not even discussed this time). Panama's application for observer status was readily endorsed, thus reconfirming the NAM's inter-regional character; however, the Bangladeshi request to be granted full membership status again stumbled upon fierce opposition from Morocco and Senegal, who demanded Dhaka normalize relations with Pakistan beforehand and only afterwards submit its official request. Therefore, on Algeria's insistence, it was agreed upon to forward the Bangladeshi case to the summit to be deliberated there, without making any prior recommendations. As for the PRGSV and Sihanouk's attendance, the Indonesian and Malaysian delegations raised the issue that both countries maintained diplomatic relations with the current regimes in Saigon and Phnom Penh, but eventually they also had to reluctantly accept this participation so as to avoid undermining the forthcoming summit.[74]

As expected, the other controversy was the consensus issue. In the document Indonesian and Malaysian delegations submitted in advance, it was stated that the consensus principle should be fully observed as a guarantee that a minority would never be marginalized by a majority, thus restoring mutual confidence in the spirit of common interest. After a heated debate, a compromise solution was found through Yugoslav and Indian mediation. This solution acknowledged respect for everyone's opinion, and also included taking into consideration the opinion of a minority. However, it was also agreed that any minority should be advised to always put additional effort into adjusting its position in the interest of overall unity, thus avoiding blocking the majority whenever important decisions had to be passed. Therefore, painful compromises had to be reached by all sides to eventually agree on an acceptable resolution for dealing with contentious issues.[75] This solution, although not perfect and involving 'lengthier and more reasonable consultations', was, nonetheless, the only way to get out of a procedural quagmire.[76]

Even during the preparatory phase for the Algiers Conference, it was already evident that this would be a gathering far more important than any other preceding it, a 'conference of action' that would strengthen the NAM's unity and bolster its proactive capability by seeking more political and economic independence for non-aligned countries. Therefore, as observed by the majority of members, global issues had to be primarily addressed by different international institutions, including the NAM, and thus not allowing the two superpowers to monopolize them as being strictly bilateral ones. Both Washington and Moscow, in the eyes of the non-aligned, shared a clear penchant for making their détente a controlled process where no one else's opinion was included or valued.[77] As a result, the forthcoming summit in Algiers triggered certain unease among the superpowers. In their view, these negative factors could ultimately prevail by either strongly pushing the entire movement in China's direction or somewhat disturbing the delicate balance of power between the blocs. This proved particularly worrisome for Moscow, since it largely appraised the NAM's anti-imperialist character not as something existing apart from Soviet policies or often being critical of them but rather as a mere continuation of them.[78]

In this respect, non-aligned countries were obliged to seek new, more adequate and more efficient means for exercising their collective influence, thus making sure that the peaceful co-existence between the two blocs would not eventually turn against them. Hence, sustainable economic co-existence between the developed and developing worlds would be ultimately secured and constructively utilized in this respect.[79] African countries, especially Tanzania and Zambia, were largely preoccupied with the economic agenda as the key for the NAM's further evolution, therefore advocating consistent implementation of decisions taken at the Lusaka and Georgetown conferences.[80] However, countries like Indonesia or Egypt opposed this somewhat simplified paradigm, considering that both political and economic factors should be equally handled, even giving certain advantage to the political ones as being the crucial precondition for any meaningful economic development ever taking place.[81]

Furthermore, the Algerian hosts aspired to see this summit as the place where the account of the Third World's economic development, its incessant pauperization and a string of UNCTAD failures would be critically addressed and then decisively presented to the developed world as a unified demand that the time was right to introduce substantial changes into the international economic system.[82] In fact, Boumedienne considered that the current pressing needs of the non-aligned were not the same as had been the case during the 1961 Belgrade Conference, since now the poor countries were compelled to tightly coordinate their efforts, while reclaiming their real independence through exercising direct control over their natural resources.[83] Furthermore, Algeria and Yugoslavia were fully engaged in jointly drafting key summit documents, thus trying to steer the future debate towards major international issues, and thus somewhat depriving the superpowers of their exclusive role as final arbiters in the matters of decolonization, disarmament and development.[84]

Nevertheless, Tito remained fearful that Algeria or any of the other future summit hosts could get the wrong impression that hosting such an event would also award them with the unchecked authority to decide everything by themselves on behalf of the entire movement. Therefore, according to him, it was necessary to establish a well-balanced and representative body that would take firm control over all future summit preparations and speak on behalf of everyone.[85] Countries such as Morocco were quite concerned that Algeria's monopolistic tendencies could surface through any new forms of institutional cooperation inside the movement.[86] Tito's ideas struck the right note with some other NAM members, like Tanzania, which raised the issue of establishing a new institution dedicated to directly overseeing the implementation of summit decisions, organizing periodic consultations and being in charge of the coordination of different activities, thus keeping the entire movement active and vibrant in world affairs but outside anyone's exclusive control.[87]

However, nations like Egypt were more concerned with the fact that the majority of non-aligned countries were going to Algiers basically unaware of the sweeping changes already enveloping the world. As seen in Cairo, it was not only the two superpowers who were engaged in a negotiating process but other rising centres of power, such as China, Japan and Western Europe, were all shaping the face of the international order for decades to come. Therefore, in this respect, the NAM was endowed with a huge responsibility to define seriously its specific role in this newly emerging world order.[88] For very different reasons, other countries were also staging attempts to redefine the basic role and principles of non-alignment (Libya, Cuba), either by adjusting them to their regional necessities or projecting their individual policies on the entire Third World. These 'Third Worldist' leanings were still strong, a tendency that would come to haunt the NAM in the future.[89]

The Preparatory Committee held its last meeting on 29–30 August. This meeting adopted the summit's final agenda without any additional remarks, but the decision concerning acceptance of new members still fomented discord. While Peru, Oman, Qatar, Argentina and Bhutan were endorsed as full participants, alongside the reconfirmation of Cambodian and PRGSV permanent status, nonetheless, the Bangladeshi request still did not enjoy proper recommendation, so it was left again to the forthcoming ministerial meeting to end this dilemma (Panama was endorsed as an observer, while Austria, Sweden and Finland were accepted as guests). Malta's application for full membership was also forwarded to the ministerial meeting, since some participants opposed its participation due to the existence of a NATO base on its soil. This was an obvious transgression of one of the basic principles of non-alignment, but other participants considered that this base would be closed in six years anyway, while Malta, as a former colony should be, nonetheless, welcomed into NAM's ranks. For example, Cyprus was a founding member of the group despite having a British base on its soil.[90]

Another misunderstanding was the Algerian attempt to forward to the summit only their draft of the final declaration, thus preventing other drafts (Yugoslav, Indian and Cuban) from being circulated in advance. Nevertheless, on Yugoslavia's strong insistence, resolutely backed by others, it was finally decided to set up Political and Economic Committees with India and Chile chairing them, which would, based on all submitted draft proposals, immediately start with putting together final documents.[91] Yet Cuban delegates fiercely opposed any formulations in these drafts where the USSR was openly criticized or it was treated in an even-handed manner as the US.[92] In fact, Moscow was clearly counting on Cuban active presence at this summit, particularly emphasizing Havana's progressive stance, thus aspiring not to have final documents being formulated in the Maoist spirit of anti-hegemonic struggle against the two superpowers.[93]

Before the Algiers Conference was officially opened, a ministerial meeting was held on 2–4 September. During these proceedings, it was decided to establish a new body, Conference Bureau, consisting of a chairman (summit host) and twelve vice-chairman (one from Europe, four from Asia, four from Africa and three from Latin America) that would be responsible for all organizational and procedural work during the summit. Even though there were far less Asian than African countries as NAM members, this decision was still a compromise solution to strike a balance between different regions and their particular interests.[94] As for accepting new participants, recommendations made during the Kabul and Algiers preparatory meetings were stressed again, with both Bangladesh and Malta eventually endorsed as full members. Contrary to earlier decisions, Cuba wanted to accord national-liberation movements with the full membership status; nevertheless, African countries managed to block such proposals, leaving the OAU or AL to decide on their future status. It was generally accepted that only independent countries should be recognized as NAM members.[95]

However, on the issue of summit agenda, certain controversies still surfaced. It was the Libyan foreign minister who insisted on expanding it by including new topics, such as redefinition of the principles of non-alignment or providing financial compensation to non-aligned countries victims of 'imperialist aggression'. This demand, although not officially pursued by Algeria, was somewhat reiterated in Bouteflika's speech when he implicitly expounded that the Soviet bloc was the NAM's natural ally in the struggle against imperialism. Libyan and Algerian representatives were also discretely advocating that dedicated anti-imperialist forces inside the movement should assume more responsibility in running it, since, according to them, quality of membership was far more important than quantity. However, when it came to the majority of participants, such diatribes were more than they could tolerate, so the summit agenda was finally adopted and forwarded without any major changes ever being introduced.[96]

The Algiers Conference

The Algiers Conference was held on 5–9 September 1973, with seventy-five full participants, nine countries, sixteen national-liberation movements and four international organizations present as observers (UN Secretary General Kurt Waldheim was also there), while three European neutrals were also guests of this event. This was not only the largest gathering of non-aligned countries so far but it was also the most representative event in the world after the UNGA. This summit was formally organized in the same fashion as any previous NAM meetings, but in many other respects it became another defining moment in the movement's history. This was the event where the process of institutionalization initiated at Lusaka had been brought to its successful completion, while the political and economic role of this organization had been redefined and expanded.[97] Non-aligned countries understood well that increased concentration of all their political and material resources through mutually binding cooperation and coordination ultimately enabled them to restart comprehensive negotiations with the developed world from, as it seemed, a position of bolstered strength and elevated moral high ground. This summit was more inspired by the spirit of anti-imperialist and anti-colonial struggle than before, thus also being more critical towards the US, but without ever leaning to the side of Moscow either.[98]

Three sets of issues dominated the discussion in Algiers: reassessment of the world situation and the NAM's respective role, priority of economic issues for the future functioning of the developing world and creation of the movement's institutional mechanisms as a fundamental factor of its protracted integration and existence. The entire general debate was dedicated to the topic of détente, while questions were also raised whether such fundamental strategic changes had altered the wider role of the non-aligned and what their adequate response to such developments should be. Many participants, especially African ones, had clearly put a sign of equality between non-alignment and the struggle for national liberation, observing the enhanced capacity for collective action and mutual assistance against the background of any exploitation or subjugation, as a means for introducing substantial changes into the existing world order.[99]

The majority of attendees agreed with Tito's assessment that world peace was basically indivisible, while the European détente could not be separated from the introduction of stability, prosperity and the spirit of cooperation into other regions of the world. Otherwise, such instability and chaos roaming in the adjacent areas would eventually spill over into Europe and the rest of the developed world. According to him, the greatest danger emanated from the selective implementation of the principles of co-existence by projecting them exclusively on relations between the developed countries, irrespective of them being capitalist or socialist. What he particularly stressed in the end was the fact that non-aligned countries did not 'seek from anyone to recognise their right to equal participation in the resolution of world problems', they had 'fought for this right, they have it and they are firmly determined to use it'.[100] However, Yugoslavia largely failed to make the Cold War, peaceful co-existence and disarmament as yet another focus point of this summit, since the anti-imperialist and anti-colonial agenda, although somewhat mitigated, still became its central ethos.

Therefore, leaders like Boumedienne, Bourgiba, Banadaranike and others also expressed their strong resentment with the manner in which great powers were handling the international situation, indicating their profound fears that stabilization in Europe would implicitly mean exporting intensified great power competition into the Third World. They issued a clear warning to both blocs not to perceive the individual weakness of developing countries as carte blanche to manage world affairs without any extended responsibility. 'World rested on more than two legs', as it was colourfully put by the Algerian president. Thus the role of the UN had to be strengthened through the substantial role accorded to the NAM, other non-great power factors and different multilateral institutions. Leaders like Muammar El Qaddafi were even more pessimistic in their appraisals, projecting a not so bright future for the movement and the world at large, other than the imminent continuation of a fierce armed struggle against imperialism and neo-colonialism.[101]

Nevertheless, in the political sense, this summit succeeded in transforming the existing moral strength of the NAM into a more tangible one, largely underpinned not only by the overwhelming numbers in the UN but also by threatening to assume more direct control over some of the key world commodities, like crucial raw materials (oil, rare earths). This new action concept was also supplemented by the idea of launching a collective endeavour in this respect, thus giving boost to the NAM's active component, both in its political and economic spheres.[102] These ideas were largely presented in the summit's 'Political Declaration' and the 'Declaration on National Liberation', as well as in some specific regional resolutions, where support for national-liberation movements and condemnation of different colonial or racist regimes was even more harshly reiterated than before, especially with respect to Israel and South Africa.[103]

Closely related to this debate was the one on the role of blocs, their relationship with the NAM and how to eventually overcome all bloc divisions. This triggered a heated debate between Qaddafi and Castro, each representing an opposite pole. In essence, this was a clash of two concepts where Qaddafi often spoke in Tito's terms about whether the movement should maintain equidistance as before or seek 'natural alliance' with the Soviet bloc. This was the so-called 'theory of two imperialisms', one putting the sign of equality between the two superpowers. In fact, continuous discussion over the future of the NAM participation criteria, whether it should be made more flexible to include more countries or revolutionary quality as opposed to quantity should be used as the ultimate benchmark, was also closely linked to this dispute.[104] Indonesian officials considered such artificially imposed dilemmas as indicators that some countries still had not properly understood the depth and significance of changes then occurring in the world, where addressing a quite different set of issues would be crucial for the preservation of political stability, while also boosting economic prosperity.[105]

The Libyan leader, in his colourful manner, stated that, under the pressure of US imperialism the Soviets had also transformed themselves into imperialists of their own kind, seeking spheres of influence and new frontlines around the world to protect their narrow interests. In response, Castro immediately stood up against such claims, passionately indicating the positive score card of the USSR in its selfless assistance to the anti-imperialist and anti-colonial struggle and extension of unconditional economic aid to many Third World countries, thus issuing a formal call for setting up a natural alliance of all progressive forces in the world.[106] Moscow was quite satisfied that Qaddafi's position did not receive wider endorsement, while Castro's firm stance was lavishly praised, particularly when he suddenly announced breaking off diplomatic relations with Israel.[107] Up to a point, Tito found a way out of this quarrel by making a constructive proposal that the NAM should define its own standpoint on different world issues irrespective of the views of the two blocs, while the movement, on the other hand, should judge specific policies of the superpowers based on its own interests, thus promoting NAM's own agenda, and not acting in line with how both Washington or Moscow aspired them to think.[108]

Figure 4 Fourth Summit of the Non-Aligned Movement: closing plenary session, Algiers, 9 September 1973. © Museum of Yugoslavia.

Another outstanding feature of this gathering was its strong advocacy of the issues of economic development as those predating superpower confrontation. This summit had launched a new NAM slogan, one gaining more international prominence in 1974, and it was the call for the establishment of the NIEO as an expression of creating a more balanced, inclusive and mutually beneficial world order, one more attuned to the needs of its most deprived members. Economic issues of the developing world were not defined as primarily of their own making, but as a result of these nations being subjected to unfair treatment by their more affluent counterparts in the North who sought their natural resources on terms more advantageous to themselves.[109] This entire concept was primarily inspired by the works of economists like Raul Prebisch who argued for transforming international trade practices to less discriminate developing nations, increasing South–South trade, while introducing certain protective mechanisms, as well as creating cartels of producers of primary commodities, which, together with the establishment of alternative international institutions (UNCTAD, G77, NAM) to the existing ones (GATT, IMF, World Bank), would provide a necessary political impulse for staging a substantial global economic overhaul that implied redistribution of economic power not further liberalization.[110] As indicated by some British officials, if the non-aligned would be able to successfully pursue such a line, they would for sure become 'a formidable force in international negotiations'.[111]

During discussions to chart the new economic action plan, the principle of individual and collective self-reliance promoted at Lusaka was reaffirmed again as the paramount one, while its realization was closely related to the implementation of internal socioeconomic reforms in member states. By creating an economic leverage of collective action, the non-aligned nations had oriented themselves towards cooperation and not confrontation with the global North. However, this new level of cooperation needed to be extracted from the developed world as a kind of concession in order for the NAM to take active part in the inner workings of the international economic system, henceforth more efficiently bolstering the economic aspect of non-aligned world's independence.[112] Some Algerian officials were even proposing to set up a working partnership between the NAM and the European Economic Community (EEC), since Europe could provide to the non-aligned both finances and technologies, 'without breathing too heavily down their necks' as the superpowers and China did.[113]

In fact, in the words of the NAM leaders, the Third World needed to reassert itself through nationalization of natural resources, cartelization and establishment of the Solidarity Fund for financing economic and social development. These measures should also be accompanied by an increase in assistance for stimulating food production, doubling mutual trade exchanges, providing each other with non-discriminatory treatment, promoting closer monetary coordination between central banks, while enhancing cooperation in conducting multilateral trade negotiations, as well as expanding economic cooperation with other developed countries besides Western ones.[114] These ideas were defined in the summit's 'Economic Declaration' and the 'Action Program for Economic Cooperation'. The first step was to summon a UNGA special session in 1974, one that would be solely dedicated to economic and developmental issues.[115] Furthermore, during the summit, Tito even proposed founding a non-aligned bank that would gather funds from all members and strategically invest them not only into non-aligned countries but also into other parts of the world and different key development projects.[116] This idea was reiterated again by Sri Lanka at the next summit.

As mentioned previously, the Algiers Conference was also a defining moment in the process of the NAM's institutionalization. However, what had spurred controversies in the Political Committee was the contentious character of these newly established mechanisms: whether the non-aligned should seek tighter institutionalization or continue with advocating more flexible and looser means of conducting cooperation. This issue was also closely related to the one concerning the nature of leadership in the movement. A small group of countries headed by Algeria presented a resolution in which they insisted on the establishment of a permanent secretariat of seven members situated in Algiers that would ultimately run the movement on a daily basis. This radical institutional change also implied the abolition of the Standing Committee in New York, while ministerial meetings would be held only once between the two summits. This was an evident attempt of a creeping takeover of the NAM by a group of nations.[117] Essentially, this was just another way for leaders like Boumedienne, Castro or Qaddafi to minimize the role of the old guard represented by Tito, Selassie, Bourgiba and others.[118] Therefore, Boumedienne proposed to Tito that a new permanent coordinating body should be set up to organize NAM activities and monitor the world situation. However, Tito responded that any increased level of institutionalization, like establishing a secretariat, could trigger negative responses from all sides, so he suggested founding a number of new bodies that would deal flexibly with the issue of the movement's continuity and daily functioning.[119]

It was Tito's proposal that eventually gained massive positive reception, one which implied the establishment of a new and more representative coordinating body that would narrow down the role of the summit host, while both members of this body and other non-members would have an equal say in launching initiatives and participating in corresponding discussions.[120] In the end, it was decided to set up a Coordinating Bureau (CB) of fifteen plus two members in the place of the Standing Committee (Algeria, Cuba, Guyana, Kuwait, Liberia, Malaysia, Nepal, Peru, Senegal, Somalia, Sri Lanka, Syria, Tanzania, Yugoslavia, Zaire plus India and Mali as chairman of Political and Economic committees). The primary task of this new institution was to run the preparatory work for the next summit, organize ministerial and other gatherings, while continuously coordinating the activities of the movement from New York or, in special cases, from other places too (Boumedienne attempted to exclude India, but Yugoslavia strongly opposed it). In order to reach a compromise with the Algerians, the CB chairman, who was also the host of the previous summit, was endowed with the expanded authority in the matters of summoning different meetings or defining their specific agendas.[121] This became an excellent way to effectively implement all decisions adopted during the previous summit, thus guaranteeing the continuity of the movement, while this new executive body, without major decision-making capacity, would be also able to generate the NAM's adequate responses to different situations.

Taking all these aspects into consideration, the Algiers Conference was a turning point when the majority of non-bloc and developing countries succeeded in speaking in one voice, clearly defining not only the final institutional form of this organization but also charting its future strategy, while also boosting the general adherence to a more proactive policy vis-à-vis the blocs and the developed world in general.[122] Furthermore, this summit achieved tangible results in enriching and expanding the non-aligned platform by taking into consideration the rapidly evolving international situation and new problems arising globally, providing equal attention to political, economic and social issues causing serious concern among its members. It seemed to the majority of observers that the Third World had finally prevailed in taking destiny into its own hands.[123] Concurrently, a dangerous feature had also become prominent – the NAM's potential excessive institutionalization which could have produced a detrimental effect on the nature, quality and significance of non-alignment for years to come.[124]

This was, indeed, a stellar moment for Boumedienne himself, a moment when the hosts demonstrated that without the non-aligned no other global issues could be substantially deliberated or resolved, while the movement's agenda with respect to economic issues or wider assessment of détente substantially reflected Algeria's position.[125] In his words, the non-aligned world had 'developed a new mood', 'it no longer feels that it is a petitioner', 'it has the right to make its voice heard, and the right to demand the correction of historical inequalities', since so far 'all the important decisions are made by the rich, though the consequences are often borne by the poor'.[126] However, some British analysts called the newly found confidence at this summit as 'truculent determination borne out of frustration', one propelled by awareness that these nations could not yet exercise considerable political influence or still being economically marginal.[127] Nevertheless, this was Algeria's prime moment when it had positioned itself at the centre of world politics, making the rest of the world 'sit up and take notice', thus somewhat eclipsing Yugoslavia's and India's earlier dominant influence.[128] Nevertheless, this call from Algiers was not a call for confrontation but for a substantial dialogue between the North and South, one that would, as hoped, eventually chart a new course of world politics and economics.[129]

Conference Aftermath

As for international reactions, both Washington and Moscow were almost equally dissatisfied with the results, since both superpowers were primarily treated as two developed countries being essentially different from the Third World and somewhat working against its interests. Brezhnev's attempt to influence the conference proceedings by dispatching a congratulatory telegram did not produce any major impact. As for the US, the White House was particularly concerned with the possibilities of non-aligned countries scaling down petroleum or other raw material supplies to North America and Europe, ominously forseeing future events. In fact, it was only China that was modestly satisfied with this outcome, considering that its personal agenda of opposition to both superpowers had somewhat gained prominence.[130] The only thing that eclipsed these positive results was the sudden overthrow of the Chilean leader Salvador Allende in a US-sponsored *coup d'état* right in the wake of the summit, which directly affected not only the destiny of one NAM member but further infuriated many others against Washington's aggressive Third World policies.[131]

What the subsequent 28th UNGA session had also demonstrated was the evident growing cohesion of the non-aligned bloc and especially the Afro-Arab group within it, where one side extended unconditional support for the local issues important to the other, while also directing joint action with respect to major political and economic issues. An inter-regional response to the great powers inside the UN was more than necessary, at least at the level of potentially blocking certain superpower activities, while also influencing decisions made at the UNGA related to crucial programme and budgetary matters. This tendency was the direct outcome of the Algiers summit when the non-aligned sensed 'power they could wield'. Even moderate non-aligned countries, like Yugoslavia, were now voting for resolutions adverse to US interests like the overt support for seating Sihanouk's representatives in New York, criticizing the Chilean coup or supporting Panama's eventual takeover of the Canal, causing a lot of disturbance in Washington.[132] Essentially, this was the official beginning of the non-aligned voting bloc in the UN, demonstrating its substantial impact on the organization's internal decision-making process. In his speech at this gathering, Kissinger, although very critical of the non-aligned becoming a collective tool for exerting more pressure on the West, nonetheless, also had to openly admit that from then onwards their opinion had to be seriously taken into account in some way.[133]

Conclusion

What the Algiers Conference clearly stressed was the notion that the NAM's new agenda was fully embraced by even the most radical members of the movement, compelling them to give their own constructive contributions, despite the fact that future events would require heightened attention from other members in curbing any extreme positions ultimately affecting the movement's unhindered functioning. In addition, some principal differences coming to the forefront at Georgetown were generally settled in Algiers, thus spurring a comprehensive dialogue where African countries were largely dealing with colonialism, Arabs dedicated their attention to the Middle Eastern situation, Asian countries mostly elaborated Indochina and some economic issues, while Latin American delegations stressed political and economic independence as their obvious priority. However, what would become the greatest legacy of this summit would be the official initiation of the NIEO as a comprehensive action programme for the non-aligned and developing countries in their attempts to trigger the gradual restructuring of the international economic system.[134]

This new world order, as they saw it, truly had to be an inter-national, equitable and cooperative one, closely linking security and economic issues and permitting free development of national economies without excessive foreign interference, following a prescript of equal opportunities and mutual respect for each and every member of the international community. This newly reformed system also had to fully recognize the sovereign rights of each nation and redress lingering grievances of the developing world, while erasing all outstanding inequalities hitherto dividing the world into two distinctive clusters, the 'privileged and underprivileged, dominant and dominated, autonomous and dependent, rich and poor, powerful and weak'.[135] In fact, some authors detected this change in NAM's character as an outright expression of an evident decline in the classical form of non-alignment which was previously propelled by the skilfully maintained balancing act between the great powers, while also being closely related to the active search for foreign aid or avoidance of a global conflict.

However, détente had pushed the movement to eventually transform itself into a 'joint alignment against all industrial countries', an extension of socioeconomic import-substitution policies of industrialization, basically just another form of an 'international class war' now waged through major international institutions, with a more nuanced approach and more sophisticated tools of operation.[136] Regardless, the NIEO was still not a revolutionary cry for retribution by the world's deprived, it was a call for introducing fundamental evolutionary changes into the world system, those that would bring more balance and predictability into the deteriorating global economic situation. Nevertheless, against the background of a new Middle Eastern crisis, the NAM would initiate its active search for a new world order, right until the next summit in Colombo in August 1976, one which would surprisingly pose the most serious challenge to Western hegemony in the second half of the twentieth century.

Notes

1 Odd Arne Westad, *The Cold War: A World History* (New York, NY: Basic Books, 2017), 365–93; Jeremy Suri, 'Counter Culture: the Rebellions against the Cold War Order', in *The Cambridge History of the Cold War*, 2, 465–80.
2 Raymond L. Garthoff, *Détente and Confrontation: American-Soviet Relations from Nixon to Reagan* (Washington, DC: Brookings Institution, 1994), 123–45; Georges-Henry Soutou, 'The Linkage between European Integration and Détente: Contrasting Approaches of de Gaulle and Pompidou, 1965–74' and Andreas Wilkens, 'New Ostpolitik and European Integration: Concepts and Policies in the Brandt Era', in *European Integration and the Cold War: Ostpolitik-Westpolitik, 1965–73*, N. Piers Ludlow (ed.) (London: Routledge, 2007), 11–35, 67–80.
3 Raymond L. Garthoff, *Détente and Confrontation*, 27–73; Marc Trachtenberg, 'The Structure of Great Power Politics', in *The Cambridge History of the Cold War*, 2, 486–99.
4 Raymond L. Garthoff, *Détente and Confrontation*, 100–22, 146–223; Vladislav Zubok, *A Failed Empire: the Soviet Union in the Cold War from Stalin to Gorbachev* (Chapel Hill, NC: The University of North Carolina Press, 2007), 207–26; Thomas Crump, *Brezhnev and the Decline of the Soviet Union* (London: Routledge, 2014), 121–48.
5 Raymond L. Garthoff, *Détente and Confrontation*, 325–403; Robert S. Litwak, *Détente and the Nixon Doctrine: American Foreign Policy and the Pursuit of Stability, 1969-1976* (Cambridge: Cambridge University Press, 1984), 48–149; William Bundy, *A Tangled Web: the Making of Foreign Policy in the Nixon Presidency* (New York, NY: Hill and Wang, 1998), 57–399.
6 Chris Tudda, *A Cold War Turning Point: Nixon and China, 1969–1972* (Baton Rouge, LA: Louisiana State University Press, 2012), 1–201; Yukinori Komine, *Secrecy in U.S. Foreign Policy: Nixon, Kissinger, and the Rapprochement with China* (London: Routledge, 2008), 71–227; Yafeng Xia, *Negotiating with the Enemy: U.S.-China Talks during the Cold War, 1949–1972* (Bloomington, IN: Indiana University Press, 2006), 135–212.
7 Odd Arne Westad, *The Global Cold War*, 195–201; Mark Atwood Lawrence, 'Containing Globalism: the United States and the Developing World in the 1970s', in *The Shock of the Global: The 1970s Perspective*, Niall Ferguson, Charles S. Maier, Erez Manela and Daniel J. Sargent (eds) (Cambridge, MA: Harvard University Press, 2010), 207–11; Svetlana Savranskaya and William Taubman, 'Soviet Foreign Policy, 1962–1975', 149–54.
8 DAMSPS, PA, 1972, F-141, 43586, 'Foreign Secretariat's telegram', 4 February 1972.
9 DAMSPS, PA, 1972, F-141, 45632, 'Telegram from Egypt', 11 February 1972.
10 Bojana Tadić, *Nesvrstanost u teoriji i praksi međunarodnih odnosa*, 211–13.
11 Jeffrey Kimbal, *Nixon's Vietnam War* (Lawrence, KS: University of Kansas Press, 1998), 63–285; Lien-Hang T. Nguyen, *Hanoi's War*, 153–228; Ilya V. Gaiduk, *The Soviet Union and the Vietnam War*, 194–245; Qiang Zhai, *China and the Vietnam Wars*, 193–215.
12 Wilfred P. Deac, *Road to the Killing Fields: The Cambodian War of 1970–1975* (College Station, TX: Texas A&M Press, 1997), 54–153; Robert D. Sander, *Invasion of Laos, 1971: Lam Son 719* (Norman, OK: University of Oklahoma Press, 2014), 81–191.

13 Lien-Hang T. Nguyen, *Hanoi's War*, 231–99; Pierre Asselin, *A Bitter Peace: Washington, Hanoi, and the Making of the Paris Agreement* (Chapel Hill, NC: The University of North Carolina Press, 2002), 31–180.
14 Boaz Vanetik, Zaki Shalom, *The Nixon Administration and the Middle East Peace Process, 1969–1973: From the Rogers Plan to the Outbreak of the Yom Kippur War* (Brighton: Sussex Academic Press, 2013), 54–201; Craig Daigle, *The Limits of Détente*, 48–227.
15 Kirk J. Beattie, *Egypt during the Sadat Years* (London: Palgrave Macmillan, 2000), 39–92.
16 Alvin Z. Rubinstein, *Red Star on the Nile: the Soviet-Egyptian Influence Relationship since the June War* (Princeton, NJ: Princeton University Press, 1977), 129–248; Isabella Ginor, Gideon Remez, *The Soviet–Israeli War*, 215–99.
17 Craig Daigle, *The Limits of Détente*, 228–93; Mohamed Heikal, *The Road to Ramadan* (Glasgow: Fontana Collins, 1976), 113–205; Lorenz M. Lüthi, *Cold Wars*, 230–4.
18 S. Nihal Singh, *The Yogi and the Bear: A Study of Indo-Soviet Relations* (New Delhi: Allied Publishers, 1986), 60–98.
19 Srinath Raghavan, *1971: A Global History of the Creation of Bangladesh* (Cambridge, MA: Harvard University Press, 2013), 34–263; Garry J. Bass, *The Blood Telegram: Nixon, Kissinger, and a Forgotten Genocide* (New York, NY: Alfred A. Knopf, 2013), 24–324.
20 Assassi Lassassi, *Non-Alignment and Algerian Foreign Policy*, 120–9.
21 Mohammed Lakhdar Ghettas, *Algeria and the Cold War*, 19–90; Ardavan Amir-Aslani, *L'âge d'or de la diplomatie algerienne* (Paris: Editions du Moment, 2015), 91–109, 116–21.
22 DAMSPS, PA, 1971, f-190, 44854, 'Foreign Secretariat's telegram', 12 February 1971.
23 DAMSPS, PA, 1971, f-190, 49987, 'Telegram from Tanzania', 17 March 1971.
24 DAMSPS, PA, 1971, f-190, 418612, 'Foreign Secretariat's telegram', 18 May 1971.
25 DAMSPS, PA, 1971, f-190, 410670, 'Telegram from India', 22 March 1971.
26 DAMSPS, PA, 1971, f-190, 420815, 'Telegram from Zambia', 28 May 1971.
27 DAMSPS, PA, 1971, f-190, 412544, 'Telegram from Algeria', 2 April 1971.
28 DAMSPS, PA, 1971, f-190, 423256, 'Telegram from UN', 15 June 1971.
29 DAMSPS, PA, 1971, f-190, 429907, 'Telegram from Zambia', 11 August 1971.
30 NAI, MEA, HI/121(24)/71, 'Non-aligned consultative meeting held in New York', 26 October 1971.
31 DAMSPS, PA, 1971, f-190, 433336, 'Foreign Secretariat's telegram', 8 September 1971.
32 NAI, MEA, HI/121(24)/71, 'Non-aligned consultative meeting held in New York', 26 October 1971.
33 AJ, 837, KPR, I-4-a/10, 'Program of activities', 10 April 1972.
34 DAMSPS, PA, 1972, f-142, 424377, 'Foreign Secretariat's telegram', 6 July 1972.
35 DAMSPS, PA, 1972, f-141, 47082, 'Foreign Secretariat's telegram', 29 February 1972.
36 Mourad Ahmia (ed.), *The Collected Documents of the Group of 77*, 6 (Oxford: Oxford University Press, 2015), 43–96.
37 NAI, MEA, HI/121(10)/72, 'First meeting of the Preparatory Committee', 14 March 1972.
38 DAMSPS, PA, 1972, f-141, 413556, 'Foreign Secretariat's telegram', 7 April 1972.
39 DAMSPS, PA, 1972, f-141, 419618, 'Telegram from Malaysia', 28 May 1972.
40 NARA, RG 59, CFPF, 1970–1973, box 1968, POL 8, 'Telegram from Guyana', 8 August 1972.

41 DAMSPS, PA, 1972, f-141, 425578, 'Telegram from Egypt', 10 July 1972.
42 DAMSPS, PA, 1972, f-141, 424001, 'Telegram from Zambia', 23 June 1972.
43 NARA, RG 59, CFPF, 1970–1973, box 1968, POL 8, 'Status report on the non-aligned foreign ministers conference', 1 August 1972.
44 DAMSPS, PA, 1972, f-142, 431366, 'Telegram from Cuba', 4 September 1972.
45 DAMSPS, PA, 1972, f-141, 428105, 'Foreign Secretariat's telegram', 31 July 1972.
46 NARA, RG 59, CFPF, 1970–1973, box 1968, POL 8, 'Telegram from Sri Lanka', 2 August 1972.
47 DAMSPS, PA, 1972, f-141, 424377, 'Telegram from UN', 25 July 1972.
48 DAMSPS, PA, 1972, f-141, 427921, 'Telegram from Algeria', 28 July 1972.
49 DAMSPS, PA, 1972, f-142, 429008, 'Foreign Secretariat's telegram', 18 August 1972.
50 Ibid.
51 Leo Mates, *Počelo je u Beogradu*, 88–90.
52 *Documents of the Gatherings of the Non-Aligned Countries*, 1, 68–73.
53 NARA, RG 59, CFPF, 1970–1973, box 1968, POL 8, 'Telegram from Guyana', 11 August 1972.
54 NARA, RG 59, CFPF, 1970–1973, box 1968, POL 8, 'Telegram from Malaysia', 14 August 1972.
55 DAMSPS, PA, 1972, f-142, 432136, 'Telegram from Sri Lanka', 30 August 1972.
56 DAMSPS, PA, 1972, f-142, 429008, 'Foreign Secretariat's telegram', 18 August 1972.
57 TNA, FCO 63/954, 'Letter from India', 24 August 1972.
58 NARA, RG 59, CFPF, 1970–1973, box 1968, POL 8, 'Telegram from Guyana', 19 August 1972.
59 DAMSPS, PA, 1973, f-131, 46980, 'Conditions in non-aligned countries', 7 March 1973.
60 NARA, RG 59, CFPF, 1970–1973, box 1968, POL 8, 'The non-aligned conference', 8 December 1972.
61 DAMSPS, PA, 1973, f-131, 415970, 'Telegram from UN', 13 April 1973.
62 NARA, RG 59, CFPF, 1970–1973, box 1968, POL 8, 'Non-aligned conference implications for Soviet foreign policy', 25 August 1972.
63 DAMSPS, PA, 1972, f-142, 438476, 'Telegram from UN', 28 October 1972.
64 NARA, RG 59, CFPF, 1970–1973, box 1968, POL 8, 'Telegram from Singapore', 30 August 1972.
65 DAMSPS, PA, 1973, f-131, 432372, 'Telegram from Egypt', 1 February 1973.
66 DAMSPS, PA, 1973, f-131, 411476, 'Telegram from Indonesia', 16 March 1973.
67 AJ, 837, KPR, I-4-a/15, 'Bulletin on the preparations for the 4th NAM summit, no. 2', 7 May 1973.
68 DAMSPS, PA, 1973, f-131, 411868, 'Foreign Secretariat's telegram', 23 March 1973.
69 DAMSPS, PA, 1973, f-132, 418638, 'Telegram from UN', 3 May 1973.
70 NARA, RG 59, CFPF, 1970–1973, box 1969, POL 8, 'Telegram from Indonesia', 2 May 1973.
71 AJ, 837, KPR, I-4-a/13, 'Preparatory Committee meeting in Kabul, 13-15 May 1973', 23 May 1973.
72 Ibid.
73 DAMSPS, PA, 1973, f-132, 421128, 'Foreign Secretariat's telegram', 18 May 1973.
74 Ibid.
75 AJ, 837, KPR, I-4-a/13, 'Preparatory Committee meeting in Kabul, 13-15 May 1973', 23 May 1973.

76 NARA, RG 59, CFPF, 1970–1973, box 1969, POL 8, 'Telegram from Malaysia', 5 June 1973.
77 DAMSPS, PA, 1973, f-132, 432576, 'Foreign Secretariat's telegram', 31 July 1973.
78 PAAA, C483/77, 'Talks with the first secretary of the Soviet embassy in Algeria', 23 July 1976.
79 DAMSPS, PA, 1973, f-132, 430859, 'Telegram from Tunisia', 17 July 1973.
80 DAMSPS, PA, 1973, f-132, 430654, 'Telegram from Tanzania', 14 July 1973.
81 DAMSPS, PA, 1973, f-132, 430428, 'Telegram from Indonesia', 12 July 1973.
82 DAMSPS, PA, 1973, f-132, 431588, 'Telegram from Algeria', 25 July 1973.
83 TNA, FCO 93/6, 'Letter from Algeria', 22 August 1973.
84 DAMSPS, PA, 1973, f-132, 433585, 'Foreign Secretariat's telegram', 10 August 1973.
85 AJ, 837, KPR, I-4-a/12, 'Tito's speech at the session of the preparatory committee', 12 April 1973.
86 NARA, RG 59, CFPF, 1973–1979, Electronic Telegrams (ET), 1973RABAT03444, 27 July 1973.
87 AJ, 837, KPR, I-4-a/15, 'Bulletin of preparations for the 4th NAM summit, no. 6', 26 July 1973.
88 DAMSPS, PA, 1973, f-133, 435860, 'Telegram from Egypt', 30 August 1973.
89 DAMSPS, PA, 1973, f-132, 433582, 'Foreign Secretariat's telegram', 15 August 1973.
90 DAMSPS, PA, 1973, f-133, 436052, 'Telegram from Algeria', 31 August 1973.
91 AJ, 837, KPR, I-4-a/15, 'Conference bulletin, no. 1', 1 September 1973.
92 DAMSPS, PA, 1973, f-133, 435926, 'Telegram from Algeria', 30 August 1973.
93 PAAA, C483/77, 'Short information on the NAM conference', 10 August 1973.
94 AJ, 837, KPR, I-4-a/15, 'Conference bulletin, no. 4', 4 September 1973.
95 DAMSPS, PA, 1973, f-134, 436537, 'Telegram from Algeria', 4 September 1973.
96 AJ, 837, KPR, I-4-a/15, 'Conference bulletin, no. 2 and no. 3', 2–3 September 1973.
97 AJ, 837, KPR, I-4-a/15, 'Report of the Yugoslav delegation', 12 September 1973.
98 DAMSPS, PA, 1973, f-135, 438085, 'Foreign Secretariat's telegram', 12 September 1973.
99 AJ, 837, KPR, I-4-a/15, 'Conference bulletin, no. 5, no. 6, no. 7, and no. 8', 5–8 September 1973.
100 AJ, 837, KPR, I-4-a/15, 'Tito's speech', 7 September 1973.
101 AJ, 837, KPR, I-4-a/15, 'Conference bulletin, no. 5, no. 6, and no. 7', 5–7 September 1973.
102 Bojana Tadić, *Nesvrstanost u teoriji i praksi međunarodnih odnosa*, 220–2.
103 *Documents of the Gatherings of the Non-Aligned Countries*, 1, 81–6, 95–7.
104 DAMSPS, PA, 1973, f-134, 437126, 'Telegram from Algeria', 5 September 1973.
105 DAMSPS, PA, 1973, f-135, 439443, 'Telegram from Indonesia', 17 September 1973
106 AJ, 837, KPR, I-4-a/15, 'Conference bulletin, no. 6 and no. 7', 6–7 September 1973.
107 PAAA, C483/77, 'NAM conference in Algiers', 17 September 1973.
108 AJ, 837, KPR, I-4-a/15, 'Tito's speech', 7 September 1973.
109 NAI, MEA, FIII/102/33/81, 'Non-aligned summit conferences (1961–1979)'.
110 Vijay Prashad, *The Darker Nations*, 67–70; Jürgen Dinkel, *The Non-Aligned Movement*, 202–4; Mark Mazower, *Governing the World: the History of an Idea* (London: Penguin, 2012), 300–3.
111 TNA, FCO, 93/7, 'The 4th NAM summit conference', 19 September 1973.
112 AJ, 837, KPR, I-4-a/15, 'Conference bulletin, no. 5 and no. 8', 5 and 8 September 1973.

113 TNA, FCO, 93/8, 'Meeting with Lakhdar Brahimi', 24 September 1973.
114 DAMSPS, PA, 1973, f-135, 438085, 'Foreign Secretariat's telegram', 10 September 1973.
115 *Documents of the Gatherings of the Non-Aligned Countries*, 1, 86–95.
116 AJ, 837, KPR, I-4-a/15, 'Tito-Boumedienne talks', 2 September 1973; 'Tito-Gandhi talks', 4 September 1973.
117 DAMSPS, PA, 1973, f-134, 437398, 'Telegram from Algeria', 8 September 1973; AJ, 837, KPR, I-4-a/15, 'Note of talks during a dinner given by Boumedienne', 7 September 1973.
118 NARA, RG 59, CFPF, 1973–1979, ET, 1973STATE180471, 11 September 1973.
119 AJ, 837, KPR, I-4-a/15, 'Tito-Boumedienne talks', 2 September 1973.
120 AJ, 837, KPR, I-4-a/15, 'Tito-Gandhi talks', 4 September 1973; 'Tito-Selassie talks', 4 September 1973.
121 DAMSPS, PA, 1973, f-135, 438085, 'Foreign Secretariat's telegram', 10 September 1973.
122 MMFA, 'Non-Alignment Movement', Research Division, 1978.
123 NARA, RG 59, CFPF, 1973–1979, ET, 1973NATO04630, 1 October 1973.
124 M. S. Rajan, *Nonalignment and Nonaligned Movement*, 229–30.
125 Assassi Lassassi, *Non-Alignment and Algerian Foreign Policy*, 130–3; Mohammed Lakhdar Ghettas, *Algeria and the Cold War*, 107–8; Ardavan Amir-Aslani, *L'age d'or de la diplomatie algerienne*, 141–4.
126 TNA, FCO 93/7, 'Letter from Algeria', 19 September 1973.
127 TNA, FCO 93/7, 'The 4th NAM summit conference', 19 September 1973.
128 NAI, MEA, HI/1011(79)/74, 'Annual political report from Algeria, 1973', 15 April 1974.
129 TNA, FCO, 93/8, 'Letter to PM's Private Secretary', 19 September 1973.
130 DAMSPS, PA, 1973, f-135, 437974, 'Foreign Secretariat's telegram', 5 September 1973.
131 Lubna Z. Qureshi, *Nixon, Kissinger, and Allende: U.S. Involvement in the 1973 Coup in Chile* (Lanham, MD: Lexington Books, 2009), 47–144.
132 NARA, RG 59, CFPF, 1973-1979, ET, 1973STATE238777, 6 December 1973.
133 DAMSPS, PA, 1973, f-96, 440497, 'Telegram from U.S.', 25 September 1973.
134 AJ, 837, KPR, I-4-a/15, 'Report of the Yugoslav delegation on the results of the 4th NAM summit', 12 September 1973.
135 Janez Stanovnik, 'Non-Alignment and the New International Economic Order', in *Non-Alignment in the Eighties*, 157–8.
136 Robert L. Rothstein, 'Foreign Policy and Development Policy: From Nonalignment to International Class War', *International Affairs* 52.4 (1976), 613–16.

6

Searching for a New Order: the 1976 Colombo Conference

The Colombo Conference and all historical events preceding it had become the stellar moment of the NAM when its global influence and potential to push through substantial changes into the world order, especially the economic ones, had reached an undisputed apex. For the very first time, decisions made by the entire movement were starting to produce greater impact on the great powers and the developed world as a whole, thus demonstrating that the developing world represented much more than a mere object of great power politics and a simple passive recipient of external aid. These were the years when the developing world in its NAM emanation had succeeded in inflicting a certain amount of pain on its more developed counterpart by prolifically playing the raw materials card, while compelling the Global North to unwillingly offer some incentives, compromises and concessions.

The period between the Algiers and Colombo Conferences had ushered in an era of a dynamic collective search for a restored economic sovereignty of developing nations – essentially, an attempt at the final realization of a long-term objective pursued by the non-aligned ever since 1961. This new agenda was principally implemented through an active inducement of a constructive dialogue between the North and South, one which primarily entailed potential accommodation between the two major parts of the world over some of the fundamental features of the current economic system (trade tariffs, prices of raw materials and finished goods, technology transfers, debts, international financial institutions). Some of the highlights of this newly proclaimed undertaking were also manifested through careful application of direct pressure on industrialized nations by skilful manipulation of prices of basic commodities, together with the additional curbing of outside access to different raw materials by introducing nationalization, imposing unilateral embargos or by forming producer cartels.[1]

In fact, many changes introduced into the Bretton Woods system by the US in the early 1970s, reflecting the relative decline in the overwhelming primacy of the West,[2] eventually stimulated a drive for the gradual reshuffle of international economic relations that would ultimately engender a necessary shift in the balance between North and South, though less in favour of the former. The key to introducing such sweeping changes was in the promotion of the notion of interdependence that awarded both sides with an equal say in shaping the subsequent future of the world, since each of these two parts eventually contributed to the general peace and stability in one way or the other. These aspirations had become an integral part of a rallying cry for the NIEO, basically the way in which a structurally different global economic system would be ultimately assembled, one clearly accompanied by a qualitatively new level of socioeconomic interdependence and tighter global transnational integration based on the redistribution of economic power. This kind of a new systemic solution promoted by the NAM was directly associated with the notion of enhanced economic sovereignty and diversified equality for developing nations then striving to more quickly catch up with their developed counterparts. In many ways, the NIEO reflected some of the ideas of the welfare state characteristic in East–West development since 1945, but this concept was then applied more globally, expanding it to envelop almost half of humanity.[3]

Declining Détente and the Third World

As soon as the superpower détente achieved significant political breakthroughs, on the US domestic front opponents of the entire process were rapidly gaining ground, particularly inside the US Congress, increasingly imposing restrictions on some of the dealings between the two sides (the Soviet's most-favoured-nation status, liberalization of Jewish emigration), thus also influencing the subsequent fate of SALT II negotiations. What also did not help to ease this burden was the Watergate Affair which almost totally paralysed Nixon's ability to follow up on any new initiatives, which the new summit with Brezhnev in June 1974 clearly demonstrated. This stalemate would continue until Nixon's resignation in August, while the ascension to power of the new President, Gerald Ford, did not significantly alter the deterioration trend, in spite of the good will still present on both sides. With the intensification of the superpower competition in the Third World in 1975–6, détente was rapidly being dismantled both at home and abroad, with the two superpowers discovering fewer and fewer incentives to invest more efforts into overcoming this deadlock.[4]

In spite of everything, the greatest achievement of détente in this period was the convening of the Conference for Security and Cooperation in Europe (CSCE), lasting between September 1973 and June 1975, which gathered in a pan-European forum the delegations of thirty-three countries, plus the US and Canada. In many ways, the CSCE would become an extension of policies previously pursued by France and West Germany vis-à-vis the Soviet bloc, followed by reluctant US participation at first. While Moscow and its allies would concentrate their attention on the Baskets I and II related to the issues of postwar borders, security and bringing down economic and technological barriers, the West primarily stressed Basket III, dealing with humanitarian issues such as human rights, people-to-people exchanges in education and culture, freedom of movement and information. These conflicting perspectives would somewhat stall the entire process for almost two years, but still each party had to make necessary concessions in order to push through whatever was pertinent to their interests. In the end, even though the Soviet bloc managed to gain recognition of its postwar borders, although with a caveat of potential peaceful changes, as well as certain economic benefits, it still had to introduce the human security part of internal legislation, thus slowly degrading its ideological grip. When the Helsinki Final Act was solemnly signed on 1 August 1975, it seemed that everyone involved finally triumphed, even though very soon each bloc would start interpreting its provisions as they saw fit.[5]

The neutral and non-aligned states, which formed a separate group inside the CSCE process, encompassing Finland, Sweden, Switzerland, Austria, Yugoslavia, Cyprus and Malta, eventually significantly impacted certain stages of negotiations, especially in the cases of the introduction of the concept of baskets, decision-making by consensus or organization of follow-up conferences instead of establishing a permanent organization as was sought by the USSR. Yugoslavia also argued for creating a direct link between the CSCE and the NAM in the Mediterranean, thus strengthening Europe's security along its southern flank. However, this proposal was widely rejected by other participants, although non-aligned countries, like Algeria or Egypt, were expressing strong interest in the Yugoslav initiative.[6]

However, the danger of direct bloc interference into the internal affairs of non-aligned countries had not diminished due to the development of the superpower détente. Moreover, this kind of tendency would only escalate on both sides of the Cold War division. One obvious example was the 1974 Cyprus crisis when two NATO members, Greece and Turkey, openly interfered into the island's domestic affairs by either trying to overthrow its leader, Archbishop Makarios, in July, as was sought by Greek military junta, or staging two concurrent military interventions in July and August under the pretext of protecting the Turkish minority. This was an outright attack by two bloc nations against a non-aligned country, although it did not stir up much opposition among Western countries and was even tacitly endorsed by the US as a means to boost Western presence in the Eastern Mediterranean.[7]

The NAM was, nonetheless, very active in the UN during this crisis, denouncing bloc aggression, submitting different resolutions, resolutely demanding that the sovereignty and territorial integrity of Cyprus be respected, while also criticizing the imposition of unilateral measures.[8] The primacy of the UN in brokering a political compromise was crucial for the non-aligned, therefore, in September, a contact group of five member states (Algeria, Guyana, India, Mali and Yugoslavia) was established with a clear mandate to closely monitor developments in Cyprus.[9] Eventually, a compromise non-aligned Resolution 3212 was adopted during the 29th UNGA session in November, calling for direct negotiations between the island's two main communities, respect for country's independence, sovereignty and territorial integrity to be stressed, while the withdrawal of all foreign troops was demanded, as well as the return of all refugees to their previous places of residence. This gave a new impetus to future negotiations, temporarily stabilizing the situation, but without precluding any final settlement.[10]

However, two events served as a turning point in the superpower relationship in the Third World, marking the beginning of active Soviet military involvement there. These two significant events, which proved Moscow's thesis that Marxist forces were globally on the rise, were the fall of Indochina and the Cuban involvement in Angola. Therefore, differing perceptions of the impact détente would have on the wider world eventually contributed to this new Soviet awareness that pursing more assertive policies in the Third World would be in accordance with its ideological principles but it would not effectively undermine the relationship with Washington. This, nonetheless, proved as an illusion, since the US was still not ready to give up on the Third World without a serious fight, while increasing domestic pressures eventually compelled the Ford administration to act regardless of détente concerns.[11]

The origins of this new Soviet assertiveness should be also sought in the way détente was playing out in the shadow of the next major conflict in the Middle East, the 1973 Yom Kippur (October) War. When Egypt and Syria launched their coordinated attack against Israel on 6 October, achieving initial success on two fronts, this acted as a total shock for both Israel and the US, while the USSR, although aware of Arab preparations for war, did not openly encourage such an action so as not to endanger its interactions with the US. Nevertheless, both sides would soon initiate airlifts to supply arms to their regional allies. However, Sadat, unbeknown to others, was pursuing a limited war strategy, essentially a political one through military means, that aimed at inducing the superpower conflict which would then create conditions for a political solution. He was also intensively signalling to the Americans that any acceptance of a ceasefire had to be closely related to the concrete progress achieved in reaching the final settlement that implied liberation of occupied territories.[12]

However, the tide of war would soon turn against the Arabs, primarily facilitated by massive US arms shipments, thus resulting in the swift Syrian defeat in the Golan Heights and the encirclement of the entire Egyptian Third Army along the Suez Canal. This soon triggered serious unease in Moscow that the Arabs could end up losing yet another war. Consequently, Brezhnev started threatening direct Soviet involvement, while at the same time inviting the US to act jointly in the spirit of détente. Kissinger's visit to Moscow on 20 October had managed to secure a ceasefire agreement that was implemented through the UNSC Resolution 338 two days later. However, with Washington's silent nod, Israel, nonetheless, continued with its counteroffensive, thus creating a full-blown crisis in relations with the Kremlin invoking Moscow's right to unilaterally intervene, while Nixon responded with a DEFCON III nuclear alert. Soon enough, the Soviets backed down, while the Americans compelled the Israelis to halt their operations and honour the ceasefire agreement. Despite this, the damage to détente had been already done.[13]

For the USSR, the Yom Kippur War stood as a clear example that détente in the Third World implied a completely different thing to the Americans than they had initially thought, indicating that the Nixon administration was ready to cooperate only as long as its main interests were safeguarded. This would become even more evident when Sadat soon drifted in the US direction, using his new partnership with Washington as leverage in securing the Sinai I disengagement agreement with Israel in January 1974. This initial disengagement was complemented by another significant Israeli withdrawal based on the Sinai II agreement in September 1975. Kissinger's astute shuttle diplomacy achieved great success in bringing Egypt into US orbit, while consequently reducing Soviet influence in the region, except in places like Syria or Iraq. In fact, Sadat was gaining back his country's territory but he was concurrently losing his ground with other Arab governments and diminishing his country's influence in the NAM.[14]

Therefore, changes to the Soviet thinking on the US role in the Third World had come to fruition in the aftermath of these events. After the speedy end of US military involvement in Indochina, North Vietnam, although dedicated to economic reconstruction of a devastated nation, while also paying lip service to a political settlement in the South, nevertheless, endorsed the military option for the ultimate takeover of power there. Since Hanoi was convinced that in the light of the Watergate affair renewed US military intervention was off the table, a new offensive was launched in early 1975 which resulted in total disintegration of South Vietnam by the end of April. Even though the PRGSV would officially rule the South, in July 1976 a unified Socialist Republic of Vietnam was proclaimed, triggering celebrations in Moscow and causing a sombre atmosphere in both Washington and Beijing. This sudden and total Vietnamese victory also had a serious impact on both Laos and Cambodia where indigenous communist forces also seized power by force. However, while Pathet Lao's government in Vientiane would be a loyal Vietnamese ally, the Khmer Rouge regime in the newly formed Democratic Kampuchea (DK) would become a fierce Maoist outpost in Indochina, engaged in relentless bickering with Hanoi.[15] Even though the USSR was not directly engaged in all these events, this was yet another signal to the US that Moscow was changing its posture in the Third World.

However, the sudden decolonization of the Portuguese African colonies stood as evidence of how increasing domestic concerns and perceived international obligations led to a more open confrontation between the blocs. A civil war broke out in Angola in early 1975, resulting in a conflict between three rivalling factions, where the one closest to socialist countries – MPLA – was far better positioned to assume power than the two other pro-Western and pro-Chinese factions – FNLA and UNITA. Eventually, South Africa launched an invasion of Angola in October 1975, enjoying strong US backing of its scheme. Even though the MPLA enjoyed material assistance from the Soviet bloc and Yugoslavia, it was the direct Cuban military intervention in November, one set in motion against Soviet advice but one which Moscow was bound to support soon enough, that ultimately pushed the South African forces back into Namibia, thus forcing the US to back off and humiliatingly withdraw from the entire affair. Regardless of certain disagreements between Moscow and Havana, this entire episode left the strong impression on the White House that it was the USSR and not Cuba that was exploiting Washington's weaknesses.[16] In fact, in Angola the US had a taste of its own medicine, i.e. unilateralism used against the Soviets after the Yom Kippur War, but the eventual consequences of all these actions rapidly led to a total breakdown of détente in a matter of years.

OPEC's Oil Embargo as an Impetus for the NIEO Offensive

In response to the outbreak of the Yom Kippur War, the OPEC decided to raise oil prices by 70 per cent. Very soon Persian Gulf members of the cartel also adopted total embargo of all oil supplies to the US and other Western countries, ultimately endorsing the cut of exports by a maximum of 25 per cent in November, with an additional 5 per cent cut planned in December and the following months. By implementing such measures, the Arabs were trying to induce an early Israeli withdrawal from the occupied territories through imposition of direct economic pressure on Tel Aviv's sponsors. Between mid-October 1973 and January 1974, global oil prices had quadrupled, causing worldwide economic crisis, recession, inflation, unemployment, drop in industrial production and financial instability. Oil had thus become a new weapon in the hands of non-aligned and developing countries to try to extract Western concessions related to this crisis situation. Futhermore, they also received a huge moral boost to finally make their move and attempt to trigger the fundamental restructuring of the international economic system. The era of cheap oil, keeping many Western economies prospering for decades, had thus effectively ended. Oil prices were now being set not only by consumers but also by producers too, thus creating a new sensitive balance of interests not only between these two key sectors of the oil market but also between the developing and developed worlds in general as well.[17] In Kissinger's words, 'we are living in a never-never land ... in which tiny, poor, and weak nations can hold up for ransom some of the industrialised world'.[18]

Nevertheless, those non-aligned countries which did not possess such crucial natural resources such as oil were seriously affected by this sudden hike in prices, thus contributing to their further impoverishment. Taking this adverse situation into account, some non-aligned officials pointed out that it was in the interest of the developed world to back up developing nations in their efforts to become more prosperous societies, ones fully capable of absorbing industrial goods from the North and fulfilling all their financial obligations. Otherwise, economic, financial and social instability would gradually engulf most of the Third World, soon to be followed by a dangerous spillover effect. In essence, the oil shock had greased the wheels of the NIEO diplomatic offensive in 1974–5.[19] By that time, the developed world would become painfully aware that the developing one was slowly building up all kinds of institutional mechanisms, among them also the NAM, for launching collective initiatives aimed at safeguarding its fundamental interests, while also stimulating a comprehensive global change.[20]

As well as the oil embargo, the Middle Eastern conflict also acted as a catalyst for a new concerted action of the non-aligned. Therefore, during the Tito–Boumedienne meeting in mid-October, the Yugoslav president warned his Algerian counterpart that Arab countries should handle the powerful oil weapon wisely, since its excessive use could only cause a serious backlash from the West, thus also missing another precious opportunity to effectively drive a wedge between the US and their Western European allies. Boumedienne proposed to immediately hold a CB meeting dedicated to the Middle Eastern crisis, which Tito initially did not endorse, but Israel's loose interpretation of the ceasefire resolution ultimately changed his mind, concluding that the unity of Arab and other non-aligned countries was now subjected to an aggressive assault from the West.[21] However, the majority of the other NAM members were far more interested in organizing a gathering that would tackle all critical issues affecting the non-aligned, particularly the current economic crisis, then just dealing with one regional conflict that was just a fraction of all the global challenges they were then facing.[22]

In this respect, India, Sri Lanka and Yugoslavia seemed dissatisfied with the Algerian management of the CB not only due to its excessive insistence on Middle Eastern issues but also for the obvious lack of any new initiatives dealing with the immediate aftermath of the oil crisis. Therefore, any future discussions organized by the CB, as perceived by these countries, had to be expanded to include all dominant political and economic issues and not only those relevant to one group of nations, and thus also mitigating fears from non-alignment's further regionalization.[23] However, the oil crisis, having serious impact on the world's poor also, spurred a serious rift between the non-aligned countries themselves, with Tito being significantly concerned about the negative effect it produced on Asian nations, his closest allies. For example, Bandaranaike was even contemplating how Third World oil-consumers could bring more pressure on oil-producers to finally take their economic plight into consideration when setting the future oil prices.[24]

During their next meeting in New Delhi in early 1974, both Tito and Indira Gandhi were entirely dissatisfied with Algeria's lack of initiative in a time of grave crisis, which, as they saw it, further debilitated the NAM's capacity to act decisively and in a well-organized manner. The Indian side was particularly annoyed with the way the CB was being run by the Algerians, while Bandaranaike, also then present for tripartite talks, insisted on radically expanding the membership of this body, labelling it as still being 'unrepresentative'. Therefore, as the three leaders agreed, holding the next CB meeting was essential for further boosting movement's continuity, thus shaping an adequate collective response to recent international developments. However, this event would be just a prologue to holding similar ones in the nearest future, since such gatherings would be also supplemented by constructive exchanges of opinion between the NAM experts on trade, monetary and energy issues.[25]

Nevertheless, what particularly worried the majority of NAM members were the US attempts to handle the energy crisis either within the ranks of the most developed countries or through direct talks between the rich oil-consumers and oil-producers. In this way, the interests of poor non-aligned consumers, also adversely affected by the crisis, would not be either acknowledged or respected, thus directly affecting movement's unity. What also had to be avoided was an overt tendency to lay down the burden of aid solely on rich oil-producers, due to their recently earned profits, while developed countries would still strive to preserve the international economic system as it was. Therefore, a collective action in the UN had become a pressing issue for many non-aligned nations.[26]

Hence, it was decided to hold the next CB ministerial meeting in late March 1974, while concurrently Boumedienne, without holding additional consultations with other NAM members, proposed to the UN Secretary General to hold a special session of the UNGA in April, one that would be exclusively dedicated to the issues of raw materials, economic development and economic inequalities in general.[27] As reported by some British diplomats, this entire initiative was mainly inspired by a covert Algerian agenda of forestalling OPEC's growing political isolation from the rest of the Third World, while also trying to shield oil producers from the wrath of other developing countries labelling them as prime culprits for the dire economic situation.[28] This clearly indicated that Algeria sensed that the fallout from the oil embargo was not doing it any favours with other NAM allies. The promotion of Third World economic solidarity had become a new rallying cry for pushing forward the 'unholy alliance' between the oil-producers and oil-consumers within the developing world.[29]

In this way, the agenda of this extraordinary session would be largely dedicated to the status of developing countries, since they were hardest hit by this oil shock. Therefore, it would be necessary for the NAM to find a meaningful way in which additional oil revenues acquired during this crisis would not end up financing the industrialized world again, as it would be eventually the case, but they would be diverted to the constructive needs of the Third World, thus further strengthening its economic integration and bolstering its bargaining position in any future North–South negotiations.[30] As an attempt to mitigate such resentment, the Arab countries decided to extend loans in the amount of US$200 million to African nations, while an additional US$500 million was provided to the Arab-African Bank.[31] However, Asian countries, hardest hit by this crisis, were not included in this financial scheme, thus causing their additional consternation with the evident lack of progress in the Solidarity Fund negotiations or implementation of the preferential pricing for non-aligned oil-consumers as it had been adopted at Georgetown.[32]

However, Boumedienne was mindful enough that similar problems would also dominate the CB agenda, so he aspired to strike a sensitive balance between the demands to extend aid to non-aligned countries facing economic downturn and the sovereign rights of oil producers to adjust commodity prices accordingly. Furthermore, the Algerians insisted again on the establishment of the NAM's permanent secretariat as a way to deal with this crisis, but this proposal came against strong opposition, with some countries considering this blackmail in order for the aid to be provided.[33] During Algerian–Yugoslav consultations, both sides stressed that clear unity had to be achieved with respect to Middle East and international economic relations. This basically implied an active search for long-term solutions for diverting the increased financial potential of parts of the non-aligned world into stimulating its general economic progress.[34]

The CB meeting in Algiers on 19–21 March 1974 was attended by twenty-four observers, alongside the original seventeen CB members, despite Algerian and Syrian opposition. This reflected a constructive atmosphere where all NAM members, irrespective of their formal participation in certain bodies, were all invited to discuss crucial issues. In a way, this meeting was a dress rehearsal for the UNGA special session, therefore the bulk of the issues discussed were related to economic matters. During this event, it was also agreed to hold a special conference on raw materials in early 1975 as an integral part of this struggle to reclaim sovereign rights over natural resources.[35] Therefore, as a means of setting up a readjusted system of economic relations, participants decided to initiate work on the establishment of the Solidarity Fund, with Kuwait also promising to increase its funding to US$3 billion in the future. In addition, in order to patch up any current rifts, it was also agreed that all non-aligned countries should resolutely back their oil-producing partners in this new trial of strength with the US, while in return these more affluent NAM members would strive to ease the financial burden of countries hardest hit by the oil shock.[36]

However, this meeting also adopted some key institutional decisions: first, the CB would be permanently in charge of coordinating all activities in the UN; next, ministerial meetings could be held more frequently than once between the two summits; finally, the next NAM ministerial meeting, i.e. a conference, would be held in Lima in the latter half of 1975. In this way, the Algerian concept of unilaterally running the CB while restricting the number of ministerial conferences suffered an ultimate defeat, although the concurrent Yugoslav and Indian proposal for convening another ministerial meeting in 1974 was also rejected as part of this compromise.[37] This gathering also adopted the radical 'Declaration on the Middle East and the Palestinian Question', which basically negated the very existence of Israel, while a call was also issued to ban the Jewish state from the UN and other international organizations (Guyana broke off relations with Israel during this event, with seventeen African nations following suit). This document was the direct outcome of the rising Arab financial influence in the NAM against the backdrop of the oil crisis.[38]

The Role of the 6th UNGA Special Session

The 6th UNGA Special Session took place on 9 April–2 May 1974 and it represented the first significant international event where new principles and concepts of international economic relations were defined and promoted through the constructive North–South dialogue, while adequate and globally applicable solutions were also actively sought for. The overall aspiration of the majority of the participants was to introduce balanced improvements into the economic order through seeking gradual rather than revolutionary change, thus avoiding this important event degenerating into a showdown between the world's 'haves' and 'have nots'.[39] During the preparatory phase, the joint NAM-G77 working group managed to chart the general agenda: interdependence between developed and developing countries, general principles of economic cooperation, practical measures for dealing with long-term issues, balancing the price ratio between raw materials and industrial goods, non-discriminatory treatment, technology transfers, financing development, role of multinational corporations, debt burden, strengthening UN economic mechanisms, expanding the role of developing nations in international financial institutions, etc.[40]

However, the US and its allies were also preparing for a head-on encounter with the non-aligned, while simultaneously adopting a flexible approach. Nevertheless, the majority was still prone to carry out only limited improvements to the international economic system, without endorsing the entire NIEO concept.[41] In fact, Washington aspired to diplomatically curb vociferous demands for equal sovereign rights, thus the non-aligned had to invest additional effort in decisions adopted at the previous NAM summit to find their reflection in the documents of the special session.[42] The way the US treated non-aligned countries largely depended on their outright capability to clearly and efficiently present their policies and demands, backing them up with their newfound unity and diversified cooperation.

In his opening speech at this event, Boumedienne stressed all the basic points non-aligned countries advocated during the Lusaka, Georgetown and Algiers gatherings, thus indicating the progressive evolutionary potential of the NAM in forwarding such an agenda: development was the chief priority and, if not treated adequately, it could become the source of instability; world income needed to be redistributed according to the needs and interests of all nations; world economy in the hands of developed countries was the key obstacle to any substantial development of the Third World; developed and developing countries should seek constructive dialogue; direct control over natural resources was a clear priority for the developing world; industrialization and the agricultural development of developing nations should be further encouraged; new mechanisms of international aid should be established; the Third World's debt burden should be substantially alleviated.[43]

In his response, Kissinger emphasized the overall importance of interdependence where confrontation and division between the rich and poor was not the dominant feature of the international system any more, since the world economy had become a vibrant interconnection of different sets of interests and aspirations of both developed and developing countries further aspiring for prosperity and stability for all. However, he also admonished the developing world that such high goals could not be imposed on others through the arbitrary application of pressure and raising different threats, like the oil producers had, since ganging up against developed countries, still crucial for introducing substantial changes, could not yield any positive results in the long-run. Therefore, Kissinger stressed externally stimulated growth as the key aspect for elevating the Third World out of poverty, clearly opposed to the notion of redistribution demanded by the NIEO proponents.[44]

What the subsequent general debate corroborated was that, for the very first time, non-aligned countries had succeeded in pushing through their specific agenda as the key topic of UN deliberations. It was the successful treatment of economic issues that had become a crucial precondition for the realization of the global détente enveloping all nations promoted by the NAM. Most of the issues raised by the Algerian president were also emphasized in the speeches presented by other non-aligned representatives. However, the majority of Western delegates stressed their strong opposition to imposing any restrictions on the free access to raw materials, the forceful adjustments of prices, as well as to the potential creation of new cartels of producers of raw materials. Non-aligned countries also resolutely opposed the attempt to divide them as rich and poor developing nations, thus basically driving a wedge between them. Effectively, the NAM had managed to uphold the initiative throughout this gathering, more or less successfully dictating some of its demands.[45]

Finally, this UNGA special session unanimously adopted two crucial documents: one was the 'Declaration on the Establishment of the NIEO' (Resolution 3201) and the other one was the 'Program of Action' (Resolution 3202). In these two documents, the existing international system was proclaimed to be basically obsolete, new requirements for rectifying inequalities and addressing injustices were defined, sovereign control of developing nations over their natural resources was recognized, as was the growing role of producer cartels, while the influence of multinational corporations was set to be effectively curbed. Stress was particularly laid on the industrialization of the developing world, while the UN Emergency Relief Fund was also established as a step to diversify multilateral aid institutions. Even though implementation of all these measures was still being debated, nonetheless, the NAM succeeded in presenting itself as the chief promoter of the socioeconomic interests of the entire developing world, an outright expression of the shifting global balance of power.[46]

Yet some US officials considered this event to be a strong catalyst for the increased economic role of the NAM, where radicals, like Algeria, had started to set its agenda, with many moderate countries now seeking safety in numbers and tacitly going along with this new trend. Therefore, separating moderate Asian, Latin American and some African countries from the radical Afro-Arab group, while extending individual economic incentives, would eventually become the backbone of the US strategy to ultimately weaken the movement's will.[47] Essentially, this was Kissinger's 'southern strategy', a constructive appeasement aiming to divide developing countries along the lines of their individual economic interests. Nevertheless, the White House was also ready to mitigate some of the Third World's grievances and satisfy some of their demands, pragmatically engaging these nations over certain key issues, thus constructively integrating them into the Western-dominated economic system.[48]

Some US diplomats even considered this newfound NAM cohesion to be a direct product of common emotions and aspirations of the postcolonial world, an expression of its deep sense of wounded pride, now also linked to present socioeconomic difficulties, and often very uncertain future prospects. In the minds of many non-aligned leaders, as they concluded, all this was directly associated with the long history of unjust policies of the developed world. This kind of perception was only fuelling strong beliefs among these nations that collective strength and wielding power through manipulation of natural resources would eventually provide them with enough capacity to state their demands and openly present their grievances, thus increasingly assisting the cause of aligning their individual interests with the NAM's stated goals.[49]

This tendency also continued during the 29th UNGA session when Bouteflika was elected as its president. This proved to be a valuable opportunity for the NAM to finally set some of the UN agenda. This was quite evident when the UNGA expelled South Africa from its ranks (ninety-one votes for, twelve against, nineteen abstained), though not from UN membership. This decision set a serious legal precedent, implying that other countries, like Israel, could also face a similar fate when being at odds with the NAM. Moreover, the PLO delegation had also been accorded with observer status in this body, much to the open Western chagrin, with Yasser Arafat giving his first speech in front of the international organization.[50] Under the impression of these developments, Ford publicly admonished the non-aligned against introducing the 'tyranny of majority', while also utilizing commodities as a weapon for gaining political objectives.[51] Based on these specific historical circumstances, the NAM had finally managed to unearth concrete political power in its rising numbers.

As part of the NAM's new diplomatic onslaught, on 12 December, the UNGA passed the 'Charter on Economic Rights and Duties of States', initially proposed by the Mexican President Luis Echeverria, which stipulated the sovereign right of every country to independently determine conditions for the use of its natural resources and freely set their prices. Essentially, this document implied freedom of action for the developing world to nationalize any foreign assets at home, with or without handing out any adequate compensation, while correspondingly it could also independently raise commodity prices without consulting developed countries. This document was perceived by some as a demand for restitution for centuries of colonial exploitation, which was not basically the case. In the end, it was also agreed to hold the 7th UNGA special session on economic issues in September 1975.⁵²

During his subsequent meeting with Tito, Kissinger pointed out that due to the confrontation between the developed and developing countries, these complex economic issues could not be resolved overnight as the non-aligned aspired. In his words, in spite of the unreasonable and radical character of recently passed documents by the UNGA, the US was, nonetheless, ready to assist in the search for a constructive way out of the recent deadlock.⁵³ It is true that the non-aligned had finally succeeded in outvoting the West in the UN; however, this caused some concerns in Yugoslavia that, if such a procedural weapon was used far too often, while implementation of different resolutions was still not imminent due to strong Western opposition, the NAM could end up in an adverse situation with Washington paying even less heed to the authority of the UN in a moment when the international organization had become far more relevant to the cause of small countries than ever before. Therefore, the spirit of cooperation and compromise, naturally backed by certain gains, had to eventually prevail over any revanchist drive.⁵⁴ The Yugoslavs were on the right track in their fears that in the future the US might seek a reduction of their role in the UN, while utilizing that move to launch a counteroffensive that would eventually re-establish their control by marginalizing the international organization in favour of free market forces, instead of the NIEO, and nongovernmental human rights in place of state sovereignty.⁵⁵

Comprehensive Struggle for the NIEO

In spite of achieving some propaganda success, it quickly became clear that the developed world was starting to fight back in order to turn the tables in its favour. It was doing this primarily by trying to drive a wedge between the oil-producing and oil-consuming developing countries by using their obvious material contradictions.⁵⁶ Bandaranaike, as the host, was putting additional efforts into making South–South cooperation the main topic of the future summit, since recent developments had demonstrated that the disparity between the rich and poor non-aligned countries produced a far more negative effect on the movement's unity than previously expected.⁵⁷ Therefore, the Conference on Raw Materials in Dakar in early February 1975 issued a call for a more integrated sub-regional and regional cooperation between different cartels of raw materials producers, as well as for establishing a new model of a more preferential economic treatment. In essence, non-aligned and developing countries fully comprehended that the staunch defence of their immediate control over natural resources was also their strongest card in any future talks with the developed world.⁵⁸

In spite of the complex international situation, economic issues still dominated the NAM agenda. The immediate goal of the forthcoming CB ministerial meeting in Havana, originally planned in late February 1975, was to readdress developments since the last UNGA session, reassess what had been done since the Algiers summit and initiate preparations for the NAM ministerial conference in Lima planned for late August. Essentially, one of the main goals of this gathering was to implement new measures directed at easing the economic burden of the least-developed countries, while expanding mutual cooperation into new areas, like food production, peaceful use of nuclear energy, health care, education, culture, etc.[59]

The CB ministerial meeting was held in the Cuban capital on 17–19 March, with seventeen observers also attending this gathering. Since this meeting was held for the second time in Latin America, countries like Cuba and Peru clearly aspired for regional issues to dominate the meeting's agenda. They wanted to use this opportunity to stress that the 'tyranny of minority' represented by Washington and its allies had officially ended. However, such a direction was only partially endorsed by other participants, since the movement's unity and mutual solidarity were still paramount, regional affiliation notwithstanding.[60] In fact, many delegations did not want to see this meeting acting as a catalyst for triggering new divisions along the lines of being more or less 'progressive', as it was sometimes advocated by Cuba. The Yugoslav, Indian and Algerian representatives finally managed to steer this meeting in a more constructive way, ultimately inducing a more conciliatory approach even from the hosts.[61] Furthermore, this was the very first meeting where the NAM was officially mentioned in its final documents under such a name.

The general debate, as well as the one in the political and economic committees, revolved around the draft submitted by the Cubans, one dealing equally with both different regional crises and North–South relations. Even though, under Cuban guidance, the political part of this declaration was characterized by a more critical tone towards the US, thanks to the prevailing moderate line of thinking, this document was eventually passed with no references being made to the movement potentially aligning itself with any of the great powers. Nevertheless, fears from attempts of overthrowing legal NAM governments by outside factors, as it was the case with Allende or Makarios, were reiterated again, while all members were called upon to work out a more effective mechanism for extending timely assistance to any affected nations. In this respect, this declaration also issued a stern warning to all great powers that aggression against one non-aligned country was aggression against all of them.[62] This provision, although declaratory in its nature, was largely inspired by the successful experience of OPEC's oil embargo.

This meeting also welcomed the successful epilogue of liberation struggle in Portuguese colonies, firm support was again extended to the peoples of South Africa, Namibia and South Rhodesia (Zimbabwe) in their just struggle, as well as to the formation of the zone of peace in the Indian Ocean. The lack of progress in the withdrawal of foreign troops from Cyprus was again condemned. Furthermore, the DPRK, on Yugoslavia's, Zaire's and Senegal's initiative, was officially invited to join the NAM's ranks as a full member at the forthcoming Lima conference (South Korea's application was rejected). However, the Syrian proposal for the expulsion of Israel from the UN by annulling its 1949 accession resolution, as well as the introduction of UN sanctions against that nation, was rejected by some delegations, like Yugoslavia or India, which considered this meeting as being without an adequate format for adopting such far-reaching decisions.[63]

As for the economic part of the declaration, it highly appreciated the NAM's recent contributions to the realization of the NIEO, as well as the character and pace of current preparations for the 7th UNGA special session. However, developed countries were also publicly condemned for their relentless opposition, even though they were often laying blame for the global economic crisis on developing nations, without even remotely contemplating bringing down any trade barriers. Therefore, based on decisions made in Dakar, the CB proposed to initiate work on setting up a coordinating body – a council of producers and exporters of raw materials, especially strategic ones like oil, bauxite, copper, uranium, etc. In addition, a special fund for financing buffer stocks of raw materials had to be promptly established. This meeting also raised the issue of founding a new international trade organization that would primarily cater to the needs of developing countries. Industrialization and food production were also devised as clear priorities for any successful economic development. OPEC's assistance to other developing nations was officially praised, although internally its limited scope was also criticized.[64] Work on the establishment of the NAM Solidarity Fund would also continue, spearheaded by Kuwait, expecting its final completion in Lima (the initial plan was for each NAM member state to contribute at least US$1 million).[65]

Even though cooperation rather than confrontation with the developed world was promoted at this meeting, Kissinger was annoyed with the text of the declaration and especially with the DPRK's acceptance as a future member. In his mind, the non-aligned nations had become a more rigid bloc than the aligned ones, with many among them cheering for an open confrontation with the West, despite the fact that this was a battle they could never win.[66] However, Yugoslavia's promotion of North Korean membership was primarily directed at getting Romania to also attend the NAM conferences as a special guest, since some members were also lobbying for other bloc countries such as Australia, Portugal and the Philippines to receive the same status.[67] In the meantime, what also irritated Washington was the NAM's new initiative to officially endorse and actively lobby the application for UN membership for both Vietnamese states, thus eventually opening doors for subsequent legal, UN-backed reunification of that nation.[68]

However, developed countries intended to conduct negotiations with developing countries from the position of strength. The formation of the exclusive club of six major Western industrialized powers (G6) also heralded a concerted response to the NIEO initiative and the NAM's takeover of the UNGA. In fact, industrialized nations were continuing with their tactics of separating oil-producers from the least developed nations, as well as radicals from the moderates within the NAM, while reasserting their global financial authority.[69] In mid-July, Kissinger made another speech in Milwaukee in which he admonished the non-aligned from falling into a trap where the UN would be frequently used to settle the score with the developed world through using its bodies as a political weapon. Therefore, the US Secretary of State called for the new spirit of cooperation and mutual adjustments to be introduced, one based on new foundations and practices of interdependence.[70]

Truthfully speaking, it seemed to some NAM members that recent means of applying pressure on developed countries had still not yielded positive results, thus forcing the movement's hand to expand its arsenal of political and economic measures stimulating the next phase of the North–South dialogue. This was a deliberate attempt to find a delicate balance between the developmental necessities of the South and the financial interests of the North, where economic and financial integration of developing countries would eventually stem the impact of multinational corporations as a clear priority.[71] As a sign of good faith, during Ford's visit to Yugoslavia in early August, Kissinger suddenly proposed to fly directly to Lima and address this conference as an observer. Since everything related to the NAM was decided through consensus, the Yugoslavs could not unilaterally commit themselves to such an unexpected offer, so nothing came of this idea.[72]

The Lima Conference, taking place on 25–30 August 1975, had become the largest NAM gathering thus far, with 108 delegations attending, among them eighty-one full members, eight countries and ten organizations present as observers, while nine countries were guests, among them Romania, Australia, the Philippines and Portugal. As for newly accepted NAM members, they were DR Vietnam, the DPRK, Cape Verde, PLO, Panama and Guinea Bissau. This selection was the outcome of decisions adopted at Lima that membership criteria would not be altered but they would be somewhat expanded and made more flexible so as to encompass a growing number of countries and organizations now aspiring to receive observer or guest status. This was an encouraging sign for the movement that even bloc members were sometimes contemplating changing the nature of their engagement.[73] This conference was also held at the specific moment when it seemed that the NAM was still on the offensive; nevertheless, the West was rapidly consolidating its economic and financial positions, while the North–South dialogue was facing a growing deadlock.

During the general debate, all participants stressed the NAM's rising international role, its incessant membership expansion into four continents, as well as its increased capacity to exercise a more tangible role in both political and economic spheres. As for the political issues present at this conference, all major crisis hotspots were equally covered by all speakers, and the recent successes in these regions were generally praised by everyone, with the majority of them avoiding any radical outbursts beyond just customary criticism of the US. The Yugoslav delegation also managed to actively discourage attempts to identify the movement with the Third World, since that would seriously narrow down the role of European members.[74] What also dominated the political debate were new demands for a more efficient coordination of NAM activities, thus further empowering the movement's collective response to any crisis situations involving its members. This tendency, as concluded, would materialize through more frequent CB meetings.[75]

However, what this gathering also brought forward was a serious split and lack of cohesion inside the previously formidable Afro-Arab group. Syrians tabled again the proposal for the expulsion of Israel from the UN, in spite of some Arab countries, like Algeria, only opting for the introduction of UN economic sanctions. However, the majority of African delegations, committed to earlier OAU decisions, stood up against such extreme ideas, labelling them as both counterproductive and irresponsible. A similar outcome occurred when Syria also tried to publicly condemn Egypt's disengagement agreements with Israel as a Zionist plot. Therefore, as a compromise, the political part of the 'Lima Program for Mutual Assistance and Solidarity' recommended that all NAM members study the issue of potential application of UN sanctions against Israel, without ever criticizing Egypt's respective position.[76] Moreover, Bandaranaike was already very much annoyed with the Arab handling of NAM affairs, considering that there was too much influence of the AL and OAU in the movement's functioning.⁷⁷ This tendency also proved to be quite true for India. In spite of receiving full backing from all Lima participants for its UNSC non-permanent seat candidacy, when the vote finally took place the majority of Muslim countries, except some such as Algeria and Egypt, backed Pakistan's candidacy, even though it was not a NAM member, thus foiling New Delhi's bid.⁷⁸

As for the economic issues that dominated the text of the 'Lima Program' and thirteen additional separate resolutions, all participants reiterated their strong commitment to the full implementation of the NIEO. They frequently emphasized that the economic gap between the developed and developing countries had been rapidly increasing, in spite of all solemn promises previously made by industrialized nations to introduce substantial changes into the world economic system. External accusations that nationalization of foreign assets was primarily responsible for the global economic crisis were outright rejected. The origins of this crisis were sought in the monopolistic position of the developed world and its reluctance to ease the financial burden of developing countries and offer them equal trading opportunities, as well as management responsibilities in running the world economy. Therefore, as concluded by this conference, the NAM's solidarity and unity of action were paramount to the successful completion of these goals. However, some African members also stressed that more prosperous developing countries were not always ready to demonstrate such a proactive stance towards their less fortunate partners.⁷⁹

In this respect, this conference redefined South–South cooperation in a number of fields, like raw materials, trade, finances, agriculture, transportation, technology transfers, peaceful use of nuclear energy, education, healthcare, information, etc., thus promoting the spirit of global economic inclusiveness. Furthermore, the 'Solidarity Fund for Economic and Social Development in Non-Aligned Countries' was finally set up, aimed to officially start at the next summit (the contribution of each member was 500 SDRs in a convertible equivalent), while the establishment of two specialized centres was also proposed by Yugoslavia and Peru: the 'Centre for Research and Information', dealing with the analysis of the world economic situation, and the 'Centre for Science and Technology', promoting cooperation in these two spheres. This event also passed two resolutions initiating administrative work for the establishment of the 'Special Fund for Financing Buffer Stocks of Raw Materials' and the 'Council of Associations of the Developing Countries Producers-Exporters of Raw Materials'. In addition, two inter-governmental groups were set up, one monitoring the cooperation between the NAM central banks and the other providing advice on the international monetary reform. Essentially, all these decisions created new institutional mechanisms for regulating the practices for trading commodities.⁸⁰

In fact, all the economic documents adopted at Lima were couched in moderate terms, avoiding any confrontationist rhetoric, thus preparing the NAM for the next round of dialogue with developed countries.⁸¹ The overall significance of these decisions could not even escape Kissinger's attention, who saw this entire conference as NAM's dress rehearsal for the 7th UNGA special session planned in September, a means of directly strengthening its bargaining position.⁸² In his instruction to all diplomatic posts, Kissinger indicated that the US policy would reflect Washington's newly found readiness to satisfy some demands, while also offering some concrete incentives related to trade, commodities, food production and financial matters. His tactic also entailed assuming a positive stance with respect to budgetary, disarmament and human rights issues (although the US was ready to oppose any criticism regarding Israel, South Korea and South Africa).[83] However, some members, like Yugoslavia, also drew important conclusions that any attempts by the NAM to impose radical unilateral solutions during the special session could only backfire. Therefore, Belgrade started advocating a new approach, one suggesting having more patience and increased readiness to reach even limited compromises at least on a number of trade, industrial and financial issues, without raising high the banner of radicalism and confrontation.[84]

Essentially, Kissinger understood well that the protracted confrontation with the NAM could stir new disturbances in the world market. Therefore, assuming direct control over this dialogue would ultimately keep the US firmly in the saddle, splitting the non-aligned countries along moderate and radical lines. In one of his internal deliberations, Kissinger indicated that he did not 'want to accept a New Economic Order' nor did he aspire 'to confront Boumedienne'. However, on another occasion, he was even blunter: 'Obviously we can't accept the new economic order, but I would like to pull its teeth and divide these countries up, not solidify them.'[85] This pragmatic approach implied avoiding ideological skirmishes with the NAM, carrying a drawn-out struggle on many technical issues, while playing on differences among the opposition, thus making the entire debate eventually pointless. Kissinger was concerned that the US would stand alone without European support if it was to get bogged down in an ideological fight with the NAM over the issue of whose economic system was better.[86] He once indicated the rationale behind this entire scheme:

> Our basic strategy must be to hold the industrialized powers behind us and to split the Third World. We can only do that if we start with a lofty tone and a forthcoming stance ... Bloc formation in the Third World can be inhibited only if we focus attention on practical measures in which they have a tangible stake. We must speak early in the session and put forward specific and progressive ideas.[87]

This kind of strategy was evident in his speech made at the 7th UNGA special session, read out by the US ambassador Daniel Patrick Moynihan in his absence, in which Kissinger, while admonishing against the formation of new blocs of rich and poor and criticizing recent NAM and OPEC practices, presented a number of constructive proposals aimed at ensuring global economic stability: partial reform of existing international financial institutions, stimulating economic growth through the infusion of capital and introduction of new technologies among developing countries, assisting their industrialization, developing new energy sources, regulating the practices of multinational corporations, promoting special trade incentives, establishing producer-consumer forums, boosting food production and providing additional financial aid to the least developed countries.[88] When the US delegation submitted its draft paper everyone was pleasantly surprised by some of the ideas raised in them, some seeming even revolutionary. However, many substantial economic issues were also not encompassed by this document.[89]

During the subsequent heated debate, developed countries, in spite of their negative comments, still expressed their openness to endorsing some of the ideas proposed by developing nations, although they did not include raw materials, price indexation, easing the debt burden and monetary reform into this package. Essentially, developed nations were only improving the existing system but not fundamentally reforming it. Nevertheless, the US, Western Europe and Japan indicated their readiness to start working on certain compromise solutions, like allowing the preferential treatment of developing countries in the North–South trade, stabilizing their export revenues through different financial mechanisms, allowing technology transfers and endorsing the International Monetary Fund (IMF) and the International Financial Corporation (IFC) financing of Third World development. This change in attitude was somewhat praised by the non-aligned, even though they were well aware that the positive US stance was primarily motivated by attempting to break up their solidarity and unity, while only making limited concessions.[90] Nevertheless, recent events still garnered some hope for opening a new chapter in the North–South dialogue. Concurrently, Moscow also sought to present itself as the NAM's most reliable ally in pursuing the NIEO agenda, extending substantial economic aid to different developing nations and verbally backing intentions to restructure the international economic system, although without providing concrete ideas how to achieve that goal in a constructive manner.[91]

Troubled NAM on the Road to Colombo

Despite the general belief, many non-aligned countries were left with ambiguous conclusions about the second special session. This was evident during the subsequent 30th UNGA session where, as witnessed by US officials, militancy of the Arab-African group was already in decline, as was Algerian leadership, with some disenchantment evidently present within their ranks, while some poor African countries were clearly aspiring to avoid US sanctions over some of their UN voting habits. Washington was, therefore, hoping that the recent non-aligned bloc-like unity in the UN would fracture due to its artificial character and disparate individual interests.[92] In this respect, by utilizing the economic downturn in the Third World, a special task group was established in the State Department to closely monitor all activities of non-aligned countries, taking down their reactions, speeches, voting patterns, and, based on that, implementing specific US policies towards individual countries based on the 'stick and carrot' approach, rewarding their proper behaviour with economic aid and punishing more critical countries by withdrawing it, thus affecting the movement's future unity.[93]

However, what also contributed to the NAM's internal divisions was the controversial vote for Uganda's resolution at that UNGA session which declared Zionism as a form of racism and a direct threat to world peace, when some non-aligned countries abstained from voting or even voted against it. This kind of unpopular decision left a serious blemish on the NAM's reputation, even if these abstaining countries could not be considered individually as being pro-Israeli.[94] Hence, key NAM leaders were well aware of these inherent weaknesses and divisive undercurrents plaguing the movement, ranging from bilateral conflicts, different regionalist initiatives (ASEAN, Third World and Islamic conferences) to ideological divisions between 'progressive' and 'reactionary' members. All this was closely related to the increased interference undertaken by the two superpowers, either directly or via proxies.[95] The Soviets even attempted to influence Colombo to turn the forthcoming summit into a major anti-imperialist gathering. However, this was immediately rejected by Sri Lankan officials who stressed that the NAM was based on the principles of independence, negotiations and cooperation, not on divisions and confrontation.[96]

Yugoslavia and Algeria were particularly concerned that, under the conditions of a détente in crisis, both superpowers were stepping up the ante against the movement, especially the USSR, which aspired to decisively sway the NAM towards a fully fledged alliance with the Soviet bloc. This kind of overt tendency, as both Belgrade and Algiers saw it, had to be resolutely denounced.[97] Nyerere also agreed with this assessment, considering Soviet attempts at reining in the movement through Cuba, Vietnam and other leftists as very dangerous, indicating that non-alignment had moved well beyond anti-imperialist policies and had already become a far more complex doctrine clearly emphasizing independence, equality, stability, emancipation, development, cooperation and peaceful resolution of conflicts.[98] However, ideas about creating the NAM's secretariat as its main body were still relevant among some members, especially the ones edging closer to Moscow (Cuba, Vietnam, Libya and Iraq), which then triggered staunch opposition from others advocating a more independent stand (Yugoslavia, India, Sri Lanka, Tanzania and Egypt).[99]

Furthermore, Asian countries had gained a strong impression that they were facing growing isolation inside the movement, becoming increasingly marginalized by the Arab-African majority, especially with respect to their intent to focus more on economic and developmental rather than political and ideological issues.[100] In addition, India still firmly opposed giving any status to Pakistan, since it was an aligned country through CENTO. New Delhi also did not want Islamabad being accorded observer status, since it could then also influence some of the NAM's internal proceedings through its physical presence at some sessions. Indian officials were less reserved with respect to the Philippines and Thailand potentially attending as guests, since from 1975 SEATO was being phased out and New Delhi maintained far better relations with both these countries.[101] However, so as to remain unbiased, India adamantly opposed the Lima formula for inviting guests and observers to the NAM events, since this precedent, according to them, could not only open doors for potential Pakistani attendance but could also create a niche for any other overt bloc interference into the movement's affairs.[102] Nevertheless, this issue of uncritically expanding membership in order to gradually push back bloc structures, which was essentially the Yugoslav idea of increasing the NAM's global relevance but without taking into account the 'quality' of new members and what kind of effect this could produce on the movement's functioning, eventually triggered a serious principled debate between the Yugoslav and Indian diplomats and scholars for years to come.[103]

The CB ministerial meeting in Algiers was held on 30 May–2 June 1976 and it was attended by twenty-nine observers. Initially, this event was to be held in New Delhi, but Algeria pressed to be the host, so India reluctantly withdrew its candidacy.[104] The main goal of this CB meeting was to coordinate all preparations for the Colombo Conference, especially with respect to setting down its agenda and drafting the final documents. Some participants also aspired to discuss the current complex international situation, as well as to review the participation criteria for observers and guests. Furthermore, Yugoslavia wanted to expand the CB's mandate by defining precisely the principles of its functioning, as well establishing its working core for launching rapid reactions to any unforeseen world developments.[105] Iraq and Libya raised again the issue of officially setting up the movement's secretariat, an initiative strongly opposed by Algeria, Yugoslavia and others, while North Korea also proposed to hold the NAM ministerial conferences twice a year, an idea that was considered by many as quite unpractical.[106]

During the general debate, most of the attention was dedicated to major political issues and different crisis hotspots, with the majority of participants sharing similar views in this respect. This constructive spirit also found its reflection in the final declaration. Only serious disagreements could be found between Syria and Egypt over Cairo's negotiations with the US and Israel, as well as regarding Syria's role in the Lebanon crisis, with some dissenting tones also tackling the Algerian–Moroccan conflict in Western Sahara or trying to tone down the uncritical praise of the USSR by some attendees. Algerian and Yugoslav delegations dominated the debate, often backed by India, thus blunting Cuban, Syrian and Libyan criticism, while the Sri Lankan delegation, even though the host of the next summit, demonstrated a serious passivity, thus leaving many doubts about its ability to hold off the potential radical onslaught in Colombo.[107] As for economic issues, decisions adopted in Algiers and Lima were reiterated again, while serious concern was raised over the deteriorating economic situation. The paralysis in the functioning of the Solidarity Fund was particularly criticized, since only seventeen out of forty necessary signatories ultimately decided to join this body and extend their contributions.[108]

However, what seemed to be another major controversy at this event was again the participation criteria for bloc nations, whether they could be invited as guests or observers or not invited at all. India again strongly rejected any attendance of bloc members, while Yugoslavia advocated a more flexible approach on an ad hoc basis. Since no compromise could be found, it was decided for the Colombo summit to finally determine the status of Romania, Portugal, Australia and the Philippines, and previous guests and observers were invited again, thus indirectly implying the final abandonment of the Lima formula. In addition, Angola, Comoros, Seychelles and Maldives were now accepted as NAM members, while Belize was accorded with special status, since it was still not formally independent.[109]

As previously noted, this meeting had a far-reaching impact regarding the CB's future role and shape, since many participants reached an agreement that as many countries as possible should become its members, thus making this body more democratic and regionally representative, with the rotation of membership within each regional group intended to prevent any monopoly of power. Therefore, Yugoslavia's initial proposal was adopted with only minor alterations, with four key principles set as the basis for this reform: membership expansion, permanent character, rotation of the chairman and balanced geographic presence. It was recommended to the summit to expand the CB's membership to twenty-five countries, with this body regularly meeting once a year at a ministerial level and once a month at the level of permanent representatives in New York. Based on this, the CB's role was more precisely determined: implementation of summit decisions, coordination of preparations for summits and different NAM meetings, deliberations of crucial international events, organization of collective actions and coordination of all activities in the UN.[10]

Yet another tendency was also becoming increasingly present among different members. There was a fear that the Colombo summit would become a stage for a new round of struggles for leadership among different countries or groups, where bilateral conflicts would eventually dominate the debate, instead of general issues, with new divisions coming to the forefront, thus bringing into peril movement's hard-won unity.[111] It seemed to some members, like Malaysia, that this event would not have the capacity to deal with major issues like before, since it would be preoccupied with internal disputes and bilateral conflicts.[112] In the mind of Egyptian officials, this summit would not be a venue for confrontation between the 'progressive' and 'conservative' forces as claimed by some, but a showdown between truly non-aligned countries and the ones acting on behalf of the US or the USSR.[113] Even Sri Lankan hosts were concerned that profound polarization between different groups would leave a lasting stamp on this event.[114] This was, in fact, an early harbinger of ominous trends affecting the NAM until the next summit in Havana.

Furthermore, the NAM was also trying to break up the monopoly on information compilation and distribution of a handful of Western and Eastern news agencies predominantly shaping the worldwide public opinion (AP, AFP, UPI, Reuters, DPA, TASS, Xinhua). The majority of non-aligned countries considered these agencies as either being not objective enough to their respective situation, often pointing out the negative side, or holding out some key information necessary for the policy-planning activities of these nations.[115] Therefore, as a precursor to the 'New International Information Order' (NIIO) being officially launched at a seminar in Tunisia in March 1976, the Non-Aligned News Agency Pool (NANAP) was established in Belgrade on 20 January 1975. This was a fully fledged alliance of twelve major non-aligned news agencies, not any supra-national institution, initially headed by the Yugoslav news agency 'Tanjug'.[116] These decisions heralded an undertaking aimed at completing total decolonization of information, while liberating the non-aligned public sphere from outside information manipulation. Essentially, the NAM's immediate strategic goal was to distribute around the world unedited information about its member states, thus trying to reclaim direct control over the image they produced both internally and externally. This work was officially completed at a special conference organized in New Delhi on 8–13 July 1976.[117]

The Colombo Conference

Based on the decisions made at Lima, the Colombo Conference finally took place on 16–19 August 1976, preceded by a CB preparatory meeting on 9–11 August and the NAM ministerial conference occupying the three days after the event. This was a moment when the movement, due to its active role in the North–South dialogue and the successful completion of national-liberation struggle in Indochina and most of Africa, seemed to be in its prime, ready to assert a more influential role in world affairs. In order for the hosts to organize a successful summit, a number of countries extended their considerable financial and technical support to the Sri Lankan government so as to secure this goal (Iraq and Libya offered US$1 million each, Algeria US$600,000, Qatar US$500,000, North Korea US$500,000, Kuwait US$250,000, while China assisted in constructing the conference hall).[118] For example, Yugoslavia extended its assistance in the amount of US$500,000 for the purchase of dozens of teleprinters, typewriters, office equipment, cars, flags and an internal television system for the conference hall and the airport, while Yugoslav experts gave advice with respect to organizing everything related to the conference infrastructure, protocol, hosting of delegations and security.[119]

The initial role of the CB preparatory meeting was to discuss the drafts of the summit's political and economic declarations, a work which was then transferred to the ministerial conference, while the CB prepared the final proposal for the reform of its mandate, structure and functions based on the revised Yugoslav document.[120] As for the NAM ministerial conference, its main duty was to adopt the summit agenda, establish political and economic committees to deal with the final documents (chairmen from Tanzania and Panama), elect the summit chairman and eighteen vice-chairman (six from Asia, six from Africa, four from Latin America and two from Europe) and finally decide upon the observer and guest status of some countries. However, a heated debate erupted between the Indian and some African delegations over the CB's regional representation, i.e. who would have more seats in this body. In the end, it was decided that until the next summit Europe would only have one representative (Yugoslavia), Latin America four (Cuba, Peru, Guyana and Jamaica), while Asia and Africa would have eight and twelve respectively, eventually leaving it for each group to choose its candidates.[121] New composition of the CB included the following countries: eleven old members (Algeria, Cuba, Guyana, India, Liberia, Peru, Sri Lanka, Syria, Tanzania, Yugoslavia and Zaire) and fourteen new ones (Afghanistan/Bangladesh, Angola, Botswana, Chad, Guinea, Indonesia, Iraq, Jamaica, Niger, Nigeria, PLO, Sudan, Vietnam and Zambia). It was decided that Bangladesh would serve for the first eighteen months, then yield its seat to Afghanistan for the second half of that term. It is conspicuous that Egypt, one of the founding members, was excluded from this structure due to strong Arab opposition.[122]

Nevertheless, the bulk of attention at this ministerial conference was dedicated to the role and character of non-alignment, the criteria for participation, as well as to defining new ways of coordinating the NAM's collective activities. The tendency to advocate closer association with the Soviet bloc was effectively sidelined by Yugoslavia, Algeria and India, while Saudi and Libyan attempts to project decisions of the last Islamic Conference were also subverted by them.[123] The Yugoslav Foreign Secretary directly raised the issue of the 'natural alliance' with the Cuban Foreign Minister Raul Roa, admonishing him that any similar initiatives would seriously affect the unity and solidarity of the movement. Under such pressure, the Cuban and Vietnamese delegations eventually decided to withdraw their proposals.[124] However,

India and Yugoslavia were also pursuing a line that this summit should clearly define the role of non-aligned countries inside the G77, especially since some other Third World initiatives, launched by Pakistan or Mexico, were aimed at decreasing the NAM's influence inside that group.[125]

In fact, the most heated debate at this event occurred again over the presence of bloc members such as Romania, Australia, Portugal, Pakistan and the Philippines as guests of this summit. The majority of delegations were ready to award some of these countries with guest status, but eventually it was decided to accept only Romania, Portugal and the Philippines, with other applications being rejected until the next summit (Pakistan did not even submit its application). This was, indeed, a compromise between different groups led by Yugoslavia and India, hesitantly opening the NAM to the remote possibility of eventually embracing into its ranks some bloc defectors, while still preserving the essence of old participation criteria for any future applicants. Therefore, members and observers were still being subjected to very strict vetting, while, conversely, rules for summit guests were loosened up a bit.[126]

The 5th NAM summit in Colombo was hitherto the largest event in the movement's history and the biggest gathering of international leaders in Asia after Bandung. It was meticulously organized, with three thousand foreign guests attending, among them more than six hundred journalists from all over the world.[127] This conference was attended by 114 delegations, among them eighty-six full members, twenty-one observers (nine countries, seven national-liberation movements and five international organizations), as well as seven guest countries, most of them from Europe, even though there were fewer heads of state or government present compared to the Algiers Conference. As for the conference agenda, the main issues were: the role and place of non-alignment in international affairs, its strategic orientation, and its concrete contribution during the previous fifteen years, assessments of the world situation, crisis hotspots, mutual political and economic cooperation, disarmament, role of the UN, etc. This gathering, similar to previous NAM summits, eventually adopted the 'Political and Economic Declarations', the 'Action Program for Economic Cooperation' and the 'Decision Regarding the Composition and Mandate of the CB', as well as thirty-two different resolutions dealing with specific political and economic issues.[128]

During the general debate, as well as in the summit's 'Political Declaration', all participants praised the consistent role of the NAM in forwarding the struggle for ending decolonization. Its concrete contribution to overcoming the threat of a nuclear war and bloc divisions was again stressed, as was its continuous advocacy of the establishment of a new model of international political and economic relations based on the paramount principles of independence and equality. Therefore, as agreed by all, the movement had become an unavoidable factor in world affairs, one strictly promoting further democratization of state-to-state relations and ending any kind of domination. Furthermore, the economic component of international relations was being observed by NAM leaders as closely related to the political one, thus becoming a dominant feature of the Colombo Conference to firmly integrate the political and economic contexts. Therefore, as attendees believed, the efforts involved in establishing the NIEO had become an integral part of the greater struggle for the general overhaul of the entire world order to create a viable global political and economic alternative encompassing all nations and moving beyond the narrow policies of bloc divisions, balance of power, arms race and spheres of influence.[129]

Yet the majority of participants were also very critical with respect to détente, considering that any lessening of inter-bloc tensions only further induced the superpowers to increase their Third World interference. For the first time in Colombo, détente was not praised but openly brought into question by the NAM. Support for the liberation struggle around the world was reiterated, while a separate 'Solidarity Fund for the Liberation of Southern Africa' was also established. Israel was again threatened to be ultimately expelled from the UN, also due to its close relationship with South Africa, while a special NAM committee on the Middle East was also set up. In addition, based on Yugoslavia's proposal, it was also endorsed to hold a UNGA special session on disarmament in 1978, thus finally bringing the discussion on arms control issues fully under the auspices of the UN.[130] In fact, despite a certain degree of radicalization of the NAM, closer coordination between Sri Lanka, India and Yugoslavia with respect to all proceedings and drafting of final documents ultimately managed to grind down the radical steamrolling tactics and steer the entire summit in a more moderate direction.[131]

Nevertheless, some participants, like Sadat and Qaddafi, stressed that the gravest danger to non-aligned countries now came from their immediate neighbours. In this respect, countries in peril often decided to seek support and protection from different great powers first and only afterwards from the NAM, thus demonstrating their lack

Figure 5 Fifth Summit of the Non-Aligned Movement: President Tito's speech on plenary session, Colombo, 17 August 1976. © Museum of Yugoslavia.

of trust in the movement's capacity to resolutely act. This negative tendency, in their opinion, had to be overcome in order to preserve the movement's coherence, and thus bilateral conflicts had to be either avoided or quickly settled, before the great powers could eventually interfere.[132] Therefore, during this summit, Tito even made a tentative proposal for establishing a special body within the NAM that would exclusively deal with bilateral conflicts between different members and try to effectively mediate them, since, in his opinion, such ideological, religious, historical or geographic divisions were causing serious harm to the movement's unity, downgrading its capacity to act, not to mention its international prestige.[133]

As for economic issues, a very pessimistic assessment of the current international economic situation was offered, one where the overall socioeconomic situation in the developing world, above all due to its rising indebtedness (from US$12.2 billion in 1973 to over US$40 billion in 1975), which had been continuously deteriorating. In the view of many NAM leaders, the obvious responsibility of all developed nations, both capitalist and socialist, for this kind of adverse situation was clear, especially due to their overt resistance to implementing decisions passed at the two previous UNGA special sessions and consecutive UNCTAD meetings. However, the role of the spike in oil prices in the additional pauperization of the developing world was not mentioned at all, obviously due to the presence of some influential OPEC members. Despite everything, the spirit of cooperation with the Global North ultimately prevailed, although it was coated in a certain amount of scepticism. Therefore, concrete efforts for the establishment of the NIEO were praised again, while, as all participants agreed, more had to be done in the future with respect to restructuring the world trade and production, establishing new monetary arrangements, enabling adequate transfers of resources and technologies, reducing external debt and extending adequate financial assistance.[134]

In order to start implementing these economic decisions, the NAM undertook the institutionalization of cooperation in fifteen different economic areas, each having a country-coordinator in charge of procuring finances and developing new initiatives. Besides, the 'Special Fund for Financing Buffer Stocks' was finally set up. Mutual cooperation in the fields of industrialization, agriculture, transportation, telecommunications, insurance, healthcare, education, science and technology, culture, tourism, media, sports, etc. were again promoted through the establishment of specialized centres dealing with some of these areas (science and technology in Peru, public enterprises in Yugoslavia, multinational corporations in Cuba). Other economic initiatives included: establishing a joint NAM currency, as well as a payment union; founding a commercial bank for the developing world; and integrating financial institutions for financing sub-regional and regional projects. All these proposals were guided by the overarching idea to fundamentally reform the international financial and monetary systems as a necessary precondition for the successful establishment of the NIEO.[135] However, certain disagreements were inevitable, since some participants aspired to preserve their preferential treatment with some developed markets, like the oil producers, while others wanted to protect their exports from competition, thus receiving better prices for a certain category of raw materials. All this went against the general intention to support the least-developed nations.[136] Ideas were diverse, desire for their realization sincere, but there was still a lot of work to be done. At the same time many divisive issues were emerging, which affected the NAM's capacity to primarily become an economic and not only political pressure group.

Conference Aftermath

According to US analysts, the Colombo Conference, unlike its predecessor, was generally marked by moderation, at least verbally moving away from the spirit of confrontation, further nurturing universalist tendencies at the expense of regionalist ones, advocating primacy of economic development over political divergence, but being increasingly plagued by a rising trend that the movement should eventually become a Soviet-affiliated anti-imperialist bloc. However, as a countervailing point to such tendencies, moderates were also beginning to stand up and start to fight back, thus announcing the future trial of strength between these two major groupings.[137] Nevertheless, the radicalization drive still had not prevailed. As noted by British diplomats present on the sidelines, this summit's strong point was the achievement of a clear consensus on South Africa and the NIEO, but its greatest weakness stemmed from the fact that it also tried to seek out common ground on so many diverse issues on a too simplistic basis, thus contributing to the lack of clarity in forwarding the NAM's general agenda, irrespective of individual policies of its members.[138]

However, the USSR was not quite satisfied with the outcome of this gathering that was less inspired by an anti-imperialist agenda, considering that Moscow's intensive propaganda efforts and its work through proxies to sway the movement in its favour had still not borne fruit, similar to its attempt to trigger an internal ideological split that would push the NAM into a more confrontationist mood vis-à-vis the West and China. Furthermore, countries like Sri Lanka were pursuing total neutralization of the Indian Ocean, thus also limiting Soviet access to that region, which also proved to be frustrating for the Kremlin.[139] In fact, China was the only one among the great powers that was pretty content with the results of this summit, considering that Beijing's approach to the issues of consistent opposition to superpower hegemony, especially the Soviet one, economic cooperation between developing nations and establishment of different zones of peace had ultimately gained prominence at this event.[140]

Conclusion

The Colombo Conference, in spite of its modest success, nonetheless became a place where two contradictory tendencies in the history of the movement finally met in one place, further adding to the internal polarization that would mark the latter half of the 1970s. On one side, there were long-standing aspirations for the achievement of lofty goals set by the NIEO, aimed at restructuring the entire world order, while, on the other, there were concrete difficulties acting in the opposite direction that increasingly affected NAM's efficiency and cohesiveness (economic crisis, rise of radicalism, ideological divisions, factionalism and foreign interference). With the extensive expansion of its membership, the NAM had become, in the words of a Yugoslav diplomat, 'vulnerable' to outside interference with respect to certain issues, thus discovering a lesser number of common points on which they could all achieve a unified position. This also meant that Belgrade was slowly reconsidering its earlier concept of loose membership criteria.[141] Under the banner of positive messages being sent out from the Sri Lankan capital, much more sombre prospects were lurking in the background, those which Tito linked in his summit speech to an outright danger of imposing monolithic unity on the movement, a tendency which could have produced dire consequences and eventually contributed to its final split into two camps, almost along Cold War lines.[142]

The choice of Havana as the venue for the next summit in 1979, which was primarily motivated by the obvious desire to avoid any further conflicts and prevent any new fissures with the radicals, demonstrated that a growing number of members, both those moderate ones and the ones more or less openly tilting towards the West, could still not easily reconcile themselves with the increasing influence of pro-Soviet radicalism within the NAM that could have pushed more timid and reluctant members to eventually acquiesce with the Cuban and Vietnamese line. Furthermore, profound wealth disparities between the rich and poor non-aligned countries, with the former being increasingly less ready to share their affluence with the latter, instead investing it into the North's financial markets, also contributed to the emergence of new splinters inside the NAM, even more so than the evident reluctance of the developed world to give in to the movement's demands. Sometimes it seemed that the individual needs of certain member states were gradually gaining the upper hand over the collectivist demands of the entire movement, thus making somewhat pointless the entire effort for the successful advancement of the NIEO.[143] With time, conciliatory remarks and a certain degree of understanding expressed by some circles in the West gave ground to a more biased stand that depicted the NIEO as being an irrational, vindictive, self-serving and basically revolutionary concept, thus creating a coalition of intertwined interests directed against all the movement's efforts in this respect.[144] Therefore, the NAM's fundamental search for a new world order, still without achieving any major breakthroughs at Colombo, had slowly evolved into a frantic search for its own soul, one that would test the movement's unity and purpose to the very limit, thus triggering serious repercussions for its subsequent future.

Notes

1 Jeffrey A. Hart, *The New International Economic Order: Conflict and Cooperation in North-South Economic Relations, 1974–77* (London: Palgrave Macmillan, 1983), 30–61; Nils Gilman, 'The New International Economic Order: A Reintroduction', *Humanity* 6.1 (2015), 2–8.
2 Charles S. Meier, 'Malaise: the Crisis of Capitalism in the 1970s', in *The Shock of the Global*, 25–48.

3 Giuliano Garavini, *After Empires*, 174–83; Sara Lorenzini, *Global Development*, 119–23; Victor McFarland, 'The New International Economic Order, Interdependence, and Globalization', *Humanity* 6.1 (2015), 219–22.
4 Raymond L. Garthoff, *Détente and Confrontation*, 458–525, 594–620; Vladislav Zubok, *A Failed Empire*, 229–47; Thomas Crump, *Brezhnev and the Decline of the Soviet Union*, 149–202; Daniel J. Sargent, *A Superpower Transformed: The Remaking of America's Foreign Relations in the 1970s* (Oxford: Oxford University Press, 2015), 100–97.
5 Michael Cotey Morgan, *The Final Act: The Helsinki Accords and the Transformation of the Cold War* (Princeton, NJ: Princeton University Press, 2018), 108–235.
6 Thomas Fischer, *Neutral Power in the CSCE: the N+N States and the Making of the Helsinki Accords 1975* (Baden-Baden: Nomos, 2009); Jovan Čavoški, 'On the Road to Belgrade: Yugoslavia's Contribution to the Defining of the Concept of European Security and Cooperation, 1975–1977', in *From Helsinki to Belgrade: The First CSCE Follow-up Meeting and the Crisis of Détente*, Vladimir Bilandžić, Dittmar Dahlmann and Milan Kosanović (eds) (Bonn: Bonn University Press, 2012), 84–100.
7 Jan Asmussen, *Cyprus at War: Diplomacy and Conflict during the 1974 Crisis* (London: I.B. Tauris, 2008), 21–239.
8 DAMSPS, PA, 1974, f-174, 443179, 'Foreign Secretariat's telegram', 6 September 1974.
9 DAMSPS, PA, 1974, f-174, 448834, 'Telegram from UN', 12 September 1974.
10 DAMSPS, PA, 1974, f-174, 452361, 'Foreign Secretariat's telegram', 4 November 1974.
11 Alvin Z. Rubinstein, *Moscow's Third World Strategy* (Princeton, NJ: Princeton University Press, 1990), 32–8, 47–77, 95–124; Bruce D. Porter, *The USSR in Third World Conflicts: Soviet Arms and Diplomacy in Local Wars, 1945–1980* (Cambridge: Cambridge University Press, 1984), 26–35, 147–81.
12 Abraham Rabinovich, *The Yom Kippur War: The Epic Encounter that Transformed the Middle East* (New York, NY: Shocken Books, 2004), 85–440; Craig Daigle, *The Limits of Détente*, 294–331.
13 Victor Israelyan, *Inside the Kremlin during the Yom Kippur War* (University Park, PA: The Pennsylvania State University Press, 1995), 55–210; Alistair Horne, *Kissinger: 1973, the Crucial Year* (New York, NY: Simon and Schuster, 2009), 227–331.
14 Kenneth W. Stein, *Heroic Diplomacy: Sadat, Kissinger, Carter, Begin, and the Quest for Arab-Israeli Peace* (London: Routledge, 1999), 117–86; William B. Quandt, *Peace Process: American Diplomacy and the Arab-Israeli Conflict since 1967* (Washington DC, Berkeley: Brookings Institution Press, University of California Press, 2005), 130–73.
15 George J. Veith, *Black April: the Fall of South Vietnam, 1973–1975* (New York, NY: Encounter Books, 2012), 35–499; Ben Kiernan, *How Pol Pot Came to Power: Colonialism, Nationalism, and Communism in Cambodia* (New Haven, CT: Yale University Press, 2004), 297–393.
16 Raymond L. Garthoff, *Détente and Confrontation*, 556–93; Odd Arne Westad, *The Global Cold War*, 218–41; Piero Gleijeses, *Conflicting Missions*, 246–372.
17 Fiona Venn, *The Oil Crisis* (London: Pearson Education, 2002), 7–21, 154–63.
18 FRUS, 1969–1976, 35, National Security Policy 1973–76 (2014), 134.
19 Christopher R. W. Dietrich, *Oil Revolution: Anticolonial Elites, Sovereign Rights, and the Economic Culture of Decolonization* (Cambridge: Cambridge University Press, 2017), 263–301.
20 Dinesh Singh, 'Non-Alignment and New International Economic Order', in *Non-Alignment in the Eighties*, 161.

21 *Југословенско-алжирски односи 1956–1979* (Београд: Архив Југославије, 2014), 252–4, 257–8.
22 DAMSPS, PA, 1973, f-136, 453148, 'Foreign Secretariat's telegram', 14 December 1973.
23 DAMSPS, PA, 1974, f-173, 4178, 'Foreign Secretariat's telegram', 8 January 1974.
24 NARA, RG 59, CFPF, 1973–1979, ET, 1974COLOMB00466, 15 February 1974.
25 AJ, 837, KPR, I-2/56, 'President's visit to India, Bangladesh, Nepal, and Syria', 12 February 1974.
26 DAMSPS, PA, 1974, f-198, 48898, 'Telegram from UN', 25 February 1974.
27 DAMSPS, PA, 1974, f-198, 45175, 'Telegram from UN', 2 February 1974.
28 TNA, FCO 59/1231, 'Reflections on the Sixth Special Session', 12 June 1974.
29 FRUS, 1969-1976, 31, Foreign Economic Policy 1969–76 (2009), 428–31.
30 AJ, 837, KPR, I-4-a/16, 'CB meeting and the UNGA special session', 22 February 1974.
31 DAMSPS, PA, 1974, f-198, 45092, 'Telegram from UN', 5 February 1974.
32 DAMSPS, PA, 1974, f-198, 45567, 'Telegram from Egypt', 6 February 1974.
33 DAMSPS, PA, 1974, f-173, 412866, 'Telegram from Algeria', 17 March 1974.
34 DAMSPS, PA, 1974, f-173, 412867, 'Telegram from Algeria', 19 March 1974.
35 DAMSPS, PA, 1974, f-173, 413749, 'Foreign Secretariat's telegram', 28 March 1974.
36 DAMSPS, PA, 1974, f-173, 413845, 'Telegram from Algeria', 21 March 1974.
37 DAMSPS, PA, 1974, f-173, 417233, 'Telegram from Algeria', 22 March 1974.
38 NARA, RG 59, CFPF, 1973–1979, ET, 1974ALGIER00607, 21 March 1974.
39 NARA, RG 59, CFPF, 1973–1979, ET, 1974STATE048341, 11 March 1974.
40 DAMSPS, PA, 1974, f-198, 410983, 'Foreign Secretariat's telegram', 8 March 1974.
41 DAMSPS, PA, 1974, f-198, 415591, 'Foreign Secretariat's telegram', 5 April 1974.
42 DAMSPS, PA, 1974, f-198, 415656, 'Telegram from U.S.', 29 March 1974.
43 DAMSPS, PA, 1974, f-199, 418468, 'Telegram from UN', 11 April 1974.
44 FRUS, 1969-1976, 33, 1, Foundations of Foreign Policy (2012), 168–78.
45 DAMSPS, PA, 1974, f-198, 413683, 'Foreign Secretariat's telegram', 23 April 1974.
46 Odette Jankowitsch and Karl Sauvant, 'The Initiating Role of the Non-Aligned Countries', in *Changing Priorities on the International Agenda: The New International Economic Order*, Karl P. Sauvant (ed.) (Oxford: Pergamon Press, 1981), 68–72.
47 NARA, RG 59, CFPF, 1973-1979, ET, 1974STATE099106, 13 May 1974.
48 Daniel J. Sargent, 'North-South: the United States Responds to the New International Economic Order', *Humanity* 6.1 (2015), 207–10.
49 NARA, RG 59, CFPF, 1973–1979, ET, 1974JAKART07905, 27 June 1974.
50 DAMSPS, PA, 1974, f-174, 461984, 'Telegram from UN', 22 December 1974.
51 FRUS, 1969–1976, 38, 1, 224–9.
52 Ibid.
53 FRUS, 1969–1976, E-15, 1, Eastern Europe, doc. 71.
54 DAMSPS, PA, 1975, f-123, 42477, 'Telegram from U.S.', 16 January 1975.
55 Mark Mazower, *Governing the World*, 308–11.
56 Giuliano Garavini, *After Empires*, 215–24.
57 NARA, RG 59, CFPF, 1973–1979, ET, 1975COLOMB00294, 31 January 1975.
58 AJ, 837, KPR, I-4-a/18, 'Conference on Raw Materials, Dakar, 3–8 February 1975', 21 February 1975.
59 DAMSPS, PA, 1975, f-172, 43526, 'Foreign Secretariat's telegram', 28 January 1975.
60 DAMSPS, PA, 1975, f-172, 412777, 'Telegram from Cuba', 9 March 1975.
61 DAMSPS, PA, 1975, f-172, 413892, 'Telegram from Cuba', 18 March 1975.
62 DAMSPS, PA, 1975, f-172, 414485, 'Foreign Secretariat's telegram', 27 March 1975.
63 DAMSPS, PA, 1975, f-172, 414485, 'Foreign Secretariat's telegram', 26 March 1975.

64　AJ, 837, KPR, I-4-a/19, 'Report on the CB ministerial meeting in Havana, 17–19 March 1975', 24 March 1975.
65　NARA, RG 59, CFPF, 1973–1979, ET, 1975KUWAIT01431, 2 April 1975.
66　NARA, RG 59, CFPF, 1973–1979, ET, 1975STATE113936, 15 May 1975.
67　DAMSPS, PA, 1975, f-175, 436398, 'Foreign Secretariat's telegram', 28 July 1975.
68　DAMSPS, PA, 1975, f-174, 444707, 'Telegram from UN', 19 September 1975.
69　FRUS, 1969–1976, 31, 386–452.
70　FRUS, 1969–1976, E-14, 1, doc. 23.
71　DAMSPS, PA, 1975, f-175, 432059, 'Foreign Secretariat's telegram', 1 July 1975.
72　Југославија-САД: сусрети и разговори највиших званичника 1955–1980 (Београд: Архив Југославије, 2017), 352–3.
73　DAMSPS, PA, 1975, f-174, 441269, 'Telegram from Peru', 26 August 1975.
74　DAMSPS, PA, 1975, f-174, 44284, 'Foreign Secretariat's telegram', 11 September 1975.
75　TNA, FCO 58/855, 'The 5th non-aligned conference of foreign ministers', 8 September 1975.
76　AJ, 837, KPR, I-4-a/20, 'Telegram from Peru no. 304', 1 September 1975.
77　NARA, RG 59, CFPF, 1973–1979, ET, 1975STATE129263, 3 June 1975.
78　DAMSPS, PA, 1975, f-174, 454422, 'Telegram from India', 13 November 1975.
79　DAMSPS, PA, 1975, f-174, 441992, 'Telegram from UN', 2 September 1975.
80　AJ, 837, KPR, I-4-a/20, 'Lima ministerial conference, 25–30 August 1975', 17 September 1975.
81　TNA, FCO 58/855, 'Telegram from Peru', 4 September 1975.
82　NARA, RG 59, CFPF, 1973–1979, ET, 1975STATE238052, 6 October 1975.
83　FRUS, 1969–1976, E-14, 1, doc. 24.
84　DAMSPS, PA, 1975, f-198, 432137, 'Foreign Secretariat's telegram', 27 June 1975.
85　FRUS, 1969–1976, 31, 1003, 1012.
86　Ibid., 1006–7, 1010–11.
87　Ibid., 1014–15.
88　Henry A. Kissinger, *American Foreign Policy* (New York, NY: W.W. Norton, 1977), 239–76.
89　DAMSPS, PA, 1975, f-198, 443405, 'Telegram from UN', 10 September 1975.
90　Catherine B. Gwin, 'The Seventh Special Session: Toward a New Phase of Relations between the Developed and the Developing States?' in *The New International Economic Order: Confrontation or Cooperation between the North and South?*, Karl P. Sauvant and Hajo Hasenpflug (eds) (Boulder, CO: Westview Press, 1977), 103–14.
91　Ruslan Vasilievich Kostiuk and Ekaterina Petrovna Katkova, 'The Soviet Union and the Non-Aligned Movement', in *The 60th Anniversary of the Non-Aligned Movement*, 138–40.
92　FRUS, 1969–1976, E-14, 1, docs 36 and 38.
93　DAMSPS, PA, 1976, f-131, 42624, 'Telegram from U.S.', 16 January 1976.
94　Jürgen Dinkel, *The Non-Aligned Movement*, 192–4; Salim Yaqub, *Imperfect Strangers: Americans, Arabs, and U.S. Middle Eastern Relations in the 1970s* (Ithaca, NY: Cornell University Press, 2016), 176–80.
95　DAMSPS, PA, 1976, f-179, 413731, 'Foreign Secretariat's telegram', 17 March 1976.
96　DAMSPS, PA, 1976, f-174, 413044, 'Telegram from Sri Lanka', 6 March 1976.
97　AJ, 837, KPR, I-4-a/22, 'Boumedienne-Minić talks', 1 June 1976.
98　DAMSPS, PA, 1976, f-175, 440978, 'Telegram from Tanzania', 26 July 1976.
99　DAMSPS, PA, 1976, f-174, 41287, 'Telegram from UN', 9 January 1976.
100　DAMSPS, PA, 1976, f-174, 414385, 'Telegram from India', 15 March 1976.

101 NAI, MEA, HI/102(29)/76, 'Feasibility and eligibility of the Philippines, Thailand, and Pakistan for membership', 17 January 1976.
102 NAI, MEA, HI/103(3)/76, 'Criteria for admission of new members', 12 January 1976.
103 M. S. Rajan, *Studies on Nonalignment and the Nonaligned Movement*, 88–92.
104 NARA, RG 59, CFPF, 1973–1979, ET, 1976COLOMB00600, 17 February 1976.
105 AJ, 837, KPR, I-4-a/22, 'CB ministerial meeting in Algiers, 30 May–2 June 1976', 17 May 1976.
106 DAMSPS, PA, 1976, f-175, 430654, 'Telegram from Algeria', 1 June 1976.
107 NARA, RG 59, CFPF, 1973–1979, ET, 1976STATE176135, 16 July 1976.
108 DAMSPS, PA, 1976, f-175, 431196, 'Foreign Secretariat's telegram', 8 June 1976.
109 DAMSPS, PA, 1976, f-175, 431380, 'Telegram from Algeria', 3 June 1976.
110 AJ, 837, KPR, I-4-a/22, 'CB ministerial meeting in Algiers, 30 May–2 June 1976', 4 June 1976.
111 DAMSPS, PA, 1976, f-176, 441172, 'Telegram from Tunisia', 27 July 1976.
112 NARA, RG 59, CFPF, 1973–1979, ET, 1976USUNN02973, 21 July 1976.
113 DAMSPS, PA, 1976, f-175, 440933, 'Telegram from Egypt', 23 July 1976.
114 DAMSPS, PA, 1976, f-176, 443511, 'Telegram from Sri Lanka', 8 August 1976.
115 Herbert I. Schiller, 'Decolonization of Information: Efforts toward a New International Order', *Latin American Perspectives* 5.1 (1978), 36–44.
116 DAMSPS, PA, 1975, f-172, 43488, 'Foreign Secretariat's telegram', 27 January 1975.
117 Jürgen Dinkel, *The Non-Aligned Movement*, 196–201; AJ, 837, KPR, I-4-a/25, 'Conference of ministers of information of non-aligned countries, New Delhi, 8–13 July 1976', 21 July 1976.
118 W. M. Karundasa, *Sri Lanka and Non-Alignment*, 311–12.
119 AJ, 837, KPR, I-4-a/26, 'Sri Lanka's preparations for the 5th NAM summit', 6 October 1975.
120 DAMSPS, PA, 1976, f-176, 444130, 'Telegram from Sri Lanka', 10 August 1976.
121 DAMSPS, PA, 1976, f-177, 444685, 'Telegram from Sri Lanka', 14 August 1976.
122 Robert A. Mortimer, *The Third World Coalition in International Politics*, 89–91.
123 DAMSPS, PA, 1976, f-177, 444611, 'Telegram from Sri Lanka', 12 August 1976.
124 DAMSPS, PA, 1976, f-177, 444672, 'Telegram from Sri Lanka', 13 August 1976.
125 DAMSPS, PA, 1976, f-177, 444610, 'Telegram from Sri Lanka', 12 August 1976.
126 TNA, FCO 58/980, 'Telegram from Sri Lanka', 16 August 1976.
127 NAI, MEA, HI/1011(7)/77, 'Annual political report for 1976', 14 April 1977.
128 DAMSPS, PA, 1976, f-178, 446809, 'Foreign Secretariat's telegram', 26 August 1976.
129 AJ, 837, KPR, I-4-a/26, 'Report on the 5th NAM conference', 6 September 1976; *Documents of the Gatherings of the Non-Aligned Countries*, 1, 160–74.
130 Ibid.
131 TNA, FCO 58/982, 'The 5th non-aligned summit', 27 August 1976.
132 Dragan Bogetić, *Nesvrstanost kroz istoriju*, 368–9.
133 AJ, 837, KPR, I-4-a/26, 'Tito-Bandaranaike talks', 20 August 1976.
134 AJ, 837, KPR, I-4-a/26, 'Report on the 5th NAM conference', 6 September 1976; *Documents of the Gatherings of the Non-Aligned Countries*, 1, 174–87.
135 NAI, MEA, FIII/102/33/81, 'Non-aligned summit conferences (1961–1979)'; *Documents of the Gatherings of the Non-Aligned Countries*, 1, 174–87.
136 TNA, FCO 58/982, 'The 5th non-aligned summit', 27 August 1976.
137 NARA, RG 59, CFPF 1973–1979, ET, 1976STATE224884, 11 September 1976.
138 TNA, FCO 58/982, 'Telegram from Sri Lanka', 24 August 1976.

139 PAAA, M95 5.817, 'Information on the 5th NAM conference from the Soviet embassy in East Germany', 5 August 1976.
140 NARA, RG 59, CFPF, 1973–1979, ET, 1976STATE267007, 29 October 1976.
141 NARA, RG 59, CFPF, 1973–1979, ET, 1976BELGRA06146, 17 September 1976.
142 M. S. Rajan, *Nonalignment and Nonaligned Movement*, 241–2.
143 Mark Atwood Lawrence, 'The Rise and Fall of Nonalignment', 152.
144 Helen E. S. Nesadurai, 'Bandung and the Political Economy of North-South Relations', 81–4; Craig N. Murphy, *Global Institutions, Marginalization, and Development* (London: Routledge, 2005). 115–17.

7

For the Soul of the NAM: the 1979 Havana Conference

The late 1970s constituted a specific period when the NAM was internationally most recognizable and very influential, while it had also drawn correspondingly heightened attention from both superpowers. However, unlike the preceding years, this rapid deterioration of superpower relations directly reflected on the state and the course of the rising internal power struggle then plaguing the movement. In this way, as this chapter will demonstrate, the NAM was put again at the crossroads of the East–West conflict, though not as a potential mediator but rather as the primary arena for the new round of inter-bloc confrontation. Therefore, the East–West dimension was complemented by the new intensive South–South conflict that would put the NAM's very future into question, forcefully redirecting its major priorities from external to more pressing internal ones.

The situation after the Colombo Conference was primarily characterized by the rapid collapse of the superpower détente, triggering wide-ranging political and economic turmoil, affecting not only the state of inter-bloc relations but the overall international situation as well. In fact, it was the receding mutual trust, depleted strategic agendas, strong domestic pressures, as well as booming superpower ambitions that all contributed to the speedy downfall of détente. Therefore, aggressive bloc competition would again become the hallmark of their mutual dealings, thus ushering in an era of the so-called Second Cold War, one resembling the tense strategic situation of the late 1950s and early 1960s. This kind of a negative trend led many knowledgeable observers to conclude that détente was effectively buried in the Third World, while its superpower essence was essentially worn out after the CSCE formation.

Yet the evident failure of the North–South dialogue, marked by a clear lack of willingness on the part of the developed world, especially the US, to further compromise its established global standing, one also mirrored by a growing disillusionment of many of the NAM members in this respect, all contributed to the final dissolution of the NIEO initiative. Great hopes for the radical stabilization of the world situation and the expansion of economic progress and prosperity into the four corners of the globe had been rapidly fading away, actively replacing the well-intended ideals with escalating conflicts and social upheaval not dissimilar to those occurring around the Third World during the mid-1960s, when it had been fundamentally reshaped.

In fact, all these negative trends would indicate that the NAM had entered squarely into a precarious phase of increased factionalism, both leftist and rightist, which could have resulted in the movement ultimately tearing itself apart. Since collective undertakings of the NAM members, like the NIEO, eventually proved to be futile, some members were increasingly opting for a tentative rapprochement with certain great powers, a move which, in their mind, offered them more concrete security guarantees than the NAM's sheer numbers ever could. However, this kind of thinking gradually evolved into an outright attempt, mainly staged by countries leaning towards the Soviet bloc, to effectively side the movement with Moscow's policies. The Havana Conference would thus mark the apex of this competition between different factions inside the movement, an outright struggle for the soul of the NAM between Yugoslavia and Cuba, and thus, strangely enough, also marking the movement's high point and its greatest visibility in international history.

Collapsing Détente and the Third World

Despite earlier developments, like its predecessors, the new Carter administration decided to keep up with pursuing détente but now gave more prominence to a somewhat altered agenda, one that also emphasized other relevant topics, such as the state of human rights and democracy within the Soviet bloc countries. This controversial start in bilateral affairs was clearly perceived by the Kremlin as a basic negation of the previously reached level of mutual accommodation, thus clearly indicating that it would be very hard reaching any meaningful results on major issues if the US insistence on the domestic agenda would often prevail. In addition, Carter's decision to fully normalize relations with China and substantially increase anti-Soviet coordination with Beijing only further alienated Moscow and contributed to its sieged fortress mentality. Even the 1977–8 CSCE follow-up process in Belgrade had become embroiled in counterproductive ideological accusations, while the shattering failure to ratify the SALT II agreement in the US Congress after the first and last Carter–Brezhnev summit in Vienna in June 1979 also testified to the fact that détente had become both obsolete and irrelevant. Lack of mutual trust and common goals, a shortage of new incentives for further expansion and diversification of bilateral relations, as well as diminishing restraint in Third World engagements had all contributed to détente's final collapse.[1]

However, while Washington perceived Moscow's growing involvement in the Third World as going against the very essence of détente and US policies there, the Soviet leadership was quite convinced that any such developments could still not seriously undermine the high-priority character of the superpower relationship in areas like arms control or economic exchanges. This new wave of Soviet direct or proxy interventionism, present since 1975, although not always firmly orchestrated by Moscow, was, nonetheless, considered by the Kremlin as something ideologically acceptable, as well as part of the newly set rules of the global game. Yet this was a serious strategic miscalculation on behalf of the Soviets, since it demonstrated Moscow's inherently flawed apprehension of the US domestic situation, the impact the Vietnam War and Watergate had on the American psyche, as well as crucial differences in the foreign policy priorities advocated by the Nixon/Ford and Carter administrations. Only when the Soviets finally understood that the sudden emergence of a string of pro-Soviet regimes in places such as Angola, Ethiopia, Vietnam, South Yemen, Nicaragua, Afghanistan, etc. only added new pressures to old US sore points, causing domestic mobilization over there, it was already far too late for the USSR to backtrack. By the end of 1979, détente was effectively dead and a new round of fierce Cold War competition had just begun.[2]

In this way, any conflict in the Third World, even a minor one, was being increasingly observed by the blocs through the Cold War lens, essentially evolving into yet another part of the ongoing global confrontation. Africa had become the centre stage of such perilous developments where local frictions received significantly heightened superpower attention. What was particularly characteristic of this period, ultimately proving to be the greatest challenge to non-alignment from within, would be the rise of a new generation of radical Third World leaders that would freely embrace bloc ideologies, especially the Soviet-style Marxism, perceiving them as being the right remedies for preserving their nation's independence.[3] Conflicts between the non-aligned countries dominating the African and Asian geopolitical landscape in the latter half of the 1970s were: the Algeria–Morocco–Mauritania conflict over Western Sahara; the Angola–Zaire conflict over the province of Shaba (Katanga); the Ethiopia–Somalia conflict over the province of Ogaden; the Tanzania–Uganda conflict; the Libya–Chad conflict; the Egypt–other Arab countries conflict over the policy of reconciliation with Israel; the Syria–PLO conflict in Lebanon; and the Vietnam–Kampuchea conflict, ending in the Vietnamese invasion.[4]

Since 1975, Algeria, Morocco and Mauritania had been engaged in confrontation over the future status of the former Spanish colony of Western Sahara. While Spain was ready to hand over this territory to two neighbouring nations, Morocco and Mauritania, Algeria was vociferously advocating its full independence and closer ties to Algiers, strongly backing the local national-liberation movement, the Polisario Front. This soon triggered indirect military confrontation between the three sides, with Algeria standing firmly behind Polisario, while Morocco and Mauritania decided to dispatch their troops into Western Sahara, trying to ultimately divide its territory and take control over its rich phosphate deposits, thus becoming drawn into a protracted guerrilla war there. Military conflict between these three non-aligned nations would also get its diplomatic extension in the active and divisive political struggle often being waged inside the OAU and the NAM.[5]

The civil war in Angola was still raging on without an end in sight, with South African incursions becoming almost customary and the Cubans and Soviets standing behind the legitimate government in Luanda, while the rebel forces were receiving their fair share of support from South Africa, Zaire and the US. When on two occasions, in March 1977 and May 1978, Zairian exiles staged massive incursions from Angola into the neighbouring province of Shaba as a way to initiate the overthrow of Mobutu Sese Seko, these actions not only re-inflamed the conflict between the two countries but also resulted in a French airlift of Moroccan troops who were then used to suppress this intrusion. These actions were also closely followed by the French and Belgian reinforcements being dispatched on US planes. Shaba I and Shaba II operations had evolved into multilateral conflicts involving a number of non-aligned states, Zaire and Morocco against Angola and Cuba, with the USSR, France and the US extending their aid accordingly.[6]

However, one of the most important conflicts in Africa at that time, which stood at the crossroads of the collapsing détente, increased Soviet interventionism and triggered new conflicts to break out between non-aligned countries themselves, was related to Ethiopia. After the victory of the Ethiopian revolution in 1974, one that overthrew the monarchy and initiated a political divorce from the US, a strong leftist turn in all spheres of life was soon undertaken, embodied in the face of the military rule of the Dergue (Committee) headed by Major Haile Mariam Mengistu. This kind of political course was bound to stir trouble on the domestic front, especially in the volatile province of Eritrea, resulting in the launching of a brutal campaign of terror against all dissenters in 1976–7. Such a time of escalating internal chaos was eventually utilized by Somalia, an old-time Soviet client, to raise again its claims to the neighbouring province of Ogaden where ethnic Somalis resided, thus transforming Addis Ababa's domestic turmoil into a full-blown regional crisis.[7]

As a result, customary geopolitical roles in the Horn of Africa had started to shift by 1977, with Ethiopia receiving more scrutiny and material backing from the Soviet bloc, while the Carter administration initiated its programme of support for Somalia's leader Mohammed Siad Barre. When the Somalis launched a well-planned attack into Ogaden in late July 1977, enjoying considerable initial success, a month later it seemed that the Ethiopian revolutionary experiment was at its sorrow end. This kind of crisis situation sounded the alarm in both Moscow and Havana, eventually resulting in a massive airlift of Soviet arms, advisors and thousands of Cuban troops that lasted well into 1978, soon prompting a devastating Somali defeat (Castro was initially reluctant to intervene but he eventually went along with Soviet plans). The Soviet bloc had thus gained a strong foothold in Ethiopia not only by co-opting a new geopolitical ally in the face of Mengistu but also by embracing an ardent ideological follower, with Moscow once again proving its credentials as a global power. Yet again, as the White House perceived it, the US had primarily lost its prestige, which added more negative pressure on the immediate future of the superpower détente.[8]

Similarly with the case of Africa, the volatile situation in the Middle East was also characterized by the emerging conflicts between non-aligned countries, as well as increased regional factionalism, even though bloc involvement in this region had never reached the level of intensity characteristic of the crisis situation in Africa. As for Egypt, Sadat continued pursuing rapprochement with the US, while simultaneously exploring possibilities for a direct settlement with Israel that could finally result in the return of occupied territories under Cairo's rule. On the contrary, Syria and Iraq, as well as the PLO and South Yemen, had become new Soviet political and military strongholds in the region. However, due to the eruption of the Lebanese Civil War in 1975, which also directly involved the PLO exiled there, a Syrian response in the form of an invasion of that country soon followed, resulting in not only a conflict between Damascus and the Palestinians but a further complicated local situation.[9]

While the Middle Eastern peace process in Geneva was facing a prolonged stalemate, Sadat decided to actively pursue his own line by unexpectedly visiting Jerusalem in November 1977, thus opening direct negotiations with the new Israeli Prime Minister Menachem Begin. However, a substantial breakthrough in these initial contacts was still no closer. Nevertheless, Sadat's decision to talk to the Israelis was so strongly denounced by some 'radical' Arab countries that it only pushed Cairo to sever diplomatic relations with them. This kind of a negative trend served as yet another incentive for Sadat to turn decisively to the Carter administration as a mediator in reaching a final agreement with Israel. Carefully balancing Israel's staunch position on preserving control over West Bank and Gaza and Sadat's intention not to be publicly perceived as one concluding a separate peace against Palestinian wishes, Carter had succeeded in securing the Camp David Accords in September 1978, as well as a full peace treaty in March 1979. In spite of Sadat's uneasiness, this was essentially a separate treaty between two mutually recognized nations that clearly satisfied their individual interests without framing them into any wider regional considerations. These accords caused an uproar in the Arab world, especially due to many other outstanding regional issues being left out of this bilateral deal with rather murky prospects. Egypt was initially suspended from the AL in November 1978, while in March the following year it was finally expelled from the organization, with its headquarters also moved from Cairo to Tunis. A similar scenario occurred soon after with the Islamic Conference and the OAPEC, while the NAM was waiting next in line for Egypt's potential expulsion.[10]

On the other side of the globe, the situation in Southeast Asia was also rapidly deteriorating, with the newly established communist regimes in Kampuchea and Vietnam continuously engaged in escalating mutual confrontation. In addition, Phnom Penh's close association with China and Hanoi's with the USSR also contributed to the perpetuation of the regional conflict, holding much wider repercussions for the rest of Asia.[11] After almost two years of incessant border skirmishes, together with the brutal persecution of minorities on both sides, the Vietnamese leadership, bolstered by the recent conclusion of the Treaty of Friendship and Cooperation with the USSR, decided to launch an invasion of Kampuchea in late December 1978. This military operation resulted in a swift ousting of the Pol Pot regime, now turning to guerrilla warfare against the invaders, and the installation of a Hanoi-friendly government of the People's Republic of Kampuchea (PRK) headed by Heng Samrin. Even though everyone was aware of the genocidal nature of the Khmer Rouge reign, invasion of a non-aligned country by another NAM member, especially one almost allied with one superpower, could not be understood, tolerated nor endorsed by the majority of the NAM members, as well as by China.[12]

Therefore, as a response to such a blatant breach of Kampuchea's sovereignty, perceiving this as yet another anti-Chinese move by the Soviet Union, in mid-February 1979, Beijing decided to invade the northern part of Vietnam in a punitive military action directed at teaching Hanoi a lesson and potentially overturning the situation in Kampuchea. Even though this was not a very successful foray from a military point of view, lasting less than a month, China still managed to complete many of its immediate tactical goals, even at a great cost, while as a result drawing Vietnam into a protracted two-front conflict during the entire 1980s, thus slowly draining

Hanoi's economic potential.¹³ Such Chinese action was not strongly denounced by the NAM, primarily due to Vietnam's earlier invasion of Kampuchea, but Deng Xiaoping's controversial statement comparing the 1962 Sino-Indian border war with this one naturally caused serious consternation in India, eventually pushing New Delhi into warming up to Moscow again, although without endorsing the stance of Soviet allies inside the NAM.¹⁴

The NAM's Internal Crisis and the Cuban–Yugoslav Competition

The second half of the 1970s was clearly marked by two outstanding, though contradictory, trends in the NAM's history. One was the intensive institutionalization and expansion of the movement, both in the domain of membership and the number of organized gatherings, thus indicating that the organization was still on the rise, while the other was an increasing destabilization embodied in the form of many different conflicts erupting between its member states, which clearly demonstrated the movement's growing inherent weakness and incapacity to react adequately.¹⁵ This kind of behind-the-scenes conflict occurred between countries edging closer to either of the two blocs, on one side, and on the other, the ones advocating strict adherence to a more balanced and non-bloc understanding of the NAM's global role. In time, some of these conflicts would seriously eclipse the primary responsibility of the movement that was promoted at previous summits, namely the establishment of a fundamentally different world order.¹⁶ In addition to these precarious developments, during this period Gandhi and Bandaranaike were also forced to step down due to electoral defeats in the first half of 1977, with some of their successors now openly demonstrating less interest in the traditional forms of non-alignment.¹⁷

In fact, previous attempts at keeping bilateral conflicts from substituting the general purpose of the movement was no longer possible due to their increasing numbers and intensive superpower involvement. Fear of a small group of countries assuming control over the movement had spurred earlier initiatives to significantly expand the NAM's membership, while at the same time this overexpansion had also introduced new problems associated with the movement's excessive growth, thus often causing corresponding paralysis of its internal functioning.¹⁸ In this way, the movement had demonstrated one of its long-term disadvantages: its outright inability to prevent or end bilateral conflicts between its members.¹⁹ These profound doubts were clearly voiced by an Ethiopian diplomat when he reasonably concluded that 'when someone is vitally in danger, he is not in a position to choose between the principles and long-term interests of the NAM and the desperately needed aid offered by the USSR and socialist countries'.²⁰ This was a hard choice to make, indeed, so the movement needed to invest far more effort into strengthening its mediation capabilities, before the superpower intervention could even occur.

This tendency of seeking cover under the superpower umbrella was also closely linked to an evident growth of internal radicalism. However, during the years at stake, leftist radicalism more assertively advocated the 'natural alliance' thesis of aligning the movement with the Soviet bloc. Such projections figured even more prominently due to the fact that Cuba was to host the next summit, the result of a painful compromise previously reached at Colombo as a means to placate the leftist group and transform it into a more constructive one. These kinds of overt leanings in Havana, Hanoi, Luanda and other places, nonetheless, could have resulted in the fundamental loss of the movement's global, independent and non-bloc character, even if they initially did not want to pursue such a course to the very limit.[21] This also went hand in hand with changing Soviet perceptions of the NAM's international role which was, according to them, now more in accordance with its 'original' anti-imperialist and anti-colonial essence.[22] According to the Yugoslav Foreign Secretary Miloš Minić, individual non-aligned countries could nurture positive or negative sentiments towards either of the two blocs or argue for cooperation with them but this should remain their private stance and they should never try to impose it on the entire movement, otherwise this would create far-reaching negative consequences.[23]

As we have seen, Cuba was often acting in the Soviet interests at different NAM gatherings. In many ways, during the 1970s, Cuba's authentic revolutionary experience had started to undergo a 'Sovietization' drive in all spheres of life, thus also contributing to an increased level of internal and external rigidity, which was all part of Havana's painful awareness of the necessity for nurturing Moscow's protective role.[24] Furthermore, events in Angola clearly demonstrated that Cuba was not a mere satellite but a country often pursuing its own agenda in the world, formally non-aligned but still not fully, and this often constituted a problem with some NAM members. However, Cuba's evident freedom of action could never be observed separately from its robust relationship with Moscow, especially when Castro clearly intended to project his own agenda on the entire movement, gradually putting the NAM in line with his own revolutionary ideas and eventually Soviet ones too, thus decisively separating it from the West, although still not fully subjugating it.[25]

In fact, top Cuban officials were convinced that their ideological alignment with the Soviet bloc was still not incompatible with their membership in the NAM, whilst the movement itself, as they saw it, did not represent any separate third way but was actively promoting the socialist path of development. However, advocacy for the NAM's unity for its own sake represented for Havana one of the major blunders that eventually blunted the movement's strong anti-imperialist and anti-colonial edge.[26] Some Cuban diplomats even claimed that the so-called leftist turn was not motivated by any desire to align the movement with the Soviet bloc but was happening because the US had largely remained opposed to the NAM's basic objectives, like decolonization or the North–South dialogue.[27] This kind of statement, nevertheless, demonstrated a high level of disenchantment among many NAM members with the Western handling of the NIEO or South Africa, thus creating a much wider pool of dissatisfaction internally, going beyond even the leftist group.

However, as privately conveyed by a high-ranking Cuban diplomat, Havana still aspired to be authentically non-aligned, similar to Yugoslavia or India, but living in the US backyard eventually forced its hand to fully rely upon the USSR. Any claims of total adherence to non-alignment, according to him, thus implying strict equidistance, would have only incited the Soviets to quickly abandon the island nation, and thus de facto ending Cuba's independence from the US.[28] In one of his internal deliberations,

Tito expressed his genuine empathy for Cuba's difficult position vis-à-vis both superpowers, which ultimately forced Castro to act in a certain way, but still he could not accept such an argument as a rationale for transforming the entire NAM into a mere 'pendant' of the Soviet bloc.[29] Since Cuba was not a classical Moscow satellite, this created a hint of a possibility that Havana could even be ready to preside over a rump NAM of ideologically congenial nations.[30] Furthermore, Cuba openly advocated that the movement should be primarily defined as an anti-imperialist, anti-colonial and anti-racist organization, not open to all developing nations but instead more of an exclusive club.[31]

However, apart from this proximity to Moscow, such policies were also part of a deliberate strategy to boost Havana's 'tricontinentalization' drive through the creeping leadership takeover in the NAM, a move that was largely inspired by the evident successes Cuba gained in Africa after the intervention in Angola. During one of his private talks with a high-ranking Guyanese officials, Castro stated that he felt convinced that the Havana summit would become Cuba's stellar moment to finally mobilize the entire NAM to stand with his views. Nevertheless, he was admonished by his interlocutor that the future summit should never be perceived as a gathering of only 'Cuban friends' but of all member states, even those who would have preferred Cuba not to host. In fact, as he stressed, the NAM's newly found internal dynamism should never be associated in any way with its further radicalization or rapprochement with either of the two blocs.[32] This stance was very close to Tito's own position that a truly 'progressive' character of non-alignment entailed a 'realistic positioning that rejects radicalism and quasi-revolutionary phrases and enables activities actually leading to the resolution of problems and [facilitating] the general progress of the world'.[33]

This overt Cuban challenge eventually became Tito's nightmare, compelling him to fight for the NAM's fledgling unity at the time of his advanced age and progressing illness. US analysts accurately defined the ongoing dilemma and challenges he was facing:

> He may also be concerned that his own leadership role in the NAM may be jeopardized by Cuban strength. Nevertheless, he knows that a viable NAM requires more internal unity than exists today and surfacing the Cuban problem would not help in this regard. He is thus in a quandary. He must promote unity; he needs to deal with a potentially divisive issue of Cuban credentials. Other NAM members are aware that the issue of Cuba's credentials will have to be either addressed or deftly swept under the rug.[34]

In this respect, during his meeting with Brezhnev in August 1977, Tito expressed his concerns that any attempt to fully materialize this division between the so-called 'progressive' and 'reactionary' forces in the NAM, as advocated by Cuba, could ultimately inflict irreparable damage to the movement's integrity.[35]

Yet subversive activities were not only coming from the Cubans. Countries such as Pakistan and Saudi Arabia, enjoying tacit backing from Washington, were also trying to split the NAM along geographic or religious lines, arguing for either Third

World or Islamic integration substituting the movement's comprehensive membership format. Some other pro-Western nations, for example Zaire, were investing efforts to downscale the movement's role in favour of G77, thus limiting the NAM's responsibility strictly to political issues.[36] What caused a significant level of concern was the US's increasing insistence on the respect for individual human rights. This kind of policy was often perceived by the NAM as a move to deflect attention from the responsibility of the developed world for the current economic crisis, thus substituting the North–South economic dialogue with this alternative. Therefore, many non-aligned countries started to perceive this Western insistence on human rights as primarily directed against the unity of the movement, one also subverting sovereignty of member states; thus, as a response, they put more emphasis on collective human rights, closely linking them to the economic and social rights of both individuals and entire nations in the developing world.[37]

Evidently, challenges to the NAM's authority were coming from all sides. According to a former Guyanese foreign minister, there were two outstanding dangers currently undermining the NAM's integrity: one was an obvious tendency to transform its nature, alter its goals and thus narrow its platform by subjecting it to specific Soviet policies, while the other was the noticeable trend to eventually divide and fragmentize the movement and the remains could then be firmly integrated with the Western bloc.[38] Therefore, the movement had to initiate a parallel search for its new role in order to adapt itself to rapidly deteriorating international conditions, while still operating outside the immediate superpower control. In fact, this conceptual clash between Cuba and Yugoslavia started soon after the Colombo summit ended and it only intensified as the new summit approached.[39]

The CB as a New Arena for Competition

While preparing for the next CB ministerial meeting in New Delhi in early April 1977, this body decided to open up its meetings to all NAM members in the capacity of observers, which was a radical departure from the previous practices of avoiding any internal factions from prevailing.[40] However, even though Belgrade's candidacy for organizing the next NAM ministerial conference was well known, Mozambique unexpectedly submitted its application for hosting this event. This was obviously a covert attempt by the Cubans to situate the second most important gathering before the summit in the capital of one of its closest allies in Africa.[41] However, in spite of intensive Cuban and Mozambican lobbying during the OAU summit in Lome, a number of very influential non-aligned nations stood firmly behind their earlier promises to back Yugoslavia's bid whatever the cost. Under such intensive diplomatic pressure, Mozambique decided to tacitly withdraw its application and stand officially behind Belgrade's candidacy.[42] This proved to be a tangible setback for the Cuban effort but not serious enough to dissuade them from launching new and even bolder attempts.

The CB ministerial meeting in New Delhi on 7–11 April 1977, attended by fifty-one non-aligned foreign ministers, more than half of them present as observers, represented the most important NAM gathering during that year. Even though the general purpose of this meeting was to make a full appraisal of the international situation, its debate was largely conducted in the shadow of intensifying armed conflicts between different member states. Some of these conflicts were only superficially discussed, since it was often hard to forge even basic consensus, while others, due to their inflammatory nature, were eventually sidelined to avoid totally paralysing the proceedings. This tendency clearly indicated that the main procedural feature of the NAM, reaching decisions by consensus, was gradually becoming an impediment to its effective functioning, with some countries, like Iraq, even proposing setting up new bodies.[43]

Political debate was primarily dedicated to the non-controversial and unifying issues of eliminating colonialism and racism on the African continent or disarmament. A similar approach was assumed during the economic section of the discussion between the oil-producing and oil-consuming countries, even though general ongoing dissatisfaction with the lack of progress in propelling the Solidarity Fund was expressed.[44] Neither the US nor the USSR were excessively criticized or uncritically praised by those present. In the political section of the final declaration a formulation was adopted so that no group of countries could ever replace the irreplaceable international role of the NAM. This specific choice of words was a subtle warning addressed at some nations, like Cuba, Vietnam and others, not to insist excessively on transforming the movement into an exclusive gathering of 'progressive' forces.[45] In the end, it was decided to hold the next CB ministerial meeting in Kabul in May 1978, while the NAM ministerial conference would follow in Belgrade during the summer of that same year. In fact, the New Delhi gathering, lacking any spectacular results, did manage to temporarily patch up some of the fissures emerging inside the movement.

With the onset of 1978, it was evident to many members that the movement's unity could not be built upon the incessant reiterating of the basic principles any longer, thus more substantial efforts had to be invested in the field of increased mobilization and strengthening of mutual assistance in resolving many critical issues. The obvious decline in the level of solidarity spurred artificial dilemmas about the basic goals, fundamental character and general practices of the movement. This new subversive tendency also created a significant breach where more proactive countries, associated with the blocs, could gradually impose their views on other less involved or more reluctant members, thus decreasing the general level of the movement's autonomy. This kind of activity incited strong opposition on the side of some influential members, while many others still opted for a more passive stance, thus raising doubts about the NAM's feasibility, unity and cohesiveness.[46] Some Afghan diplomats characterized this identity crisis as a 'loss of an original philosophy of non-alignment'.[47]

In many ways, preparations for the next CB ministerial meeting in Kabul in May 1978 were progressing under increasingly tense conditions. While Yugoslavia, Sri Lanka and India argued for extended attendance, encompassing all members, observers and guests present at the Colombo summit, the Cuban line was to include the CB's full members only. Both sides aspired to have as many potential backers as possible, with the Cubans counting on a more limited presence as a plus for them, while the Yugoslavs and others considered that extended representation would only provide them with additional strength through sheer numbers.⁴⁸ Moreover, Yugoslavia and India were also actively trying to strengthen Sri Lanka's potential as the movement's chairman, especially due to Colombo's increased passivity, while Egypt was expecting the US to demonstrate more constructive understanding for such efforts, similar to what the Soviets were doing in the Cuban case.⁴⁹

The Yugoslav officials worked assiduously on expanding NAM attendance, regardless of recent reservations, primarily by embracing newly liberated countries that had not yet officially become members (Djibouti, Fiji, Papua New Guinea, Samoa, Surinam), with some observers also potentially becoming members (Bolivia), despite Cuban opposition, with some guests being upgraded to the status of observers, thus also becoming eligible to attend all NAM meetings (the Philippines).⁵⁰ Similar concerns compelled Sri Lankan officials to privately propose setting up an 'action bureau' inside the CB, like a small steering committee of five or six nations, consisting of Sri Lanka, Yugoslavia, India, Afghanistan and some others, which would run this body on a daily basis, propose and head any new initiatives, thus preventing the competitive 'radical' group from ever assuming direct control. Their Yugoslav counterparts remained very reserved to such ideas, since they essentially resembled what Havana and Hanoi were trying to promote themselves.⁵¹ Yet some Sri Lankan diplomats were convinced that Cuban attempts to radicalize the movement would ultimately fail. Therefore, Cuba's future chairmanship, in their assessment, would eventually produce a restraining effect on Castro's unilateral actions, since for sure he would not want to be the one presiding over the NAM's eventual dissolution.⁵²

In fact, an increasing number of NAM members believed that forthcoming gatherings in Kabul and Belgrade would play a decisive role in determining the movement's future. In time, the preservation of its integrity had become the primary expression of Yugoslavia's proactive approach to world affairs, with the strengthening of the 'moderate' wing as its most visible trait.⁵³ However, Cuban aspirations to turn this 'progressive' group into the NAM's driving force was not a foregone conclusion, nor was it a strong position on behalf of the 'moderates', since another economic downturn, further disenchantment with Western policies in Africa, another war in the Middle East or even Tito's death could seriously hamper their effectiveness.⁵⁴ Soon enough, the Yugoslav officials privately requested that their US counterparts scale down their public criticism of Cuba, since constant propaganda attacks were making it much harder to effectively contain Cuban initiatives.⁵⁵

Nevertheless, a sudden turn of events occured in late April 1978, when the Afghan government was overthrown in a Soviet-sponsored coup. These unfortunate events forced the NAM to postpone the CB ministerial meeting and start searching for a new venue.⁵⁶ Some high-ranking Cuban officials flew to Kabul to try to persuade the new Afghan communist leadership to remain the hosts of the event, since that would further bolster the 'progressive' faction. Regardless of such efforts, it was still impossible to safely organize this gathering there.⁵⁷ During intensive consultations in New York, despite giving strong assurances that Havana would not apply for hosting the CB meeting, the Cuban delegation, nonetheless, readily accepted a tentative proposal to organize this event in mid-May. This was an unexpected gain for the Cuban faction, with many attendees reluctantly agreeing with this so as to avoid creating any new ruptures.⁵⁸ This implied that any heightened activism on behalf of Cuba, Vietnam and others could eventually gain the acquiescence of the more hesitant NAM members.

The CB ministerial meeting in Havana (15–20 May 1978) was attended by twenty-five members and eighteen observers, although their role was further restricted by the Cuban hosts. Attendance was generally on a lower level than in New Delhi a year ago (only nine ministers present), very probably due to the venue itself which was evidently not to everyone's preference. This kind of tense atmosphere eventually forced the Cubans to act in a more pragmatic way to achieve results.⁵⁹ The general debate was dedicated to the NAM's identity crisis, with many participants stressing their opposition to the one-sided interpretation of the doctrine, particularly the one adding any kind of external ideological flavour. This kind of bloc-leaning policy was only advocated by the Cuban and Vietnamese delegates, while all others reiterated the movement's firm non-bloc orientation.⁶⁰

Both during the general debate and while drafting the final document, the Cuban hosts strived to distance the discussion from the decisions made at Colombo by insisting on constructing a principally new common ground based on emphasizing ideological and class divisions between different NAM members. This triggered strong resistance from another group of nations represented by India, Yugoslavia, Sri Lanka and others, which ultimately kept the proceedings from following the same lines as the current NAM agenda.⁶¹ In fact, the Cubans were evidently dissatisfied with this united front staged against their proposals, though they had to eventually succumb in order for this event to be generally recognized as a success.⁶² As for the economic side of the debate, everyone present strongly denounced the attempts of certain members striking separate economic deals with developed countries as going against the very purpose of the NIEO initiative. This was a worrisome trend indeed, one indicating serious internal discontent with the results hitherto achieved in this sphere.⁶³

In general, the CB ministerial meeting in Havana once again confirmed, at least verbally, the continuity of the NAM, as well as its spirit of cooperation and accommodation. However, it also revealed the unrelenting polarization between countries actively working for the revision of the NAM's basic character and those strictly opposed to such projections.⁶⁴ Nevertheless, the dubious results of this meeting soon triggered covert ideas by some pro-Western members that the CB should be immediately disbanded, while the NAM should resume its meetings with total attendance, similar to G77, having monthly rotation of the chairman and vice-chairman and also establishing different ad hoc working groups.⁶⁵ Furthermore, Egyptian officials even aspired to have Belgrade as the next summit venue, thus postponing Havana's candidacy for 1982, but Yugoslavia immediately denounced this idea, primarily avoiding being seen as directly contributing to the current tensions.⁶⁶

Recent developments raised profound fears that not only could the West try to split the movement in order to prevent Cuba and the USSR from assuming control over it but that this could also induce Cuba to respond erratically by pushing even harder to impose its own views on others.⁶⁷ Countries such as Tanzania were gravely concerned that a pro-Western political attack against Cuba would compel many attendees to reluctantly render their support to Havana as a sign of preserving the movement's fledgling unity, a move which could further encourage the Cubans to continue with their earlier agenda.[68] Furthermore, the overall situation was becoming so absurd that Tito even made a joke that in 1961 the non-aligned had issued an appeal to the superpowers to sit down and talk, while now Washington and Moscow could ask the non-aligned to do the same.[69] According to top Tanzanian officials, while proximity to either of the two blocs depended on the nature of specific issues, this should never lead to the NAM's eventual fusion with one of the blocs.[70] Cuba, as a result, had to understand that this was a heterogeneous movement, one marked by different undercurrents, and it had to tread carefully if it aspired to act as a coordinating country in the future.

Delayed Showdown in Belgrade

The forthcoming NAM ministerial conference in Belgrade had indeed become a defining moment on the road to the Havana summit. Acting as hosts, the Yugoslav officials opted for comprehensive action aimed at exchanging views with their non-aligned partners on a number of issues: whether the current direction and character of the movement were in accordance with the founding principles; inciting the movement's progressive dynamic, but one that was also divorced from the parallel process of both rightist and leftist radicalization; preventing further ideological polarization, while finding new approaches to conflict mediation; condemnation of all foreign interference; renegotiating criteria for the acceptance of new members, observers and guests; preserving the principle of decision-making by consensus; and re-evaluating the roles of the CB and the coordinating country.[71] The Cubans hoped to use the forthcoming event and the following summit to work for a 're-codification of the movement's aims along the original, i.e. anti-imperialist lines', thus openly going against Yugoslavia's intentions.[72]

During Cuban–Yugoslav bilateral talks in Belgrade in July, guests clearly pointed out that the NAM's unity should never be constructed at the expense of anti-imperialist and anti-colonial struggle, while strengthening the 'progressive' wing was a natural consequence of aggressive Western interference.[73] In spite of extending private assurances that Cuba would not seek confrontation, political heavyweights such as Vice-President Carlos Rafael Rodriguez, together with the Foreign Minister Isidoro Malmierca Peoli, were dispatched to Belgrade to galvanize the 'progressive' performance there.[74] In addition, on the eve of the central event, the Cubans submitted a document in which Yugoslavia's initial draft declaration was harshly criticized as intending to override the decisions of the Colombo summit. Yugoslavia was openly accused of colluding with the US imperialists, abandoning true non-alignment, and thus trying to subvert the NAM's authentic anti-imperialist role. The Yugoslav leadership was utterly shocked with this uncorroborated criticism.[75] Adding insult to injury, Castro also made an emotional speech in which, while accusing the US and some non-aligned countries for conspiring against Cuba, he deliberately avoided mentioning Tito's name as one of the NAM's founding fathers when listing the names of Nehru, Nasser, Sukarno and others. This would definitely not slip Yugoslavia's attention.[76]

As a consequence, when Rodriguez had a meeting with the Yugoslav Vice-President Fadilj Hodža and the new Foreign Secretary Josip Vrhovec, a heated discussion ensued. After some initial sharp exchanges, Rodriguez eventually decided to back off, and started to seek accommodation with the hosts. He then decided to submit a more moderate document, while, in response, the Yugoslav side indicated that their text of the final declaration was only the first draft and thus still needed perfecting. In this way, both sides reached a tentative compromise, leaving other members to decide which side's arguments proved to be more valid. During another round of talks, Rodriguez received firm assurances that Yugoslavia would never endanger Cuba's hosting of the future summit.[77] A monumental Cuban–Yugoslav ideological showdown in Belgrade had been suddenly avoided, regardless of their lingering differences. However, during a conversation with Carter's special envoy Averell Harriman in Belgrade, Tito stressed that he was quite ready to have a serious fight with Castro in the future.[78] Essentially, as observed by the Yugoslavs, strict non-bloc policies and ad hoc proximity to or distance from either of the two blocs, depending on the nature of certain concrete issues, were the only viable way for the movement to continue with its independent existence.[79]

The NAM ministerial conference in Belgrade finally took place on 25–30 July 1978, with 117 delegations attending it, among them eighty-five full members, one member with special status (Belize), twenty-one observers from Latin America and the African national-liberation movements and ten guests, mainly from Europe (Djibouti and SWAPO were accepted as full members, Bolivia's status was to be determined at Havana, while Pakistan and San Marino were endorsed as future guests). The main goal of this event was to initiate tangible preparations for the next summit, as well as for the forthcoming 33rd UNGA session, and to launch a reassessment of all crucial international events, including armed conflicts between non-aligned countries, relationship with blocs, anti-imperialism and the right to self-defence.[80] In fact, this was a gathering that largely surpassed the role of an ordinary ministerial conference, basically emulating a summit. This was also evident when Carter sent a congratulatory telegram to the conference, which had not happened since 1961, while Brezhnev decided not to do so for the first time since the Algiers summit – thus indicating their respective endorsement of or dissatisfaction with the hosts.[81]

In his opening speech, Tito set the tone of the general debate by trying to reaffirm the NAM's basic principles, especially its non-bloc character as the main expression of its dedication to the policies directed against imperialism, neo-colonialism, racism, domination, exploitation, hegemony and the indiscriminate use of force. Overcoming bloc divisions, in his view, was the NAM's chief goal, which had nothing to do with any shifting global balance of power. Tito's veiled criticism of any pro-bloc leanings was quite apparent when he stressed that non-aligned countries should 'allow no one to jeopardise solidarity of their movement and blunt the edge of its basic orientation', also stating that 'sectarianism of any kind is alien to non-alignment', while 'divisions based on ideological, religious, and other criteria' were unacceptable. Tito also warned against rising bloc pressure, particularly in Africa where 'new forms of colonial presence or bloc dependence, foreign influence and domination' were growing. This was an allusion not only to the Western but also Cuban and Soviet presence on the continent. Nevertheless, Tito extended his full backing to holding the next summit in

Havana, thus effectively ending any controversies in that respect.[82] In the aftermath of this speech, the Cuban delegation suddenly started postponing their initial address and rewriting speeches, thus discretely signalling that they were satisfied with the earlier arrangement.[83]

During the general debate, topics close to Tito's agenda on the movement's non-bloc and independent character, its unity in diversity, disruptive influences of bilateral conflicts, as well as stern opposition to the movement's closer association with one of the blocs were all reiterated by many delegations.[84] The proceedings of the Political and Economic Committees also advanced without incident, with only occasional, unsuccessful, attempts by Cuban delegates to steer the debate.[85] In fact, some of Tito's points were also picked up by Malmierca and Rodriguez in their statements, thus proclaiming in full Cuba's respect for the NAM's heterogeneous character. However, these two officials also stressed that anti-imperialism still had to be observed as the predominant feature of the movement, while socialism and imperialism or struggle for liberation and neo-colonialism should never be equated.[86] Nevertheless, the Cubans still tried rallying some countries behind their agenda. This was quite obvious during the discussion on the sovereign rights of non-aligned countries to seek external aid for their defence, when some African countries staunchly defended Cuban presence on the continent.[87]

Naturally, this kind of debate invited opposition from countries such as Somalia, Egypt, Zaire, Saudi Arabia, Morocco, etc. who now demanded a change of the summit venue or else threatened to boycott that event altogether. This initiative of depriving Havana from its role as the summit host, although not gaining much foothold, still succeeded in compelling Cuba to not raise the 'natural alliance' thesis again.[88] Even though the Cuban delegation was doing its best to avoid any extreme outbursts, introducing into final documents any formulations like 'hegemony' and 'bloc powers', still implied for them a sign of equation between the East and West.[89] In this respect, Minić tried to explain to Rodriguez that this notion of 'hegemony' did not pertain just to the USSR but was basically related to both superpowers and all other great powers too. In his opinion, a clear distinction should be always made between the notions of military bloc, socialist camp and socialism, since they did not represent the same thing.[90]

The final declaration, both in its political and economic sections, together with the Action Program, and four accompanying resolutions, were all basically shaped by the Yugoslav arguments, especially in areas such as fundamental principles, the orientation and character of non-alignment, the movement's independent international role, strengthening of mutual solidarity, opposition to further monopolization of power, priority of the consensus principle, together with some moderate formulations regarding the NAM's anti-imperialist and anti-hegemonic character. The Yugoslav approach also prevailed with respect to some other issues like détente, blocs, spheres of influence, crisis hotspots, disarmament, non-interference, etc. As part of the general compromise, more militant formulations were adopted concerning the Middle East, Cyprus, Southern Africa, etc., thus compensating for the lack of any extreme positions in general terms. For the very first time, the non-aligned had also provided their own interpretation of human rights, emphasizing that this issue should not be observed outside the national, economic and social context, while the rights of individuals were inseparably tied to the collective rights of nations as being key parts of the struggle for further democratization of international affairs. Finally, it was also passed to hold the Havana summit on 3–7 September 1979, and also decided to hold the 7th NAM summit in Baghdad in 1982.[91]

In general, this ministerial conference succeeded in reaffirming the movement's independent and non-bloc character, while any adversarial ideas about aligning it with one of the superpowers were effectively sidelined by the majority. However, this gathering still did not manage to eliminate ideological polarization from its ranks, thus still adding a certain dose of uncertainty to the future. Many contentious issues were left out of the final document altogether, a sign that it was trying to artificially patch up the previous unity. Furthermore, this only served to reveal the depth of incongruence of views and interests held by different leading members, which could then negatively affect any future joint activities. This was truly the most serious conceptual challenge launched from within for the previous seventeen years, shaking the movement's very foundations but still not creating an open rift that the superpowers could afterwards utilize to their advantage.[92] In the words of a Malaysian diplomat, the movement 'came out of Belgrade with numerous bruises and wounds' and it would take time for them to heal.[93]

Essentially, Yugoslavia ultimately won the day in Belgrade, but a new round of ideological struggles was expected in Havana, now depending largely on how the situation in the Third World would evolve and whether that would strengthen Cuba's hand. The most dangerous outcome, as perceived by the Yugoslavs, would be for the 'moderates' not to travel to Havana at all and leave the movement or at least its truncated version firmly in the Cuban grip. The other worst-case scenario would be for the majority to finally expel Cuba and its allies from the movement as a means of preserving some of its authority. Nevertheless, in any of these cases, the NAM's unity and future would be seriously imperiled.[94] This kind of disastrous scenario was no illusion, since one influential Cuban official revealed to the US ambassador in Belgrade that, if Cuba wanted, it could soon establish a competitive movement to the NAM and thirty to forty countries would immediately follow in its footsteps.[95] Whether this was a bluster or a veiled threat, dark clouds had definitely descended upon the NAM.

According to one top Yugoslav diplomat, the primary reason for his country's tactical victory over Cuban policies was primarily due to the Cubans themselves. In his opinion, Cuba was continuously trying to wrap up its tangible and often positive achievements in Africa into a distinct ideological framework, which was quite unnecessary, and thus only served to incite opposition from others. He believed the Cubans were their own worst enemy, since, in his words, they tried to 'accomplish today what they might better postpone until after Havana'.[96] As noted by the Guyanese foreign minister, the only lesson Cuba should draw from this gathering was to openly convey to Moscow that pursuing such a line would only endanger prospects for the next summit.[97] In fact, the Soviet bloc was somewhat dissatisfied that Yugoslavia had invested so much effort in luring the NAM away from their position, thus continuously trying to undermine the activities of the 'progressive group'.[98]

However, what was also set in motion in Belgrade was the subsequent discussion on the 'Agenda Item 15'. The main goal of this initiative was to improve the CB's and the NAM's decision-making process, thus further strengthening its democratic capacity, solidarity and action capability.[99] On the other hand, this entire effort was basically directed at limiting Cuba's future role as the movement's chairman, downscaling it from an executive to a more presiding one. As for the Cubans, they were pursuing conflicting agenda where the CB would get an enhanced executive role, with extended powers endowed upon the future NAM chairman. Furthermore, as Havana sought, importance of summit decisions would be further elevated, while the role of other ministerial meetings and conferences would be accordingly diminished.[100] It was clear to everyone that the Cubans were now using other means to reach the same goals, and thus trying to monopolize power without getting a clear majority behind them.

Splintered Non-Alignment on the Road to Havana

The year 1979 proved to be an even more turbulent one for the world and the NAM. While countries leaning towards the Soviet bloc were proceeding with their previous activities, although with more tact and acumen than before, their more moderate opponents, not including the ones openly tilting towards the West, were desperately trying to preserve some of the NAM's founding principles and its original political orientation. The bulk of their diplomatic efforts primarily focused on the following issues: the movement's non-bloc and independent stance towards all great powers; anti-imperialism and anti-colonialism having nothing in common with the 'natural alliance' thesis; the struggle against all blocs having nothing to do with either capitalism or socialism, but was instead a continuous struggle against all kinds of political, military and economic domination; the pursuance of the NAM's further democratization which would then strengthen the national security of all members outside great power arrangements; the peaceful resolution of conflicts between non-aligned countries.[101]

The situation inside the NAM was becoming so tense that pessimism was starting to taint the reasoning of some nations, inducing some of them to seriously start considering leaning to the side of different great powers or further strengthening regional integration at the expense of the movement's overall unity.[102] Even Tito was still contemplating whether to travel to Havana. He eventually decided to attend, despite his illness and advanced age, since otherwise he believed the long-term consequences would be even more serious than just another ideological row with Castro.[103] Under such difficult circumstances, Yugoslavia gradually altered its tactics by transforming this conceptual bilateral conflict between Belgrade and Havana into one between Cuba and the NAM's silent majority. Therefore, the Yugoslavs initiated a comprehensive diplomatic action, thus trying to offset the Cuban offensive aimed at extracting a number of concessions in order to gain corresponding advantages for the hosts before the summit.[104]

The situation in Southern Africa was also becoming increasingly tense, directly tackling the interests and security of not only the 'frontline states' but other key non-aligned countries, as well as major world powers. Naturally, since the USSR and Cuba directly aided the anti-colonial struggle in the region, while the US and other Western allies were still not ready to exert a tremendous amount of pressure on the local racist regimes to withdraw, as a response some African NAM members were gradually sliding towards Havana's position.[105] Therefore, an extraordinary CB ministerial meeting was held in the Mozambican capital Maputo on 26 January–2 February 1979. This gathering was attended by twenty-three CB members (Indonesia and Syria did not attend), together with twenty-four other NAM members, while the representatives of four national-liberation movements and five international organizations were also present. This event was also the first real test of strength between the two competing factions after the Belgrade conference, with one of them prompting an equal say between all CB members and non-members in preparing the meeting agenda and drafting its final documents.[106]

Nevertheless, when the Mozambican hosts, backed by Cuba, Vietnam, Angola, Ethiopia, PLO and others, submitted their draft of the final document, it was immediately evident that the radical agenda was trying to prevail again, openly arguing for a military solution for total decolonization. Many of the NAM's peaceful initiatives, like holding free elections in Namibia, were outright denounced by this group. The Yugoslavs decided to present their own draft document, one condemning the perils of bloc confrontation in Africa, which then got a strong boost from India, Sri Lanka, Peru, Nigeria, Tanzania, Zambia, Botswana and some other delegations. Eventually, it was agreed to put together a final compromised document based on both these drafts, with the Yugoslav one having more impact on the parts dealing with the basic principles and active measures, tentatively balancing between promoting new negotiations and pursuing armed struggle, and also avoiding any strong pro-Soviet sentiments while still reserving plenty of criticism for Western policies.[107]

Despite attempts at propagating radical anti-imperialist policies and a pro-Soviet agenda, the general debate was widely marked by a more moderate undertone, many earlier controversies were clearly avoided and the decisions of the previous NAM ministerial conference were confirmed again, while a general consensus on issues related to extending substantial material aid to African national-liberation movements was ultimately reached. Yugoslavia's proposal to accept the Patriotic Front of Zimbabwe as a new member was readily endorsed by all, as was India's offer to host the next NAM ministerial conference in 1981. This was yet another score gained for the 'moderate' group, since it was clear that the second most important gathering during Cuba's future chairmanship would be held in the capital of one of its competitors.[108]

However, there were two further controversial issues that eclipsed the proceedings. The first was the initial Arab attempt to suspend Egypt from the movement. Countries such as Yugoslavia, Sri Lanka and India were ready to condemn some provisions of the Camp David Accords, above all their unilateral and partial character, but none would stand firmly behind the decision for Cairo's suspension or expulsion.[109] The other issue was Kampuchea's representation, bringing back painful memories of the early 1970s dispute. The exiled Pol Pot regime insisted on Vietnam's immediate expulsion from the NAM, while its delegation was already on the way to Maputo to represent DK as the only legitimate government. Together with India, Yugoslavia strongly backed this bid, especially since DK representatives had been present at both the Colombo summit and Belgrade conference, and this government was a recognized UN member. Naturally, the Vietnamese, Laotians, Afghans, Ethiopians and some others spoke in the name of the recently established PRK, lobbying for either their presence or at least leaving out Kampuchea totally from the list of attendees. Eventually it was decided to accept Pol Pot's representatives, but as a sign of compromise they were stripped of their voting and speaking rights, and the country's name was altered to just Kampuchea, without any political prefixes.[110]

This gathering in Maputo was evidently less marked by confrontation, while one of its major contributions was the provision of additional justification to the armed struggle in the Southern Africa. However, due to the efforts of the 'moderate' group, this struggle was now also closely intertwined with a corresponding political action and it had received exclusive political and material support primarily from non-aligned countries rather than any blocs.[111] This was a transitional compromise between the two factions, since many of these controversial issues would still come to haunt the movement in the future. Nevertheless, this extraordinary CB meeting clearly indicated that the 'progressive' group was still not able to push through its own agenda against the wishes of the NAM majority.[112] Furthermore, some of the countries previously reluctant to travel to Havana, like Malaysia and Indonesia, had recently started reversing their policies, understanding that their attendance was far more conducive to the movement's proper functioning than staging any boycott.[113]

In order to secure some success at the forthcoming summit, Cuba adopted a two-pronged approach in its preparations: they were actively trying to be as constructive and accommodative as possible in any negotiations, while also pedalling even harder their advocacy of the anti-imperialist and anti-colonial essence of the movement.[114] The impression that Cuba had already reconciled itself with the fact that not all countries would attend the summit caused serious concern among some members. In order to secure a more favourable outcome, Havana tried continuously to expand its platform in order to increase wider attendance, not only counting on clearly pro-Soviet elements but also on a significantly larger number of different African and Arab nations truly disenchanted with the Western policies in Southern Africa and the Middle East. Even though many of these countries did not share Cuba's ideological leanings, nonetheless, in this respect both sides could find a lot of common ground.[115] In order to gain some additional points with the Arabs, Castro was even ready to not invite Egypt to the summit until the CB finally made its decision regarding Cairo's expulsion, knowing well that only a summit or ministerial conference had the capacity to deal with such a serious issues.[116] Furthermore, some influential Cuban officials publicly proclaimed that Yugoslavia's time had passed and Cuba's had finally come. Naturally, this stirred a lot of consternation in Belgrade, raising fears that ideological polarization was becoming the NAM's unavoidable long-term trend.[117]

These kinds of profound contradictions also produced an adverse impact on other NAM members. For example, during a visit of Castro's personal envoy to North Korea, Kim Il Sung bluntly professed that, in his opinion, due to the complex international situation and many bilateral conflicts, the Havana summit should be postponed for at last six months or even a year in order for the movement to successfully resolve some of these contentious issues. Kim also proposed that another NAM ministerial conference should be held in 1979 instead of a summit.[118] This entire idea was outright rejected by the Cubans, who saw this as a deliberate attempt to undermine their efforts. Since the North Korean foreign minister had recently been in Belgrade, suspicions about the joint Yugoslav-Korean collusion were widely present in Havana.[119] Cairo also tentatively proposed that the forthcoming summit should be held in Yugoslavia, while Havana should be the venue for the 7th summit in 1982.[120] However, Belgrade sought no changes to the summit venue, but was investing additional efforts to assemble an effective anti-radical lobby within the movement.[121]

Preparations for the next CB ministerial meeting in Colombo also included a heated debate on the 'Agenda Item 15'. After a few months, it had been tentatively decided to launch another overhaul of the CB, thus setting off a process where its membership would increase to thirty to thirty-five representatives, the institution of the vice-chairman would be introduced, all NAM members would be allowed to attend its meetings, take part in debates and submit proposals but without having the capacity to cast votes. Moreover, the CB should also assume a role in the peaceful mediation of conflicts between member states, at least on an ad hoc basis.[122] In many of these cases, 'progressive' diplomats voiced their strong discontent with such modifications, trying instead to promote some of their own ideas. Nevertheless, this kind of behaviour was strongly disputed by the majority of other participants.[123]

The Sri Lankan government was conscious that the forthcoming CB ministerial meeting could also determine the future course of the movement. This event was essentially transformed into another ministerial conference, thus eventually curbing Cuban and Vietnamese ambitions to remould the CB into an exclusive body working separately from all other members of the movement.[124] This was quite evident when the event, held on 4-9 June 1979, was attended by twenty-three CB members (Chad and Guinea did not attend), with another fifty NAM members present, accompanied by twenty-two other guests and observers from the ranks of different countries, international organizations and national-liberation movements. This was a clear signal that the CB inner workings had to be more transparent and inclusive than they had been in the past. At this meeting, the NAM's membership was expanded by five new members: Bolivia, two former colonies (Granada and Surinam) and two former bloc members (Iran and Pakistan after the dissolution of CENTO).[125]

As for the general debate, it tackled the following issues: the direction, role and character of non-alignment; expansion of the movement's membership and additional democratization of the CB's inner workings, one closely associated with a more strict definition of the rule of reservations as part of the consensus mechanism; exhaustive deliberation of some of the major crisis hotspots. In the end, the outcome remained close to the mainstream concepts of the 'moderate' group, except for Sri Lanka's proposal for establishing a permanent mechanism for conflict mediation, which was totally rejected. As for economic issues, the obvious lack of progress in the North-South dialogue was readily acknowledged, as was the lack of success in the implementation of the Action Program adopted at the last summit. Even though Cuba still did not submit its draft of the summit's final documents, thus causing a wave of criticism over its attempts to present others with a *fait accompli* as Algeria had done in 1973, it was eventually decided for the CB in New York to assume the role of a preparatory committee.[126]

Nevertheless, two outstanding issues would prove again to be quite controversial: Kampuchean attendance and Egyptian suspension. In both these cases, the movement was supposed to provide a clear answer as to whether national sovereignty should be strictly observed by all, irrespective of individual preferences, or whether imposing certain policies on individual governments or even substituting them through the use of force should be tolerated or even endorsed. Even though the CB had previously allowed Pol Pot's representatives to be present in Colombo, the Vietnamese, Cuban, Angolan and Afghan delegates denounced this decision by claiming that a consensus had not been achieved. The situation was complicated further when Sri Lankan and Indian delegations allowed Heng Samrin's representatives to suddenly show up in Colombo.[127] As a response, Indonesia and Yugoslavia started to fight back, ushering in a strange tautology that, in fact, the previous situation had not basically changed, since DK was still officially a NAM member and there was no summit to have claimed otherwise, while any current members, and they claimed DK was still one, were not encompassed by that consensus decision. Sri Lanka and India soon sided with this stretched argument, followed by strong reservations also expressed by Algeria and Iraq regarding the Vietnamese and Cuban argumentation. Eventually, the Maputo formula was passed again as a compromise solution, therefore Pol Pot's delegates would be present but they could neither speak nor vote.[128]

As for the Egyptian suspension, Iraq, Syria and the PLO were quite active in promoting this agenda, but soon many African countries – above all Tanzania, Zambia, Nigeria, Zaire, backed by some ASEAN members, India, Peru, Guyana and behind-the-scenes Yugoslavia – adamantly opposed such an initiative as constituting a dangerous precedent. Finally, this issue was removed from the meeting proceedings despite fierce Arab protests. Therefore, in order to somewhat mitigate Arab intransigence, Sri Lankan, Indian and Yugoslav foreign ministers privately agreed that the part of the Camp David Accords related to Palestine should be officially condemned, Arab unity should be further encouraged, while an adequate solution for the occupied territories should be also sought. However, they also agreed that potential Egyptian suspension should be avoided at all cost, unless, of course, Sadat opted for a fully fledged military alliance with the US.[129] These carefully drafted formulations were then introduced into the final document, while Arab delegations, for the time being, decided to drop their standing reservations.[130]

The outcome of the Colombo CB ministerial meeting largely implied that preparations for the Havana summit were becoming more embedded in the agenda of the 'moderate' group. However, the Indians were also becoming very pessimistic when analysing recent events, considering that the NAM was heading in the wrong direction altogether, primarily since many members were subordinating the movement's general well-being to their national or regional interests. Excessive expansion of membership was already producing a negative toll on the movement's quality, while forging a joint position was being increasingly marked by attempts to discipline some members along these new lines.[131] During their meeting in late June, Tito and the Indian Prime Minister Morarji Desai agreed to work hand in hand in Havana, thus not allowing Castro to privatize the summit. They also decided to leave the Cubans guessing whether they would travel to Cuba (Desai's government would be voted out of office in July, with only its foreign minister attending the summit).[132] This only surfaced a serious long-term dilemma – membership expansion was paralysing the NAM's effectiveness in a time of trouble but without it a small group of determined countries would be able to more easily assume control over it.

According to Sri Lankan diplomats, the movement was facing an unprecedented onslaught from both blocs, outside interference was at a never greater level, while assistance rendered to such policies from within the organization had become a worrisome trend. In their words, the NAM was transforming itself into a 'propaganda pressure group', one even more inefficient than the Commonwealth.[133] As a means to counterbalance Soviet influences, Egypt was privately discussing potential Chinese membership but Cairo never publicly raised that point.[134] The Soviet Foreign Ministry issued a directive to all its diplomats stationed in non-aligned countries to actively promote the concept of Cuban leadership of the movement, while giving additional assurances to host governments that the Cuban foreign policy was acting independently from Moscow, its military involvement in Africa was not guided by the USSR, while Soviet economic assistance to Havana should be continuously downplayed in front of these nations.[135]

When Cuba finally submitted its draft of the summit's final documents in early July, all these concerns had started to materialize again. The CB was presented with a document that was clearly permeated with the original Cuban stance: many basic features of non-alignment were left out, while peaceful co-existence was presented in the narrowest sense of that term; a one-sided emphasis was put on anti-imperialism, while still implying the 'natural alliance' thesis; the international situation was presented as a clash between the forces of aggression and forces of peace, while détente was analysed only through Soviet policies; opposition to blocs was reiterated but without mentioning the non-bloc character of non-alignment; advocacy of the tricontinental character of the movement was reiterated, thus quietly leaving out European members; the policy of the use of force, spheres of interest and military interventions was also circumscribed, while decisions of previous summits were not clearly named.[136] Yugoslavia considered this move as a 'double-cross', since the Cubans proved to be quite reasonable and constructive up until the Colombo CB meeting, securing wide attendance of the summit, while now they had reversed back to their old policies.[137]

Despite continuous Cuban assurances that this was just the first draft that needed to be amended, many NAM representatives were seriously distressed that future deliberations could regress back to a more confrontationist mood. A serious debate ensued in New York, with many countries questioning some of Cuba's ideologically tainted ideas and concepts, particularly with respect to Havana's obvious neglect of the basic principles of non-alignment and too obvious advocacy of some pro-Soviet policies.[138] Some non-aligned leaders were disappointed that the Cubans did not learn anything from the recent CB meeting, still holding onto the previous tactics, while often assuming an ambiguous stance depending on the interlocutor. Serious concerns were also raised over whether Castro's performance at the summit would be more flexible and pragmatic or ideologically rigid and assertive as before.[139]

In fact, based on some internal information, this ideologically rigid draft was only a part of deliberate Cuban tactics to strengthen their negotiating position by initially presenting others with maximalist demands. This would then lead to tense negotiations and finally to a compromise solution that would guarantee that criticism of Havana's pro-Soviet policies would not go beyond what had been adopted at the previous summit.[140] Well aware of such intentions, Yugoslavia privately asked the US government to refrain from undertaking any moves that could be either interpreted as direct interference into the NAM's internal affairs, since they would only further exacerbate relations between different delegations attending the summit. Similar advice was also passed on to the Chinese.[141]

As part of Cuban diplomatic efforts, in early July, Vice-President Rodriguez was dispatched on a diplomatic mission to Yugoslavia, India, Sri Lanka, Iraq and Algeria. Yugoslavia was the first country officially presented with the draft document, thus initiating a comprehensive exchange of views. Even though both sides could not find common ground on a number of issues, nonetheless, Rodriguez was still content that the constructive tone prevailed during his visit, thus enabling the Cuban–Yugoslav dialogue to continue, while avoiding a clash with Tito that could have ultimately split the movement.[142] In India, he encountered arguments similar to those in Belgrade, while in Iraq and Algeria Rodriguez had to openly admit that the first draft of the final document was not perfect and it still had to be seriously amended by considering the views of other influential NAM members.[143]

A certain amount of Cuban flexibility was also demonstrated during the visits of Indian and Yugoslav high-ranking officials to Havana in early August, when the hosts finally accepted introducing profound amendments into the text of final documents. However, the Cubans still did not invite Pol Pot's delegation to attend.[144] Yugoslavia and ASEAN members were still insistent on the Maputo and Colombo formulas, while the Cubans stressed that they would not allow the presence of DK representatives in Havana, indicating that they would invite Heng Samrin's people to come instead. Sihanouk, disgruntled with everyone, started to openly advocate for an empty seat until the situation clarified. Nevertheless, the DK delegation was still determined to attend the summit and they travelled to Havana straight from Belgrade, where they had previously exchanged views with the Yugoslav leadership.[145] However, everything remained to be decided on the eve of the central event, since the debate in the CB was facing a growing deadlock, with India, Sri Lanka and Yugoslavia now initiating work on preparing alternative texts of the final documents as a way of circumscribing any new Cuban surprises.[146]

High Noon at Havana

Since Tito was also invited to perform a state visit to Cuba on the occasion of this summit, the Yugoslav delegation, one of the most numerous at this event, was among the first ones to arrive in Havana at the very end of August. Tito was attending as a seasoned statesman, last of the movement's founding fathers, fully aware that this could be his very last summit during which the destiny of the movement could be eventually decided. Hence, he fully grasped that he had to forcefully demonstrate his utmost strength, astuteness and authority. Sri Lanka's evident passiveness as the current NAM chairman, as well as the absence of India's prime minister, together with Boumedienne's untimely death in 1978, ultimately left Tito as the last line of defence to reshape the basic outlook of the movement.[147] The complexity of the situation for Tito was evident when both Carter and Brezhnev sent him personal messages which asked for the summit not to condemn the Camp David Accords or advocate equality between the two blocs, thus putting even more responsibility on his shoulders.[148]

Based on some Yugoslav intelligence reports, Castro had informed the Kremlin beforehand that he would do everything in his power to influence Tito's stance and seek suitable compromises, since he knew well that the summit's success largely depended on his personal agreement with the Yugoslav president.[149] In fact, Moscow was quite interested in the positive outcome of the Havana summit, so assisted the Cubans by introducing all necessary corrections into their draft document, and thus mitigating its radical tone.[150] Nevertheless, as soon as Tito arrived, other members of the 'moderate' group started rallying around him. His first meeting was with the Indian Foreign Minister Mishra, when both sides agreed that they had to work together in order to preserve the NAM's basic principles without fracturing its unity. This summit, they thought, was of the utmost importance to the future, especially since both superpowers were trying to shape its outcome through different proxies.[151]

The summit itself was preceded by two events: the first was the CB ambassadorial meeting held on 28–29 August, while the other a ministerial meeting (29 August–2 September). Kampuchean representation was hotly debated at both these events. Two Kampuchean delegations were then present in Havana, although the DK one was isolated in a villa outside the city, while the PRK representatives were housed together with other delegations. However, the Cubans now openly argued for an empty seat as a provisional solution. Many attending ambassadors considered this as an insolent arbitrariness, since the hosts unilaterally monopolized some of the movement's prerogatives. This had caused a serious split at the ambassadorial meeting, where twenty-four delegates backed Pol Pot's delegation, fifteen were lobbying for accommodating Heng Samrin's representatives, while a dozen others were unable to state their preferences. Naturally, a final decision could not be reached. In the end, the CB elected twenty conference vice-chairman, as well as chairmen of the Political and Economic Committees (Iraq and Mozambique) and their deputies.[152]

When the ministerial meeting started, old controversies were bound to emerge. In his opening speech, Foreign Minister Malmierca accused the US, China and their NAM allies of scheming against Cuba. His Malaysian counterpart insisted on allowing the DK delegation to take its rightful place as previously agreed in Maputo and Colombo. This received backing from Singapore, Morocco, Gabon and, surprisingly, the PLO, while Madagascar and Benin stood behind the Cuban line. The Yugoslav Foreign Secretary Vrhovec was quite dissatisfied with the Cuban stance and their penchant to decide everything by themselves, while the Vietnamese minister openly accused Yugoslavia and Sri Lanka of undermining earlier arrangements. Nevertheless, the ministerial meeting still managed to welcome new members into the NAM's ranks: Bolivia, Granada, Iran, Nicaragua, Pakistan, Surinam and Zimbabwe, as well as new observers: Costa Rica, the Philippines, St Lucia and Dominica, while Spain was added to the list of guests.[153]

However, on the second day of this event, the old quarrel broke out again when the Singaporean Foreign Minister Rajaratnam demanded the DK delegation be allowed to attend the summit, now strongly backed by even more delegates, while the Cubans and their allies reiterated their argument for the legitimacy of Heng Samrin's representation. The ensuing discussion balanced precariously on the brink of an incident. Hence, India unexpectedly suggested a compromise offer that the Kampuchean seat ultimately be left empty, enjoying in this initiative cautious Algerian endorsement. This acted like a genuine bombshell, especially for countries defending previously adopted principles, since the Indian delegation provided the Cubans with an easy way out of this deadlock, thus enabling them to achieve the second best solution for them if Heng Samrin's representatives could not be seated at the summit.[154]

Eventually, the Yugoslav delegation recommended the ministerial meeting pass this issue to the summit in order for non-aligned leaders themselves to adopt the final decision. They pointed out three potential solutions: removing this issue from the summit agenda altogether, instructing the conference bureau to reconsider it or establishing a separate committee that would hold a new round of discussions. Malmierca basically agreed with this proposal, agreeing to postpone everything until the New Delhi ministerial conference in 1981.[155] Soon enough, Tito and his Sri Lankan counterpart Jayewarden finally reconciled themselves with an empty seat for Kampuchea, just to avoid further paralysis of the proceedings, thus leaving it to the Cubans to eventually take the heat for such an outcome.[156] When the ministerial meeting finally submitted its report, it was evident that NAM foreign ministers could not achieve consensus on another issue related to the final distribution of ten additional seats in the new CB structure (five African, four Asian, one Latin American), while Europe could not get another seat.[157] Nevertheless, Egyptian diplomats were quite content with these developments, since they thought such a display of heavy-handed tactics by the Cubans won them no favors with other delegations.[158]

Meanwhile, Tito and Castro had two private meetings. Their talks were held in a friendly and constructive atmosphere, even though their foreign ministers were often engaged in a fierce diplomatic fight. During these conversations, Tito emphasized that both sides should strive for preserving the fundamental character of the movement, while working hard to achieve even more constructive unity, despite individual differences. He clearly recognized the responsibility which both Cuba and Yugoslavia shared for the eventual success of the summit. However, Tito also had to highlight that with respect to certain issues these two countries often did not see eye to eye, which, nonetheless, should not become an obstacle for reaching a meaningful compromise. Castro readily agreed with this assessment, indicating that there were issues on which Cuba and Yugoslavia held opposite views but that should be used as an incentive to finally discover common ground.[159]

However, Castro denounced the accusations that he intended to gamble away the NAM's independence, since he, like Tito, also advocated the movement's separation from the blocs. Both leaders ultimately agreed that they should continue to resolutely oppose any schemes directed at fomenting discord between the two countries. They both eventually expressed a certain discontent with some press reports occupying headlines in their respective countries.[160] During their face-to-face conversation, Castro again provided firm assurances that there would be no unpleasant surprises occurring at the summit and he would do his utmost to further strengthen the NAM's unity.[161] Nevertheless, on the next day, Fidel's brother Raul went to see the Soviet ambassador and he conveyed the basics of these talks, stating that Tito did not want to proceed with confrontation at Havana.[162] This episode clearly indicated that Cuba and the Soviet Union were still closely coordinating everything regarding the summit, although their tactics had somewhat changed.

Since Tito and Castro had managed to patch up some of their differences, the Havana Conference finally started on 3 September 1979 and lasted for another six days. This was the largest summit attendance thus far, although with fewer heads of state or government present (only fifty-six), but still drawing the widest possible attention from all over the world. This event was attended by 131 delegations, among them ninety-two full members, twenty observers (twelve countries, three national-liberation movements and five international organizations), eighteen guests (eight countries and ten international organizations) and one country with special status (Belize). Despite months of fierce agitation to boycott the summit, only two countries ultimately refused to show up – Saudi Arabia and Chad (Chad due to its armed conflict with Libya).[163] Since the character and future course of the movement were at the heart of the general debate, Castro's and Tito's respective speeches essentially embodied the 'progressive' and 'moderate' currents crucially shaping the NAM's discourse.

Castro's opening speech, despite his assurances, was not a formal welcome extended to all attending leaders. In a fiery tone, he proclaimed some of Cuba's controversial views, avoiding formally imposing them on others but still with clear intentions to demonstrate why his position, nonetheless, proved to be more adequate for the NAM than that professed by others. Throughout his speech, Castro tried to present Cuba as a selfless anti-imperialist and anti-colonial fighter, it was no one's puppet but still nurtured close ties to the USSR. He stressed again the anti-imperialist, anti-colonial and anti-racist essence of the movement as its *raison d'être*, without ever mentioning its non-bloc orientation or stressing superpower hegemony as the NAM's true foe. In accordance with these claims, he extended his full support to the anti-imperialist struggle still being waged around the world. For Castro, the world revolutionary forces were on a successful march to triumph and the NAM was their main stage.[164]

Yet when referring to those countries aspiring to undermine this gathering, he squarely named the US and China, as well as implicitly some of their NAM allies, thus causing consternation among some delegations. He also accused some of the attendees of persistently revising the Cuban draft of the final document, thus somewhat discretely pointing his finger at Yugoslavia which initially submitted many amendments. Castro also stressed that Cuba was a socialist country, close to the Soviet Union, but still he did not want to advocate that other members follow in his footsteps – they should freely choose their own path, although, as he stressed, no one could objectively deny Soviet contribution to the national-liberation struggle.[165]

Another part of Castro's speech was, possibly, also directed against Yugoslavia, especially taking into account Tito's old policy of balancing between the two blocs:

> Some in the world have made opportunism an art, the Cuban revolutionaries will never be opportunists. We know how to sacrifice our own economic and national interests as often as necessary to defend a just principle and an honourable political line. We Cubans today will not do the opposite of what we said yesterday, nor will we do tomorrow the opposite of what we say today.

Nevertheless, in the economic part of his speech, Castro recognized all the major problems plaguing the developing world and contributing to its rapid pauperization. He also stressed that richer non-aligned countries had to take another step to help their less fortunate brothers and avoid being seduced by the imperialists.[166] The main goal of Castro's speech was to create an adequate atmosphere for promoting his specific views. Since the Cuban position basically had not changed, Tito was quite discontent, thus instructing his delegation not to stand up with others and applaud Castro's speech.[167]

After Castro's performance, speeches made by the leaders of Zambia, Sri Lanka and others were permeated with the spirit of conciliation – trying to find a middle-of-the-road position. However, since Sadat was overtly attacked by Castro, the Egyptian Foreign Minister Boutros Boutros-Ghali decided to immediately respond, which then triggered a fierce debate on Egypt. Only Nyerere's personal intervention with Castro finally put a stop to these orchestrated attacks.[168] In this tense atmosphere, on the second day of the summit, Tito was about to open the plenary session with his speech. Taking a subtle approach, he tackled all the same issues as Castro, but using a more nuanced language and sending quite the opposite messages, thus artfully promoting his own agenda. Unlike Castro's speech, which largely dealt with the NAM's future role, Tito emphasized the past and the values and principles that made the movement, thus highlighting continuity with the previous summits as the key principle which should be upheld in order to prevent the movement fundamentally changing in the future.[169]

During his address, Tito also stressed unity based on respect and understanding of the diverse views and interests of all non-aligned countries as opposed to the harsh criticism of some of their individual policies demonstrated by Castro. In this spirit, he defined again NAM's basic goals:

> Our movement is facing key problems of the world today – issues of peace, security, development, and general progress. It expresses fundamental interests of the entire humanity, not just one part of it … We should never lose from sight what is common to all of us and what unites us. We should oppose everything that separates us and what facilitates penetration of foreign interests into our ranks. Our permanent interest and our strategic goal in this moment is further affirmation of the basic principles of the policy of non-alignment and based on that we should strengthen solidarity, unity, and action capability of the NAM … Only in this way we can successfully contribute to the construction of the world we strive for.[170]

Although Tito sat down while he read his speech, due to his feeble health, his performance, nonetheless, left a remarkable impression on the majority of participants. It acted as a true boost for the 'moderate' group, with some high-ranking Soviet officials privately admitting that this was a statesmanlike, balanced and moderate address.[171]

Even though neither Castro nor Tito openly stirred confrontation, after these two speeches it was almost unavoidable that some disagreements would occur during the general debate. The pro-Cuban faction was represented by at least twenty pro-Soviet countries and in all their speeches they advocated for strong adherence to the anti-imperialist struggle, proximity to the Soviet bloc as NAM's true ally, strict division between the friends and foes of non-alignment, while openly cheering for the shift in the global balance of power. In fact, Cuban representatives also used their chairing function to steer the debate in their favour by letting their allies address the conference during the day, while leaving their opponents to speak during the evening, when attendance was far less numerous.[172] The performance of this group – assertive and loud – was perceived by the Yugoslav and Guyanese foreign ministers as 'cheap propaganda', one not having any clear goals nor leading to any concrete results.[173]

However, there was a majority of more than fifty countries comprising the opposite group, which often based their speeches on the points raised by Tito in his plenary address. In his speech, Nyerere, after naming himself as one of Tito's 'most consistent comrades-in-arms', stressed that the NAM was neither a movement of socialist or progressive countries, despite some members being socialist, nor it was a bloc, since 'it did not have permanent enemies, friends, and especially no natural allies', while it was also 'not an organisation of neutrals'. In his words, the NAM had to 'remain a group of states jealous of their independence, taking pride in their non-alignedness ... rejecting without any hesitation the idea of alliances with any blocs or any of the great powers'. Some other attendees, like those from Egypt, Singapore or Ghana, even started advocating strict equidistance and neutrality towards both blocs.[174] The extreme example in this respect was Burma, a country that demanded the movement be immediately disbanded and established again based on newly defined principles. When this proposal was rejected, Burma decided to leave the movement in protest. This was the first time a nation had dropped out of the NAM.[175]

Since a compromise could not be found regarding the Kampuchean representation, it was eventually agreed to leave the CB to study this issue until the next NAM ministerial conference in 1981. This topic was then totally dropped from the final document, largely since even countries arguing for the Maputo formula did not feel comfortable defending the genocidal Pol Pot regime any longer.[176] Nevertheless, Rajaratnam admonished the movement, openly implying that, in this way, the movement had endorsed aggression, agreed with interference into the internal affairs of member states and even turned a blind eye to launching military interventions if some members disagreed with the policies of others. This was particularly concerning, as he pointed out, if the membership credentials of the victim were now being questioned rather than the those of the aggressor.[177] This argument followed the Yugoslav conclusions that the superpowers had previously largely ignored the movement, while now they were trying to infiltrate it, while at the same time charting their own spheres

Figure 6 Sixth Summit of the Non-Aligned Movement: President Tito's speech on general debate, Havana, 4 September 1979. © Museum of Yugoslavia.

of influence.[178] In fact, some Cuban diplomats privately concluded that Havana had overplayed its hand by not allowing Pol Pot's delegation to take its seat, since this later backfired in the UNGA.[179]

There was, naturally, another issue that stirred a heated debate: potential Egyptian suspension. Before the summit even started, Iraqi leader Saddam Hussein stressed to Tito that he would strongly criticize Sadat, formally asking for Egypt's suspension, but he would still not decisively pursue that line. Something similar was also conveyed by the Syrian leader Hafez El-Assad. In both these cases, Tito advised his counterparts that some criticism of Cairo's unilateral decisions was necessary but seeking Egypt's suspension was a shortcut to finally undermining the unity and stability of the movement.[180] This kind of stance was clearly evident during the speeches made by Hussein, Assad and Arafat, since none formally raised this issue, despite reserving some very harsh language for the Egyptian leader. It was a paradox that such demands were then launched by the representatives from the leftist group, contrary to the many Arab delegations who remained reserved in this respect.[181]

Yet there were also some nations – especially the African ones like Zaire, Cote d'Ivoire, Senegal, Gabon, etc., that praised Egyptian efforts for reaching peace, while others – Zambia, Tanzania, Guinea and the majority of others – criticized the Egyptian–Israeli peace treaty as a move against the NAM's policies and an outright betrayal of Palestinian rights, although many of them privately expressed their understanding for Cairo's rationale for undertaking such a move.[182] In the end, even though Arab delegations formally submitted their demand for Egyptian suspension, thus trying to save face in front of others, the majority rejected that proposal altogether. On Kaunda's private advice, it was eventually left to the CB to further study this issue until the next ministerial conference, hoping that this would eventually relax the situation, while the peace treaty was formally denounced at this summit.[183]

As well as this heated general debate, the situation in the Political and Economic Committees was also tense, since Cuba put up strong resistance to the revision of its draft of the final document, although eventually Cuban representatives had to succumb and reach a compromise by making a trade-off with the Yugoslavs over certain issues.[184] Therefore, the political part of the declaration was substantially altered by turning it into the most complete codification of the basic principles of non-alignment. Parts on détente, peaceful co-existence, non-interference, disarmament and human rights were added, while the elements of one-sided anti-imperialism and 'natural alliance' were dropped altogether or framed in a totally different manner. All recommendations concerning the 'Agenda Item 15' were also adopted. As part of this political haggling, it was also agreed to increase the CB membership to thirty-six seats (seventeen African, twelve Asian, five Latin American, one Europe and one divided), with the thirty-sixth seat being shared between Europe and Africa for one and a half years each. This solution also clarified the practice of submitting reservations when reaching consensus, while CB members and non-members were somewhat equated, although not fully (non-members still could not vote but they could submit proposals that could sway the opinion of voting members).[185]

As for the economic problem, the debate in that committee was even more agitated, with Cuba and its allies forcefully insisting on encapsulating these issues into the notions of imperialism, colonialism and neo-colonialism, contradictions between capitalism and socialism, also leaving out many key details previously pertaining to the NIEO. Another controversial issue was energy cooperation between OPEC members and other developing nations, which went against the resistance of Iraq, Algeria and Indonesia considering this as another attempt at blackmailing the rich oil-producing nations. Nevertheless, through the active involvement of the 'moderate' group, a compromise was reached that was made in accordance with the original principles adopted at the Colombo summit, thus making energy cooperation the NAM's rallying point in this respect. Yet all participants were painfully aware that the final realization of the NIEO now seemed ever more distant.[186]

The Havana Conference ended in a solemn atmosphere when, on Kaunda's and Toure's insistence, the gathering decided to award Tito with a special recognition as the NAM's founding father. During a special session, a number of foreign leaders expressed their sincere admiration for the seasoned leader, though this was still not the case with Castro. He did not mention Tito's name in any of his speeches, including the concluding one, while one of his deputies even wanted this special ceremony to be held on the margins, without any journalists attending it. In fact, this was a small payback to Tito for not being forthcoming with respect to Castro's opening speech.[187] Even though the Yugoslav president succeeded in personally forestalling the 'radical' onslaught, largely at the expense of his deteriorating health, Yugoslavia was, nonetheless, becoming less influential in steering the NAM affairs as before.¹⁸⁸ However, concerning some of its crucial goals, like preserving the movement's original character and orientation, preventing Egyptian expulsion or not legitimizing military aggression in Southeast Asia, a tangible success had been achieved.¹⁸⁹

Conclusion

In general, regardless of the many tensions plaguing this summit, the resounding majority did manage to promote once again the independent, non-bloc and democratic essence of non-alignment, thus clearly sidelining Cuban and Vietnamese ideas about the NAM's revolutionary character, but without fomenting any new divisions. What was especially important for Yugoslavia, was that Cuba's thinking about identifying the NAM solely with the Third World was successfully foiled, while the CB was reorganized in such a way that Castro and his allies could never assume direct control over it while concurrently chairing the movement. Even the summit declaration was more of an expression of the position of the 'moderates', even though, as a sign of compromise, some radical anti-Western formulations were also adopted. Essentially, the minority was not able to impose its will on the majority, as many had feared, therefore it had to accommodate itself to the general trend of continuity along the previously established lines.¹⁹⁰

In fact, victory of the 'moderates' in Havana obviously did not guarantee that the loud minority would not try to stage the same attempt in the future. However, this would be much more complicated due to Castro's lack of willingness to further compromise his role as the new chairman. Even the Soviets did not want to further endanger the crumbling détente with the US due to increased Cuban assertiveness or to openly push for an internal takeover of the NAM.¹⁹¹ Some high-ranking Yugoslav officials were convinced that the Havana summit was the very last opportunity for the Cubans and their allies to try to take a firm stand, since anti-imperialism and anti-colonialism were currently virulent in the Third World, but soon these issues would start to fade away and other problems, primarily socioeconomic ones, would gradually start to preoccupy these nations.¹⁹² This was a far-sighted assessment indeed.

This had become quite clear when Cuba started using its chairmanship for promoting the NAM's economic agenda, often avoiding raising controversial political issues.¹⁹³ Nevertheless, some members were still seriously concerned about what would happen after Tito's death, since that would leave a huge authority gap with certain countries trying to fill that role, and thus reshaping the NAM's identity according to their own preferences.¹⁹⁴ Some eight months after Havana, Tito passed away, thus ending the 'golden age' of non-alignment. Even if the Cubans perceived his death as yet another opportunity to try their luck and complete what had been originally planned at Havana, it would be their tolerance of the Soviet invasion of non-aligned Afghanistan that would swiftly subvert all their original plans. This excessive insistence on the 'natural alliance' thesis ultimately made Cuba a hostage to an outmoded concept that would came back to haunt Castro with such dire consequences, irrespective of the fact of whether Tito was alive or not. The high noon in Havana ultimately ended in Tito's favour, but its immediate outcome was that the movement was largely drained of its previous vitality at the most perilous historical moment it had encountered since the mid-1960s.

Notes

1. Raymond L. Garthoff, *Détente and Confrontation*, 623–85, 758–824, 829–912; Melvyn P. Leffler, *For the Soul of Mankind*, 259–99; Odd Arne Westad, *The Cold War*, 475–92; Daniel J. Sargent, *A Superpower Transformed*, 229–95.
2. Raymond L. Garthoff, *Détente and Confrontation*, 732–57; Odd Arne Westad, *The Global Cold War*, 283–7; Jonathan Steele, *Soviet Power: The Kremlin's Foreign Policy – Brezhnev to Chernenko* (New York, NY: Simon & Schuster, 1984), 163–78.
3. Martin Meredith, *The State of Africa*, 218–48, 260–74, 331–43.
4. Bojana Tadić, *Sukobi među nesvrstanim zemljama: dokumentacioni prilog* (Beograd: Međunarodna Politika, 1987), 136–66.
5. Mohammed Lakhdar Ghettas, *Algeria and the Cold War*, 135–80; Ardavan Amir-Aslani, *L'âge d'or de la diplomatie algérienne*, 186–90, 195–7.
6. Piero Gleijeses, *Visions of Freedom: Havana, Washington, Pretoria, and the Struggle for Southern Africa, 1976–1991* (Chapel Hill, NC: The University of North Carolina Press, 2013), 37–44, 53–60.
7. Odd Arne Westad, *The Global Cold War*, 253–72; Gebru Tareke, *The Ethiopian Revolution: War in the Horn of Africa* (New Haven, CT: Yale University Press, 2009), 11–54; Andargachew Tiruneh, *The Ethiopian Revolution, 1974–1987: A Transformation from Aristocratic to a Totalitarian Autocracy* (Cambridge: Cambridge University Press, 1993), 37–201.
8. Radoslav Yordanov, *The Soviet Union and the Horn of Africa during the Cold War: Between Ideology and Pragmatism* (Lanham, MD: Lexington Books, 2016), 153–99; Nancy Mitchell, *Jimmy Carter in Africa: Race and the Cold War* (Washington, DC, Stanford: Woodrow Wilson Center Press, Stanford University Press, 2016), 253–302, 340–400; Piero Gleijeses, *Visions of Freedom*, 45–53.
9. Galia Golan, *Soviet Policies in the Middle East: From World War II to Gorbachev* (Cambridge: Cambridge University Press, 1990), 110–23, 140–75; Yevgeny Primakov, *Russia and the Arabs: Behind the Scenes in the Middle East from the Cold War to the Present* (New York, NY: Basic Books, 2009), 177–99.
10. Kenneth W. Stein, *Heroic Diplomacy*, 187–253; Salim Yaqub, *Imperfect Strangers*, 239–75; Lawrence Wright, *Thirteen Days in September: Carter, Begin, and Sadat at Camp David* (New York, NY: Alfred A. Knopf, 2014), 47–265.
11. Nayan Chanda, *Brother Enemy: A History of Indochina since the Fall of Saigon* (New York, NY: Collier Books, 1986), 74–262; Grant Evans and Kelvin Rowley, *Red Brotherhood at War: Vietnam, Laos, and Cambodia since 1975* (London: Verso, 1990), 35–111.
12. Stephen J. Morris, *Why Vietnam Invaded Cambodia: Political Cultures and the Causes of War* (Stanford: Stanford University Press, 1999), 88–115, 167–228; Kosal Path, *Vietnam's Strategic Thinking during the Third Indochina War* (Madison, WI: the University of Wisconsin Press, 2020), 19–109.

13 Xiaoming Zhang, *Deng Xiaoping's Long War: the Military Conflict between China and Vietnam, 1979–1991* (Chapel Hill, NC: The University of North Carolina Press, 2015), 40–140; King C. Chen, *China's War with Vietnam, 1979: Issues, Decisions, and Implications* (Stanford: Hoover Institution Press, 1987), 69–149.
14 Lorenz M. Lüthi, *Cold Wars*, 530–1.
15 A. W. Singham and Shirley Hune, *Non-Alignment in the Age of Alignments*, 167–71.
16 Bojana Tadić, *Sukobi među nesvrstanim zemljama*, 31–50, 61–73.
17 Lorenz M. Lüthi, *Cold Wars*, 525–8; W. M. Karundasa, *Sri Lanka and Non-Alignment*, 181–93.
18 Bojana Tadić, *Osobenosti i dileme nesvrstanosti*, 37–43.
19 M. S. Rajan, *The Future of Non-Alignment and the Non-Aligned Movement: Some Reflective Essays* (New Delhi: Konark Publishers, 1990), 74–5.
20 DAMSPS, PA, 1978, f-188, 429531, 'Telegram from Britain', 17 May 1978.
21 DAMSPS, PA, 1977, f-171, 411733, 'Telegram from UN', 2 March 1977.
22 Ruslan Vasilievich Kostiuk and Ekaterina Petrovna Katkova, 'The Soviet Union and the Non-Aligned Movement', 130–5.
23 Miloš Minić, *Spoljna politika Jugoslavije 1973–1979* (Novi Sad: Centar za političke studije, 1979), 578–9.
24 Piero Gleijeses, *Conflicting Missions*, 214–29; Michelle Getchell, 'Cuba, the USSR, and the Non-Aligned Movement', in *Latin America and the Cold War*, 160–5; Jacques Levesque, *The USSR and the Cuban Revolution: Soviet Ideological and Strategic Perspectives, 1959–1977* (New York: Praeger, 1978), 147–92.
25 Roy Allison, *The Soviet Union and the Strategy of Non-Alignment in the Third World*, 69–77; Theodor Tudoroiu, 'Fidel Castro and the Radicalization of Non-Alignment: A Political Psychology View', *International Studies* 53.2 (2017), 125–9.
26 DAMSPS, PA, 1977, f-173, 433752, 'Telegram from Cuba', 10 June 1977.
27 NARA, RG 59, CFPF, 1973–1979, ET, 1978USUNN00751, 3 March 1978.
28 DAMSPS, PA, 1978, f-194, 439827, 'Telegram from Zambia', 6 July 1978.
29 AJ, 837, KPR, I-4-a/31, 'First meeting of the Coordinating Commission for participation in the 6th NAM summit, Brdo kod Kranja, 9 May 1979'.
30 NARA, RG 59, CFPF, 1973–1979, ET, 1978STATE155783, 19 June 1978.
31 DAMSPS, PA, 1977, f-172, 417727, 'Consultations with Cuba in Belgrade', 25 March 1977.
32 DAMSPS, PA, 1977, f-171, 49139, 'Telegram from Guyana', 14 February 1977.
33 Josip Broz Tito, *Nesvrstanost i savremeni svijet*, 2 (Beograd: Komunist, 1982), 685.
34 FRUS, 1977–1980, 17, 1 (2016), 202–3.
35 *Југославија-СССР*, 733.
36 DAMSPS, PA, 1977, f-171, 48205, 'Foreign Secretariat's telegram', 16 February 1977.
37 Mark Mazower, *Governing the World*, 322–31; DAMSPS, PA, 1977, f-172, 415516, 'Telegram from UN', 18 March 1977.
38 DAMSPS, PA, 1978, f-188, 430698, 'Telegram from Britain', 26 May 1978.
39 NARA, RG 59, CFPF, 1973–1979, ET, 1978USUNN01534, 20 April 1978.
40 DAMSPS, PA, 1977, f-171, 42243, 'CB activities since the 5th summit', 14 January 1977.
41 DAMSPS, PA, 1977, f-171, 43114, 'Foreign Secretariat's telegram', 20 January 1977.
42 DAMSPS, PA, 1977, f-171, 412563, 'Foreign Secretariat's telegram', 9 March 1977.
43 DAMSPS, PA, 1977, f-172, 420122, 'Telegram from India', 9 April 1977.
44 DAMSPS, PA, 1977, f-172, 420553, 'Telegram from India', 12 April 1977.
45 MMFA, 'Non-Alignment Movement', Research Division, 1978.

46 DAMSPS, PA, 1978, f-187, 427404, 'Conditions in the NAM before the CB meeting in Havana', 9 May 1978.
47 NARA, RG 59, CFPF, 1973–1979, ET, 1978USUNN00931, 16 March 1978.
48 DAMSPS, PA, 1978, f-187, 418544, 'Telegram from UN', 1 March 1978.
49 NARA, RG 59, CFPF, 1973–1979, ET, 1978COLOMB01176, 13 March 1978.
50 DAMSPS, PA, 1978, f-192, 421059, 'Foreign Secretariat's telegram', 12 April 1978.
51 DAMSPS, PA, 1978, f-187, 418112, 'Telegram from Sri Lanka', 27 March 1978.
52 NARA, RG 59, CFPF, 1973–1979, ET, 1978COLOMB02250, 12 May 1978.
53 NARA, RG 59, CFPF, 1973–1979, ET, 1978STATE067645, 16 March 1978.
54 CREST, CIA-RDP80T00942A000900060001-9, 'NAM – dynamics and prospects', 30 March 1979.
55 NARA, RG 59, CFPF, 1973–1979, ET, 1978BELGRA02858, 8 April 1978.
56 TNA, FCO 58/1307, 'Yugoslavia, non-alignment, and the Soviet Union', 16 May 1978.
57 DAMSPS, PA, 1978, f-191, 426282, 'Telegram from Afghanistan', 5 May 1978.
58 DAMSPS, PA, 1978, f-187, 424561, 'Telegram from UN', 4 May 1978.
59 DAMSPS, PA, 1978, f-193, 431878, 'Foreign Secretariat's telegram', 31 May 1978.
60 DAMSPS, PA, 1978, f-191, 429715, 'Telegram from Cuba', 21 May 1978.
61 DAMSPS, PA, 1978, f-191, 428595, 'Telegram from Cuba', 17 May 1978.
62 TNA, FCO 58/1307, 'Telegram from Cuba', 31 May 1978.
63 DAMSPS, PA, 1978, f-191, 428597, 'Telegram from Cuba', 17 May 1978.
64 AJ, 837, KPR, I-4-a/29, 'CB ministerial meeting in Havana, 15–20 May 1978', 6 April 1978.
65 DAMSPS, PA, 1978, f-188, 436970, 'Telegram from UN', 22 June 1978.
66 DAMSPS, PA, 1978, f-188, 442047, 'Telegram from Sudan', 16 July 1978.
67 DAMSPS, PA, 1978, f-188, 435315, 'Foreign Secretariat's telegram', 20 June 1978.
68 DAMSPS, PA, 1978, f-194, 440703, 'Telegram from Zambia', 10 July 1978.
69 *Југословенско-алжирски односи*, 385.
70 DAMSPS, PA, 1978, f-194, 439789, 'Telegram from Tanzania', 6 July 1978.
71 AJ, 837, KPR, I-4-a/30, 'Current issues related to the NAM ministerial conference in Belgrade', 18 July 1978.
72 TNA, FCO 58/1310, 'Telegram from Cuba', 4 September 1978.
73 DAMSPS, PA, 1978, f-188, 441123, 'Consultations with Cubans in Belgrade, 6–7 July 1978'.
74 DAMSPS, PA, 1978, f-195, 442642, 'Telegram from Cuba', 17 July 1978.
75 AJ, 837, KPR, I-4-a/30, 'Cuba's rejection of the Yugoslav draft document', 23 July 1978.
76 AJ, 837, KPR, I-4-a/30, 'Information on Fidel Castro and the NAM', 27 July 1978.
77 AJ, 837, KPR, I-4-a/30, 'Talks between the Cuban delegation and Hodža and Vrhovec in Belgrade, 24 July 1978'.
78 NARA, RG 59, CFPF, 1973–1979, ET, 1978BELGRA05561, 30 July 1978.
79 AJ, 837, KPR, I-4-a/30, 'Talks between Miloš Minić and Hammadi, 28 July 1978'.
80 DAMSPS, PA, 1978, f-196, 444598, 'Foreign Secretariat's telegram', 4 August 1978.
81 NARA, RG 59, CFPF, 1973–1979, ET, 1978STATE185993, 24 July 1978; *Југословенско-алжирски односи*, 402.
82 Josip Broz Tito, *Nesvrstanost i savremeni svijet*, 2, 648–53.
83 NARA, RG 59, CFPF, 1973-1979, ET, 1978BELGRA05596, 31 July 1978.
84 TNA, FCO 58/1310, 'Non-aligned conference', 4 August 1978.
85 DAMSPS, PA, 1978, f-196, 444598, 'Foreign Secretariat's telegram', 4 August 1978.
86 Ђука Јулијус, *Хавана – сукоби или споразуми* (Београд: Политика, 1979), 13–14.

87 AJ, 837, KPR, I-4-a/30, 'Proceedings of the NAM ministerial conference', 26 and 28 July 1978.
88 AJ, 837, KPR, I-4-a/30, 'Proceedings of the NAM ministerial conference', 29 July 1978.
89 AJ, 837, KPR, I-4-a/30, 'NAM ministerial conference in Belgrade', 24 August 1978.
90 AJ, 837, KPR, I-4-a/30, 'Talks between Minić and Rodriguez, 26 July 1978'.
91 AJ, 837, KPR, I-4-a/30, 'NAM ministerial conference in Belgrade', 24 August 1978; *Documents of the Gatherings of the Non-Aligned Countries*, 1, 247–64.
92 TNA, FCO 58/1310, 'Belgrade conference of NAM foreign ministers', 2 August 1978.
93 DAMSPS, PA, 1978, f-197, 448089, 'Telegram from Malaysia', 16 August 1978.
94 NARA, RG 59, CFPF, 1973–1979, ET, 1978BELGRA05793, 8 August 1978.
95 NARA, RG 59, CFPF, 1973–1979, ET, 1978BELGRA05594, 31 July 1978.
96 NARA, RG 59, CFPF, 1973–1979, ET, 1978BELGRA05718, 4 August 1978.
97 DAMSPS, PA, 1978, f-197, 447351, 'Telegram from Guyana', 18 August 1978.
98 PAAA, M95 9.076, 'Course and results of the NAM ministerial conference', 1 August 1978.
99 Peter Willetts, *The Non-Aligned in Havana: Documents of the Sixth Summit Conference and an Analysis of their Significance for the Global Political System* (London: Frances Pinter, 1981), 12, 35–6.
100 DAMSPS, PA, 1978, f-189, 463201, 'Telegram from UN', 20 November 1978.
101 AJ, 837, KPR, I-4-a/31, 'Draft platform for the 6th summit', 26 April 1979.
102 DAMSPS, PA, 1979, f-184, 420808, 'Telegram from Sri Lanka', 9 April 1979.
103 AJ, 837, KPR, I-4-a/31, 'Tito's speech at the CC LCY Presidium session in Herceg Novi', 22 March 1979.
104 DAMSPS, PA, 1979, f-184, 47123, 'Telegram from UN', 10 February 1979.
105 DAMSPS, PA, 1979, f-205, 41293, 'Foreign Secretariat's telegram', 12 January 1979.
106 DAMSPS, PA, 1979, f-205, 410356, 'Foreign Secretariat's telegram', 28 February 1979.
107 DAMSPS, PA, 1979, f-205, 44944, 'Telegram from Mozambique', 30 January 1979.
108 DAMSPS, PA, 1979, f-205, 45678, 'Telegram from Mozambique', 3 February 1979.
109 DAMSPS, PA, 1979, f-206, 430758, 'Telegram from Sri Lanka', 20 January 1979.
110 DAMSPS, PA, 1979, f-205, 44325, 'Telegram from Mozambique', 26 January 1979.
111 DAMSPS, PA, 1979, f-205, 45679, 'Telegram from Mozambique', 3 February 1979.
112 DAMSPS, PA, 1979, f-205, 46194, 'Foreign Secretariat's telegram', 7 February 1979.
113 NARA, RG 59, CFPF, 1973-1979, ET, 1979KUALA0872, 29 March 1979.
114 PAAA, M95 10.079, 'Developments in the NAM after the Belgrade conference', 15 March 1979.
115 DAMSPS, PA, 1979, f-186, 418063, 'Telegram from Cuba', 2 April 1979.
116 DAMSPS, PA, 1979, f-186, 421963, 'Telegram from Cuba', 19 April 1979.
117 AJ, 837, KPR, I-4-a/31, 'First meeting of the Coordinating Commission for Yugoslavia's participation in the 6th NAM summit, Brdo kod Kranja, 9 May 1979'.
118 AJ, 837, KPR, I-4-a/31, 'DPRK's proposal', 1 May 1979.
119 DAMSPS, PA, 1979, f-186, 426228, 'Telegram from Cuba', 11 May 1979.
120 DAMSPS, PA, 1978, f-188, 442047, 'Telegram from Sudan', 16 July 1978.
121 NARA, RG 59, CFPF, 1973–1979, ET, 1979BELGRA01967, 15 March 1979.
122 DAMSPS, PA, 1979, f-205, 423375, 'Telegram from UN', 25 April 1979.
123 DAMSPS, PA, 1979, f-206, 426438, 'Telegram from UN', 14 May 1979.
124 DAMSPS, PA, 1979, f-206, 429825, 'Telegram from Sri Lanka', 29 May 1979.
125 DAMSPS, PA, 1979, f-206, 434099, 'Foreign Secretariat's telegram', 25 June 1979.

126 AJ, 837, KPR, I-4-a/33, 'CB ministerial meeting in Colombo, 4–9 June 1979', 19 June 1979.
127 DAMSPS, PA, 1979, f-206, 430908, 'Telegram from Sri Lanka', 4 June 1979.
128 DAMSPS, PA, 1979, f-206, 432216, 'Telegram from Sri Lanka', 8 June 1979.
129 DAMSPS, PA, 1979, f-206, 432010, 'Telegram from Sri Lanka', 6 June 1979.
130 TNA, FCO 58/1578, 'CB ministerial meeting, Colombo, 4–9 June 1979', 25 June 1979.
131 DAMSPS, PA, 1979, f-184, 435828, 'Telegram from UN', 27 June 1979.
132 AJ, 837, I-3-a, India, 'Tito-Desai talks', 20 June 1979.
133 DAMSPS, PA, 1979, f-188, 443076, 'Telegram from UN', 9 August 1979.
134 DAMSPS, PA, 1979, f-184, 444382, 'Telegram from Egypt', 22 August 1979.
135 DDRS, CK2349648041, 'Memorandum for the President', 12 July 1979.
136 DAMSPS, PA, 1979, f-187, 438226, 'Foreign Secretariat's telegram', 18 July 1979.
137 NARA, RG 59, CFPF, 1973–1979, ET, 1979USUNN03205, 1 August 1979.
138 DAMSPS, PA, 1979, f-187, 439907, 'Telegram from UN', 23 July 1979.
139 DAMSPS, PA, 1979, f-187, 441152, 'Telegram from Guyana', 26 July 1979.
140 DAMSPS, PA, 1979, f-187, 439223, 'Telegram from Cuba', 18 July 1979.
141 NARA, RG 59, CFPF, 1973–1979, ET, 1979STATE194093, 26 July 1979.
142 DAMSPS, PA, 1979, f-187, 438104, 'Foreign Secretariat's telegram', 26 July 1979.
143 DAMSPS, PA, 1979, f-187, 440622, 'Telegram from Algeria', 26 July 1979.
144 DAMSPS, PA, 1979, f-188, 443014, 'Telegram from Cuba', 11 August 1979.
145 DAMSPS, PA, 1979, f-189, 445015, 'Legitimacy of Democratic Kampuchea', 27 August 1979.
146 DAMSPS, PA, 1979, f-188, 443926, 'Telegram from Sri Lanka', 19 August 1979.
147 Vladimir Petrović, *Titova lična diplomatija: studije i dokumentarni prilozi* (Beograd: ISI, 2010), 263–9.
148 AJ, 837, KPR, I-4-a/35, 'Tito-Jayewardene talks', 1 September 1979.
149 AJ, 837, KPR, I-4-a/35, 'SID information', 31 August 1979.
150 AJ, 837, KPR, I-4-a/35, 'SID information', 2 September 1979.
151 AJ, 837, KPR, I-4-a/35, 'Tito-Mishra talks', 30 August 1979.
152 AJ, 837, KPR, I-4-a/35, 'Conference bulletin no. 1', 30 August 1979.
153 DAMSPS, PA, 1979, f-189, 446131, 'Telegram from Cuba', 31 August 1979.
154 NAI, MEA, HI/162/11/79, 'The 6th NAM summit', 26 September 1979.
155 DAMSPS, PA, 1979, f-189, 446137, 'Telegram from the Yugoslav delegation', 2 September 1979.
156 AJ, 837, KPR, I-4-a/35, 'Tito-Jayewardene talks', 1 September 1979.
157 AJ, 837, KPR, I-4-a/35, 'Conference bulletin no. 5', 3 September 1979.
158 NARA, RG 59, CFPF, 1973–1979, ET, 1979HAVANA08011, 31 August 1979.
159 AJ, 837, KPR, I-4-a/35, 'Tito-Castro talks', 31 August 1979.
160 Ibid.
161 AJ, 837, KPR, I-4-a/35, 'Tito-Castro private talks', 31 August 1979.
162 'Conversation between ambassador Vorotnikov and Raul Castro, 1 September 1979', http://digitalarchive.wilsoncenter.org/document/111249.
163 DAMSPS, PA, 1979, f-189, 449429, 'Foreign Secretariat's telegram', 27 September 1979.
164 AJ, 837, KPR, I-4-a/35, 'Castro's speech', 3 September 1979.
165 Ibid.
166 Ibid.

167 Živojin Jazić, *Moj pogled na diplomatiju (1957–2005)* (Beograd: Čigoja, 2010), 151.
168 AJ, 837, KPR, I-4-a/35, 'Conference bulletin no. 6', 4 September 1979.
169 AJ, 837, KPR, I-4-a/35, 'Tito's speech', 4 September 1979.
170 Ibid.
171 DAMSPS, PA, 1979, f-192, 448653, 'Telegram from USSR', 14 September 1979.
172 AJ, 837, KPR, I-4-a/35, 'Conference bulletin no. 7', 5 September 1979; 'Conference bulletin no. 8', 6 September 1979.
173 AJ, 837, KPR, I-4-a/35, 'Conference bulletin no. 11', 8 September 1979.
174 AJ, 837, KPR, I-4-a/35, 'Conference bulletin no. 8', 6 September 1979; 'Conference bulletin no. 9', 7 September 1979; 'Conference bulletin no. 11', 8 September 1979.
175 DAMSPS, PA, 1979, f-189, 450950, 'Talks between Šestan and U Tun Tin, 3 October 1979'.
176 AJ, 837, KPR, I-4-a/35, 'Conference bulletin no. 11', 8 September 1979.
177 NARA, RG 59, CFPF, 1973–1979, ET, 1979HAVANA08252, 8 September 1979.
178 AJ, 837, KPR, I-4-a/35, 'Tito-Rahman talks', 5 September 1979.
179 NARA, RG 59, CFPF, 1973–1979, ET, 1979USUNN03893, 21 September 1979.
180 AJ, 837, KPR, I-4-a/35, 'Tito-Hussein talks', 31 August 1979; 'Tito-Assad talks', 2 September 1979.
181 AJ, 837, KPR, I-4-a/35, 'Conference bulletin no. 6', 4 September 1979; 'Conference bulletin no. 7', 5 September 1979.
182 AJ, 837, KPR, I-4-a/35, 'Conference bulletin no. 8', 6 September 1979; 'Conference bulletin no. 9', 7 September 1979.
183 NAI, MEA, HI/162/11/79, 'The 6th NAM summit', 26 September 1979.
184 TNA, FCO 58/1584. 'The 6th non-aligned summit', 20 September 1979.
185 DAMSPS, PA, 1979, f-189, 449429, 'Foreign Secretariat's telegram', 27 September 1979; *Documents of the Gatherings of the Non-Aligned Countries*, 1, 336–66, 391–6.
186 AJ, 837, KPR, I-4-a/35, 'Conference bulletin no. 6', 4 September 1979; 'Conference bulletin no. 7', 5 September 1979; 'Conference bulletin no. 8', 6 September 1979; *Documents of the Gatherings of the Non-Aligned Countries*, 1, 366–90, 397–402.
187 Tvrtko Jakovina, *Treća strana Hladnog rata*, 238–40.
188 NARA, RG 59, CFPF, 1973–1979, ET, 1979NEWDE17523, 26 September 1979.
189 TNA, FCO 58/1586. 'The NAM summit conference', 26 September 1979.
190 DAMSPS, PA, 1979, f-189, 449429, 'Foreign Secretariat's telegram', 27 September 1979.
191 DAMSPS, PA, 1979, f-192, 456087, 'Telegram from India', 1 October 1979.
192 NARA, RG 59, CFPF, 1973–1979, ET, 1979BELGRA07098, 21 September 1979.
193 DAMSPS, PA, 1979, f-189, 465985, 'Telegram from Cuba', 25 December 1979.
194 NAI, MEA, FIII/102/33/81, 'Non-aligned summit conferences (1961–1979)'.

Epilogue: 'A House Divided Against Itself'

Unlike preceding summits, three summits held during the 1980s did not attract as much limelight as before, thus eventually producing a far less significant global impact. In fact, the respective agendas of these three gatherings were more dedicated to the NAM's growing stack of internal problems and finding ways of overcoming them than it had to do with charting new strategies and preparing the movement for the post-Cold War period. The incessant internal squabbling and evident lack of purposefulness finally contributed to the NAM's reduced global influence and diminished international footprint, leaving the movement an almost powerless reminder of a bygone era at a time when the Cold War was drawing to its end.

In the aftermath of the Havana Conference, a serious internal crisis enveloped the NAM, gradually contributing to its unhindered decline. A rapidly deteriorating international situation, both on global and regional levels, mirrored by an expanding conceptual division between key NAM members all contributed to plunging the movement into further disarray. Individual activities often overrode collectivist remedies, while member states were more frequently seeking security in great power bilateral arrangements than in multilateral actions. Any earlier discussions on the NIEO were now effectively dead, with ideas based upon free markets, private initiative, foreign direct investments and the disappearance of the welfare state slowly becoming the predominant features of the emerging world economic system. The experiences of some Asian countries with successful economic transformation, like Japan, South Korea, Singapore and ultimately China, also proved to be quite edifying in this respect for many non-aligned countries, thus further discrediting the NAM's old ways of dealing with economic underdevelopment.[1] In fact, China was the only one among the great powers that still actively sought cooperation with the NAM by tying its economic reforms to the still current call for boosting South–South cooperation, while also officially adopting non-alignment as its own foreign policy orientation.[2]

As a means of overcoming these difficulties, many developing countries turned to cheap loans and credits provided by the developed world (IMF and World Bank) in order to preserve some social stability and regain a certain level of economic vibrancy, eventually putting themselves into an even deeper debt trap. It was only the general Cold War framework and superpower competition in the Third World that still held back developed Western countries from using this obvious inherent weakness for assuming more direct control over different developing nations.[3] The Third World's indebtedness was, therefore, used as additional leverage in imposing the so-called Washington Consensus as a predominant model of neoliberal capitalist development for the entire world (budget austerity, devaluation, deregulation, price and trade liberalization, privatization, dismantling of tariffs).⁴ This kind of structural change in the economic position of the developing world, accompanied with the abrupt end of the Cold War, would largely coincide with the NAM's reduced political relevance in world affairs by the end of the 1980s.

Hence, the NAM's many internal divisions, closely wedded to the deteriorating strategic situation, ultimately proved to be the greatest obstacle to the movement resuming its role of global mediator and engine of Third World activism. Moreover, the economic dimension of non-alignment had started to lose appeal due to the ongoing debt crisis and escalating economic downturn. This double effect of rising internal and external pressures largely contributed to the NAM's overall impotence and its unwillingness to resolutely act. This only signalled that the movement had lost its original compass, it was depleted from its fundamental philosophy, while the general level of internal disenchantment was only expanding. The sense of helplessness in the face of mounting challenges was indeed widespread. Eventually, when the superpowers initiated a new period of mutual accommodations during the late 1980s, they were no longer interested in soliciting the good offices of the NAM, while the non-aligned themselves were no longer able to offer any meaningful solutions or useful advice.

The Second Cold War and the Third World

By the end of the 1970s, it was evident that détente was on its deathbed, only waiting for another major crisis to occur. That crisis was not only the Soviet intervention in Afghanistan in late December 1979 but also NATO's 'double-track' policy decision, adopted at the same time, which involved holding negotiations with the Soviets over the status of their R-16 (SS-20) medium-range missiles in Eastern Europe, while also conducting its own deployment of medium-range Pershing II and Tomahawk cruise missiles in the West. In effect, all these events totally dismantled the entire process of détente by the year 1980. The global Cold War was escalating not only in different parts of the Third World, but in Europe too, with relations inside the Soviet bloc becoming increasingly tense, as during the 1980–1 crisis in Poland. The elevation to power of the Reagan administration in early 1981, part of a wider turn towards conservatism in the West, had launched an assertive global anti-communist crusade, supported by a massive armaments programme, which encompassed gradually rolling back Soviet presence in the Third World, while also forcing Moscow into making substantial concessions in Europe.⁵

However, this new round of intensive superpower competition was also having a profound impact on the Third World, where the East was trying to preserve some of its positions acquired during the 1970s global offensive, while the emboldened West had mounted a political and economic counteroffensive in the same region.⁶ Under such complex conditions, the widening gap between different NAM members was becoming more evident and increasingly severe, while the attempts of some countries to reconcile some of their policies with the interests of either superpower were also contributing to the swift emergence of these divisive fissures. Eventually, this kind of confusion was only assisting further with radicalization of both leftist and rightist extremes in the movement, thus directly undermining any realistic approach to the NAM's policies advocated by the dominant silent majority since the Lusaka Conference.⁷

The war in Kampuchea would continue throughout the 1980s, with the West and China politically and materially backing the Khmer Rouge guerrilla struggle against the pro-Vietnamese regime in Phnom Penh,[8] somewhat similar to the ongoing confrontation between Angola and Cuba against South Africa and their proxies over the southern parts of Angola and ultimately Namibia.[9] Furthermore, the Cold War in East and Southeast Asia was already undergoing structural changes steadily leading it towards the post-Cold War period. The formation of the global Sino-US axis, the growing prominence of a number of regional organizations like ASEAN, accelerated economic modernization, as well as the parallel collapse of the communist revolutionary model had all testified to such a significant strategic shift. These concrete processes had also produced diverse effects on the NAM's diminishing profile in that part of the world.[10] Nevertheless, it was the Middle East, and to a certain extent Central America with its Cuban-modelled Sandinista Revolution in Nicaragua,[11] that would become the old/new fronts of the escalating Cold War struggle of the 1980s.

In fact, some of the earth-shattering events of those years would also announce the emergence of a new universal challenge to the ideological hegemony of both superpowers. That was the meteoric rise of Islamism in the Middle East and beyond. The Islamic Revolution in Iran and the Soviet invasion of Afghanistan, both taking place in a span of just ten months, marked the beginning of the end of the classical Cold War division in that region, thus ushering in fresh ideological challenges carried out by new players, both state and non-state ones, thus shaping their own versions of independence, sovereignty and universality, now coated in more traditionalist and non-secular forms. In many ways, political Islam would gradually substitute the Cold War dichotomy in the Middle East.[12] This new wave of Third World factionalism would also influence the NAM's cohesiveness and its future role, downscaling any intensive international activities to a more regional level of adapting to widespread disturbances.

After more than a year of internal turbulences, the Islamic Revolution finally triumphed in February 1979, with the deposed Shah disgracefully seeking asylum abroad. One of his main political opponents, Ayatollah Ruhollah Khomeini, would soon return from exile, thus heralding the rising power of the Islamist wing of Iranian politics. This tectonic geopolitical shift totally disrupted the customary Cold War alliance system in the Middle East, with the Iranian-led CENTO being quickly disbanded, and Tehran seeking NAM membership in response. In spite of being officially dedicated to non-alignment, the new Iranian authorities were increasingly advocating their own revolutionary model, thus projecting Tehran's political ambitions onto the entire region, particularly the Shia-dominant areas in Iraq, Syria and Lebanon. This radical line of thinking also suggested mounting a direct challenge to all secular ideologies represented by the superpowers, while strenuously denouncing the very international order they stood for. This not only resulted in the total estrangement of the new Iranian regime from both blocs but it also rocked the very foundations of the Middle Eastern order of states, inviting open confrontation with the leading Sunni countries (Saudi Arabia, Iraq, Egypt, etc.).[13]

However, the long-standing Arab fears from Iranian threat finally led Saddam Hussein to take advantage of Iran's protracted instability to forcefully overturn any bilateral territorial arrangements, while simultaneously crushing the Islamic Revolution by launching a full-scale war in September 1980. The Iran–Iraq War, which lasted for eight years, would be the bloodiest and the longest conflict between two non-aligned states, thus creating serious disturbances not only throughout that region but inside the NAM as well. At first, due to the general tactical surprise and forces armed with modern equipment, the Iraqi side initially achieved tangible successes until 1982. Though any luck in the battlefield gradually turned in Tehran's favour and lasted for another three years, with Iranian troops finally bringing war into the Iraqi territory. Soon enough, the entire conflict had evolved into a bloody protracted stalemate, also invoking the use of chemical weapons, eventually marked by the parallel emergence of the so-called City and Tanker Wars, where both sides tried to bomb each other's urban areas into rubble, while also destroying oil-exporting infrastructure. In the last two years of the war, luck was on the Iranian side again, but without achieving any major breakthroughs, thus eventually ending in total military and economic exhaustion of both nations. While Saddam's bid for Arab leadership effectively laid in ruins, Iran decided to opt for a less revolutionary course both at home and abroad.[14]

The Islamist challenge was also burgeoning in Afghanistan. After the communist coup led by Nur Muhammad Taraki in April 1978, the overall situation in that country was deteriorating by the day, marked by the escalating factional infighting inside the ruling People's Democratic Party of Afghanistan (PDPA), as well as by the steady rise of the Islamist opposition. Although this kind of opposition was largely domestically grown, they were also receiving substantial material support from Pakistan. Moscow was observing developments in Afghanistan with a worrisome eye, desperately trying to end internal strife, while also forestalling US and Pakistani attempts at subverting PDPA rule. The rapidly expanding insurgency, together with the treacherous coup staged by Taraki's deputy Hafizullah Amin in September 1979, all contributed to the Kremlin's final decision to launch an invasion. This action was envisaged as a move primarily directed at removing Amin, while simultaneously stabilizing the local security situation. Soon enough, this intervention would degenerate into a decade-long Soviet occupation and a bloody war that alienated much of the non-aligned world from the USSR, opened up a new phase of intense confrontation with the US and its allies (Pakistan, Saudi Arabia, Egypt, China), ultimately resulting in their dispatch of massive material aid and thousands of Islamist fighters to wage war against the Soviet and Afghan government troops. This new kind of a religious proxy war, positioned inside the old Cold War framework, eventually ended in the total destruction of the Afghan state and society, a million dead on all sides, the Soviet Union's ignoble withdrawal, with the radical Islamist fighters then being ready to aggressively export their local experiences into other parts of the world and well into the post-Cold War era.[15]

Plunging the NAM into Strife

It is true that the NAM had faced rising international pressure before and had suffered from the impact produced by different regional conflicts, but always managed to somehow extricate itself from such adverse situations. However, this time a serious doubt about the viability of the entire endeavour had occupied the minds of many members, thus largely contributing to the prevailing atmosphere of pessimism. Overcoming these newly emerging divisions, finding common ground on basic issues, openly debating controversial topics, while avoiding the cry to rally the movement behind any of the blocs had become the primary concerns of many members.[16] Countries like Sri Lanka were already talking about the 'fragmentation' of the movement, the Zambians were emphasizing its 'dislocation' and the Algerians were pointing out its 'regression', while the overwhelming majority considered this new crisis as the most serious to plague the movement in the last twenty years.[17]

According to the Algerian Foreign Minister Benyahia, the NAM could not find suitable means to cope with all these challenges, since both Washington and Moscow were acting like there was no movement at all, while the NAM, on the other hand, could not find enough inner strength to mobilize its members beyond any divisive issues for successfully launching another collective action. When decolonization was almost completed, he stressed, the movement proved not to be up to the task of preserving and strengthening the subsequent independence of its member states nor could it successfully promote the establishment of a new model of international relations. In his words, the NAM 'seemed … impotent', which could ultimately raise questions as to whether it was still viable or sustainable. Thus, key member states, like Algeria, India and Yugoslavia, had to work even more industriously to prop up its capability to immediately act whenever the situation demanded, otherwise the final outcome could prove to be rather tragic.[18]

Without ever questioning the viability or purposefulness of the NAM, the Yugoslav officials had gradually started to make the distinction between the policy of non-alignment and the movement itself, concluding that the policy had existed even before the movement was established and would continue to exist even outside this framework, since it was based on some long-lasting interests and principles that largely went beyond any institutional form. However, the individual policy of non-alignment still needed an adequate vessel to distribute its messages globally, facilitate reaching general consensus, formulate and launch collective actions, while also stimulating the spirit of overall solidarity of all non-bloc factors.[19] Nevertheless, the differences between the principles, interests and character of individual actions often produced a diverse impact on the proactive capacity of the movement by deepening its hidden antagonisms. Essentially, the individual interests and goals of member states had started to outweigh the general benefit, purpose and cause of the movement, thus representing a serious challenge to its future unity.[20]

Yet further institutionalization of the NAM also played a large part in the emergence of different internal contradictions and tensions. This clearly indicated that a joint action was welcomed, although one not determined by some concrete issues, since that could only foment new disagreements, but one specially dealing with the general context that was, paradoxically, directly contributing to the deteriorating character of a specific situation. Therefore, continuous work on the improvement and redefinition of strategic interests and the goals of the NAM, wedded to setting up a realistic balance between short-term and long-term agendas and between the general, regional and individual interests of its many members, could eventually prove to be the desirable path towards revitalizing the policy of non-alignment and the movement itself, while keeping them both outside the intensifying bloc confrontation.[21] The only tangible success achieved by the movement during these years was the establishment of black majority rule in Zimbabwe in 1980, which not only added another country to the non-aligned fold but also significantly increased political and military pressure on South Africa to cease with its occupation of Namibia and end the apartheid rule at home.[22]

However, these were also the years when all these complex issues only further contributed to the general lack of trust in Cuba's capability to lead.[23] This trend was first evident when the Pol Pot delegation was seated as the sole legal representative of Kampuchea at the 34th UNGA session, contrary to Cuba's ideas or advice, while Havana's bid to become the non-permanent member of the UNSC was also foiled, primarily by the lack of necessary NAM votes.[24] Furthermore, Havana's credibility was directly torpedoed by the Soviet invasion of Afghanistan, which caused an angry outcry all over the non-aligned world. This controversial Soviet action proved to be a far more serious obstacle to materializing Cuban ambitions than any organized internal opposition could ever be. Cuba's evident dependence on Moscow now went head to head with Havana's outright commitment to the NAM.[25] This would become even more obvious when a special session of the UNGA was held in January 1980, with Afghanistan being the main topic of deliberations. When a resolution was submitted to condemn Soviet action, fifty-seven non-aligned countries voted for, nine of them were against, core members of the 'progressive' group, while twenty-four countries abstained from voting, among them India, Zambia and Algeria. Before that vote took place, the non-aligned had also forced out a Soviet veto in the UNSC on the same issue, thus fully discrediting Moscow's stand in the Third World.[26] With such an outcome, some members were even calling for Cuban expulsion from the movement, now even more vociferously than before.[27]

Cuba had found itself caught between the Soviet anvil and the non-aligned hammer, thus desperately trying to avoid any debate on this issue at the CB. Naturally, such tactics backfired, since many CB members clearly aspired to discuss the negative consequences of the Soviet invasion against a fellow non-aligned country. Some among them, like Pakistan and Singapore, strongly criticized Cuba for defending Moscow's aggression, while others, like India and Algeria, avoided directly calling out the Soviets, primarily due to their special relationships with Moscow, but they still had to firmly oppose any military intervention in principle. However, Cuba's less than astute handling of this dispute only exacerbated things. In fact, as concluded by many, great power interventionism had become the main instrument of aggressively imposing someone else's will on small and weak countries, and everyone was well aware that this negative trend could become the NAM's most serious trial.[28]

This deadlock triggered a number of mediation initiatives launched by Yugoslavia, Cuba, India and others, primarily directed at reaching some kind of compromise between Afghanistan and Pakistan that would induce the Soviets to eventually withdraw. Some of these talks were also held during Tito's funeral in May 1980.[29] The Yugoslav basic idea was to hold an extraordinary NAM ministerial conference in the near future in order to discuss the issue of foreign interventionism, thus securing constructive participation from the majority of members, even though everyone knew that Afghanistan would, nevertheless, dominate the agenda. This proposal received backing from many Asian and African leaders. However, India was against this proposal altogether not only because it did not want to further annoy the USSR but it also perceived this initiative as a poorly thought-out idea that could only diminish India's role in the region and concurrently boost Pakistan's influence.[30]

The initial Yugoslav proposal was to hold this unplanned ministerial conference somewhere in Africa or Asia, primarily to avoid potential Cuban control over its proceedings. Since no one was too eager to accept hosting responsibilities, while others also wanted to avoid openly confronting Cuba, Havana suddenly presented itself as a potential host, proposing either to hold such conference there or at least organize a special CB meeting. Soon it became clear that this was a deliberate attempt to divert attention from Afghanistan and turn issues like Iran, Palestine, Namibia, etc. into the main topic of deliberations. Moreover, another Cuban tactic was to indefinitely extend the period of consultations, thus eventually making this conference either totally unnecessary or meaningless.[31] This kind of political manoeuvring especially enraged the Yugoslavs, while India and Sri Lanka also stood against holding this event in Havana. Since Cuba was apprehensive that there was no clear majority backing its bid, Yugoslavia pushed India to propose holding the scheduled NAM ministerial conference in January 1981, thus creating an additional guarantee that any competing proposals could not take place in the meantime.[32]

This turn of events clearly upset the Cubans who openly vented their frustrations. Nevertheless, their Yugoslav counterparts clearly indicated that such a tense situation was the direct outcome of the movement's inherent inability to openly and constructively discuss controversial issues like Kampuchea or Afghanistan, often pushing justified discontent under the carpet.[33] The Guyanese foreign minister once concluded that internal polarization along the bloc lines had reached its maximum, thus directly endangering the movement's unity, while such differences had affected many of the basic principles, prolonging the NAM's evident paralysis. He openly pointed his finger at Cuba as the main 'factor of disorientation'.[34] In a confidential conversation, one of Algeria's top officials stressed that letting Cuba become the NAM chairman was a big mistake and the primary cause for the movement's recent stagnation. According to him, Havana had proved itself incapable of successfully reforming the movement, which had become a necessity, thus triggering additional resentment and suspicion among other member states.[35]

The NAM ministerial conference in New Delhi, ultimately scheduled for early February 1981, was the first important gathering of non-aligned states after the Havana summit and the first major event since the eruption of the Iran–Iraq War. In fact, contentious issues, like the arms race, Iran–Iraq, Afghanistan and Kampuchea, would clearly dominate its agenda. This event was yet another attempt to revitalize and reinvigorate the NAM as a clear alternative to any bloc divisions, vociferously stressing its strong opposition to the escalating world chaos. These complex circumstances also contributed to the far lesser degree of assertiveness demonstrated by the 'progressive' group.[36] In addition, this ministerial conference also served its purpose to further strengthen Indira Gandhi's authority after her recent return to power. According to one of her closest advisors, she aspired to assume what used to be Tito's role in the movement, thus continuing with his general course as the NAM's chief spokesperson and key balancer.[37]

It was clear to everyone that it would be hard levelling out the many contradictions continuously tearing the movement apart, particularly if this gathering would only try to reaffirm the basic principles, without striving to consistently and objectively apply them. This had triggered concerns that India as a host would try avoiding any controversies by firmly holding middle ground, thus further blunting the edge of any new reform initiatives.[38] Furthermore, Indian officials were aware that reaching a workable consensus on certain issues would be very hard, therefore, upholding the movement's capacity to continue holding itself together had become New Delhi's overarching priority, even if that had to be done at the expense of the NAM's efficiency. Indian representatives also wanted to deal with everything in a closed circle of a few countries but Yugoslavia clearly opted for expanded consultations as a means of offsetting any kind of sectarianism. Some other participants, like Peru and Kuwait, considered that only stressing what was uniting the NAM, without determining points of discord, could, however, overshadow the pressing need of finding at least some common ground on these contentious issues. In essence, this largely implied keeping up with the unpopular Cuban practice of sweeping any controversies under the carpet.[39]

The depth of the NAM's internal crisis was also evident when everyone present in New Delhi finally realized that the CB ministerial meeting, previously organized every year, had not been summoned even once since the Havana summit. Therefore, when it did convene on the eve of the ministerial conference, its proceedings immediately faced a deadlock. A similar situation was present during the subsequent preparatory meeting when a fierce debate erupted between the two factions over Kampuchean representation and Soviet invasion of Afghanistan, thus only further amplifying the areas of disagreement. Furthermore, Iran and Iraq were also refusing to discuss a ceasefire, with some Arab countries calling again for Egypt's suspension. Essentially, the Indian hosts had a very tough time preventing a long-term split over so many divisive issues, while the situation seemed even more dramatic since the same old disputes were still raging on with undiminished intensity.[40]

However, when the ministerial conference eventually started (9–13 February 1981), the initial Indian draft of the final document attempted to accommodate the views of so many countries, and so also faced strong criticism in this respect. In the end, through skilful manoeuvring of Indian hosts and other delegations, a workable solution was eventually found. As for the Kampuchean representation, it had not yet been resolved, leaving its seat still vacant, but its people were, nonetheless, recognized with a clear right to decide their own destiny free from any foreign interference.[41] In the Afghan case, since the debate had reached a stalemate, a delicate consensus was found by calling out for a political settlement on the basis of withdrawal of all foreign troops, without explicitly naming the Soviets, and extending full respect for the independence, sovereignty and territorial integrity of a non-aligned Afghanistan. As for the Iran–Iraq War, the Committee of Good Offices, established the previous year, consisting of the Cuban, Indian, Zambian and PLO delegates, was asked to continue with its mediating efforts. The issue of Egyptian suspension was also deferred to the next summit without making any concrete recommendations.[42] Nevertheless, Cuba used some of its covert tactics to get Yugoslavia out of the Good Offices Committee. Havana skilfully used Iraqi opposition to Algerian participation to effectively sideline Yugoslavia's potential candidacy, awkwardly presenting this as a balanced approach to committee's regional composition.[43]

Even though this ministerial conference could not offer constructive solutions, it did manage to minimize the damage and mitigate some of the controversies, thus keeping the movement still functional and partially out of total paralysis. Essentially, the Havana-type consensus was largely dead. However, it still seemed that the movement had reasserted its image as an independent moral and political force in the world. In addition, on this occasion NAM foreign ministers also marked the twentieth anniversary of the Belgrade Conference, issuing an appeal to the great powers for preserving world peace and resuming top-level dialogue. This time, nonetheless, such an initiative carried far less weight than the one launched in 1961.[44] Furthermore, the New Delhi ministerial conference somewhat shifted the focus of the superpowers onto the NAM again, with the Soviets trying to court non-aligned countries so as to avoid future condemnation, while the Americans aspired to incite a more assertive stance among the 'conservative' members in order to exert more pressure on Cuba. Nevertheless, in both these cases the blocs would only step up their interference.[45]

In order for the NAM to regain some of its old dynamism, during 1981 two CB ministerial meetings were held, one extraordinary one on Namibia in Algiers in April and the other one during the 36th UNGA session in September. While the former exclusively dealt with the issue of reassessing the aid extended to the Namibian liberation movement SWAPO, the latter, with a strong anti-US undertone, made a re-evaluation of the situation in different crisis hotspots that directly tackled the NAM's interests.[46] This second meeting triggered a harsh response on behalf of the US ambassador to the UN ambassador, Jeane Kirkpatrick, who dispatched a letter to sixty-four heads of non-aligned delegations, openly criticizing them for their unfair and unbalanced treatment. This severe reaction made many 'moderates' reconsider their role when drafting similar documents in the future but also implied that the US was again taking seriously the NAM's international role, even when the outlook of this organization was not at its best.[47]

Problems with Organizing the 7th Summit

This active struggle against the blocs, which the NAM had waged from the very start, now transformed itself from largely an external one into increasingly an internal one, thus further contributing to the ideological polarization and escalating political divisions. This was closely related to the open manipulation of the consensus principle, with different factions often trying to either impose it or prevent it from ever being reached. Furthermore, a number of international crises was also on the rise. Paradoxically, in spite of such difficult conditions, the superpowers were stubbornly refusing to accept the services offered by different non-aligned countries, often blatantly trying to undermine their efforts or, even more often, completely ignoring them. Therefore, the NAM's future task was not only to promote the lessening of tensions between the superpowers but also to formulate a concrete action plan to tackle all key issues related to the well-being of all nations, irrespective of their individual preferences, thus returning again to the agenda of the 'golden years' of non-alignment.[48]

The greatest challenge to the NAM's continuity came in 1982, when the Baghdad summit was supposed to be held. A clear majority of countries was becoming increasingly sceptical that such a gathering could ever take place during wartime. Even though Tehran was initially for postponing the summit, at least until the situation on the battlefield clarified, their fresh successes inspired the Iranian leadership to actively push for changing the summit venue altogether.[49] In the meantime, the NAM held another extraordinary CB ministerial meeting in Kuwait in April, primarily dedicated to the Palestinian issue. This was a direct attempt made by the PLO to reassert its role as an independent political factor in the region. This gathering also demonstrated an obvious decline in Cuba's influence when the US was solely criticized for some of its regional policies, primarily the ones related to Israel, but not in general as an 'imperialist power' as used to be the case. Nevertheless, the Iran–Iraq War was still ominously looming in the background.[50]

In spite of everything, everyone acted as if the 7th summit would be still organized in Baghdad. The forthcoming CB ministerial meeting in Havana in late May–early June 1982 was supposed to serve the purpose of a preparatory meeting, since the future summit had to become an event where some internal NAM conflicts would be effectively remedied.[51] This gathering took place under very complex international circumstances, those marked by deteriorating conditions in the regions of Central and South America (Nicaragua, Salvador, Falklands War) and the Middle East (Israeli annexation of the Golan Heights, invasion of Lebanon, Iran–Iraq War), while negotiations on the decolonization of Namibia were already facing a protracted deadlock due to the US reluctance for totally giving up on South Africa. Despite attempts by the pro-Soviet and pro-US factions to take command of this gathering, the 'moderate' forces headed by India and Yugoslavia managed to steer the proceedings away from any extreme positions. Only on the Latin American issues more radical formulations prevailed, especially due to the Cuban chairing of the drafting committee and the NAM's stringent opposition to the US, British and South African militarization of the South Atlantic.[52]

On the margins of this meeting, Iran and Syria actively lobbied for holding the summit anywhere else but Baghdad. Nevertheless, there was still no general consensus as to whether that event would be held in Iraq or elsewhere. Naturally, the Iraqi representatives were adamant that they could still successfully organize the 7th summit, while India was already campaigning to host the 8th one, opposite Libya, Syria and North Korea.[53] Some 'radical' countries were also tacitly against Baghdad, primarily due to Iraq's recent rapprochement with the West, Saudi Arabia and Egypt, while Cuba secretly aspired to use this opportunity to extend its chairmanship for a while longer. Based on some sources, during the CB meeting Malmierca even offered to the Iraqis to hold an extraordinary NAM ministerial conference in Havana in August, and then, based on its results, assess the prospects for holding the summit in Baghdad later that same year. Furthermore, in order to get ahead of all these initiatives, Saddam soon ordered full withdrawal of his forces from the Iranian territory and declared a unilateral ceasefire. However, the Iranians were determined to continue with their offensive and they were aggressively pressing on with Saddam's removal from power.[54]

When analysing these developments, it seemed as if the movement had regressed back to the situation similar to the years of stagnation between the Cairo and Lusaka Conferences. However, international conditions were now much worse, while relations inside the movement were even tenser. Therefore, Yugoslavia was seriously considering India as the best choice to host the summit instead of Iraq, especially since some of the 'radicals' were thinking about promoting Cuba or Ethiopia as venues, while some 'conservatives', contrary to Belgrade's desires, were prepared to raise Yugoslavia's candidacy.[55] Nevertheless, during the extraordinary CB ministerial meeting on the Lebanon crisis in Nicosia in July, the Cubans finally realized that any postponement of the summit, however opportune it could seem, would only further prolong the movement's ongoing crisis. Finding a new host, preferably India, and holding the next summit in the first half of 1983 would be the best solution for overcoming all these difficulties, while restoring some of NAM's shattered credibility. The only obstacle to such a proposal could be protracted Iraqi intransigence. Therefore, launching a coordinated diplomatic action involving Cuba, India, Yugoslavia, Algeria, Zambia, Sri Lanka and some other countries, mostly former summit hosts (not Egypt due to Cuban opposition), would be the best way to collectively present to the Iraqi side what the movement's future really entailed if the next summit was not held at all.[56]

According to some Cuban sources, Saddam was also toying with the idea of holding the summit in Kuwait as a co-host or in Geneva under Iraqi chairmanship. This was unacceptable to others, since it implied that the movement was totally incapabable of even organizing its own summit, which would mark the lowest point of the NAM's existence.[57] However, since Malmierca's visit to Baghdad did not succeed in changing Saddam's mind, on the second day Castro sent a letter to all non-aligned leaders inviting their foreign ministers to a conference in Havana in late August, where the final decision on the future of the 7th summit would be passed.[58] In response, Iraq dispatched a number of delegations, arguing for holding a ministerial conference in Baghdad, thus tentatively opening doors to the possibility of Iraq eventually not hosting the summit. In a private conversation with his Yugoslav colleague, the Iraq ambassador in the UN clearly indicated that Baghdad had reconciled with the fact that it was impossible to organize the summit there but that they still wanted to save face. This was also in accordance with the earlier Yugoslav proposal to let Iraq take the initiative in this respect, while a conference in Havana should be kept on the table as a means of applying additional pressure on Baghdad if it decided to backtrack on its promises.[59]

Since Yugoslavia enjoyed considerable prestige and influence in Iraq it was agreed to dispatch a member of the Yugoslav Presidium and the Foreign Secretary to Iraq as special envoys. After their meetings with the Iraqi leadership, both sides reached the conclusion that the next summit should be held in India in 1983, while Iraq would organize a ministerial conference in early September, with only one item on the agenda: confirmation of the decision regarding the change of summit venue.

This was Saddam's red line for abandoning his role as a host, while the Cubans were supposed to drop their demands for holding a conference in Havana.[60] However, Cuba still continued with its competing conference proposal, even though its outlook was also dim. Yugoslavia was adamant against such an approach, especially since, as they considered, Iraq had made such a huge concession by deciding not to host the summit, a move that eventually preserved the NAM's credibility and unity. Everything had to be done, as observed from Belgrade, to let Saddam save his face and walk out of this desperate situation as least humiliated as possible.[61]

In fact, the majority of other members were arguing for a closer study of all these proposals, even though many of them were clearly more in favour of Baghdad than Havana for holding any ministerial conferences, regardless of the war danger. However, the Cubans and their allies were strongly against Iraq being the host of such an event, even an interim one, especially since it was still impossible to reach an across-the-board consensus in this respect, thus also promising a full-scale diplomatic confrontation with Iraq. The greatest fear was that this sideshow controversy would only instil new disturbances into the movement, even though the summit issue had been successfully resolved. Therefore, Yugoslavia, India and Zambia were trying to induce both sides to walk away from such proposals, while concurrently promoting a new ministerial meeting in New York. This kind of solution was especially important since India tied its final agreement to host the summit to the official Iraqi proposal for New Delhi to be the new summit venue.[62]

One of the reasons for demonstrating Cuban inflexibility was also to secure the venue for the future 8th summit for some of the members of the 'progressive' group, like Syria or Libya, instead of Iraq. Castro's haste to sound out his proposal for a ministerial conference, even though Iraq still had not provided Malmierca with a definitive answer, was potentially indicative in this respect.[63] Nevertheless, since it had become clear to everyone that this Cuban–Iraqi turf would effectively sabotage any future NAM events from ever taking place, during Malmierca's second visit to Baghdad in late August, he and Saddam had finally reached an agreement to hold the summit in India. Iraq would be then the next summit host, while both sides decided to drop their demands for any ministerial conferences, thus opening the way for preparations for the 7th summit to start immediately.[64] This compromise decision was officially acknowledged during the NAM ministerial meeting in New York in early October, scheduling the New Delhi summit for early March 1983.[65]

The New Delhi Conference

Despite barely getting out of a tight spot, the NAM was still preoccupied with its different internal disputes. The overall economic situation had also worsened, while outside pressures on both individual members and the entire movement were only trumped up. Nevertheless, recent developments had somewhat blunted the edge of both leftist and rightist radicalism, although still insufficiently empowering the 'moderate' group. In fact, both these extremes had realized that the Indian chairmanship provided a leeway for lessening tensions between these two factions, while also restoring some general balance into the movement's operations.⁶⁶ For example, even the Reagan administration was not observing the NAM as a lost cause or an implacable foe any longer, trying to find at least some points of accommodation. The US seemed to be even more ready to seriously discuss implementing measures for easing the economic burden of developing countries, although still based on Washington's ideas.⁶⁷

India was investing a lot of effort to assume a more dominant role as a NAM chairman, often dictating some of its key points, especially regarding the potential creation of a smaller and more efficient CB. This basically went against the Yugoslav, Sri Lankan and Zambian proposal for the CB's further democratization by turning this body into a more open and plenary one, since, as they thought, everyone had to be given the same opportunities to express their respective stance. In addition, with respect to the Kampuchean representation, India decided not to invite the DK or PRK delegations to be physically present in New Delhi. Yugoslavia and Sri Lanka protested such a decision, firmly upholding the Maputo formula, considering that this issue needed to be further elaborated at the summit, while, in the meantime, the DK delegation should be at least present in the city. Nevertheless, the Indian side was adamant not to allow either the DK or Sihanouk delegations to attend, a position which naturally enjoyed strong Vietnamese support.⁶⁸

The very first test of all these initiatives was the extraordinary CB ministerial meeting in Managua in January 1983, one dedicated to the complex security situation in Latin America. Although Nicaragua was the host, everything was done under Cuban guidance, ranging from drafting the final document to some procedural issues. This gathering proved to be a valuable opportunity for the Cubans to restore some of their receding influence by boosting Havana's anti-US position among some of its neighbours. In this way, Latin America would become Castro's secure stage for transmitting Cuban influences inside the NAM. This was tested during the preparatory meeting when the Cuban chairman aspired to exclude some Latin American observers (Mexico, Columbia, Venezuela) from the process of drafting documents, a proposal strongly protested by Yugoslavia, Algeria, Sri Lanka, Peru and some other countries. Many 'moderate' participants, nonetheless, succeeded in tempering the tone of the final document, allowing only general criticism of the US and its policies towards Cuba and Nicaragua. Essentially, the tense situation in Central and South America was generally put into a wider context of inter-bloc confrontation, without accusing the US as being the sole culprit.⁶⁹

In order to guarantee a successful outcome of the forthcoming summit, countries such as India, Yugoslavia and Egypt, but also Cuba and its allies, decided to dispatch a number of high-level delegations to travel across the non-aligned world and present their respective ideas, proposals and agendas.⁷⁰ Furthermore, New Delhi's middle-of-the-road tactics when drafting the summit's documents was primarily aimed at securing the widest possible consensus, any militant formulations were clearly avoided, thus allowing the hosts to eventually reach compromises with the 'radicals' on certain side points, while standing firm on some fundamental issues. This proposed document treated both superpowers in an even-handed manner, the US was not that frequently mentioned, crisis hotspots were more or less objectively treated, while economic and disarmament issues evidently dominated its contents.⁷¹

Most of the time India and Yugoslavia were working hand in hand to prepare the forthcoming event, while adequately covering some of the most important points so as to avoid any surprises. At the preparatory meeting in New York in mid-February 1983, India circulated a number of proposals for a radical overhaul of the CB structure and its competences, waiting for a final say in this respect to be made during the summit. This meeting also recommended that Colombia, Barbados, Bahamas and Vanuatu be accepted as full members, while the Venezuelan application was postponed indefinitely due to the Guyanese opposition. In addition, Honduras was not endorsed as an observer, primarily due to its close military relationship with the US and its specific role in the regional confrontation with Nicaragua.[72] Nevertheless, on the controversial bilateral issues both India and many other countries were still bracing themselves for bitter divisions and acrimony.

The New Delhi Conference proved to be the last stand for the majority of members aspiring to see the NAM extricating itself from a lingering crisis and preserving some of its international prestige without compromising its essence. Since this gathering was organized under very tense conditions, expectations for maintaining the movement's continuity were very high. This summit was held on 7–12 March 1983, attended by ninety-nine full members (out of 101), eighteen observers and twenty-seven guests, preceded by ambassadorial (1–2 March) and ministerial (3–5 March) meetings. While India was the conference chairman, together with twenty-two vice-chairman, Yugoslavia and Nicaragua were elected as heads of the Political and Economic Committees. In addition, a recommendation was passed to the summit to expand CB membership to seventy-four representatives, thus formally boosting its democratic capacity and equal regional representation, but, as time would tell, only contributing to its growing ineffectiveness.[73]

The first controversy erupted at the ministerial meeting when a heated debate was initiated by Singapore on the issue of Kampuchea. In fact, the Singaporean delegation wanted to use this occasion as a suitable pretext to continue hammering Cuba's policies. Foreign Minister Rajaratnam largely based his argument on recent UNGA decisions regarding DK presence in that body, although without gaining much ground with others. Thus, despite three days of intensive exchanges, it was again agreed to keep the Kampuchean seat vacant until the next NAM ministerial conference in Luanda in 1985.[74] This failure served as an incentive for Rajaratnam to openly circulate a letter in which he raised serious questions about the NAM's future and the imminent dangers of becoming irrelevant. Due to the astute Indian handling of this affair, without also allowing Cuba or Vietnam to set off a new round of clashes, another conflicting debate was smoothly avoided. Nevertheless, some of the points raised by Singapore made many members consider the movement's prospects generally bleak.[75]

In her opening speech, Indira Gandhi gave a very constructive and balanced overview of India's position on the current state of affairs, primarily stressing points of agreement between different views. She did not mention either of the two superpowers, but she did criticize the arms race and interventionism, while continuously emphasizing the non-bloc and peaceful character of the NAM. Gandhi also presented some of the basic principles and strategic goals of the movement in accordance with its fundamental values, especially with respect to different crisis hotspots, economic problems and the failure of the North–South dialogue taking the bulk of her elaboration. She issued a new call for the establishment of the NIEO, while encompassing peace, independence, development and disarmament as one set of closely interrelated issues. In order to avoid any new disputes, Gandhi formally praised Castro's performance as the preceding chairman, in spite of privately reserving a lot of criticism for him.[76] In this spirit of cooperation, Gandhi provided us with one of the key definitions of non-alignment:

> Non-alignment is national independence and freedom. It stands for peace and the avoidance of confrontation. It aims keeping away from military alliances. It means equality among nations and the democratisation of international relations, economic and political. It wants global cooperation for development on the basis of mutual benefit. It is a strategy for the recognition and preservation of the world's diversity.[77]

Her entire address had nothing to do with the ideological messages sounded out at Havana, thus restoring the principles, ideas and visions of the 1976 Colombo Conference. This ultimately proved to be beneficial to the current stabilization of the movement.

In the soothing atmosphere set by this speech, the general debate proceeded in a constructive and balanced manner, thus avoiding further deepening of the crisis. The majority of participants managed to find common denominators that bonded together their individual interests, while still putting the burden of blame for the deteriorating situation in the world on both superpowers. This part of the summit proceedings was primarily dedicated to economic issues, largely avoiding different political controversies. However, issues like Korea, Afghanistan, the Iran–Iraq War and the Indian Ocean had the potential to set off another round of tense exchanges.[78] Nevertheless, a compromise was eventually found through either resorting back to the decisions of the 1981 New Delhi ministerial conference, as in the case of Afghanistan, or using them as a basis for applying a similar formula for Korea, while on other issues where no compromise was at hand (Iran–Iraq), further deliberations were deferred to future NAM gatherings. India also succeeded in removing the Egyptian suspension issue from the agenda, in spite of some Arab protests.[79]

The text of the Political Declaration was prepared under the Yugoslav chairmanship of the Political Committee. In this document the NAM's traditional goals were reiterated, while all non-aligned leaders rejected domination of all great powers as directly threatening their independence and stability, especially stressing economic inequality as having a major impact on the unfortunate state of political conditions. Therefore, they insisted on an interdependent world where all countries, irrespective of their size and strength, took an equal part in the global decision-making process. These leaders also criticized attempts at transforming the just wars of national-liberation into unjust ones closely related to the East–West conflict. The US role in Central America was particularly singled out in this respect. A special Committee for the Middle East was also established, especially as a means of assisting the PLO after the Israeli invasion of Lebanon, while the venue for the 8th summit was still left undetermined. In the end, the so-called 'New Delhi Message' was issued as an appeal to the great powers to end the arms race, reduce tensions, restart their dialogue and assist the economic development of the South by releasing necessary funding through decreasing their defence expenditures.[80]

A similar situation was observed with the Economic Declaration, drafted under the Nicaraguan chairmanship of the Economic Committee, surprisingly leaving out any ideological influences from this subject. This document advocated a multilateral framework for resolving economic plight of the developing world through comprehensive North–South dialogue, as well as by setting up a new international monetary system that would end the financial domination of certain nations or currencies. The non-aligned leaders also adopted a two-stage approach by arguing for initially resolving key monetary and financial issues (debts, the role of the IMF and the World Bank, trade, raw materials, food, monetary issues), while later turning to other important areas that needed to be addressed (science and technology, nuclear energy, environment, human resources, refugees). South–South cooperation was particularly stressed as a means for developing countries to enhance their bargaining position, although that was becoming increasingly difficult due to their direct competition in the same commodities markets and growing debt burden.[81] Unfortunately, none of the funds or centres established during the 1970s ever moved beyond the planning stage, thus marking another obvious failure of the NAM.

Even though the NAM was not totally out of crisis, India's hosting of this summit and its subsequent chairmanship could be summarized by two words: restoration and balance. India had succeeded in restoring importance to the movement's fundamental principles, while also bringing back balance into its dealings with both superpowers. The New Delhi Conference heralded an effective end to the pro-Soviet tilt launched by Cuba, without ever shifting the movement towards the US as a response. In her closing address, Gandhi called the NAM 'a vital historical process', one being 'not dogmatic but dynamic'. Without such an emergency leeway provided by India, it would have been quite impossible for the movement to survive that decade, perhaps even the following few years.[82] In fact, neither Washington nor Moscow were totally content with the outcome of this summit, but it still proved far less worrisome for both than they had previously expected.[83] However, the East was disturbed by the fact that the concept of equidistance was regaining its importance, shifting the NAM's loyalties decisively away from the Soviet bloc.[84]

At this event, a constructive spirit and general pragmatism had ultimately ruled the day, thus bringing back into the mainstream the 'universalist' agenda of the past. Basic unity had been restored but that did not mean that the NAM was totally out of peril. This only implied that its existential crisis had somewhat receded as compared to the previous couple of years. Furthermore, some authors even labelled this summit as 'the obituary of the Third World' when the neoliberal economic agenda had gradually started overtaking the NAM's economic discourse instead of the NIEO, with many nations now opting for the modernization agenda which was made along the lines dictated by the developed world. Asian nations were leading the way in this respect, with some Latin American countries joining in this, thus effectively undermining the entire NIEO project.[85] What the Egyptians also noticed was the fact that Yugoslavia's role was far less prominent than before, while the absence of Tito's towering figure did not go unnoticed by many attendees.[86]

However, the only other major event that same year, besides the extraordinary meeting of nine non-aligned foreign ministers in New Delhi in April dedicated to the next UNCTAD session in Yugoslavia, was the 38th UNGA session. At that time, India once again strongly assumed its leadership role as the chairman. While addressing the UN, Indira Gandhi primarily tackled economic and disarmament issues as central topics, thus demonstrating to the world the NAM's new constructive international role, one not seen in years. For some 'radicals', this could have seemed as tantamount to impotence, although the movement's moderate policies never stood for a lack of willingness to act.[87] This time, nonetheless, willingness was still verbally there but the sense of purpose had started to slowly fade away.

NAM's Deepening Crisis during the 1980s

Nevertheless, in spite of the generally positive atmosphere in New Delhi, external pressure was still on the rise, while India was often acting very cautiously, trying to maintain delicate balance between the superpowers. Such a tentative situation had slowly led the NAM into a period of stagnation. A sense of helplessness had started to taint relations between different members, nudging them to increasingly undertake individual actions, fully aware that the blocs were actively pushing the movement to the margin of world politics (US invasion of Granada in October 1983 only caused restrained protests from the movement). The continuous inability of the movement to find an adequate mechanism for resolving bilateral conflicts between member states had still remained its Achilles heel, thus affecting all other areas of activity. It seemed as if the 'progressive' group was very much in retreat, while the 'conservative' one was further emboldened by a proactive US engagement in the Third World.[88]

The situation inside the movement would somewhat intensify in 1984, especially in the realm of promoting the NIIO (Namedia Conference of the non-aligned printed and electronic media organized in December 1983). However, this increased level of activism still could not shatter the pervasive feeling that the NAM was slowly lagging behind world events and it could not formulate a timely and adequate response to them, not to mention undertaking any serious initiatives.[89] In spite of regular CB meetings in New York, the only noticeable event in the movement's history during 1984 was the meeting of heads of delegations during the 39th UNGA session, which, as in many other cases, satisfied itself only with issuing a lengthy document, a mere overview of international developments, without building up any corresponding actions.[90] In addition, Indira Gandhi's tragic assassination in October 1984 only further aggravated this unwelcoming trend, since eventually no one was left to fill in that leadership void left after her. The situation was very similar to Tito's recent departure, while Castro, who perhaps possessed the authority and charisma to assume command, was seriously crippled by his earlier controversial performance as the movement's chairman.[91]

With the onset of 1985, the first signs of potential easing of international tensions had become noticeable with first Reagan–Gorbachev contact. However, many of the armed conflicts undermining the NAM's unity were still raging on with undiminished intensity. When accompanied by a deteriorating economic situation, especially in the sphere of indebtedness, prospects were not so bright for the movement and many of its members. The two extremes of non-aligned politics were basically locked in a protracted stalemate, while the centrist forces were lacking potential, sometimes even willpower, to revitalize the NAM's global role, without inducing any new splintering. Due to so many disagreements, the only other topic where the majority of members could forge a united front was the decolonization of Namibia and the end of apartheid in South Africa (the Palestinian issue could be also put into this category). Therefore, by the mid-1980s, the 'frontline states' and other African nations had gradually assumed control of the movement by turning it into an organization frequently dealing with continental problems, in parallel to the OAU.[92]

While this kind of approach injected a new sort of dynamism into the NAM's functioning, such a trend also demonstrated that the movement was incapable of successfully resolving many conflicting situations, thus becoming increasingly mired in some regional issues that offered a well-tested rallying point for anti-colonial and anti-racist struggle. Therefore, for many members the easiest way to participate in the NAM often resembled sleepwalking into future gatherings. Nevertheless, this turn of events also indicated that the movement was essentially undergoing regionalization where the Southern African problematic would clearly dominate its agenda. The obvious confirmation was the extraordinary CB ministerial meeting in New Delhi in April 1985, primarily dedicated to Namibia and finding ways of completing its liberation, while also applying additional measures to reignite the UN debate to exert additional pressure on South Africa and its Western supporters.[93]

With this increasing 'Africanization' of the NAM, the 'progressive' group saw this as yet another opportunity to bolster their influence by linking their efforts to general African aspirations. This was quite evident when behind-the-scenes discussions opened regarding the 8th summit venue, since Iraq was no longer a viable candidate. Many countries aspiring to become hosts, like Syria, Libya and North Korea, had also withdrawn their candidacies. Therefore, new venue proposals were emerging, like Tanzania, Algeria, Tunisia, Indonesia and Argentina, but countries like India and Iraq were also lobbying for Yugoslavia to be a potential host, in spite of Belgrade's obvious reluctance.[94] Nevertheless, the Cubans understood well what would happen if the next summit was held in Yugoslavia or if India prolonged its chairmanship for longer, so they started pedalling for Zimbabwe to host that event. Due to Cuba's large military presence in Angola, it would be much easier to promote a more radical agenda at such a gathering. This proved to be quite problematic for Yugoslavia, since it did not want to be seen as obstructing the ongoing African struggle in any way. Therefore, the Yugoslav side also started tacitly pushing for Harare's candidacy, thus aspiring to bring the African group closer to its position.[95]

The ultimate decision would be passed at the forthcoming NAM ministerial conference in Luanda in early September 1985, the most important event scheduled for that year. Luanda proved to be conducive to Cuban attempts to use the explosive situation in Southern Africa as a springboard for strengthening the 'progressive' group. However, this venture largely backfired due to the opposition of many other delegations. In fact, the leftist group could not garner wider backing any longer, even among some countries that used to be close to them, like Mozambique or Ethiopia. In order to forestall the Cuban diplomatic offensive, Yugoslavia, backed by India, Algeria and other countries, decided to officially render its full support to the Zimbabwean candidacy. Therefore, Harare was chosen as the venue of the next summit scheduled for late August 1986, while Yugoslavia also assisted in constructing the hall where the summit would held. As compensation, Yugoslavia was elected as the G77 chairman in order to successfully push through plans for restarting the already moribund North–South dialogue. However, the deteriorating security and economic situation in the Third World, set against the background of receding tensions between the two blocs, still created a potential recipe for the 'radicals' to try to exercise a far more influential role than they truly deserved.[96]

The lessening of inter-bloc tensions was a promising sign for the NAM indeed, since the pressure of both blocs could soon recede, but this, nevertheless, also opened up prospects for a new deal being struck between the superpowers, one also potentially involving the re-definition of the spheres of influence. Evidently, the movement was mired in its passive phase, having less and less impact on international developments, facing serious economic downturn and desperately clinging to the Southern African and Palestinian issues as a last resort to produce at least some positive and moral effect on world politics. The NAM primarily aspired to make a contribution in the sphere of disarmament and economic development but these were still two central topics where the great powers did not seek their opinion or advice any more. In spite of a positive spirit still permeating official documents, prospects for the movement as an agency of change were becoming increasingly dim.[97] When the potential to act was far greater, especially after the Colombo Conference, valuable time had been lost on unnecessary ideological disputes which had eventually drained a lot of enthusiasm or strength for staging any meaningful actions with a long-term impact. Now, even if there was enthusiasm, and unfortunately there was not, the capability to act had been significantly reduced due to the ongoing economic strife, thus forcing many countries to disregard the bigger picture and solely concentrate on their everyday troubles.[98]

This kind of atmosphere was quite conspicuous at the CB ministerial meeting in New Delhi in April 1986, convened in the immediate aftermath of the US bombing of Libya after a terrorist attack in West Berlin. As well as the customary criticism of aggression against a non-aligned country, this meeting also dealt primarily with the situation in Namibia and South Africa. However, the remaining part of the discussion was dedicated to the issues of economic cooperation, tackling different means of alleviating economic trouble. In the end, only recent economic failures were clearly recognized, no new ideas were ever presented, while even some innovative proposals, like the idea of establishing a permanent economic committee, could not garner enough support. During this event it was becoming increasingly evident that even the most prominent members, like Algeria or Tanzania, seemed aloof, passive or even disinterested to act, while, on the other hand, India and Yugoslavia were desperately trying to keep everything alive for the foreseeable future.[99]

The Harare Conference was held on 1–7 September 1986, preceded, as had been the case in the past, by ambassadorial and ministerial meetings. This was a summit summoned on the occasion of the 25th anniversary of the movement, when, for the very first time, there were no new countries becoming NAM members, while there were even fewer heads of state or government attending this gathering than used to be the case at the New Delhi and Havana summits. Even the final document was more extensive than ever before, but still elaborated on the same old ideas and concepts, thus clearly indicating the obvious lack of innovation and comprehension of the new situation developing in the world. These facts clearly indicated that an increasing number of countries did not recognize the NAM as a crucial expression, advocate or protector of their individual aspirations any longer, but the majority still went along with the current since there was no other similar multilateral mechanism to stimulate or steer collective actions of the non-bloc world.[100] Even the behind-the-scenes presence of the two superpowers, an unavoidable fact in the past, was no longer evident, since both Washington and Moscow were now holding direct negotiations, without any outside interferences, and not paying much attention to this summit. Moscow was somewhat encouraged with the radical atmosphere created by the hosts, also extending its support for the NAM idea of setting up different zones of peace and pursuing disarmament talks, but none of that went beyond enthusiastic proclamations.[101]

Alongside discussing major international issues, primarily disarmament, the world economy and South–South cooperation, the situation in Southern Africa clearly dominated the proceedings (a fund for fighting colonialism and apartheid was established and South African sanctions were collectively introduced). For the very first time, this summit issued an official document dealing with the Iran–Iraq conflict, six years after it had erupted. This revealed a lot about the NAM's capability to effectively cope with internal conflicts. However, it was already clear that the strength of the 'progressive' group had been irretrievably diminished, while the conservatives were now looking up to the West for preserving their interests. Robert Mugabe as the host tried to promote the establishment of the movement's secretariat as its permanent governing body but that idea was immediately rejected by other attendees. In fact, unlike many earlier summits, this one did not even determine the venue of the 9th summit, leaving it for the 1988 ministerial conference in Nicosia to finally elect a candidate.[102] The decision not to choose the next summit venue was a serious transgression against the very essence of the principle of continuity. This proved to be a serious blow to the movement's future, creating an omnipresent sentiment of uncertainty.

NAM's Outlook for the Future

In the late 1980s, not only was the NAM undergoing profound crisis, it also seemed as if the Cold War was almost at its end, with Gorbachev opening strategic talks with Reagan over nuclear arms reductions, further lessening of inter-bloc tensions in Europe and also substantially downscaling of the Soviet involvement in the Third World. The latter was signified by the Soviet withdrawal from Afghanistan in February 1989, thus leaving many of the recently established Marxist regimes in Asia, Africa and Central America without any significant economic or military backing. Many of them would soon disappear from the world map, often leaving internal turmoil and extremism behind them, with only Vietnam, Cuba and North Korea being notable exceptions. Some Third World conflicts were slowly disappearing from the headlines, ending in different ways, with the agreement between the superpowers, Cuba, Angola and South Africa to end regional conflict standing as a bright example and a rare exception to a sombre rule (Namibia would gain independence in 1990). In the structural sense of the word, the classical Cold War was basically over in Asia, the Middle East, Africa and, one could say even Europe by the mid-1980s, with the new post-Cold War trends already firmly in place.[103]

In many ways, the basic problem with the NAM's role in the 1980s was also connected to its outright lack of ability to correctly assess and comprehend major shifts taking place in the world. However, the NAM was still adapting itself to old Cold War conditions and not to the international order that was coming after it. Therefore, concurrent expectations of many members were either for the movement to change its concept, purpose and direction or face growing irrelevance in world affairs. When the NAM ministerial conference finally met in Nikosia in September 1988, Yugoslavia, irrespective of its growing internal troubles, was ready to host the next summit, thus finally bringing the movement back to its point of origin, while also promoting a new modernized agenda. With Nicaragua and Indonesia both withdrawing their candidacies, the Yugoslav delegation finally succeeded in realising its bid, scheduling the next summit for September 1989.[104] This summit was essentially the 'swan song' of Cold War non-alignment. Nevertheless, it would also become the first step on the NAM's long journey of transformation and modernization for the post-Cold War era.

In that new epoch, as set by the Belgrade Conference, earlier ideological confrontation would no longer reign high in NAM's projections (eight bloc members were then accepted as guests, both East and West, Venezuela became a full member), while social, economic, humanitarian and ecological issues would definitely dominate the future Third World agenda – sustainable development and corresponding integration in terms of markets, capital flows and technology. The Yugoslav draft of the final document was revolutionary in its sense that it only emphasized disarmament, development and the global economy, without resorting to any old topics or ideological mantras. By firmly linking economic and environmental dimensions, affecting equally both the developed and developing countries, a new way for rebooting the North–South dialogue had been found. The radical agenda of some participants, coming from both sides of the spectre, had failed miserably at this summit.[105]

Accommodation with the great powers and not open confrontation would be the primary expression of these new aspirations, thus signalling the NAM's constructive integration into the existing world order, one going beyond bipolarity, without eventually establishing a new one as had been previously intended. The Yugoslavs and some other members, like India and Algeria, understood well that foreign and domestic issues had become firmly intertwined as compared to before and they needed a completely altered approach to international political and economic affairs, both on individual and collective levels. In this way, what had been initially argued by countries such as Yugoslavia or India ultimately found its expression in all the conference documents. Therefore, an executive group of fifteen non-aligned countries (G15) was established to spearhead this new socioeconomic agenda in the UN, thus signalling the birth of some new Third World multilateral initiatives.[106]

Nevertheless, neoliberal globalization substituted the Third World project by gradually deconstructing it into a new system of ideas, although with a different degree of success and often with dubious results.[107] This would be an arduous, bumpy road where the NAM would often not successfully locate its new focus or it would be plagued by new divisions or some radical attempts to initiate a new overhaul. Yugoslavia's bloody break up and its disappearance from the list of key NAM members had also removed one of the main driving forces from the historical scene. Thanks to such pragmatic guidelines laid down at Belgrade in 1989, the NAM has prolonged its existence during the entire post-Cold War era (nine summits after that). Nevertheless, during the subsequent years the movement faced growing irrelevance or was frequently ignored by the great powers. Furthermore, during those years, the US also did its best to dismantle many of the constructive things the NAM had arduously strived to establish, like the UNCTAD, also continuing with its unabated foreign interventionism.[108] However, with the rising multipolarity in the world today, with so many new centres of power or different regional organizations acting as pillars of the international order, many of them coming from the Third World, the NAM will be forced to reinvent itself along these new lines, laboriously adapting to these new conditions, preserving some of its fundamental identity, perhaps talking in a louder voice than before, while trying to move beyond the image of just a debate club or a vent for certain frustrations.[109] It might even become a Third World version of the Commonwealth: still present, everyone has grown accustomed to it, but no one really takes it too seriously, except as some kind of prestige by only being its member.

In this future endeavour, summits might play an even lesser role than before, while the emphasis on non-alignment as a foreign policy doctrine would be an integral part of the old efforts of developing countries to achieve independence, equal treatment and freedom to choose their own path of development. In this way, the NAM might be ultimately rendered obsolete but a new form of non-alignment, often called multi-vector foreign policy or similar, could remain quite current.[110] Altogether, this will be a challenging feat indeed, one definitely with an uncertain outcome, especially since some of the regional and international competitors (ASEAN, SADC, SAARC, G20, BRICS, etc.) have also started advocating and promoting similar agendas (economic development, the role of the UN, South–South cooperation, security challenges, etc.), often enjoying more credibility or popularity in that respect than the NAM today (G77 still holding the old banner high).[111] Only history will be the final judge of such an undertaking, but what has remained undisputed until today is the undiminished spirit and capacity of the Third World/Global South for multilateralism, its aspirations to act collectively, its desires to jointly protect its interests and its undiminished efforts to set the entire global agenda or at least crucial parts of it. This approach was initially launched by the non-aligned group and the subsequent NAM and it was embodied by them for decades afterwards, thus keeping that strong spirit of independence, solidarity and equality alive for others to continue down that path with the same vigour.

Notes

1. Odd Arne Westad, *The Global Cold War*, 334–8, 357–62; Martin Meredith, *The State of Africa*, 368–77; Guy Arnold, *The End of the Third World* (London: Palgrave, 1993), 27–55, 89–102; Vijay Prashad, *The Darker Nations*, 245–59.
2. Xinyao Liu and Hongwei Fan, 'Chinese Policies towards the Non-Aligned Movement', in *The 60th Anniversary of the Non-Aligned Movement*, 154–5.
3. Leo Mates, 'Variations in East-West Relations and Non-Alignment', in *The Policy and Movement of Non-Alignment – New Tendencies and Options: International Round Table, Petrovaradin, Yugoslavia, 1–3 November 1985* (Belgrade: IIPE, 1986), 20–1.
4. Vijay Prashad, *The Darker Nations*, 229–44; Mark Mazower, *Governing the World*, 348–56; Susan George, *A Fate Worse than Debt: A Radical New Analysis of the Third World Debt Crisis* (London: Penguin, 1989), 11–71.
5. Lorenz M. Lüthi, *Cold Wars*, 539–61; Odd Arne Westad, *The Cold War*, 501–26; Raymond L. Garthoff, *The Great Transition: American-Soviet Relations and the End of the Cold War* (Washington, DC: Brookings Institution Press, 1994), 7–194; Robert Service, *The End of the Cold War, 1985–1991* (London: Macmillan, 2015), 13–116.
6. Raymond L. Garthoff, *The Great Transition*, 678–733.
7. DAMSPS, PA, 1981, f-201, 454550, 'Telegram from UN', 2 November 1981.
8. Xiaoming Zhang, *Deng Xiaoping's Long War*, 141–68, 193–210; Kosal Path, *Vietnam's Strategic Thinking during the Third Indochina War*, 113–66.
9. Piero Gleijeses, *Visions of Freedom*, 166–313.
10. Odd Arne Westad, *The Cold War*, 553–64; Lorenz M. Lüthi, *Cold Wars*, 535–7, 576–7.
11. Odd Arne Westad, *The Global Cold War*, 339–47; John H. Coatsworth, 'The Cold War in Central America, 1975–1991', in *The Cambridge History of the Cold War*, 3, 205–18.
12. Lorenz M. Lüthi, *Cold Wars*, 502–18, 542–4; Amin Saikal, 'Islamism, the Iranian Revolution, and the Soviet Invasion of Afghanistan', in *The Cambridge History of the Cold War*, 3, 114–32.
13. Odd Arne Westad, *The Global Cold War*, 289–99; James Buchan, *Days of God: the Revolution in Iran and its Consequences* (London: John Murray, 2012), 198–382; Michael Axworthy, *Revolutionary Iran: A History of the Islamic Republic* (London: Penguin, 2014), 76–185.
14. Williamson Murray and Kevin M. Woods, *The Iran–Iraq War: A Military and Strategic History* (Cambridge: Cambridge University Press, 2014), 85–335; Pierre Razoux, *The Iran–Iraq War* (Cambridge: Harvard University Press, 2015), 1–473.
15. Odd Arne Westad, *The Global Cold War*, 299–326, 348–57; Gregory Feifer, *The Great Gamble: the Soviet War in Afghanistan* (New York, NY: Harper Collins, 2009), 9–217; Rodric Braithwaite, *Afgantsy: the Russians in Afghanistan, 1979–1989* (Oxford: Oxford University Press, 2011), 9–246; Artemy M. Kalinovsky, *A Long Goodbye: the Soviet Withdrawal from Afghanistan* (Cambridge, MA: Harvard University Press, 2011), 54–177.
16. DAMSPS, PA, 1980, f-220, 46136, 'Foreign Secretariat's telegram', 20 February 1980.
17. DAMSPS, PA, 1980, f-217, 416387, 'Telegram from Sri Lanka', 14 March 1980.
18. DAMSPS, PA, 1982, f-162, 4385, 'Telegram from Algeria', 3 January 1982.
19. DAMSPS, PA, 1980, f-178, 49458, 'Telegram from UN', 13 February 1980.
20. Hanspeter Neuhold, 'Non-Alignment in 1985: Problems and Prospects', in *The Policy and Movement of Non-Alignment*, 52–4.
21. DAMSPS, PA, 1980, f-178, 49458, 'Telegram from UN', 13 February 1980.

22 Sue Onslow, 'The South African Factor in Zimbabwe's Transition to Independence', in *Cold War in Southern Africa*, 111–26; Chris Saunders, 'The Non-Aligned Movement, Namibia, and South Africa over Sixty Years', in *The 60th Anniversary of the Non-Aligned Movement*, 334–40.
23 C. Russel Riechers, *Cuba and the Non-Aligned Movement: Interactions of Pragmatic Idealism* (Washington, DC: SIS AU, 2012), 52–5.
24 DDRS, CK2349717210, 'The Non-Aligned Movement', 1 March 1980.
25 Lorenz M. Lüthi, *Cold Wars*, 533–4; Richard L. Jackson, *The Non-Aligned, the UN and the Superpowers*, 68.
26 TNA, FCO 973/81, 'Prospects for the NAM', February 1980.
27 Michelle Getchell, 'Cuba, the USSR, and the Non-Aligned Movement', 165–6.
28 DAMSPS, PA, 1980, f-178, 411187, 'Telegram from UN', 22 February 1980.
29 Tvrtko Jakovina, *Treća strana Hladnog rata*, 319–67.
30 DAMSPS, PA, 1980, f-217, 431397, 'Foreign Secretariat's telegram', 30 May 1980.
31 DAMSPS, PA, 1980, f-217, 433546, 'Telegram from Cuba', 4 June 1980.
32 DAMSPS, PA, 1980, f-217, 434361, 'Foreign Secretariat's telegram', 20 June 1980.
33 DAMSPS, PA, 1980, f-218, 454707, 'Telegram from UN', 8 October 1980.
34 DAMSPS, PA, 1981, f-202, 41251, 'Telegram from UN', 11 January 1981.
35 DAMSPS, PA, 1981, f-202, 44044, 'Telegram from Algeria', 27 January 1981.
36 DAMSPS, PA, 1981, f-202, 4254, 'Platform for the Yugoslav delegation', 10 January 1981.
37 DAMSPS, PA, 1981, f-202, 44125, 'Telegram from India', 28 January 1981.
38 DAMSPS, PA, 1981, f-202, 44316, 'New important moments', 29 January 1981.
39 DAMSPS, PA, 1981, f-202, 42293, 'Telegram from UN', 16 January 1981.
40 Renu Srivastava, *India and the Nonaligned Summits*, 70–1.
41 M. S. Rajan, *Studies on Nonalignment and the Nonaligned Movement*, 189–91.
42 DAMSPS, PA, 1981, f-203, 412673, 'Report on the NAM ministerial conference', 11 March 1981; *Documents of the Gatherings of the Non-Aligned Countries*, 2, 419–51; Tvrtko Jakovina, *Treća strana Hladnog rata*, 441–70.
43 DAMSPS, PA, 1981, f-201, 442094, 'Telegram from Cuba', 20 August 1981.
44 S. B. Jain, *India's Foreign Policy and Non-Alignment*, 244–52.
45 DAMSPS, PA, 1981, f-203, 412211, 'Telegram from UN', 6 March 1981.
46 *Documents of the Gatherings of the Non-Aligned Countries*, 2, 452–63.
47 Richard L. Jackson, *The Non-Aligned, the UN and the Superpowers*, 220–1.
48 DAMSPS, PA, 1982, f-158, 46601, 'Telegram from Cuba', 9 February 1982.
49 DAMSPS, PA, 1982, f-158, 49120, 'Telegram from Iran', 23 February 1982.
50 DAMSPS, PA, 1982, f-145, 419261, 'Extraordinary CB meeting on Palestine, Kuwait, 5–8 April 1982', 10 April 1982.
51 DAMSPS, PA, 1982, f-159, 421223, 'Foreign Secretariat's telegram', 7 May 1982.
52 DAMSPS, PA, 1982, f-145, 430062, 'Foreign Secretariat's telegram', 15 June 1982.
53 DAMSPS, PA, 1982, f-159, 28841, 'Telegram from Cuba', 3 June 1982.
54 DAMSPS, PA, 1982, f-159, 433291, 'Dilemmas about holding the 7th summit in Baghdad', 12 July 1982.
55 DAMSPS, PA, 1982, f-159, 430308, 'Telegram from Cuba', 10 June 1982.
56 DAMSPS, PA, 1982, f-159, 437921, 'Telegram from UN', 30 July 1982.
57 DAMSPS, PA, 1982, f-159, 438068, 'Telegram from Cuba', 1 August 1982.
58 DAMSPS, PA, 1982, f-159, 437618, 'Foreign Secretariat's telegram', 4 August 1982.
59 DAMSPS, PA, 1982, f-160, 438744, 'Telegram from UN', 9 August 1982.

60 DAMSPS, PA, 1982, f-159, 432329, 'Foreign Secretariat's telegram', 11 August 1982.
61 DAMSPS, PA, 1982, f-160, 439095, 'Foreign Secretariat's telegram', 16 August 1982.
62 DAMSPS, PA, 1982, f-162, 440348, 'Telegram from UN', 20 August 1982.
63 DAMSPS, PA, 1982, f-160, 439929, 'Efforts to move the 7th NAM summit to New Delhi', 24 August 1982.
64 DAMSPS, PA, 1982, f-160, 440932, 'Telegram from Iraq', 29 August 1982.
65 *Documents of the Gatherings of the Non-Aligned Countries*, 2, 498–502.
66 DAMSPS, PA, 1983, f-128, 43, 'Situation in the NAM and preparations for the 7th summit', 30 December 1982.
67 DAMSPS, PA, 1983, f-152, 48142, 'Telegram from U.S.', 22 February 1983.
68 DAMSPS, PA, 1982, f-160, 456659, 'Telegram from UN', 11 December 1982.
69 DAMSPS, PA, 1983, f-128, 42791, 'Extraordinary CB meeting on Latin America and the Caribbean', 25 January 1983.
70 Renu Srivastava, *India and the Nonaligned Summits*, 78–9.
71 CREST, CIA-RDP85T00287R000700650001-5, 'The NAM: India's chairmanship and relations with the superpowers', 1 March 1983.
72 DAMSPS, PA, 1983, f-152, 46966, 'Telegram from UN', 15 February 1983.
73 DAMSPS, PA, 1983, f-153, 411263, 'Proceedings and results of the 7th NAM summit', 14 March 1983; Kumar Awadhesh Raman, *Mrs. Indira Gandhi and the Non-Aligned Movement* (Patna: Janaki Prakashan, 2011), 138–52.
74 DAMSPS, PA, 1983, f-153, 49731, 'Telegram from India', 6 March 1983.
75 A. W. Singham and Shirley Hune, *Non-Alignment in the Age of Alignments*, 313–14.
76 DAMSPS, PA, 1983, f-153, 410022, 'Telegram from India', 8 March 1983.
77 Renu Srivastava, *India and the Nonaligned Summits*, 176.
78 DAMSPS, PA, 1983, f-153, 411263, 'Proceedings and results of the 7th NAM summit', 14 March 1983.
79 Renu Srivastava, *India and the Nonaligned Summits*, 91–7.
80 DAMSPS, PA, 1983, f-153, 411263, 'Proceedings and results of the 7th NAM summit', 14 March 1983; *Documents of the Gatherings of the Non-Aligned Countries*, 2, 520–41.
81 Ibid.; ibid., 541–70.
82 A. W. Singham and Shirley Hune, *Non-Alignment in the Age of Alignments*, 330–5.
83 DAMSPS, PA, 1983, f-154, 412924, 'Telegram from USSR', 22 March 1983; 413039, 'Telegram from U.S.', 23 March 1983.
84 PAAA, M95 17.966, 'Arguments for equidistance of the NAM', 7 March 1983.
85 Vijay Prashad, *The Darker Nations*, 209–15; Jürgen Dinkel, *The Non-Aligned Movement*, 235–7.
86 DAMSPS, PA, 1983, f-153, 411723, 'Telegram from Egypt', 15 March 1983.
87 *Non-Aligned Movement under India's Chairmanship* (New Delhi: IINS, 1986), 7–13.
88 DAMSPS, PA, 1984, f-156, 431444, 'NAM after the 7th summit', 20 June 1984.
89 S. B. Jain, *India's Foreign Policy and Non-Alignment*, 262–8; Jürgen Dinkel, *The Non-Aligned Movement*, 238–42.
90 *Documents of the Gatherings of the Non-Aligned Countries*, 2, 583–95.
91 DAMSPS, PA, 1984, f-156, 443471, 'Ministerial meeting of the Mediterranean NAM members, La Valetta, 10–11 September', 14 September 1984.
92 DAMSPS, PA, 1985, f-131, 415057, 'Situation in the NAM before the extraordinary CB meeting in New Delhi', 26 March 1985.
93 DAMSPS, PA, 1985, f-131, 424035, 'Extraordinary CB ministerial meeting in New Delhi, 19–21 April', 27 April 1985.

94 DAMSPS, PA, 1985, f-152, 424275, 'The issue of hosting the 8th summit', 14 May 1985.
95 DAMSPS, PA, 1985, f-154, 439828, 'Foreign Secretariat's telegram', 30 August 1985.
96 DAMSPS, PA, 1985, f-154, 448840, 'Situation in the NAM in the light of decisions adopted at the Luanda ministerial conference', 31 October 1985; *Documents of the Gatherings of the Non-Aligned Countries*, 2, 627–71.
97 DAMSPS, PA, 1986, f-152, 430464, 'Platform for the activity of the Yugoslav delegation at the 8th NAM summit', 8 July 1986.
98 Narender P. Jain, 'Non-Aligned Movement: An Unfinished Revolution', in *Non-Aligned Movement*, 162–5.
99 DAMSPS, PA, 1986, f-130, 419637, 'CB ministerial meeting in New Delhi, 16–19 April', 28 April 1986.
100 M. S. Rajan, *The Future of Non-Alignment and the Non-Aligned Movement*, 85–104.
101 PAAA, LS-A 704, 'Report on the 8th NAM summit', 23 September 1986; Ruslan Vasilievich Kostiuk and Ekaterina Petrovna Katkova, 'The Soviet Union and the Non-Aligned Movement', 140–1.
102 DAMSPS, PA, 1986, f-155, 440034, 'Report on the 8th NAM summit', 22 September 1986; *Documents of the Gatherings of the Non-Aligned Countries*, 2, 727–89.
103 Robert Service, *The End of the Cold War*, 119–426; Melvyn P. Leffler, *For the Soul of Mankind*, 365–450; Raymond L. Garthoff, *The Great Transition*, 197–408; Lorenz M. Lüthi, *Cold Wars*, 565–91; Odd Arne Westad, *The Global Cold War*, 365–95; different chapters in *The End of the Cold War in the Third World: New Perspectives on Regional Conflict*, Artemy M. Kalinovski and Sergey Radchenko (eds) (London: Routledge, 2011).
104 TNA, FCO 973/562, 'NAM – search for more effective role', October 1988; Tvrtko Jakovina, *Budimir Lončar – od Preka do vrha svijeta* (Zagreb: Fraktura, 2020), 437–41; *Documents of the Gatherings of the Non-Aligned Countries*, 2, 837–81.
105 Renu Srivastava, *India and the Nonaligned Summits*, 125–31; Tvrtko Jakovina, *Budimir Lončar – od Preka do vrha svijeta* (Zagreb: Fraktura, 2020), 443–7; *Documents of the Gatherings of the Non-Aligned Countries*, 2, 930–76.
106 Sally Morphet, 'Three Non-Aligned Summits: Harare 1986, Belgrade 1989 and Jakarta 1992', in *Diplomacy at the Highest Level*, 150–7.
107 Kevin Gray and Barry K. Gills, 'South-South Cooperation and the Rise of Global South', *Third World Quarterly* 37.4 (2016), 557–74.
108 Jürgen Dinkel, *The Non-Aligned Movement*, 259–65; Dragan Bisenić, 'An Exit from Contradictions in the Post-Cold War Development of the Non-Aligned Movement', in *The 60th Anniversary of the Non-Aligned Movement*, 406–7.
109 Hennie Strydom, 'The Non-Aligned Movement and the Reform of International Relations', in *Max Planck Yearbook of United Nations Law*, 11, A. Von Bogdandy and R. Wolfrum (eds) (2007), 1–46.
110 Sunil Khilnani and Rajiv Kumar et al., *Nonalignment 2.0: A Foreign and Strategic Policy for India in the 21st Century* (New Delhi: Penguin Viking, 2013).
111 S. I. Keethaponcalan, 'Reshaping the Non-Aligned Movement: Challenges and Vision', *Bandung: Journal of the Global South* 3.4 (2016), 1–14.

Conclusion

As we have seen, the NAM was definitely one of the major transcending political and social phenomena of the second half of the twentieth century, in this respect perhaps only comparable to the UN, one of the very few similar international organizations still active and recognizable around the world today, regardless of its fluctuating level of influence and wider impact exercised during different time periods. This was, one could say, the only significant international actor outside the realm of great powers that stood right at the crossroads of the East–West and North–South conflicts during the entire Cold War period, thus making the NAM indeed a unique historical occurrence. What is even more fascinating from a current standpoint was the movement's clear capacity and relentless ability to gather together at free will and in one place so many geographically, historically, culturally, socially, politically and economically diverse nations, differing in size and potential, and eventually make them function, more or less successfully, as one independent, self-conscious and collective institutional actor.

Non-Aligned Movement Summits, although basically envisaged as a history of the first seven major NAM summits, with only a generalized treatment of the following two which coincided with the end of the Cold War, in many ways also explores some of the internal history of the movement's emergence and subsequent evolution during well over two decades. These were years when the movement's international standing and respective global influence ultimately reached their apex. Essentially, international historiography largely lacked this kind of approach in tackling the NAM's history from the very beginning, predominantly concentrating on analysis of different publicly available summit documents or producing general institutional overviews, and often suffering from lack of clear insight into the inner functioning or behind-the-scenes relationships between its central actors. This was understandable when no one could gain access to the archives of key non-aligned countries for a very long time, but in the past decade or so this situation has changed radically, allowing us to readdress these historical issues and begin observing the non-aligned world from its own perspective as an independent international factor, not just as a mere sideshow to the superpower confrontation. Therefore, this study has aimed to put every single fact, event or personality into the proper historical context of the major events, summits and similar gatherings, so that we can finally grasp what the NAM truly was, what kind of role it exercised globally, and what was really taking place before, during and after these major events that left a lasting stamp on the history of the movement.

In this way, *Non-Aligned Movement Summits* follows in the footsteps of recent academic trends transforming the study of the Cold War in the Third World into a new current gradually assuming visibility and popularity in this realm of scholarship, the so-called Third World's Cold War. This is a largely forgotten and understudied topic of the internal struggle for leadership and prestige between so many different regional centres of power in the Global South, one that often acted outside superpower projections but still had a sizeable impact on their respective policies, as well as on the regional and international distribution of power and influence. Therefore, through such elaboration we can observe that the Third World in general, and the NAM in particular, had far greater impact on world developments during the Cold War years than had been previously perceived, despite being economically underdeveloped and only having huge demographic numbers on its side.

This study has also tried to enhance comprehension of the historical role of non-alignment, as it is presented in the first chapter, not only by utilizing older theoretical literature and speeches of non-aligned leaders but also by interpreting many new archival findings, thus trying to rethink and often challenge the established theoretical narrative of the NAM. Therefore, this book directly engages with the following issues, while trying to provide a different framework for positioning this phenomenon in world history: specific relationships between neutrality, neutralism and non-alignment; independent, non-bloc, active and pragmatic characters of non-alignment; its basic principles and what separated non-alignment from other parallel historical currents, such as Afro-Asianism or Third Worldism; non-alignment as an expression of the aspirations of small and medium powers to be ultimately treated in a manner equal to all other participants in the international system; whether the non-aligned struggle for peace and development was marked by strict equidistance towards both blocs or was much more flexible and pragmatic in its conduct; controversies about the connections between the notions of non-alignment and the third bloc; the specific contributions of India, Yugoslavia and Egypt to the conceptual emergence and evolution, as well as the practical application, of non-alignment.

Unlike the general NAM discourse up to the present day, this study does not treat the Bandung Conference as the starting point of the movement; instead it primarily observes the NAM and the concurrent Afro-Asian Movement as two competing organizations acting as the embodiment of superficially similar but somewhat conflicting ideas and principles. This is quite evident in the second and third chapters, as well as partially in the theoretical introduction. It is true that the Bandung Conference raised high the banner of anti-colonial struggle which was also one of the NAM's chief goals. It also instilled postcolonial nations with a strong sense of political self-awareness, thus boosting their international prestige and domestic authority, and also inspired them to freely state their claims to the great powers, demonstrating their own capability to assess the world situation and offer corresponding solutions (feats strongly present in the NAM as well). However, this was still a gathering marked by serious geographic and conceptual constraints, where similar historical experiences or shared memories could not substitute real bloc obligations and corresponding duties of many attendees. Eventually, it was clear to everyone where the essential adherence of bloc members originated and it was definitely not with the Afro-Asian community.

In fact, the non-bloc character, despite different nuances in its interpretation and practical application, was the crucial criterion for defining one country as being truly non-aligned and becoming a NAM member afterwards, irrespective of the geographic location, historical experiences or political and socioeconomic systems it upheld. Furthermore, both non-alignment and the NAM were primarily transcontinental phenomena and they could not be limited to only two continents, as was the case with its failed Afro-Asian counterpart. Therefore, the Bandung Conference could obviously not meet the elaborate standards set by non-alignment, especially with so many bloc participants being actively involved, and so many non-bloc countries outside Afro-Asia largely ignored. When one takes all this into consideration, there could not be a straighter line connecting Bandung and the subsequent NAM, with the exception of certain more general topics, such as anti-colonialism, summitry or similar, apparent in their respective discourses. Essentially, non-alignment and the movement embodying it were primarily tailored for the non-bloc world where the majority of countries taking part were acting not as a mere extension of the policies and interests of outside powers, but as more or less independent and uncommitted actors of world politics. This kind of remark could never be applied to Bandung, all other similarities notwithstanding, but it was characteristic of the Belgrade Conference which this book identifies as the true starting point of a protracted historical process that would eventually transform separate political initiatives into a fully fledged international movement.

Moreover, what *Non-Aligned Movement Summits* has brought to the fore, similar to some recent trends, is the difference between the initial non-aligned group and the subsequent NAM, since the Belgrade Conference was actually not the immediate birthplace of the movement as often claimed in the international literature, because the movement came about only later on. This event was only the initial testing ground, the movement's remote point of origin, an initial cry for action of different non-bloc factors to determine whether they could act successfully in a collective fashion to establish a joint agenda they could forcefully advocate. As we have seen, the NAM was properly established only at the Lusaka Conference, nine years after Belgrade, while it was finally institutionally shaped at the next summit in Algiers. In this way, we can observe two different historical levels: the history of the less tightly organized non-aligned group during the 1960s when summits were held on an ad hoc basis, and not connected with any organizational requirements; and then the history of these gatherings during the 1970s and 1980s, when they were regularly convened every three years, followed by frequent CB and NAM ministerial meetings, which were then already firmly related to the institutional evolution of the movement as a proper international organization.

Furthermore, when compared to the majority of the preceding literature on the NAM, it was only events like the 1961 Belgrade Conference that enjoyed detailed documentary corroborated elaboration; however, this was not the case when referring to the summits and the movement's global role during the 1970s and 1980s. Two-thirds of this book focuses on that crucial decade and a half, not by primarily scrutinizing the NAM in the institutional sense but largely by reconstructing and dissecting different events and processes that clearly left a deep imprint on the entire period when the movement's complete institutionalization finally materialized. This kind of approach primarily relies upon many newly declassified archival materials, thus providing us with a plethora of lesser-known facts, details and stories which shed new light on the inner functioning of the NAM and many internal rivalries occurring during that period, and also focuses on the roles particular countries and historical figures exercised in all these developments.

Conversely, in the same vein as some recent studies of the NAM, *Non-Aligned Movement Summits* also bases its narrative on an analysis of two separate but closely interrelated dimensions where both political and economic issues figured prominently on the movement's agenda, with both national and international security and individual and collective socioeconomic development constituting the two overarching topics driving the NAM's external engagements. In this respect, throughout this book we can follow the evolution of non-alignment, the non-aligned group and the subsequent NAM in the context of both the East–West and North–South interactions and conflicts. Non-alignment and the NAM had initially started as a byproduct of the superpower conflict, where countries outside the blocs strived to act as mediators, building bridges between conflicting parties, and thus trying to prevent this global confrontation from escalating into a full-blown nuclear war that would ultimately decimate the entire human civilization. These non-bloc nations also clearly intended to avoid eventually being compelled by the superpowers to take sides in their bipolar confrontation. This dimension figured quite prominently during the Belgrade Conference, it was somewhat present in Cairo, although largely overshadowed by some internal Third World disagreements, while during the Lusaka Conference and after, despite the NAM's economic agenda gaining the upper hand, it was still visible as a part of the movement's intensive interactions with international détente.

Nevertheless, this security dimension had again gained prominence at the end of the 1970s and especially during the 1980s, at the time of new escalating tensions between the blocs, when the world was brought almost to the brink of a nuclear war again, thus directly threatening the integrity and future of the NAM, among other things. However, the NAM's primary role as the central actor of the North–South conflict was characteristic of the entire 1970s and the summits taking place during that decade, as well as for the post Cold War period that goes beyond the scope of this book. This was the time when the NAM launched several constructive attempts to restructure and reform the entire international system, above all its economic part by stressing the NIEO initiative, while eventually transforming it into a more balanced, equitable and adjustable world order, one more suited to the needs and aspirations of developing countries. In this way, the NAM, often acting in concordance with some other similar organizations, like G77 or OPEC, eventually managed to centralize the issue of North–South relations in world politics, regardless of its subsequent failure to successfully resolve these inherent contradictions between the developed and developing parts of the world.

What *Non-Aligned Movement Summits* also reveals in detail are the numerous conflicts between the non-aligned countries themselves, primarily directed at the establishment of control over the initial group or the subsequent movement. This kind of behind-the-scenes rivalry was closely related not only to historical or political differences existing between so many diverse countries but also its roots could be found in the different interpretations of the notions of anti-imperialism and peaceful co-existence, thus often being closely related to the proximity of some member states to one of the superpowers. Non-alignment and the NAM were initially inspired by anti-imperialist and anti-colonial struggle, since without the successful attainment of these goals it would have been quite impossible to have that many postcolonial nations present in the world in order to ultimately establish a movement. However, while some countries were mired in the anti-imperialist and anti-colonial discourse, refusing to go beyond this narrow understanding of international relations, others were intensively opting for peaceful co-existence as a stable framework for promoting the NAM's security and developmental agendas. These differing approaches and perceptions, on certain occasions, induced serious clashes between different opposing groups, some of them leaning to the more radical leftist agenda, others promoting the conservative rightist concepts, with the majority still choosing a moderate path encompassing both the strong sentiments of independence and equality and the pragmatic drive for cooperation with different international actors.

This kind of trend, as discussed in chapters 3 and 7, but also occasionally in other chapters, was clearly tainted by the conflicts between Afro-Asianism and non-alignment and between the 'progressive' and 'moderate' groups later on, sometimes also being closely related to the concurrently deteriorating relations between the blocs. These conflicts often heralded a profound split in the non-aligned ranks from which the movement could only recuperate at a great price and through investing enormous internal efforts. This was the case in the late 1960s and early 1970s, when the NAM, after a few years of a lingering crisis, had ultimately discovered a new focus for its global agenda, primarily its economic priorities, in order to level out all these outstanding differences from the past, thus shifting attention from individual issues to a more general one related to the North–South relationship. Nevertheless, the Cuban–Yugoslav confrontation of the late 1970s and early 1980s had ultimately depleted the movement from its internal vibrancy. It had also stirred a protracted disorientation in the NAM's priorities during the 1980s, thus leaving the movement almost totally unprepared for the tectonic geopolitical changes brought about when the Cold War ceased in 1989–91.

When we look back at the first twenty-five years of the NAM's history, which largely coincided with all the major developments of the Cold War period, we can draw some general conclusions about the role exercised by the non-aligned world during those decades and the impact it produced on international relations in general. This book, similar to some other publications, sees neither the history of the NAM as an epic narrative of the Third World's continuous struggle against the oppressors and exploiters from the developed world nor the movement's historical presence during those years as being a total failure, as has become quite common from the vantage point of the post-Cold War period. Even though this book tends to present the key events shaping global non-alignment and the movement in a linear fashion, nonetheless, with the exception of the common timeline and the general structure of this book, we can clearly see that the NAM's history was largely characterized by a series of ups and downs, periods of advancements and times of crisis, thus leaving an indelible imprint on its dynamic, convoluted and controversial progress. Although the NAM always fluctuated between the East–West and North–South conflicts, between its political and economic agendas, between different groups of member states influencing its general course and between its considerable successes and miserable failures, it has still remained one of the key historical phenomena of world history after 1945, especially in the domain of multilateralism and the political role of the Third World. In this respect, the movement managed to successfully push through the process of total decolonization as its chief achievement, while it also put socioeconomic issues at the centre of demands and aspirations cherished by the Global South, a tendency that remains relevant even today. At the same time, the movement also succeeded in instilling in all its members a strong sense of independence and self-respect which still inspires developing nations to continue with their constructive struggle for different types of political and economic relations in the world.

However, when we consider the role the NAM purports to have in the world today, it still continues to imagine an international role for itself, since issues of great power hegemony, economic inequality, problems of globalization, foreign political, economic and military interference, radicalism and terrorism, environmental degradation, etc. still represent the downsides of the existing world order, thus often laying down, deliberately or by chance, different impediments to the struggle of developing countries for preserving their sovereignty and furthering their modernization. Furthermore, aspirations for a just, equitable and democratic world order have not receded in recent decades, despite all the major international shifts. In the same vein as the 1970s, issues of under-development, poverty and social insecurity have regained their prominence on the agenda of the Global South today, while crucial challenges such as debt burden, unfair trade practices, decline in foreign aid, as well as lack of transparency in international financial institutions, have not disappeared. Furthermore, the regrettable examples of great power interventionism since 1991 have also demonstrated that old instruments of misuse of military power have not been totally sidelined and still represent a direct threat to the independence, sovereignty and even existence of some developing nations.

In fact, the NAM has largely not outlived its utility in the contemporary world, regardless of its often problematic existence over the past thirty years, when it has lost some of its focus and purpose of existence. Many developing nations are rapidly losing confidence in any kind of alignment with the great powers, particularly in military alignments; a lesson unwillingly adopted at the end of the Cold War, since these specific arrangements have often proved to be detrimental to their freedom of choice and action. Even though membership in the movement is often not portrayed as a primary choice for some of these nations, independent foreign policy is still a clear-cut decision taken by all of them, which constitutes an important legacy of the old NAM. Concurrently, the UN has remained the principal stage for discussing and promoting the general agenda of the developing world, as well as the particular interests of its member states still trying to snatch away the international organization from the exclusive control of one or only a few great powers. Creating an influential world public opinion critical to the acts of great powers and poised to impose certain moral checks on their unilateral actions has also remained one of the crucial roles established by the NAM during the Cold War years.

In the future, in order to to return to its past glory, the NAM should think more about reinventing its role and rejuvenating itself beyond the ideas, concepts and principles previously prized by the movement, while still cherishing some of them as a stable foundation and clear guidelines for the twenty-first century. The NAM's future role will largely depend on its inner strength, unity and cohesion, as well as on its outright ability to formulate clear and effective general policies, while avoiding new internal conflicts. Hence, instead of using the UN merely as a platform for presenting ideas, launching initiatives and submitting complaints, the movement and its member states should focus more on reforming and strengthening the international organization by making it a more responsible and representative instrument of the Global South. Enhanced and diversified South–South cooperation, as well as new mechanisms for boosting structural leverages of the developing world, have also come out of the old NAM playbook. Essentially, the NAM and some of its sister organizations should aim for reducing the gap among developing countries themselves, where richer developing countries should provide advice and backing to those less fortunate, but not just financially as considered before, while a constructive North–South dialogue based on common interests, good will, mutual understanding and cooperation should also be stimulated beyond just reluctant adjustments. Selective collaboration with different great powers should also be encouraged for the mutually inclusive future, especially in the field of economic, social and environmental issues, thus reflecting a fairer and more balanced international political and economic order.

Nevertheless, one of the main challenges that the NAM is facing today is a growing rift between the adherence to the policy of non-alignment, in different shapes and forms as perceived today, and direct participation in the movement. In order to strike a new balance between the relevance of this foreign policy orientation, often closely associated with the notion of national interest of individual countries, and the international organization that tends to represent it, consolidation of the NAM through necessary reforms should be an overarching goal: unity should be promoted through solidarity going beyond just particular interests of member states. Therefore it would be necessary to identify new points of convergence; membership criteria should be less liberal, thus making a more exclusive club of influential developing nations; any radicalization or advocacy of a showdown with some great powers, particularly the Western ones, should be initially isolated and henceforth totally rejected, thus bringing credibility and objectivity to the North–South dialogue; attempts at imposing bilateral conflicts on the entire movement, similar to the Cold War years, unless they are undermining basic international principles, should be largely avoided; the self-discipline of many members should be further strengthened, while ways of striking a consensus should be readdressed; and a new mechanism of monitoring global challenges and tailoring adequate responses should be established, thus either changing or establishing new, more permanent institutional mechanisms.

Both then and now, the existence of the NAM is still necessary, together with other multilateral organizations, especially since many unresolved political, economic, social, security and environmental issues still haunt the developing world. Resuming a responsible role in this respect would only further boost the movement's relevance in the twenty-first century. The fact remains that these developing nations still need strong institutional support outside the UN, together with separate regional frameworks to operate effectively within an international order that is still dominated by powerful Western political and economic interests and institutions and generally by different great powers in all parts of the world. Taking into account that some major developing countries, especially Asian ones, are exercising an increasingly influential international role which will only expand in the future, the reality is that the world system is gradually evolving and, sooner or later, it will transform itself into a multipolar world order for which the Global South should be better prepared institutionally, structurally and practically. The NAM still has a major role to play in this respect, particularly if it succeeds in overcoming some of the inherent deficiencies present in its internal functioning and engagement since the end of the Cold War.

Bibliography

Unpublished Sources

Archives of the Russian Foreign Ministry
Archives of Yugoslavia
Chinese Foreign Ministry Archives
CIA Records Search Tool
Declassified Documents Reference System
Diplomatic Archives of the Serbian Foreign Ministry
Myanmar Ministry of Foreign Affairs Archive
National Archives of India
National Archives of Myanmar
National Archives and Records Administration, United States
Nehru Memorial Museum and Library
Political Archive of the Office for Foreign Affairs of Germany
Russian State Archive for Contemporary History
The National Archives, United Kingdom
Woodrow Wilson Center Digital Archive

Published Sources

Ahmia, Mourad, ed. *The Collected Documents of the Group of 77*, 6. Oxford: Oxford University Press, 2015.
Артизов, А. Н. and Наумов, В. П. и др., ред. *Никита Хрущев 1964: стенограммы пленума ЦК КПСС и другие документы*. Москва: МФД, 2007.
Asian Relations: Report of the Proceedings and Documentation of the First Asian Relations Conference, New Delhi, March–April 1947. New Delhi: Asian Relations Organization, 1948.
Conference of Heads of State or Government of Non-Aligned Countries, Belgrade, September, 1–6, 1961. Belgrade GOY, 1964.
Consultative Meeting of Special Government Representatives of Non-Aligned Countries: Belgrade, July 8–12, 1969. Beograd: Medjunarodna politika, 1970.
Documents of the Gatherings of the Non-Aligned Countries 1–2. Beograd: IMPP, 1989.
Foreign Relations of the United States, 1969–1972, 22. Washington: USGPO, 2007.
Foreign Relations of the United States, 1969–1976, 31. Washington: USGPO, 2009.
Foreign Relations of the United States, 1969–1976, 38.1. Washington: USGPO, 2012.
Foreign Relations of the United States, 1969–1976, E-14.1.
Foreign Relations of the United States, 1969–1976, E-15.1.
Foreign Relations of the United States, 1977–1980, 17.1. Washington: USGPO, 2016.
Jawaharlal Nehru's Speeches: September 1946–May 1949. New Delhi: GOI, 1958.

Jawaharlal Nehru's Speeches 1949–1953. New Delhi: GOI, 1954.
Југословенско-алжирски односи 1956–1979. Београд: Архив Југославије, 2014.
Југославија-СССР: сусрети и разговори на највишем нивоу руководилаца Југославије и СССР 1965–1980. Београд: Архив Југославије, 2016.
Југославија-САД: сусрети и разговори највиших званичника 1955–1980. Београд: Архив Југославије, 2017.
Kahin, George McTurnan, ed. *The Asian-African Conference*. Ithaca, NY: Cornell University Press, 1956.
Kissinger, Henry A. *American Foreign Policy*. New York, NY: W.W. Norton, 1977.
Minić, Miloš. *Spoljna politika Jugoslavije 1973–1979*. Novi Sad: Centar za političke studije, 1979.
Nehru, Jawaharlal. *India's Foreign Policy: Selected Speeches, September 1946–April 1961*. New Delhi: GOI, 1961.
Non-Aligned Movement under India's Chairmanship. New Delhi: IINS, 1986.
Non-Alignment in the 1970s: Opening Address by J.K. Nyerere. Dar-es-Salaam: Government Printer, 1970.
Pancha Shila: Its Meaning and History: A Documentary Study. New Delhi: Lok Sabha Secretariat, 1955.
Selected Works of Jawaharlal Nehru (Second Series) 2. New Delhi: Nehru Memorial Fund, 1984.
Selected Works of Jawaharlal Nehru (Second Series) 24. New Delhi: Nehru Memorial Fund, 1999.
Selected Works of Jawaharlal Nehru (Second Series) 27. New Delhi: Nehru Memorial Fund, 2000.
Selected Works of Jawaharlal Nehru (Second Series) 34. New Delhi: Nehru Memorial Fund, 2005.
Tito, Josip Broz. *Govori i članci* 10. Zagreb: Naprijed, 1959.
Tito, Josip Broz. *Govori i članci* 18. Zagreb: Naprijed, 1966.
Tito, Josip Broz. *Nesvrstanost i savremeni svijet* 2. Beograd: Komunist, 1982.
Willetts, Peter. *The Non-Aligned in Havana: Documents of the Sixth Summit Conference and an Analysis of their Significance for the Global Political System*. London: Frances Pinter, 1981.
Yugoslavia – From "National Communism" to National Collapse: US Intelligence Community Estimative Products on Yugoslavia, 1948–1990. (Washington, DC: National Intelligence Council, 2006.
Zhou Enlai waijiao wenxuan. Beijing: Zhongyang wenxian chubanshe, 1994.

Articles

Ajami, Fouad. 'The Fate of Nonalignment', *Foreign Affairs* 59.2 (1980).
Anabtawi, Samir N. 'Neutralists and Neutralism', *The Journal of Politics* 27.2 (1965).
Ayoob, Mohammed. 'The Third World in the System of States: Acute Schizophrenia or Growing Pains?', *International Studies Quarterly* 33.1 (1989).
Babaa, Khalid E. and Crabb, Cecil V. Jr. 'Non-Alignment as a Diplomatic and Ideological Credo', *Annals of the American Academy of Political and Social Science* 362 (1965).
Bebler, Aleš. 'Non-Alignment and the Theory of Equidistance', *Review of International Affairs* 12 (1961).

Berger, Mark T. 'After the Third World? History, Destiny and Fate of Third Worldism', *Third World Quarterly* 25.1 (2004).

Čavoški, Jovan. 'Ideološki prijatelj iz daleka: Jugoslavija i Azijska socijalistička konferencija', *Istorija 20. veka* 1 (2019).

Choucri, Nazli. 'The Nonalignment of Afro-Asian States: Policy, Perception, and Behaviour', *Canadian Journal of Political Science* 2.1 (1969).

Ewing, Cindy. 'The Colombo Powers: Crafting Diplomacy in the Third World and Launching Afro-Asia at Bandung', *Cold War History* 19.1 (2019).

Gerits, Frank. 'When the Bull Elephants Fight: Kwame Nkrumah, Non-Alignment, and Pan-Africanism as an Interventionist Ideology in the Global Cold War, 1957–1966', *The International History Review* 37.5 (2015).

Gilman, Nils. 'The New International Economic Order: A Reintroduction', *Humanity* 6.1 (2015).

Gray, Kevin and Gills, Barry K. 'South-South Cooperation and the Rise of Global South', *Third World Quarterly* 37.4 (2016).

Hershberg, James G. 'High-Spirited Confusion: Brazil, the 1961 Belgrade Non-Aligned Conference, and the Limits of an "independent" Foreign Policy during the High Cold War', *Cold War History* 7.3 (2007).

Keenleyside, T. A. 'Prelude to Power: the Meaning of Non-Alignment before Indian Independence', *Pacific Affairs* 53.3 (1980).

Keethaponcalan, S. I. 'Reshaping the Non-Aligned Movement: Challenges and Vision', *Bandung: Journal of the Global South* 3.4 (2016).

Kumar, Satish. 'Nonalignment: International Goals and National Interests', *Asian Survey* 23.4 (1983).

Lüthi, Lorenz M. 'Non-Alignment, 1946–1965: Its Establishment and Struggle against Afro-Asianism', *Humanity* 7.2 (2016).

Lyon, Peter. 'Non-Alignment at the Summits: From Belgrade 1961 to Havana 1979 – A Perspective View', *The Indian Journal of Political Science* 41.1 (1980).

McFarland, Victor. 'The New International Economic Order, Interdependence, and Globalization', *Humanity* 6.1 (2015).

Nayudu, Swapna Kona. *'When Elephant Swallowed the Hedgehog'*: the Prague Spring and Indo-Soviet Relations. CWIHP Working Paper No. 83 (2017).

Niebuhr, Robert. 'Nonalignment as Yugoslavia's Answer to Bloc Politics', *Journal of Cold War Studies* 13.1 (2011).

Nikezić, Marko, 'Why Uncommitted Countries Hold that They Are Not Neutral?', *The Annals of the American Academy of Political and Social Science* 336 (1961).

Rajak, Svetozar. 'No Bargaining Chips, No Spheres of Interest: the Yugoslav Origins of Cold War Non-Alignment', *Journal of Cold War Studies* 16.1 (2014).

Rajan, M. S. 'India and World Politics in the Post-Nehru Era', *International Journal* 24.1 (1968–9).

Rakove, Robert B. 'The Rise and Fall of Non-Aligned Mediation, 1961–6', *The International History Review* 37.5 (2015).

Rakove, Robert B. 'Two Roads to Belgrade: the United States, Great Britain, and the First Nonaligned Conference', *Cold War History* 14.3 (2014).

Rao, R. V. R. Chandrasekhara. 'India and Non-Aligned Summitry', *The World Today* 26.9 (1970).

Rothstein, Robert L. 'Alignment, Nonalignment, and Small Powers: 1945–1965', *International Organization* 20.3 (1966).

Rothstein, Robert L. 'Foreign Policy and Development Policy: From Nonalignment to International Class War', *International Affairs* 52.4 (1976).

Sargent, Daniel J. 'North-South: the United States Responds to the New International Economic Order', *Humanity* 6.1 (2015).

Schiller, Herbert I. 'Decolonization of Information: Efforts toward a New International Order', *Latin American Perspectives* 5.1 (1978).

Smith, Tony. 'New Bottles for New Wine: A Pericentric Framework for the Study of the Cold War', *Diplomatic History* 24.4 (2000).

Strydom, Hennie. 'The Non-Aligned Movement and the Reform of International Relations', in A. von Bogdandy and R. Wolfrum, eds. *Max Planck Yearbook of United Nations Law*, 11 (2007).

Tomlinson, B. R. 'What was the Third World?', *Journal of Contemporary History* 38.2 (2003).

Vitalis, Robert. 'The Midnight Ride of Kwame Nkrumah and other Fables of Bandung', *Humanity* 4.2 (2013).

Tudoroiu, Theodor. 'Fidel Castro and the Radicalization of Non-Alignment: A Political Psychology View', *International Studies* 53.2 (2017).

Westad, Odd Arne. 'The New International History of the Cold War: Three (Possible) Paradigms', *Diplomatic History* 24.4 (2000).

Životić, Aleksandar and Čavoški, Jovan. 'On the Road to Belgrade: Yugoslavia, Third World Neutrals, and the Evolution of Global Nonalignment, 1954–1961', *Journal of Cold War Studies* 18.4 (2016).

Books

Aburish, Said. *Nasser: The Last Arab*. New York, NY: St Martin's Press, 2004.

Aćimović, Ljubivoje, ed. *Politika nesvrstanosti u savremenom svetu*. Beograd: IMPP, 1969.

Agung, Ide Anak Agung Gde. *Twenty Years Indonesian Foreign Policy 1945–1965*. The Hague: Mouton, 1973.

Alden, Chris, Morphet, Sally and Vieira, Marco Antonio. *The South in World Politics*. London: Palgrave Macmillan, 2010.

Allison, Roy. *The Soviet Union and the Strategy of Non-Alignment in the Third World*. Cambridge: Cambridge University Press, 1988.

Amir-Aslani, Ardavan. *L'âge d'or de la diplomatie algérienne*. Paris: Editions du Moment, 2015.

Armah, Kwesi. *Peace without Power: Ghana's Foreign Policy 1957–1966*. Accra: Ghana Universities Press, 2004.

Arnold, Guy, *The End of the Third World*. London: Palgrave, 1993.

Asmussen, Jan. *Cyprus at War: Diplomacy and Conflict during the 1974 Crisis*. London: I.B. Tauris, 2008.

Asselin, Pierre. *A Bitter Peace: Washington, Hanoi, and the Making of the Paris Agreement*. Chapel Hill, NC: The University of North Carolina Press, 2002.

Axworthy, Michael. *Revolutionary Iran: A History of the Islamic Republic*. London: Penguin, 2014.

Bajpai, U. S., ed. *Non-Alignment: Perspectives and Prospects*. New Delhi: Lancers Publishers, 1983.

Bass, Garry J. *The Blood Telegram: Nixon, Kissinger, and a Forgotten Genocide*. New York, NY: Alfred A. Knopf, 2013.

Beattie, Kirk J. *Egypt during the Sadat Years*. London: Palgrave Macmillan, 2000.
Bell, Corall. 'Non-Alignment and the Power Balance', in Davis B. Bobrow, ed. *Components of Defense Policy*. Chicago, IL: Rand McNally & Co., 1965.
Bisenić, Dragan. 'An Exit from Contradictions in the Post-Cold War Development of the Non-Aligned Movement', in Duško Dimitrijević and Jovan Čavoški, eds. *The 60th Anniversary of the Non-Aligned Movement*. Belgrade: IIPE, 2021.
Boden, Ragna. *Die Grenzen der Weltmacht: Sowjetische Indonesienpolitik von Stalin bis Brežnev*. Stuttgart: Franz Steiner Verlag, 2006.
Bogetić, Dragan. *Jugoslovensko-američki odnosi 1961–1971*. Beograd: ISI, 2012.
Bogetić, Dragan. *Koreni jugoslovenskog opredeljenja za nesvrstanost*. Beograd: ISI, 1990.
Bogetić, Dragan. *Nesvrstanost kroz istoriju: od ideje do pokreta*. Beograd: Zavod za udžbenike, 2019.
Bogetić, Dragan. *Nova strategija spoljne politike Jugoslavije 1956–1961*. Beograd: ISI, 2006.
Bogetić, Dragan and Dimić, Ljubodrag. *Beogradska konferencija nesvrstanih zemalja 1–6. Septembar 1961. Prilog istoriji Trećeg sveta*. Beograd: Zavod za udžbenike, 2012.
Bogetić, Dragan and Životić, Aleksandar. *Jugoslavija i arapsko-izraelski rat 1967*. Beograd: ISI, 2010.
Bott, Sandra, Hanhimäki, Jussi M., Schaufelbuehl, Janick Marina and Wyss, Marco, eds. *Neutrality and Neutralism in the Global Cold War: Between or Within the Blocs?* London: Routledge, 2016.
Bradley, Mark Philip. 'Decolonization, the Global South, and the Cold War, 1919–1962', in Odd Arne Westad and Melvyn Leffler, eds. *The Cambridge History of the Cold War* 1. Cambridge: Cambridge University Press, 2010.
Braithwaite, Rodric. *Afgantsy: the Russians in Afghanistan, 1979–1989*. Oxford: Oxford University Press, 2011.
Braveboy-Wagner, Jacqueline Anne. *Institutions of the Global South*. London: Routledge, 2009.
Buchan, James. *Days of God: the Revolution in Iran and its Consequences*. London: John Murray, 2012.
Bundy, William. *A Tangled Web: the Making of Foreign Policy in the Nixon Presidency*. New York, NY: Hill and Wang, 1998.
Burton, J. W., ed. *Nonalignment*. New York, NY: James H. Heineman Inc., 1966.
Byrne, Jeffrey James. *The Mecca of Revolution: Algeria, Decolonization, and the Third World Order*. Oxford: Oxford University Press, 2016.
Castigliola, Frank. 'US Foreign Policy from Kennedy to Johnson', in Odd Arne Westad and Melvyn Leffler, eds. *The Cambridge History of the Cold War* 2. Cambridge: Cambridge University Press, 2010.
Čavoški, Jovan. 'Between Great Powers and Third World Neutralists: Yugoslavia and the Belgrade Conference of the Nonaligned Movement 1961', in Nataša Mišković, Harald Fischer-Tine and Nada Boškovska, eds. *The Non-Aligned Movement and the Cold War: Delhi-Bandung-Belgrade*. London: Routledge, 2014.
Čavoški, Jovan. 'Constructing Nasser's Neutralism: Egypt and the Rise of Nonalignment in the Middle East', in Lorenz Lüthi, ed. *The Regional Cold Wars in Europe, East Asia, and the Middle East: Crucial Periods and Turning Points*. Washington, DC, Stanford: Woodrow Wilson Center Press, Stanford University Press, 2015.
Čavoški, Jovan. *Distant Countries, Closest Allies: Josip Broz Tito, Jawaharlal Nehru and the Rise of Global Nonalignment*. New Delhi: Nehru Memorial Museum and Library, 2015.
Čavoški, Jovan. *Jugoslavija i kinesko-indijski konflikt 1959–1962*. Beograd: INIS, 2009.
Čavoški, Jovan. 'On the Road to Belgrade: Yugoslavia's Contribution to the Defining of the Concept of European Security and Cooperation, 1975–1977', in Vladimir Bilandžić,

Dittmar Dahlmann and and Milan Kosanović, eds. *From Helsinki to Belgrade: the First CSCE Follow-up Meeting and the Crisis of Détente*. Bonn: Bonn University Press, 2012.

Čavoški, Jovan. 'On the Road to the Coup: Indonesia between the Nonaligned and China', in Bernd Schaefer and Baskara T. Wardaya, eds. *1965 – Indonesia and the World*. Jakarta: Gramedia Publishers, 2013.

Čavoški, Jovan. 'Saving Non-Alignment: Diplomatic Efforts of Major Non-Aligned Countries and the Sino-Indian Border Conflict', in Lorenz Lüthi and Amit Das Gupta, eds. *The Sino-Indian War of 1962: New Perspectives*. London: Routledge, 2017.

Čavoški, Jovan. 'The Evolution of NAM's Role in World Affairs during the Cold War Decades', in Duško Dimitrijević and Jovan Čavoški, eds. *The 60th Anniversary of the Non-Aligned Movement*. Belgrade: IIPE, 2021.

Chacko, Priya. 'Indira Gandhi, the "Long 1970s", and the Cold War', in Manu Bhagavan, ed. *India and the Cold War*. Chapel Hill, NC: The University of North Carolina Press, 2019.

Chamberlin, Paul T. *The Cold War's Killing Fields: Rethinking the Long Peace*. New York, NY: Harper Collins, 2018.

Chamberlin, Paul T. *The Global Offensive: the United States, the Palestine Liberation Organisation, and the Making of the Post-Cold War World Order*. Oxford: Oxford University Press, 2012.

Chanda, Nayan. *Brother Enemy: A History of Indochina since the Fall of Saigon*. New York, NY: Collier Books, 1986.

Chaudhary, K. C. *Non-Aligned Summitry*. New Delhi: Capital Publishing House, 1988.

Chen, Duide. *Zhou Enlai feiwang Wanlong*. Beijing: Jiefangjun wenyi chubanshe, 2005.

Chen, King C. *China's War with Vietnam, 1979: Issues, Decisions, and Implications*. Stanford, CA: Hoover Institution Press, 1987.

Cheriet, Lazhari. 'Alternative to the Bipolarization', in Bojana Tadić and Ranko Petković, eds. *Non-Alignment in the Eighties: International Round Table, Petrovaradin, Yugoslavia, 28–31 August 1981*. Beograd: IMPP, 1982.

Coatsworth, John H. 'The Cold War in Central America, 1975–1991', in Odd Arne Westad and Melvyn Leffler, eds. *The Cambridge History of the Cold War* 3. Cambridge: Cambridge University Press, 2010.

Connelly, Matthew. *A Diplomatic Revolution: Algeria's Fight for Independence and the Origins of the Post-Cold War Era*. Oxford: Oxford University Press, 2002.

Crabb, Cecil V. Jr. *The Elephants and the Grass: A Study of Nonalignment*. New York, NY: Praeger, 1965.

Crump, Thomas. *Brezhnev and the Decline of the Soviet Union*. London: Routledge, 2014.

Daigle, Craig. *The Limits of Détente: the United States, the Soviet Union, and the Arab-Israeli Conflict, 1969–1973*. New Haven, CT: Yale University Press, 2012.

Das Gupta, Amit. 'India and Non-Alignment – Formative Years', in Duško Dimitrijević and Jovan Čavoški, eds. *The 60th Anniversary of the Non-Aligned Movement*. Belgrade: IIPE, 2021.

Das Gupta, Amit. 'The Non-Aligned and the German Question', in Nataša Mišković, Harald Fischer-Tine and Nada Boškovska, eds. *The Non-Aligned Movement and the Cold War: Delhi-Bandung-Belgrade*. London: Routledge, 2014.

Das Gupta, Amit. *Serving India: A Political Biography of Subimal Dutt, India's Longest Serving Foreign Secretary*. New Delhi: Manohar, 2017.

Das Gupta, Anirudha and Shahid, A. S. 'Ghana's Non-Alignment under Kwame Nkrumah', in K. P. Mishra, *Non-Alignment: Frontiers and Dynamics*. New Delhi: Vikas Publishers, 1982.

Deac, Wilfred P. *Road to the Killing Fields: the Cambodian War of 1970–1975*. College Station, TX: Texas A&M Press, 1997.
DeRoche, Andy. 'Non-Alignment on the Racial Frontier: Zambia and the USA, 1964–1968', in Sue Onslow, ed. *Cold War in Southern Africa: White Power, Black Liberation*. London: Routledge, 2009.
Dietrich, Christopher R. W. *Oil Revolution: Anticolonial Elites, Sovereign Rights, and the Economic Culture of Decolonization*. Cambridge: Cambridge University Press, 2017.
Dimić, Ljubodrag. *Jugoslavija i Hladni rat: ogledi o spoljnoj politici Josipa Broza Tita (1944–1974)*. Beograd: Arhipelag, 2014.
Dinkel, Jürgen. *The Non-Aligned Movement: Genesis, Organization and Politics (1927–1992)*. Leiden: Brill, 2018.
Dunn, David H., ed. *Diplomacy at the Highest Level: The Evolution of International Summitry*. London: Macmillan Press, 1996.
Engerman, David C. *The Price of Aid: The Economic Cold War in India*. Cambridge, MA: Harvard University Press, 2018.
Evans, Grant and Rowley, Kelvin. *Red Brotherhood at War: Vietnam, Laos, and Cambodia since 1975*. London: Verso, 1990.
Fanon, Frantz. *The Wretched of the Earth*. London: Penguin, 2001.
Feifer, Gregory. *The Great Gamble: The Soviet War in Afghanistan*. New York, NY: Harper Collins, 2009.
Ferris, Jesse. *Nasser's Gamble: How Intervention in Yemen Caused the Six-Day War and the Decline of Egyptian Power*. Princeton, NJ: Princeton University Press, 2013.
Fischer, Thomas. *Neutral Power in the CSCE: the N+N States and the Making of the Helsinki Accords 1975* Baden-Baden: Nomos, 2009.
Friedman, Jeremy. *Shadow Cold War: The Sino-Soviet Competition for the Third World*. Chapel Hill, NC: The University of North Carolina Press, 2015.
Fursenko, Aleksandr and Naftali, Timothy. *Khrushchev's Cold War: The Inside Story of an American Adversary*. New York, NY: W.W. Norton, 2006.
Gaddis, John Lewis. 'On Starting All over Again: A Naïve Approach to the Study of the Cold War', in Odd Arne Westad, ed. *Reviewing the Cold War: Approaches, Interpretations, Theory*. London: Frank Cass, 2001.
Gaiduk, Ilya. 'New York, 1960: Die Sowjetunion und die dekolonialisierte Welt auf der Funfzehnten Sitzung der UN-Vollversammlung', in Andreas Hilger, ed. *Die Sowjetunion und die Dritte Welt: UdSSR, Staatssozialismus und Antikolonialismus im Kalten Krieg*. Munchen: R. Oldenbourg Verlag, 2009.
Gaiduk, Ilya V. *The Soviet Union and the Vietnam War*. Chicago, IL: Ivan R. Dee, 1996.
Garavini, Giuliano. *After Empires: European Integration, Decolonization, and the Challenge from the Global South*. Oxford: Oxford University Press, 2012.
Garthoff, Raymond L. *Détente and Confrontation: American-Soviet Relations from Nixon to Reagan*. Washington, DC: Brookings Institution, 1994.
Garthoff, Raymond L. *The Great Transition: American-Soviet Relations and the End of the Cold War*. Washington, DC: Brookings Institution Press, 1994.
George, Susan. *A Fate Worse than Debt: A Radical New Analysis of the Third World Debt Crisis*. London: Penguin, 1989.
Getchell, Michelle. 'Cuba, the USSR, and the Non-Aligned Movement', Thomas C. Field Jr., Stella Krepp and Vanni Pettina, eds. *Latin America and the Cold War*. Chapel Hill, NC: The University of North Carolina Press, 2020.
Ghettas, Mohammed Lakhdar. *Algeria and the Cold War: International Struggle for Autonomy*. London: I B. Tauris, 2018.

Gilman, Nils. *Mandarins of the Future: Modernization Theory in Cold War America*. Baltimore, MD: The Johns Hopkins University Press, 2003.

Ginat, Rami. *Syria and the Doctrine of Arab Neutralism: From Independence to Dependence*. Brighton: Sussex Academic Press, 2005.

Ginor, Isabella and Remez, Gideon. *The Soviet-Israeli War 1967–1973: the USSR's Military Intervention in the Egyptian-Israeli Conflict*. Oxford: Oxford University Press, 2017.

Gleijeses, Piero. *Conflicting Missions: Havana, Washington, and Africa, 1959–1976*. Chapel Hill, NC, and London: The University of North Carolina Press, 2002.

Gleijeses, Piero. *Visions of Freedom: Havana, Washington, Pretoria, and the Struggle for Southern Africa, 1976–1991*. Chapel Hill, NC: The University of North Carolina Press, 2013.

Golan, Galia. *Soviet Policies in the Middle East: From World War II to Gorbachev*. Cambridge: Cambridge University Press, 1990.

Golan, Galia. *Yom Kippur and After: The Soviet Union and the Middle East Crisis*. Cambridge: Cambridge University Press, 1977.

Good, Robert C. 'State-Building as a Determinant of Foreign Policy in the New States', in Laurence W. Martin, ed. *Neutralism and Nonalignment: The New States in World Affairs*. New York, NY: Praeger, 1962.

Gopal, Sarvepalli. *Jawaharlal Nehru: A Biography* 2–3. Cambridge, MA: Harvard University Press, 1979.

Goyal, D. R., ed. *Non-Aligned Movement: From Belgrade to Harare*. New Delhi: 21st Century Publications, 1986.

Grow, Michael. *U.S. Presidents and Latin American Interventions: Pursuing Regime Change in the Cold War*. Lawrence, KS: University Press of Kansas, 2008.

Gupta, Vijay. 'Nature and Content of Tanzanian Non-Alignment', in K. P. Mishra, *Non-Alignment: Frontiers and Dynamics*. New Delhi: Vikas Publishers, 1982.

Gwin, Catherine B. 'The Seventh Special Session: Toward a New Phase of Relations between the Developed and the Developing States?', in Karl P. Sauvant and Hajo Hasenpflug, eds. *The New International Economic Order: Confrontation or Cooperation between the North and South?* Boulder, CO: Westview Press, 1977.

Hahn, Peter. 'The Cold War and the Six Day War: US Policy towards the Arab-Israeli Crisis', in Nigel J. Ashton, ed. *The Cold War in the Middle East: Regional Conflict and the Superpowers, 1967–73*. London: Routledge, 2007.

Hart, Jeffrey A. *The New International Economic Order: Conflict and Cooperation in North-South Economic Relations, 1974–77*. London: Palgrave Macmillan, 1983.

Heikal, Mohamed. *The Cairo Documents*. New York, NY: Doubleday & Company, 1973.

Heikal, Mohamed. *The Road to Ramadan*. Glasgow: Fontana Collins, 1976.

Hershberg, James. 'The Cuban Missile Crisis', in Odd Arne Westad and Melvyn Leffler, eds. *The Cambridge History of the Cold War* 1. Cambridge: Cambridge University Press, 2010.

Hilger, Andreas, ed. *Die Sowjetunion und die Dritte Welt: UdSSR, Staatssozialismus und Antikolonialismus im Kalten Krieg*. Munchen: R. Oldenbourg Verlag, 2009.

Hilger, Andreas. *Sowjetisch-indische Beziehungen 1941–1966: Imperiale Agenda und nationale Identität in der Ära von Dokolonisierung und Kaltem Krieg*. Köln: Böhlau Verlag, 2018.

Horne, Alistair. *Kissinger: 1973, the Crucial Year*. New York, NY: Simon & Schuster, 2009.

Irwin, Ryan M. *Gordian Knot: Apartheid and the Unmaking of the Liberal World Order*. Oxford: Oxford University Press, 2012.

Israelyan, Victor. *Inside the Kremlin during the Yom Kippur War*. University Park, PA: The Pennsylvania State University Press, 1995.

Jackson, Richard L. *The Non-Aligned, the UN and the Superpowers*. New York, NY: Praeger, 1983.

Jain, Narender P. 'Non-Aligned Movement: An Unfinished Revolution', in D. R. Goyal, ed. *Non-Aligned Movement: From Belgrade to Harare*. New Delhi: 21st Century Publications, 1986.

Jain, S. B. *India's Foreign Policy and Non-Alignment*. New Delhi: Anamika Publishers, 2000.

Jakovina, Tvrtko. *Budimir Lončar – od Preka do vrha svijeta*. Zagreb: Fraktura, 2020.

Jakovina, Tvrtko. *Treća strana Hladnog rata*. Zagreb: Fraktura, 2011.

James, Laura M. 'Egypt: Dangerous Illusions', in Wm. Roger Louis and Avi Shlaim, eds. *The 1967 Arab-Israeli War: Origins and Consequences*. Cambridge: Cambridge University Press, 2012.

Jankowitsch, Odette and Sauvant, Karl. 'The Initiating Role of the Non-Aligned Countries', in Karl P. Sauvant, ed. *Changing Priorities on the International Agenda: The New International Economic Order*. Oxford: Pergamon Press, 1981.

Jansen, G. H. *Afro-Asia and Nonalignment*. London: Faber and Faber, 1966.

Jazić, Živojin. *Moj pogled na diplomatiju (1957–2005)*. Beograd: Čigoja, 2010.

Jones, Matthew. *Conflict and Confrontation in South East Asia 1961–1965: Britain, the United States, Indonesia, and the Creation of Malaysia*. Cambridge: Cambridge University Press, 2002.

Јулијус, Ђука. *Хавана – сукоби или споразуми*. Београд: Политика, 1979.

Kahin, Audrey R. and Kahin, George McT. *Subversion as Foreign Policy: the Secret Eisenhower and Dulles Debacle in Indonesia*. New York, NY: The New Press, 1995.

Kalinovsky, Artemy M. *A Long Goodbye: the Soviet Withdrawal from Afghanistan*. Cambridge, MA: Harvard University Press, 2011.

Kalinovski, Artemy M. and Radchenko, Sergey, eds. *The End of the Cold War in the Third World: New Perspectives on Regional Conflict*. London: Routledge, 2011.

Kardelj, Edvard. *Istorijski koreni nesvrstavanja*. Beograd: Komunist, 1975.

Karundasa, W. M. *Sri Lanka and Non-Alignment: A Study of Foreign Policy from 1948 to 1982*. Dehiwela: Image Lanka Publishers, 1997.

'Kautilya'. 'The Philosophy of Non-Alignment', in *India 1962: Annual Review*. London: Information Service of India, 1962.

Kerr, Malcolm H. *The Arab Cold War: Gamal Abd al Nasir and His Rivals, 1958–1970*. Oxford: Oxford University Press, 1971.

Khilnani, Sunil, Kumar, Rajiv et al., *Nonalignment 2.0: A Foreign and Strategic Policy for India in the 21st Century*. New Delhi: Penguin Viking, 2013.

Kiernan, Ben. *How Pol Pot Came to Power: Colonialism, Nationalism, and Communism in Cambodia*. New Haven, CT: Yale University Press, 2004.

Kimbal, Jeffrey. *Nixon's Vietnam War*. Lawrence, KS: University of Kansas Press, 1998.

Kimche, David. *The Afro-Asian Movement: Ideology and Foreign Policy of the Third World*. Jerusalem: Israel Universities Press, 1973.

Komine, Yukinori. *Secrecy in U.S. Foreign Policy: Nixon, Kissinger, and the Rapprochement with China*. London: Routledge, 2008.

Korany, Bahgat. *Social Change, Charisma and International Behaviour: Toward a Theory of Foreign Policy-making in the Third World*. Geneva: IUHHEI, 1976.

Kostiuk, Ruslan Vasilievich and Katkova, Ekaterina Petrovna. 'The Soviet Union and the Non-Aligned Movement', in Duško Dimitrijević and Jovan Čavoški, eds. *The 60th Anniversary of the Non-Aligned Movement*. Belgrade: IIPE, 2021.

Kullaa, Rinna. *Non-Alignment and Its Origins in Cold War Europe: Yugoslavia, Finland, and the Soviet Challenge*. London: I.B. Tauris, 2012.

Kurlansky, Mark. *1968: The Year that Rocked the World*. New York, NY: Ballantine Books, 2003.

Laron, Guy. *Origins of the Suez Crisis: Postwar Development Diplomacy and the Struggle over Third World Industrialization, 1945–1956*. Washington, DC: Woodrow Wilson Center Press, 2013.

Laron, Guy. *The Six-Day War: The Breaking of the Middle East*. New Haven, CT: Yale University Press, 2017.

Lassassi, Assassi. *Non-Alignment and Algerian Foreign Policy*. Aldershot: Avebury, 1988.

Latham, Michael E. 'The Cold War in the Third World', in Odd Arne Westad and Melvyn Leffler, eds. *The Cambridge History of the Cold War* 2. Cambridge: Cambridge University Press, 2010.

Lawrence, Mark Atwood. 'Containing Globalism: the United States and the Developing World in the 1970s', in Niall Ferguson, Charles S. Maier, Erez Manela and Daniel J. Sargent, eds. *The Shock of the Global: the 1970s Perspective*. Cambridge, MA: Harvard University Press, 2010.

Lawrence, Mark Atwood. 'The Rise and Fall of Nonalignment', in Robert J. McMahon. *The Cold War in the Third World*. Oxford: Oxford University Press, 2013.

Lefever, Ernest V. 'Nehru, Nasser, and Nkrumah on Neutralism', in Laurence W. Martin, ed. *Neutralism and Nonalignment: The New States in World Affairs*. New York, NY: Praeger, 1962.

Leffler, Melvyn P. *For the Soul of Mankind: the United States, the Soviet Union, and the Cold War*. New York, NY: Hill and Wang, 2007.

Legum, Colin. *Pan-Africanism: A Short Political Guide*. New York, NY: Praeger, 1965.

Legum, Margaret. 'Africa and Nonalignment', in J. W. Burton, ed. *Nonalignment*. New York, NY: James H. Heineman Inc., 1966.

Levesque, Jacques. *The USSR and the Cuban Revolution: Soviet Ideological and Strategic Perspectives, 1959–1977*. New York, NY: Praeger, 1978.

Li, Qianyu. *Cong Wanlong dao Aerjier: Zhongguo yu liu ci YaFei guoji huiyi*. Beijing: Shijie zhishi chubanshe, 2016.

Litwak, Robert S. *Détente and the Nixon Doctrine: American Foreign Policy and the Pursuit of Stability, 1969–1976*. Cambridge: Cambridge University Press, 1984.

Liu, Xinyao and Fan, Hongwei. 'Chinese Policies towards the Non-Aligned Movement', in Duško Dimitrijević and Jovan Čavoški, eds. *The 60th Anniversary of the Non-Aligned Movement*. Belgrade: IIPE, 2021.

Lorenzini, Sara. *Global Development: A Cold War History*. Princeton, NJ: Princeton University Press, 2019.

Lüthi, Lorenz M. *Cold Wars: Asia, Middle East, Europe*. Cambridge: Cambridge University Press, 2020.

Lüthi, Lorenz M., ed. *The Regional Cold Wars in Europe, East Asia, and the Middle East: Crucial Periods and Turning Points*. Washington, DC, Stanford: Woodrow Wilson Center Press, Stanford University Press, 2015.

Lüthi, Lorenz M. *The Sino-Soviet Split: Cold War in the Communist World*. Princeton, NJ: Princeton University Press, 2008.

Lyon, Peter. *Neutralism*. Leicester: Leicester University Press, 1963.

MacFarlane, S. Neil. *Superpower Rivalry and Third World Radicalism: The Idea of National Liberation*. Baltimore, MD: The Johns Hopkins University Press, 1985.

Madan, Tanvi. *Fateful Triangle: How China Shaped U.S.-India Relations during the Cold War*. Washington, DC: Brookings Institution Press, 2020.
Malley, Robert. *The Call from Algeria: Third Worldism, Revolution, and the Turn to Islam*. Berkeley, CA: University of California Press, 1996.
Mao, Yufeng. 'When Zhou Enlai met Gamal Abdel Nasser', in Derek McDougall and Antonia Finnane, eds. *Bandung 1955: Little Histories*. Caulfield: Monsah University Press, 2010.
Marshall, Charles Burton. 'On Understanding the Unaligned', in Laurence W. Martin, ed. *Neutralism and Nonalignment: The New States in World Affairs*. New York, NY: Praeger, 1962.
Martin, Laurence W., ed. *Neutralism and Nonalignment: The New States in World Affairs*. New York, NY: Praeger, 1962.
Mastny, Vojtech. 'Europe and the Making of Détente', in Lorenz Lüthi, ed. *The Regional Cold Wars in Europe, East Asia, and the Middle East: Crucial Periods and Turning Points*. Washington, DC, Stanford: Woodrow Wilson Center Press, Stanford University Press, 2015.
Mates, Leo. *Koegzistencija*. Zagreb: Školska knjiga, 1974.
Mates, Leo. *Nesvrstanost: teorija i savremena praksa*. Beograd: IMPP, 1970.
Mates, Leo. *Počelo je u Beogradu ... 20 godina nesvrstanosti*. Zagreb: Globus, 1982.
Mates, Leo. 'Variations in East-West Relations and Non-Alignment', in *The Policy and Movement of Non-Alignment – New Tendencies and Options: International Round Table, Petrovaradin, Yugoslavia, 1–3 November 1985*. Belgrade: IIPE, 1986.
Мазов, С.В. *Политика СССР в Западной Африке 1956–1964: неизвестные страницы холодной войны*. Москва: Наука, 2008.
Mazower, Mark. *Governing the World: The History of an Idea*. London: Penguin, 2012.
Mazrui, Ali A. *On Heroes and Uhuru-Worship: Essays on Independent Africa*. London: Longmans, 1974.
McMahon, Robert J. *The Cold War on the Periphery: The United States, India and Pakistan*. New York, NY: Columbia University Press, 1994.
McMahon, Robert J., ed. *The Cold War in the Third World*. Oxford: Oxford University Press, 2013.
Meier, Charles S. 'Malaise: the Crisis of Capitalism in the 1970s', in Niall Ferguson, Charles S. Maier, Erez Manela and Daniel J. Sargent, eds. *The Shock of the Global: The 1970s Perspective*. Cambridge, MA: Harvard University Press, 2010.
Meredith, Martin. *The State of Africa: A History of Fifty Years of Independence*. London: Free Press, 2006.
Milne, June. *Kwame Nkrumah: A Biography*. London: Panaf Books, 1999.
Mishra, K. P. *Non-Alignment: Frontiers and Dynamics*. New Delhi: Vikas Publishers, 1982.
Mishra, K. P. and Narayanan, K. R., eds. *Non-Alignment in Contemporary International Relations*. New Delhi: Vikas Publishers, 1981.
Mišković, Nataša, Fischer-Tine, Harald and Boškovska, Nada, eds. *The Non-Aligned Movement and the Cold War: Delhi-Bandung-Belgrade*. London: Routledge, 2014.
Mitchell, Nancy. *Jimmy Carter in Africa: Race and the Cold War*. Washington DC, Stanford: Woodrow Wilson Center Press, Stanford University Press, 2016.
Morgan, Michael Cotey. *The Final Act: The Helsinki Accords and the Transformation of the Cold War*. Princeton, NJ: Princeton University Press, 2018.
Morozov, Boris. 'The Outbreak of the June 1967 War in Light of Soviet Documentation', in Yaacov Ro'i and Boris Morozov, eds. *The Soviet Union and the June 1967 Six Day War*. Washington, DC, Stanford: Woodrow Wilson Center Press, Stanford University Press, 2008.

Morris, Stephen J. *Why Vietnam Invaded Cambodia: Political Cultures and the Causes of War*. Stanford, CA: Stanford University Press, 1999.

Morphet, Sally. 'Three Non-Aligned Summits: Harare 1986, Belgrade 1989 and Jakarta 1992', in David H. Dunn, ed. *Diplomacy at the Highest Level: The Evolution of International Summitry*. London: Macmillan Press, 1996.

Mortimer, Robert A. *The Third World Coalition in International Politics*. Boulder, CO: Westview Press, 1984.

Moss, Richard A. *Nixon's Back Channel to Moscow: Confidential Diplomacy and Détente*. Lexington, KY: University Press of Kentucky, 2017.

Mukherjee, Rohan. 'Nuclear Ambiguity and International Status: India in the Eighteen-Nation Committee on Disarmament, 1962–1969', in Manu Bhagavan, ed. *India and the Cold War*. Chapel Hill, NC: The University of North Carolina Press, 2019.

Murphy, Craig N. *Global Institutions, Marginalization, and Development*. London: Routledge, 2005.

Murray, Williamson and Woods, Kevin M. *The Iran–Iraq War: A Military and Strategic History*. Cambridge: Cambridge University Press, 2014.

Namikas, Lise. *Battleground Africa: Cold War in the Congo, 1960–1965*. Washington, DC, Stanford: Woodrow Wilson Center Press, Stanford University Press, 2013.

Nanda, B. R., ed. *Indian Foreign Policy: The Nehru Years*. New Delhi: Radiant Publishers, 1976.

Nesadurai, Helen E. S. 'Bandung and the Political Economy of North-South Relations: Sowing the Seeds for Re-Visioning International Societies', in See Seng Tan and Amitav Acharya, eds. *Bandung Revisited: The Legacy of the 1955 Asian-African Conference for International Order*. Singapore: NUS Press, 2008.

Neuhold, Hanspeter. 'Non-Alignment in 1985: Problems and Prospects', in *The Policy and Movement of Non-Alignment – New Tendencies and Options: International Round Table, Petrovaradin, Yugoslavia, 1–3 November 1985*. Belgrade: IIPE, 1986.

Nguyen, Lien-Hang T. *Hanoi's War: An International History of the War for Peace in Vietnam*. Chapel Hill, NC: The University of North Carolina Press, 2012.

Onslow, Sue. 'Tanzania, the Non-Aligned Movement, and Non-Alignment', in Duško Dimitrijević and Jovan Čavoški, eds. *The 60th Anniversary of the Non-Aligned Movement*. Belgrade: IIPE, 2021.

Onslow, Sue. 'The South African Factor in Zimbabwe's Transition to Independence', in Sue Onslow, ed. *Cold War in Southern Africa: White Power, Black Liberation*. London: Routledge, 2009.

Oren, Michael B. *Six Days of War: June 1967 and the Making of the Modern Middle East*. New York, NY: Ballantine Books, 2002.

Path, Kosal. *Vietnam's Strategic Thinking during the Third Indochina War*. Madison, WI: University of Wisconsin Press, 2020.

Petković, Ranko. *Nesvrstana Jugoslavija i savremeni svet: spoljna politika Jugoslavije 1945–1985*. Zagreb: Školska knjiga, 1985.

Petković, Ranko. *Nesvrstanost: nezavisan, vanblokovski i globalni faktor u međunarodnim odnosima*. Zagreb: Školska knjiga, 1981.

Petković, Ranko. *Teorijski pojmovi nesvrstanosti*. Beograd: Rad, 1974.

Petrović, Vladimir. *Titova lična diplomatija: studije i dokumentarni prilozi*. Beograd: ISI, 2010.

Porter, Bruce D. *The USSR in Third World Conflicts: Soviet Arms and Diplomacy in Local Wars, 1945–1980*. Cambridge: Cambridge University Press, 1984.

Prados, John. *Vietnam: The History of an Unwinnable War, 1945–1975*. Lawrence, KS: University Press of Kansas, 2009.

Prasad, Bimla. 'Opšte iskustvo i perspektive nesvrstanosti', in Ljubivoje Aćimović, ed. *Politika nesvrstanosti u savremenom svetu*. Beograd: IMPP, 1969.

Prashad, Vijay. *The Darker Nations: A People's History of the Third World*. New York, NY, and London: The New Press, 2007.

Primakov, Yevgeny. *Russia and the Arabs: Behind the Scenes in the Middle East from the Cold War to the Present*. New York, NY: Basic Books, 2009.

Quandt, William B. *Decade of Decisions: American Policy toward the Arab-Israeli Conflict, 1967–1976*. Berkeley, CA: University of California Press, 1977.

Quandt, William B. *Peace Process: American Diplomacy and the Arab-Israeli Conflict since 1967*. Washington, DC, Berkeley: Brookings Institution Press, University of California Press, 2005.

Quandt, William B. *Revolution and Political Leadership: Algeria, 1954–1968*. Cambridge, MA: MIT Press, 1969.

Qureshi, Lubna Z. *Nixon, Kissinger, and Allende: U.S. Involvement in the 1973 Coup in Chile*. Lanham, MD: Lexington Books, 2009.

Rabinovich, Abraham. *The Yom Kippur War: The Epic Encounter that Transformed the Middle East*. New York, NY: Shocken Books, 2004.

Radchenko, Sergey. *Two Suns in the Heavens: The Sino-Soviet Struggle for Supermacy, 1962–1967*. Washington, DC, Stanford: Woodrow Wilson Center Press, Stanford University Press, 2009.

Raghavan, Srinath. *1971: A Global History of the Creation of Bangladesh*. Cambridge, MA: Harvard University Press, 2013.

Raghavan, Srinath. *War and Peace in Modern India: A Strategic History of the Nehru Years*. Ranikhet: Permanent Black, 2010.

Rajan, M. S. *The Future of Non-Alignment and the Non-Aligned Movement: Some Reflective Essays*. New Delhi: Konark Publishers, 1990.

Rajan, M. S. *Non-Alignment: India and the Future*. Mysore: Mysore University Press, 1970.

Rajan, M. S. *Nonalignment and Nonaligned Movement: Retrospect and Prospect*. New Delhi: Vikas Publishing, 1990.

Rajan, M. S. *Studies on Nonalignment and the Nonaligned Movement: Theory and Practice*. New Delhi: ABC Publishers, 1986.

Rakove, Robert B. *Kennedy, Johnson, and the Nonaligned World*. Cambridge: Cambridge University Press, 2013.

Raman, Kumar Awadhesh. *Mrs. Indira Gandhi and the Non-Aligned Movement*. Patna: Janaki Prakashan, 2011.

Razoux, Pierre. *The Iran-Iraq War*. Cambridge, MA: Harvard University Press, 2015.

Reynolds, David. *Summits: Six Meetings that Shaped the Twentieth Century*. New York, NY: Basic Books, 2007.

Richardson, Sophie. *China, Cambodia, and the Five Principles of Peaceful Co-Existence*. New York, NY: Columbia University Press, 2010.

Riechers, C. Russel. *Cuba and the Non-Aligned Movement: Interactions of Pragmatic Idealism*. Washington, DC: SIS AU, 2012.

Ro'i, Yaacov. 'Soviet Policy toward the Six Day War through the Prism of Moscow's Relations with Egypt and Syria', in Yaacov Ro'I and Boris Morozov, eds. *The Soviet Union and the June 1967 Six Day War*. Washington, DC, Stanford: Woodrow Wilson Center Press, Stanford University Press, 2008.

Rubinstein, Alvin Z. *Moscow's Third World Strategy*. Princeton, NJ: Princeton University Press, 1990.

Rubinstein, Alvin Z. *Red Star on the Nile: the Soviet-Egyptian Influence Relationship since the June War*. Princeton, NJ: Princeton University Press, 1977.

Rubinstein, Alvin Z. *Yugoslavia and the Non-Aligned World*. Princeton, NJ: Princeton University Press, 1970.

Saikal, Amin. 'Islamism, the Iranian Revolution, and the Soviet Invasion of Afghanistan', in Odd Arne Westad and Melvyn Leffler, eds. *The Cambridge History of the Cold War* 3. Cambridge: Cambridge University Press, 2010.

Sanchez-Sibony, Oscar. *Red Globalization: Political Economy of the Soviet Cold War from Stalin to Khrushchev*. Cambridge: Cambridge University Press, 2014.

Sander, Robert D. *Invasion of Laos, 1971: Lam Son 719*. Norman, OK: University of Oklahoma Press, 2014.

Sargent, Daniel J. *A Superpower Transformed: The Remaking of America's Foreign Relations in the 1970s*. Oxford: Oxford University Press, 2015.

Saunders, Chris. 'The Non-Aligned Movement, Namibia, and South Africa over Sixty Years', in Duško Dimitrijević and Jovan Čavoški, eds. *The 60th Anniversary of the Non-Aligned Movement*. Belgrade: IIPE, 2021.

Savranskaya, Svetlana and Taubman, William, 'Soviet Foreign Policy, 1962–1975', in Odd Arne Westad and Melvyn Leffler, eds. *The Cambridge History of the Cold War* 2. Cambridge: Cambridge University Press, 2010.

Schmidt, Elizabeth. *Cold War and Decolonization in Guinea, 1946–1958*. Athens, OH: Ohio University Press, 2007.

Service, Robert. *The End of the Cold War, 1985–1991*. London: Macmillan, 2015.

Sharnoff, Michael. *Nasser's Peace: Egypt's Response to the 1967 War with Israel*. New York, NY: Transaction Publishers, 2017.

Simpson, Bradley R. *Economists with Guns: Authoritarian Development and U.S.-Indonesian Relations, 1960–1968*. Stanford, CA: Stanford University Press, 2008.

Singh, Dinesh. 'Non-Alignment and New International Economic Order', in Bojana Tadić and Ranko Petković, eds. *Non-Alignment in the Eighties: International Round Table, Petrovaradin, Yugoslavia, 28–31 August 1981*. Beograd: IMPP, 1982.

Singh, S. Nihal. *The Yogi and the Bear: A Study of Indo-Soviet Relations*. New Delhi: Allied Publishers, 1986.

Singham, A. W. and Hune, Shirley. *Non-Alignment in an Age of Alignments*. London: Zed Books, 1986.

Soutou, Georges-Henry. 'The Linkage between European Integration and Détente: Contrasting Approaches of de Gaulle and Pompidou, 1965–74', in N. Piers Ludlow, ed. *European Integration and the Cold War: Ostpolitik-Westpolitik, 1965–73*. London: Routledge, 2007.

Spohr, Kristina and Reynolds, David, eds. *Transcending the Cold War: Summits, Statecraft, and the Dissolution of Bipolarity in Europe 1970–1990*. Oxford: Oxford University Press, 2016.

Srivastava, Pramila, ed. *Non-Aligned Movement: Extending Frontiers*. New Delhi: Kanishka Publishers, 2001.

Srivastava, Renu. *India and the Nonaligned Summits: Belgrade to Jakarta*. New Delhi: Northern Book Centre, 1995.

Stanovnik, Janez. 'Non-Alignment and the New International Economic Order', in Bojana Tadić and Ranko Petković, eds. *Non-Alignment in the Eighties: International Round Table, Petrovaradin, Yugoslavia, 28–31 August 1981*. Beograd: IMPP, 1982.

Statler, Kathryn C. and Johns, Andrew L., eds. *The Eisenhower Administration, the Third World, and the Globalization of the Cold War*. Lanham, MD: Rowman & Littlefield, 2006.

Steele, Jonathan. *Soviet Power: the Kremlin's Foreign Policy – Brezhnev to Chernenko*. New York, NY: Simon & Schuster, 1984.

Stein, Kenneth W. *Heroic Diplomacy: Sadat, Kissinger, Carter, Begin, and the Quest for Arab-Israeli Peace*. London: Routledge, 1999.

Stojković, Momir. *Tito, Nehru, Naser: nastanak i razvoj politike i Pokreta nesvrstanosti*. Zaječar: RO Zaječar, 1983.

Stolte, Carolien. 'The Asiatic Hour: New Perspectives on the Asian Relations Conference, New Delhi, 1947', in Nataša Mišković, Harald Fischer-Tine and Nada Boškovska, eds. *The Non-Aligned Movement and the Cold War: Delhi-Bandung-Belgrade*. London: Routledge, 2014.

Stueck, William. *The Korean War: An International History*. Princeton, NJ: Princeton University Press, 1995.

Suri, Jeremy. *Power and Protest: Global Revolution and the Rise of Détente*. Cambridge, MA: Harvard University Press, 2003.

Suri, Jeremy. 'Counter Culture: the Rebellions against the Cold War Order', in Odd Arne Westad and Melvyn Leffler, eds. *The Cambridge History of the Cold War* 2. Cambridge: Cambridge University Press, 2010.

Tadić, Bojana. *Nesvrstanost u teoriji i praksi međunarodnih odnosa*. Beograd: IMPP, 1976.

Tadić, Bojana. *Osobenosti i dileme nesvrstanosti*. Beograd: Komunist, 1982.

Tadić, Bojana. *Sukobi među nesvrstanim zemljama: dokumentacioni prilog*. Beograd: Međunarodna Politika, 1987.

Tadić, Bojana and Petković, Ranko, eds. *Non-Alignment in the Eighties: International Round Table, Petrovaradin, Yugoslavia, 28–31 August 1981*. Beograd: IMPP, 1982.

Tareke, Gebru. *The Ethiopian Revolution: War in the Horn of Africa*. New Haven, CT: Yale University Press, 2009.

Thompson, W. Scott. *Ghana's Foreign Policy 1957–1966: Diplomacy, Ideology, and the New State*. Princeton, NJ: Princeton University Press, 1969.

Tiruneh, Andargachew. *The Ethiopian Revolution, 1974–1987: A Transformation from Aristocratic to a Totalitarian Autocracy*. Cambridge: Cambridge University Press, 1993.

Trachtenberg, Marc. 'The Structure of Great Power Politics', in Odd Arne Westad and Melvyn Leffler, eds. *The Cambridge History of the Cold War* 2. Cambridge: Cambridge University Press, 2010.

Tudda, Chris. *A Cold War Turning Point: Nixon and China, 1969–1972*. Baton Rouge, LA: Louisiana State University Press, 2012.

Tudda, Chris. *Cold War Summits*. London: Bloomsbury Press, 2015.

VanDeMark, Brian. *Road to Disaster: A New History of America's Descent into Vietnam*. New York, NY: Custom House, 2018.

Vanetik, Boaz and Shalom, Zaki. *The Nixon Administration and the Middle East Peace Process, 1969–1973: From the Rogers Plan to the Outbreak of the Yom Kippur War*. Brighton: Sussex Academic Press, 2013.

Veith, George J. *Black April: the Fall of South Vietnam, 1973–1975*. New York, NY: Encounter Books, 2012.

Venn, Fiona. *The Oil Crisis*. London: Pearson Education, 2002.

Vratuša, Antun. 'Possibilities for Promoting Mutual Cooperation of Non-Aligned and Other Developing Countries on the Basis of the Principle of Collective Self-Reliance', in Bojana Tadić and Ranko Petković, eds. *Non-Alignment in the Eighties: International Round Table, Petrovaradin, Yugoslavia, 28–31 August 1981*. Beograd: IMPP, 1982.

Westad, Odd Arne. *The Cold War: A World History*. New York, NY: Basic Books, 2017.
Westad, Odd Arne. *The Global Cold War: Third World Interventions and the Making of Our Times*. Cambridge: Cambridge University Press, 2005.
Wilkens, Andreas. 'New *Ostpolitik* and European Integration: Concepts and Policies in the Brandt Era', in N. Piers Ludlow, ed. *European Integration and the Cold War: Ostpolitik-Westpolitik, 1965–73*. London: Routledge, 2007.
Willetts, Peter. *The Non-Aligned Movement: The Origins of a Third World Alliance*. London: Frances Pinter Publishers, 1978.
Win, Kyaw Zaw, 'The 1953 Asian Socialist Conference in Rangoon: Precursor to the Bandung Conference', in Derek McDougall and Antonia Finnane, eds. *Bandung 1955: Little Histories*. Caulfield: Monsah University Press, 2010.
Wright, Lawrence. *Thirteen Days in September: Carter, Begin, and Sadat at Camp David*. New York, NY: Alfred A. Knopf, 2014.
Wright, Richard. *The Color Curtain*. New York, NY: Banner Books, 1994.
Xia, Yafeng. *Negotiating with the Enemy: U.S.-China Talks during the Cold War, 1949–1972*. Bloomington, IN: Indiana University Press, 2006.
Yaqub, Salim. *Containing Arab Nationalism: the Eisenhower Doctrine and the Middle East*. Chapel Hill, NC: The University of North Carolina Press, 2004.
Yaqub, Salim. *Imperfect Strangers: Americans, Arabs, and U.S. Middle Eastern Relations in the 1970s*. Ithaca, NY: Cornell University Press, 2016.
Yordanov, Radoslav. *The Soviet Union and the Horn of Africa during the Cold War: Between Ideology and Pragmatism*. Lanham, MD: Lexington Books, 2016.
Zelikow, Philip and May, Ernest. *Suez Deconstructed: An Interactive Study in Crisis, War, and Peacemaking*. Washington, DC: Brookings Institution Press, 2018.
Zhai, Qiang. *China and the Vietnam Wars, 1950–1975*. Chapel Hill, NC: The University of North Carolina Press, 2000.
Zhang, Xiaoming. *Deng Xiaoping's Long War: The Military Conflict between China and Vietnam, 1979–1991*. Chapel Hill, NC: The University of North Carolina Press, 2015.
Zhou, Taomo. *Migration in the Time of Revolution: China, Indonesia, and the Cold War*. Ithaca, NY: Cornell University Press, 2019.
Životić, Aleksandar. *Jugoslavija i Suecka kriza 1956–1957*. Beograd: INIS, 2008.
Zubok, Vladislav. *A Failed Empire: The Soviet Union in the Cold War from Stalin to Gorbachev*. Chapel Hill, NC: The University of North Carolina Press, 2007.

Index

18 Nations Disarmament Committee 1962 (UN) 63
1961 Belgrade Conference see Belgrade Conference
1970 Lusaka Conference see Lusaka Conference
1976 Colombo Conference see Colombo Conference

AAPSO see Afro-Asian People's Solidarity Organisation
Accra conferences 46–47
'Action Program for Economic Cooperation' 149, 181
'Action Program for International Economic Cooperation' 138–139
Action Program/Havana Conference 210–211
Addis Ababa 76, 108, 109, 110, 115, 116
Adoula, C. 59
Afghanistan
  Colombo Conference 180
  First Conference at Belgrade 59
  Havana Conference 192–193, 200, 201, 211
  Lusaka Conference 110, 113
Africa
  Algiers Conference 120, 131–132, 137–141, 143
  Cairo Conference 73, 74, 76, 79, 88, 89
  challenges of Belgrade Conference 54–55
  Colombo Conference 163, 166, 169, 171, 179–180, 182
  further boost to Belgrade 49
  Havana Conference 193–194, 197–201, 205–208, 214–215, 219–220
  initiative of the five 47–48
  Lusaka Conference 102, 107, 108, 110, 112–113, 114, 115, 117, 118
  non-aligned impetus of Belgrade Conference 46–47
  regionalism and non-alignment 26
  see also individual African countries...; South Africa
Afro-Asian People's Solidarity Organisation (AAPSO) 103
Afro-Arab group
  Algiers Conference 151
  Colombo Conference 169, 173–174
Afro-Asianism
  aftermath of Belgrade 61–62
  aftermath of Belgrade Conference 62–63
  Cairo Conference 71–97
  further boost to Belgrade 49, 50, 51–52
  Lusaka Conference 101, 102–105
  NAM's Afro-Asian predecessors 39
  non-aligned impetus of Belgrade Conference 40–45
  pillars of non-alignment 28
  Preparatory Meeting at Belgrade 53
  regionalism and non-alignment 24, 25–26
'Agenda Item 15' 210, 220
AL see Arab League
Alexandria, Lusaka Conference 103–104
Algeria
  Algiers Conference 129–157
  Ben Ella 81, 91–92
  Cairo Conference 77, 79, 80, 91–92
  Colombo Conference 161, 165–167, 173–174, 176, 180–181
  further boost to Belgrade 50, 51
  Havana Conference 193, 213, 215, 220
  initiative of the five 47
  Lusaka Conference 104, 105, 108, 110, 111–112, 113, 115, 116, 117, 118
  Preparatory Meeting at Belgrade 53
  regionalism and non-alignment 26
  see also Ben Ella, A.; Boumedienne, H.
Algerian national-liberation struggle of 1962 73

280   *Index*

Algerian-Yugoslav consultations, Colombo Conference 166
Algiers
    and Colombo Conference 167–168, 177–178
    and Lusaka Conference 116
Algiers Conference 129–157
    aftermath 151
    and Colombo Conference 181
    détente 129–134
    fourth summit preparations 141–145
    Georgetown meeting 136–141
    New York and NAM continuity 134–136
Allende, S. 151, 171
Angola 161–162, 163
    Colombo Conference 178, 180
    FNLA 163
    Havana Conference 192–193, 198, 208, 211
    Lusaka Conference 102
    MPLA 163
    regionalism and non-alignment 25
    UNITA 163
anti-Chinese sentiment of the USSR 195–196
anti-colonialism/imperialism
    Algiers Conference 147
    Belgrade Conference 52–53, 60
    Cairo Conference 73, 74, 82, 84, 87
    Colombo Conference 184
    Havana Conference 203, 204–205, 208, 220
    regionalism and non-alignment 25
anti-communist and pan-Arab policies 46
anti-Soviet sentiment, challenges of Belgrade Conference 55
anti-Western bias
    aftermath of Belgrade 61
    Belgrade Conference 62
    Cairo Conference 82
    Preparatory Meeting at Belgrade 52
anti-Western Casablanca groups 49
'Appeal of 17 Non-Aligned Nations' 91
'Appeal for Peace' 61
Arab boycotts and Israel 43
Arab League (AL) 101–102
    Algiers Conference 137, 145
    Colombo Conference 173–174
    Havana Conference 195
Arab/Afro-Asian groups and Belgrade Conference 41
Arab-African Bank, Colombo Conference 166
Arab-African bloc, Algiers Conference 140
Arab-African group, Colombo Conference 176
Arabic countries
    Algiers Conference 140–141
    Cairo Conference 89
    Colombo Conference 162, 173
    further boost to Belgrade 49
    Havana Conference 193, 209–211
    Lusaka Conference 110, 115, 117, 118, 121
    OAPEC 195
    see also individual Arabic countries...
Arab–Israeli relations, Cairo Conference 74
Arafat, Y. 169, 219
ARC *see* Asian Relations Conference
ASC *see* Asian Socialist Conference
ASEAN countries
    Colombo Conference 176–177
    Havana Conference 211
    see also individual ASEAN countries...
Asia
    Algiers Conference 135
    Cairo Conference 73, 74
    Colombo Conference 169, 180
    Havana Conference 193, 215, 220
    Lusaka Conference 100–101, 104, 107, 110, 115, 117
    see also Afro-Asianism; *individual Asian countries...*
Asian Relations Conference (ARC) 40
Asian Socialist Conference (ASC) 29–30
Assad, B. 219
Australia
    Colombo Conference 172, 173, 178, 181
    NAM's Afro-Asian predecessors 40–41
Austria
    Carter-Brezhnev summit 192
    Colombo Conference 161
    Lusaka Conference 117–118
authoritarianism 74

Bahrain, Algiers Conference 138–139
Bandaranaike, S.
    Algiers Conference 146–147
    Belgrade Conference 46–47, 57–58
    Cairo Conference 77, 79, 81–82
    Colombo Conference 164–165
Bandung Conference 43–44, 77–85, 104, 108–109
Bangladesh
    Algiers Conference 134, 142, 145
    Colombo Conference 180
    independence 134
Barre, S. 194
Basic Treaty between Germanies 1972 130
basket concepts 160–161
bauxite 171–172
Bay of Pigs 51
Begin, M. 195
Beijing
    aftermath of Belgrade Conference 62
    Algiers Conference 131
    Cairo Conference 72–75, 77, 78–80, 83–84, 90, 91–92, 723
    challenges of Belgrade Conference 56
    Colombo Conference 163
    further boost to Belgrade 49
    Lusaka Conference 101, 104
    NAM's Afro-Asian predecessors 44
    non-aligned impetus of Belgrade Conference 46–47
Belgium, Havana Conference 193–194
Belgrade
    aftermath 61–63
    and Algiers Conference 135
    and Cairo Conference 74–75, 78
    and Havana Conference 203–207
    and Lusaka Conference 106, 107, 108–109, 110, 112–114
    pillars of non-alignment 26
Belgrade Conference 18, 39–69, 77–85
    Afro-Asianism 40–45
    Algiers Conference 143
    and Cairo Conference 78–79
    challenges 54–56
    first conference 56–61
    further boost to 49–52
    initiative of the five 47–49
    and Lusaka Conference 104, 108–109
    non-aligned impetus 45–47

Preparatory Meeting 52–54
    Third Bloc non-alignment 30
Belize, Colombo Conference 178
Ben Ella, A. 81, 91–92
Bengali refugees 133–134
Benin (Republic of) 214–215
Berlin, Belgrade Conference 54–55, 61
'big three of non-alignment' see Egypt; India; Yugoslavia
Biinh, Nguyen Thi (PRGSV) 118
Bizerte (French base) 51
bloc antagonisms 24
Bolivia, Havana Conference 204, 214–215
bombing campaigns 81
Borneo, Cairo Conference 74
Botswana
    Colombo Conference 180
    Havana Conference 208
Boumedienne, H.
    Algiers Conference 146–147, 149–151
    Cairo Conference 91–92
    Colombo Conference 164, 165, 166, 167–168, 175
    Lusaka Conference 108
Bourgiba, H.
    Algiers Conference 146–147, 149–150
    Belgrade Conference 51, 57, 78–79
    Lusaka Conference 108
Boutros-Ghali, B. 217
Bowles, C. 54–55
Brandt, W. 130
Brazil
    challenges of Belgrade Conference 55–56
    Preparatory Meeting at Belgrade 53
Breton Woods system 159–160
'Brezhnev Doctrine' 109
Brezhnev, L. 107, 151, 160
Brioni Isles 45
Britain
    Algiers Conference 134, 150–151
    Cairo Conference 74
    challenges of Belgrade Conference 55–56
    Colombo Conference 184
    Lusaka Conference 113–114
buffer stocks 174, 183
Burma
    Algiers Conference 138–139, 140

282 *Index*

Belgrade Conference 62
Cairo Conference 79
challenges of Belgrade Conference 54
essence of NAM 17
Lusaka Conference 115
NAM's Afro-Asian predecessors 42–43
see also Nu, U.
Burnham, L. F. S. 137

Cairo
  Algiers Conference 137–138, 144
  Belgrade Conference 63
  Economic Conference of Developing Countries 63
  further boost to Belgrade 50, 51–52
  Havana Conference 194
  and Havana Conference 195, 209–210, 212, 219–220
  Lusaka Conference 106, 107
  NAM's Afro-Asian predecessors 41
  non-aligned impetus of Belgrade Conference 46
  Preparatory Meeting at Belgrade 52–54
Cairo Conference 71–97
  aftermath 90–92
  itself 85–89
  and Lusaka Conference 104, 108–109, 110, 112
  parallel offensives of Belgrade/Bandung Conferences 82–85
  parallels of Belgrade/Bandung Conferences 80–82
  resumption of Afro-Asianism 75–77
  second Belgrade/Bandung Conferences 77–80
  superpowers and the Third World 72–75
Cairo Prepatory Meeting for the Belgrade Conference 18
Cambodia
  Algiers Conference 138–139, 144
  Belgrade Conference 62
  Cairo Conference 83
  Colombo Conference 162
  First Conference at Belgrade 59
  Lusaka Conference 104, 116–117
  see also Vietnam War
Camp David Accords 195, 208–209, 211
Canada, Colombo Conference 160

Cape Verde, Colombo Conference 173
capitalism
  Havana Conference 220
  'troika' proposal 47
Carter, J. 192–193, 204
Carter-Brezhnev summit in Vienna 192
Castro, F. 47, 147, 149–150
  see also Havana Conference
Castro, R. 215–216
CB *see* Coordinating Bureau
Ceaușescu, N. 107
Central African Federation 43
Central Treaty Organisation (CENTO) 43, 177, 210
'Centre for Research and Information' 174
'Centre for Science and Technology' 174
Ceylon
  Algiers Conference 135
  Belgrade Conference 46–47, 54, 62
  Cairo Conference 71–72, 77, 79, 81, 83, 84–85, 88, 89
  essence of NAM 16
  Lusaka Conference 109, 113, 115
  NAM's Afro-Asian predecessors 42–43
Chad
  Algiers Conference 138–139
  Colombo Conference 180
  Havana Conference 216
challenges of Belgrade Conference 55–56
'Charter on Economic Rights and Duties of States' 169–170
Charter, UN 44
Chiang, K.-S. 40–41
Chile, Algiers Conference 135, 137, 138–139, 144–145, 151
China
  aftermath of Belgrade Conference 62
  Algiers Conference 130, 131, 138, 143, 144, 151
  Cairo Conference 72–80, 82–84, 86, 90–92
  challenges of Belgrade Conference 54, 56
  Colombo Conference 180, 184
  Havana Conference 192, 195–196, 213, 216
  initiative of the five 47–48
  Lusaka Conference 101, 104, 105, 109, 110–112, 115, 117, 120–121

NAM's Afro-Asian predecessors 41, 42–43, 44
non-aligned impetus of Belgrade Conference 46
PRC 120–121, 131, 136
Preparatory Meeting at Belgrade 52
see also Beijing
Civil War 163, 194
Cold War framework of non-alignment 20–23
Colombo
   and Algiers Conference 142
   Cairo Conference 75
   and Cairo Conference 81
   and Havana Conference 196–197
   Havana Conference 211–212
   and Lusaka Conference 108
Colombo Conference 159–190
   aftermath 184
   and Belgrade Conference 42–43
   détente 160–163
   and Havana Conference 200–201, 208–209
   itself 179–184
   OPEC oil embargo 163–167
   struggle for the NIEO 170–176
   troubled NAM 176–179
   UNGA 167–170
colonialism
   Belgrade Conference 50, 56–57
   Havana Conference 204–205, 220
   Lusaka Conference 102
   see also anti-colonialism/imperialism
Committee of Ambassadors (Belgrade Conference) 53
Communist Party of Indonesia (PKI) 91–92
Comoros, Colombo Conference 178
Composition and Mandate of the CB 181
Conference on Raw Materials in Dakar 170
Conference for Security and Cooperation in Europe (CSCE) 160, 161, 191, 192
Congo
   Cairo Conference 85
   Preparatory Meeting at Belgrade 53
Congo Crisis 73–74
Congo-Brazzaville, Lusaka Conference 113

Coordinating Bureau (CB)
   Algiers Conference 150
   Colombo Conference 164–167, 170–172, 177–180, 181
   Havana Conference 199–203, 207, 208, 209–212, 215, 218–220
copper 171–172
Costa Rica, Havana Conference 214–215
Côte d'Ivoire 219–220
'Council of Associations of the Developing Countries Producers-Exporters of Raw Materials' 174
Creswell, Michael 61–62
Crimea, challenges of Belgrade Conference 55
CSCE *see* Conference for Security and Cooperation in Europe
Cuba
   aftermath of Belgrade Conference 62
   Algiers Conference 144, 145, 150
   Bay of Pigs 51
   Cairo Conference 84–85, 88, 91
   challenges of Belgrade Conference 55–56
   Colombo Conference 161–162, 170–171, 177, 178, 180–181, 183
   further boost to Belgrade 51
   independence from US 197–198
   initiative of the five 47
   involvement in Angola 161–162
   Lusaka Conference 103, 111–112, 116, 117
   Preparatory Meeting at Belgrade 52, 53
   regionalism and non-alignment 25
   see also Havana; Havana Conference
Cuban Missile Crisis 71, 72
Cuban–Yugoslav bilateral talks in Belgrade 203–204
Cuban–Yugoslav competition/Havana Conference 196–199
Cultural Revolution in China 101
culture 160–161
Cyprus
   Algiers Conference 120, 144
   Colombo Conference 161, 171
   Havana Conference 205–206
   initiative of the five 47
   Lusaka Conference 113
Czechoslovakia 109, 111–112, 118

Dakar, Conference on Raw Materials 170
Dalai Lama 46
Danger of War and the Appeal for Peace (Statement) 60–61
Dar-es-Salaam 114, 115–116
De Gaulle, C. 107, 130
'Decision Regarding the Composition and Mandate of the CB' 181
decision-making by consensus 160–161
'Declaration on the Establishment of the NIEO' 168
'Declaration on the Friendly Relations between Countries' 120
'Declaration on the Granting of Independence to Colonial Countries and Peoples' 48–49
'Declaration of the Heads of State or Government of Non-Aligned Countries' 60–61
'Declaration on the International Strategy of Development' 120
'Declaration on National Liberation' 147
'Declaration on Non-Alignment and Economic Progress' 120
'Declaration on Peace, Independence, Development, Cooperation, and Democratisation of International Relations' 120
'Declaration on the Security and Peace' 120
decolonization
    Algiers Conference 120
    Belgrade Conference 40
    Havana Conference 197
    Lusaka Conference 107–108
    Third Bloc non-alignment 32
    see also anti-colonialism/imperialism
DEFCON III nuclear alerts 162
Democratic Kampuchea (DK) 163, 208–209, 211, 213–215
Democratic Kampuchea (KP) 163
Democratic People's Republic of Korea (DPRK) 171, 172, 173
    see also North Korea
Deng, X. 82, 195–196
Dergue (Committee) 194
Desai, M. 211–212
détente
    Algiers Conference 129–134, 146

    Colombo Conference 160–163
    Havana Conference 192–196
    Lusaka Conference 100–102
Dhaka authorities 137
disarmament 138–139
    Algiers Conference 120
    Cairo Conference 83–84
    Third Bloc non-alignment 32
Disarmament Committee 1962 (UN) 63
Djibouti 201, 204
Dominica 214–215
DPRK see Democratic People's Republic of Korea
DR Vietnam, Colombo Conference 173

East Africa
    Havana Conference 214–215
    Lusaka Conference 102, 108, 114
East Germany, Algiers Conference 130
East Pakistan, Algiers Conference 135–136
Echeverria. L. 169–170
Economic Committee
    Algiers Conference 138–139, 144–145, 150
    Havana Conference 205, 214, 220
Economic Conference of Developing Countries, Cairo 63
Economic Cooperation, Action Program 138–139, 149, 181
economic crisis 163–164
'Economic Declarations' 149, 181
economic incentives and Cold War framework of non-alignment 22
economic independence and development
    Algiers Conference 148
    Cairo Conference 83–84
    and Colombo Conference 159–190
    Lusaka Conference 107–108, 115–116
economic inequality, Belgrade Conference 58
Economic Progress (Declaration) 120
Economic Rights and Duties of States Charter 169–170
economic underdevelopment 13
    Cairo Conference 84
    see also Third World
education and culture 160–161
EEC see European Economic Commission

Egypt
  Algiers Conference 132, 133, 134, 141, 143
  Boutros-Ghali 217
  Colombo Conference 161, 162, 173–174, 177, 180
  essence of NAM 17
  Havana Conference 193, 194–195, 200–201, 205, 209, 211, 212, 217, 219–221
  Lusaka Conference 101, 103–104
  NAM's Afro-Asian predecessors 40–41
  non-aligned impetus of Belgrade Conference 45–46
  as pillar of non-alignment 26–29
  see also Cairo; Nasser, G. A.; United Arab Republic
Egyptian–Israeli peace talks 219–220
Egyptian–Syrian state union 63
Egypt–India–Yugoslavia axis 137–138
Eisenhower, D. 48
embargoes 163–167
Emergency Relief Fund of the UN 168
energy crisis 163–167
equality
  Lusaka Conference 107–108
  Third Bloc non-alignment 32
Equatorial Guinea, Algiers Conference 138–139
escalation
  Algiers Conference 131
  Cuban Missile Crisis 71, 72
Establishment of the NIEO (Declaration) 168
Ethiopia
  Cairo Conference 71–72, 84–85
  Havana Conference 192–193, 194, 208
  and Lusaka Conference 108–109
  Lusaka Conference 110–111, 113, 114
  NAM's Afro-Asian predecessors 40–41
  regionalism and non-alignment 25
Europe
  Algiers Conference 130, 138, 144, 151
  Belgrade Conference 62–63
  Cairo Conference 73, 78, 79–80, 89
  Colombo Conference 160–161, 164, 176, 180, 181
  CSCE 160, 161, 191, 192
  Havana Conference 204, 212, 214–215
  Lusaka Conference 104, 110
  non-aligned impetus of Belgrade Conference 45
  regionalism and non-alignment 25
  see also individual European countries…; United Nations
European détente 146
European Economic Commission (EEC) 149

'familyhood' 115–116
Fiji 201
Financing Buffer Stocks 174, 183
Finland
  Colombo Conference 160–161
  Lusaka Conference 117–118
Five Principles of Peaceful Co-Existence (*Panscheel*) 29
FNLA *see* National Front for the Liberation of Angola
Ford, G. 160, 169, 192–193
Four Power agreement on Berlin 1971 130
France
  Algiers Conference 130, 134
  further boost to Belgrade 51
  Havana Conference 193–194
  Lusaka Conference 117
freedom of movement and information 160–161
Friendly Relations between Countries (Declaration) 120

G77 meetings
  Algiers Conference 136–137, 148
  Colombo Conference 180–181
  Havana Conference 198–199, 202
Gabon
  Algiers Conference 138–139
  Havana Conference 193, 205, 214–215
Gafurov, B. 62
Gandhi, I.
  Algiers Conference 134
  Colombo Conference 165
  Lusaka Conference 103–104, 107, 108–109, 119
gas industries 134
  see also oil and gas industries
GATT *see* General Agreement on Tariffs and Trade

Gaza Strip 101
General Agreement on Tariffs and Trade (GATT) 148
General Assembly (GA) 32
  see also UN General Assembly
Geneva conference 1954 42
'Georgetown Declaration' 136–141, 143, 167–168
Germany
  Algiers Conference 130
  Belgrade Conference 54–55, 57–58, 59, 61
  Colombo Conference 160–161
  see also Berlin
Ghana
  Cairo Conference 71–72, 73–74, 79, 81, 84–85, 88
  First Conference at Belgrade 57, 59
  further boost to Belgrade 49, 50
  Preparatory Meeting at Belgrade 53
  see also Nkrumah, K.
Gizenga, A. 59
global non-alignment 14, 15–16
Global North
  Belgrade Conference 58
  Colombo Conference 183
  essence of NAM 15–16
global oil prices 163–164
global power dynamics 20–21
Global South
  Algiers Conference 129
  essence of NAM 15–16
Golan Heights 101, 162
Granada, Havana Conference 214–215
great power politics 16–17
Greece, Colombo Conference 161
guiding principles of non-alignment 28
Guinea
  aftermath of Belgrade Conference 62
  Algiers Conference 138–139
  Cairo Conference 71–72, 79, 81, 84–85, 88
  challenges of Belgrade Conference 54
  Colombo Conference 180
  First Conference at Belgrade 57–58
  further boost to Belgrade 49
  Havana Conference 219–220
  Lusaka Conference 113
  Preparatory Meeting at Belgrade 53

Guinea Bissau, Colombo Conference 173
Guyana
  Algiers Conference 136–137, 150
  Colombo Conference 161, 180
  Havana Conference 198, 199, 211
  Lusaka Conference 112

Hanoi
  and Colombo Conference 163
  and Havana Conference 195–197, 201
Hassan (King) 50
Havana
  Cairo Conference 85
  Colombo Conference 163, 170–171, 179
  Preparatory Meeting at Belgrade 53
Havana Conference 191–227
  Belgrade showdown 203–207
  collapsing détente 192–196
  Cuban–Yugoslav competition 196–199
  high noon 213–221
  NAM internal crisis 196–199
  splintered non-alignment 207–213
Heads of State or Government of Non-Aligned Countries (Declaration) 60–61
Helsinki Final Act 160–161
historical exclusiveness, NAM's Afro-Asian predecessors 44–45
historical meaning of non-alignment 13–37
  Cold War framework 20–23
  essence of NAM 14–18
  neutralism 18–19
  pillars of non-alignment 26–29
  regionalism and non-alignment 23–26
  Third Bloc non-alignment 29–32
Hodža, F. 204
human rights 160–161, 198–199
humanitarian initiatives 160–161
Hussein, S. 219

ideologies and bloc antagonisms 24
IFC see International Financial Corporation
IMF see International Monetary Fund
imperialism
  Cairo Conference 78–79, 91
  Havana Conference 203, 204–205, 220
  see also anti-colonialism/imperialism

Index 287

Independence to Colonial Countries and
 Peoples (Declaration) 48–49
India
 aftermath of Belgrade Conference 63
 Algiers Conference 133–136, 137–138,
  140, 142–143, 144–145, 150
 Belgrade Conference 62
 Cairo Conference 71–72, 74–76, 77,
  80–82, 84–85, 88–89, 90
 challenges of Belgrade Conference 54
 Colombo Conference 161, 164–165,
  171, 177, 180–181, 182
 delegates over Palestine 40–41
 essence of NAM 17
 First Conference at Belgrade 60–61
 further boost to Belgrade 50
 Havana Conference 200–201, 208–209,
  211, 213–214
 Lusaka Conference 103, 105, 106,
  108–109, 110, 113, 115, 118
 NAM's Afro-Asian predecessors
  40–41, 42–43
 non-aligned impetus of Belgrade
  Conference 45, 46
 as pillar of non-alignment 26–29
 regionalism and non-alignment 25–26
 see also New Delhi
Indian National Congress 27
Indian Ocean 184
 Colombo Conference 171
 see also East Africa
Indochina
 Algiers Conference 132–133, 137
 Colombo Conference 161–162, 163,
  179–180
 Lusaka Conference 118, 120
 NAM's Afro-Asian predecessors 42
 see also Vietnam War
Indonesia
 Algiers Conference 139–140, 141–142
 Cairo Conference 71–72, 74, 75,
  76–78, 79–80, 81, 82–83, 84, 86, 88,
  91–92
 challenges of Belgrade Conference 54
 Colombo Conference 180
 Havana Conference 220
 Lusaka Conference 109, 110, 113, 115,
  118
 NAM's Afro-Asian predecessors 42–43

non-aligned impetus of Belgrade
 Conference 46
PKI 91–92
Preparatory Meeting at Belgrade 52
see also Jakarta; Sukarno
inflation 163–164
initiative of the five 47–49
inter-bloc relations in Europe, Algiers
 Conference 129–130
International Economic Cooperation,
 Action Program 138–139
International Financial Corporation (IFC)
 176
International Monetary Fund (IMF) 176
 Algiers Conference 148
International Security and Disarmament
 (Statement) 138–139
International Strategy of Development
 (Declaration) 120
Internationalism, Afro-Asian, regionalism
 and non-alignment 24
interventionism 100–102, 192–193
Iran
 Belgrade Conference 46
 Cairo Conference 77–78
 further boost to Belgrade 50
 Havana Conference 214–215
Iraq
 Colombo Conference 177–178, 180
 Havana Conference 194, 211, 213, 214,
  220
 non-aligned impetus of Belgrade
  Conference 46
Islamabad, Colombo Conference 177
Islamic Conferences 176–177, 180–181, 195
Islamic integration/Havana Conference
 198–199
Israel 40–41
 Colombo Conference 162, 173–174, 178
 Havana Conference 193, 219–220
 Lusaka Conference 101–102, 118
 NAM's Afro-Asian predecessors 43
 Sinai I disengagement 162
 'The Three No's' 101–102

Jakarta
 Belgrade Conference 52
 Cairo Conference 75, 77, 79–80, 82–83
 Lusaka Conference 117

Jamaica
  Colombo Conference 180
  Lusaka Conference 112
Japan
  Algiers Conference 144
  Colombo Conference 176
  joining a bloc 14–15
Jordan, Lusaka Conference 101

Kabul 141–142, 145, 201–202
Kampuchea, Havana Conference 193, 195–196, 208–209, 214, 215
Kaul, T. N. 25–26
Kaunda, K.
  Algiers Conference 135, 137–138
  Havana Conference 219–221
  Lusaka Conference 117–118, 119
Keita, M. 61, 79, 81, 86
Kennan, G., Belgrade conference 52, 55, 61–62
Kennedy administration 55, 61, 63
Kenya, Cairo Conference 91
Khan, A. 78
Khartoum 101–102
Khmer Rouge regime 163
Khrushchev, N.
  aftermath of Belgrade Conference 62
  challenges of Belgrade Conference 55
  initiative of the five 47
  pillars of non-alignment 29
Kim, I. S. 209–210
Kissinger, H. A. 120–121
  Algiers Conference 131, 151
  Colombo Conference 162, 164, 168, 169, 172, 174–175
Korean War 41, 42
Kremlin
  Algiers Conference 131–132, 140–141
  Belgrade Conference 62
  challenges of Belgrade Conference 55
  Colombo Conference 163
  Havana Conference 192
Kuala Lumpur 137
Kuwait
  Algiers Conference 140, 150
  Colombo Conference 166, 172, 180

Lao, P. 163
Laos
  Algiers Conference 139–140
  Colombo Conference 162, 163
  see also Vietnam War
Latin America
  Cairo Conference 73, 74, 75, 78
  challenges of Belgrade Conference 55–56
  Colombo Conference 169, 171, 180
  Havana Conference 215, 220
  Lusaka Conference 110, 117–118
  regionalism and non-alignment 24
  see also individual Latin American countries...
least-developed countries 170–171, 183–184
  see also Third World
Lebanese Civil War 194
Lebanon
  Algiers Conference 136–137
  Havana Conference 193
Lenin, V. 29
Liberia
  Algiers Conference 150
  Colombo Conference 180
  further boost to Belgrade 49
Libya
  Algiers Conference 140, 144
  Colombo Conference 177–178, 180–181
  Lusaka Conference 114
Libya–Chad conflict, Havana Conference 193
Lima, and Colombo Conference 172, 174–175, 178, 179–180
Lima conference 171
Lima G77 meetings 136–137
Limited Nuclear Test Ban Treaty (LNTBT) 72, 88, 90
LNTBT *see* Limited Nuclear Test Ban Treaty
Lon, N. 115, 116–117, 140
Luanda, and Havana Conference 196–197
Lusaka
  Belgrade and NAM 112–114
  and Colombo Conference 167–168
Lusaka Conference 99–127
  Afro-Asianism 102–105
  aftermath 120–121
  and Algiers 143, 145–146, 148–149

coming out of paralysis 109–112
Détente/interventionism 100–102
new initiatives 106–109
preparations for 114–117

Madagascar, Havana Conference 214–215
Makarios (Archbishop) 161, 171
Malagasy Republic, Algiers Conference 138–139
Malawi, Algiers Conference 138–139
Malaysia
    Algiers Conference 139–140, 141–142, 150
    Cairo Conference 74
    Colombo Conference 179
    Lusaka Conference 112, 115
Maldives, Colombo Conference 178
Mali
    Algiers Conference 150
    Belgrade Conference 4, 9, 53, 57, 62
    Cairo Conference 71–72, 79, 81, 84–85, 91
    Colombo Conference 161
    see also Keita, M.
Malta
    Algiers Conference 145
    Colombo Conference 151
Maputo, S. S. 213, 214–215, 218–219
Marxism 161–162, 193
Mauritania, Havana Conference 193
Mauritius, Algiers Conference 138–139
Mengistu, H. M 194
Mexico
    Colombo Conference 180–181
    Preparatory Meeting at Belgrade 53
Middle East
    Algiers Conference 120, 131–132, 135
    Belgrade Conference 62–63
    Colombo Conference 164, 182
    Havana Conference 201, 205–206
    Lusaka Conference 101, 104, 107, 112–113, 118
    non-aligned impetus of Belgrade Conference 46
    pillars of non-alignment 28
Middle Eastern monarchies, Cairo Conference 74
Minić, M. 197
Mishra, K. P. 214

Missile Crisis in Cuba 71, 72
Mobuto, S. S. 193–194
moderate/progressive movements 198, 200–203, 206, 209–210, 216, 218
moderates and radicals 62–63
Morocco
    Algiers Conference 140, 142, 144
    Belgrade Conference 49, 57
    Cairo Conference 78–79
    Havana Conference 193, 205, 214–215
Moscow
    Algiers Conference 130–131, 140–141, 143, 146, 147, 151
    Cairo Conference 72–73
    challenges of Belgrade Conference 55
    Colombo Conference 161–162, 163, 177, 184
    Havana Conference 192–193, 194, 197, 206
    Lusaka Conference 104, 107, 109, 110–111
Moynihan, D. P. 175
Mozambique
    Havana Conference 208, 214
    Lusaka Conference 102
MPLA *see* People's Movement for the Liberation of Angola
mutual respect/sovereignty 29

Namibia
    Colombo Conference 171
    Lusaka Conference 102
NANAP *see* Non-Aligned News Agency Pool
Nasser, G. A.
    aftermath of Belgrade Conference 62, 63
    Cairo Conference 74, 75, 76–77, 78, 84, 86, 90
    challenges of Belgrade Conference 54
    essence of NAM 15
    First Conference at Belgrade 57–58, 59
    further boost to Belgrade 50, 51
    Havana Conference 203
    initiative of the five 47–48
    Lusaka Conference 101–108, 116, 117
    non-aligned impetus of Belgrade Conference 45, 46–47
    as pillar of non-alignment 27, 28

290 Index

regionalism and non-alignment 24
Third Bloc non-alignment 30
National Front for the Liberation of Angola (FNLA) 163
National Liberation (Declaration) 147
National Union for the Total Independence of Angola (UNITA) 163
Nationalist Chinese delegates over Tibet 40–41
national-liberation movements
 Algiers Conference 137, 147
 Belgrade Conference 56–57, 59
 Cairo Conference 73, 82
 Colombo Conference 179–180
 Havana Conference 216
 Organization of African Unity (OAU) 117–118
NATO (North Atlantic Treaty Organization) 144, 161
'natural alliance' thesis
 Algiers Conference 147
 Colombo Conference 180–181
 Havana Conference 196–197, 205, 207, 212, 220–222
 Lusaka Conference 101
Nehru, J.
 aftermath of Belgrade Conference 62, 63
 Cairo Conference 74–75, 76–77, 86
 challenges of Belgrade Conference 54, 55
 Cold War framework of non-alignment 20, 21
 essence of NAM 14–15
 First Conference at Belgrade 57, 60
 further boost to Belgrade 50, 51–52
 Havana Conference 203
 initiative of the five 47
 Lusaka Conference 116
 NAM's Afro-Asian predecessors 40, 42–44
 neutralism 19
 non-aligned impetus of Belgrade Conference 45–47
 as pillar of non-alignment 27, 28, 29
 Preparatory Meeting at Belgrade 53–54
 Third Bloc non-alignment 30–31
neo-colonialism

 Belgrade Conference 56–57
 Cairo Conference 84
 Havana Conference 204–205, 220
 see also colonialism
Nepal
 Algiers Conference 139–140, 150
 Cairo Conference 91
neutralism and non-alignment 18–19
neutralization of Indian Ocean 171, 184
New Delhi
 Algiers Conference 133–134, 135
 Belgrade Conference 62–63
 Cairo Conference 74–76, 79, 80–81
 Colombo Conference 165, 173–174, 177–178
 Havana Conference 199–200
 Lusaka Conference 103–104, 106, 108, 110, 115, 116–117
 NAM's Afro-Asian predecessors 40–41
 neutralism 19
 Preparatory Meeting at Belgrade 52, 53–54
New Economic Order (Colombo Conference) 159–190
'new emerging forces' 84, 86, 87–88
New International Economic Order (NIEO) 129, 148
 Algiers Conference 139
 Colombo Conference 181–182, 183–184
 Establishment Declaration 168
 Havana Conference 191, 192, 197, 202, 220
 OPEC oil embargo 163–167
 struggle for 170–177
'New International Information Order' (NIIO) 179
New York
 Algiers Conference 134–136, 149–150, 151
 further boost to Belgrade 49
 Havana Conference 201–202
 Lusaka Conference 116–117
Nicaragua
 Havana Conference 192–193, 214–215
 regionalism and non-alignment 25
NIEO see New International Economic Order
Niger, Colombo Conference 180

Nigeria
  Colombo Conference 180
  Havana Conference 208
  Lusaka Conference 115
Nixon administration
  Algiers Conference 131–132, 133
  Lusaka Conference 120–121
  see also Kissinger, H. A.
Nixon, R. 160, 162, 192–193
Nixon–Breshnev summits 1972 131
Nkrumah, K. 15
  Cairo Conference 73–74, 79
  challenges of Belgrade Conference 54
  First Conference at Belgrade 57–58, 59
  further boost to Belgrade 50
  initiative of the five 47, 48
  Lusaka Conference 103
  neutralism 19
Non-Aligned News Agency Pool (NANAP) 179
Non-Alignment movement 26–29
non-bloc policies/non-alignment 16, 18–19
'non-nuclear third force' 47
North Africa, Lusaka Conference 108, 114
North America
  Algiers Conference 151
  see also Canada; United States
North Korea
  Algiers Conference 138
  Colombo Conference 172, 180
  Havana Conference 209–210
North Vietnam
  Cairo Conference 91–92
  Colombo Conference 163
North–South confrontations and regionalism 24–25
North-South dialogue
  Colombo Conference 171–173, 176, 179–180
  Havana Conference 197
Nu, U.
  Belgrade Conference 57, 62
  NAM's Afro-Asian predecessors 43–44
  regionalism and non-alignment 24
nuclear alerts 162
Nuclear Test Ban Treaty (LNTBT) 72, 88, 90
nuclear testing

Belgrade Conference 61
First Conference at Belgrade 59
nuclear war
  Cold War framework of non-alignment 20–21
  Cuban Missile Crisis 71, 72
Nyerere, J. K.
  Havana Conference 217
  Lusaka Conference 115–116, 118, 119

OAPEC see Organization of Arab Petroleum Exporting Countries
OAU see Organization of African Unity
Ogaden province 193, 194
oil and gas industries 134
  Colombo Conference 163–167, 171–172
  Havana Conference 200, 220
  OPEC oil embargo 163–167
Organization of African Unity (OAU) 76, 82, 113
  Algiers Conference 145
  Cairo Conference 78
  Colombo Conference 173–174
  Havana Conference 193, 199
  Lusaka Conference 103
Organization of African Unity (OAU), Lusaka Conference 117–118
Organization of Arab Petroleum Exporting Countries (OAPEC) 195
organization of follow-up conferences 161
Organization of the Petroleum Exporting Countries (OPEC) 163–167, 172, 183, 220
Ostpolitik 130

Pahlavi, R. 107
Pakistan
  Algiers Conference 133–136, 142
  Cairo Conference 75, 76–78, 79, 82–83
  Colombo Conference 173–174, 180–181
  Havana Conference 198–199, 214–215
  Lusaka Conference 103–104, 108, 109
  NAM's Afro-Asian predecessors 42–43
Palestine
  Havana Conference 219–220
  Lusaka Conference 101, 118
  NAM's Afro-Asian predecessors 40–41

Palestine Liberation Organisation (PLO)
112, 116, 117, 137
  Algiers Conference 137
  Colombo Conference 169, 173, 180
  Havana Conference 193, 194, 208, 211, 214–215
pan-Africanism 73–74
Panama, Colombo Conference 173, 180
Panama Canal 151
pan-Arab policies 46
Panscheel (mutual respect/sovereignty) 29
Pant, A. B. 106
Papua New Guinea 201
Paris Summit 46, 47
Pavićević, M. 83
Peace, Appeal for 61
Peace, Independence, Development, Cooperation, and Democratisation of International Relations (Declaration) 120
Peace and International Cooperation, Program for 88
peaceful co-existing
  Cairo Conference 83–84, 86, 88
  Third Bloc non-alignment 32
Penh, P. 195
Peoli, I. M. 203, 205, 214–215
People's Movement for the Liberation of Angola (MPLA) 163
People's Republic of China (PRC) 120–121, 131, 136
People's Republic of Kampuchea (PRK) 195, 214
people-to-people humanitarian exchanges 160–161
Persian Gulf members of the cartel 163–164
Peru
  Algiers Conference 150
  Colombo Conference 172, 174, 180, 183
  Havana Conference 208, 211
petroleum *see* oil and gas industries
Philippines
  Colombo Conference 172, 173, 177, 178, 181
  Havana Conference 214–215
PKI *see* Communist Party of Indonesia
Pol Pot 195, 208–209, 211–214, 218–219

Poland, Warsaw Pact 109
polarization
  Cairo Conference 74
  see also radical non-alignment
policy of alignment 16–17
Polisario, Havana Conference 193
Political and Economic Committees
  Algiers Conference 144–145, 150
  Havana Conference 205, 214, 220
'Political and Economic Declarations' 147, 181
political liberation 13
Pope Paul VI 107
Popović, K. 52
Portugal, Colombo Conference 172, 173, 178, 181
poverty, Third Bloc non-alignment 32
PRC *see* People's Republic of China
Prebisch, R. 148
Preparatory Committee 134–135, 138–139, 141–142, 144
  see also Standing Committee
Preparatory Meeting for the Belgrade Conference 18, 52–54
privileged 'white' minorities 44–45
PRK *see* People's Republic of Kampuchea
pro-Chinese factions, Colombo Conference 163
'Program of Action' (Resolution 3202) 168
'Program for Peace and International Cooperation' 88
progressive movements 198, 200–203, 206, 209–210, 216, 218
propaganda 212
pro-Soviet regimes, Havana Conference 192–193
pro-Soviet tilt in Soviet-Yugoslav relationships 109
Provisional Government of Algeria 51
Provisional Revolutionary Government of South Vietnam (PRGSV)
  Algiers Conference 137, 138–140, 142, 144
  Colombo Conference 163
  Lusaka Conference 101, 115, 116, 117, 118
pro-Western African countries, Algiers Conference 139–140

pro-Western factions, Colombo
    Conference 163
pro-Western Middle Eastern monarchies,
    Cairo Conference 74
pro-Western sentiment
    Havana Conference 199
    Lusaka Conference 109
Puerto Rico 138

El Qaddafi, M. 146-147, 182-183
Qatar, Colombo Conference 180
Quadros, J. 55-56

racial closeness, regionalism and non-
    alignment 24-25
racial confrontations, regionalism and
    non-alignment 24-25
racial exclusiveness, NAM's Afro-Asian
    predecessors 44-45
racial polarization, Cairo Conference 74
racism/discrimination
    Algiers Conference 120
    Colombo Conference 176-177
    Lusaka Conference 102, 107-108
radical non-alignment
    anti-Western Casablanca groups/
        further boost to Belgrade 49
    Belgrade Conference 62-63
    Cairo Conference 83-84
    Cold War framework of non-
        alignment 22-23
    Colombo Conference 169
    Havana Conference 195
    Lusaka Conference 105
    regionalism and non-alignment 25
radical unilateralism, Colombo
    Conference 174-175
raw materials 171-172, 174
recession 163-164
refugees 133-134
regional exclusiveness, NAM's Afro-Asian
    predecessors 44-45
regionalism and non-alignment 23-26
'Resolution on the Strengthening of the
    Role of Non-Aligned Countries'
    119-120
Roa, R. 180-181
Rodriguez, C. R. 203, 204, 205, 213
'Rogers Plan' 133

'Rolling Thunder' bombing campaign 91
Romania, Colombo Conference 172, 173,
    178, 181
Russia *see* Moscow; USSR

El Sadat, A. 133, 182-183, 194-195
St Lucia 214-215
SALT I agreements 131
Salt II agreement 192
Samoa 201
Samrin, H. 195
Sastroamidjojo, A. 42-43
Saudi Arabia
    Cairo Conference 74
    Colombo Conference 180-181
    Havana Conference 198-199, 205,
        216
    Lusaka Conference 101, 115
SEATO *see* Southeast Asia treaty
    Organisation
Second World War 40, 49-50
Secretary General, Colombo Conference
    165
Security Council (SC) 32
Security and Peace (Declaration) 120
Selassie, H. 16, 107, 108, 110, 119,
    149-150
self-reliance principles 148-149
Senegal
    Algiers Conference 137, 142, 150
    Colombo Conference 171
    Havana Conference 219-220
    Lusaka Conference 113
Serbia *see* Belgrade
Seychelles, Colombo Conference 178
Shaba province 193-194
Shastri, L. B. 84, 103
Sihanouk, N.
    Algiers Conference 138, 141, 151
    Belgrade Conference 45, 57
    Cairo Conference 83
    Lusaka Conference 115, 116-117
    US coup against 115
Sinai I disengagement 162
Sinai Peninsula 101
Singapore
    Algiers Conference 139-140, 141
    Havana Conference 214-215
    Lusaka Conference 112, 115

294 Index

Sino-Ghanaian relations, Cairo
  Conference 79
Sino-Indian border 74–75
Sino-Indian relations, non-aligned
  impetus of Belgrade Conference
  46–47
Sino-Pakistan–US coalitions 133–134
Sino-Soviet border clashes 110–111
Sino-US dealings 131, 132–133, 134
Six-Day War 101
social and racial polarization
  Cairo Conference 74
  regionalism and non-alignment
  24–25
  see also racism
Social-Democrats, Algiers Conference 130
socialism
  Asian Socialist Conference 29–30
  Colombo Conference 163
  Havana Conference 196, 205, 220
  Lusaka Conference/Ujamaa 115–116
  Third World and 'troika' proposal 47
  see also Marxism
Socialist Republic of Vietnam 163
socioeconomic development 115–116, 118
Solidarity Fund
  Colombo Conference 166, 172
  Havana Conference 200
'Solidarity Fund for Economic and Social
  Development in Non-Aligned
  Countries' 174
solidarity and regionalism 24–25
Somalia
  Algiers Conference 150
  Cairo Conference 78
  Havana Conference 194, 205
South Africa
  Colombo Conference 163, 169, 171,
  182
  Havana Conference 193–194, 197
South Asia, Algiers Conference 135
South Korea, Lima conference 171
South Rhodesia
  Colombo Conference 171
  Lusaka Conference 102
South Vietnam
  Cairo Conference 91
  see also Provisional Revolutionary
  Government of South Vietnam

South West Africa People's Organisation
  (SWAPO) 204
South Yemen
  Havana Conference 192–193, 194
  Lusaka Conference 112
Southeast Asia
  Algiers Conference 135
  Lusaka Conference 100–101
  non-aligned impetus of Belgrade
  Conference 46
Southeast Asia treaty Organisation
  (SEATO) 43, 177
Southern Africa
  Algiers Conference 131–132
  Havana Conference 205–206, 207–208
  Lusaka Conference 102, 108
South-South cooperation/Colombo
  Conference 174
sovereignty 29
Soviet Asian republics, NAM's Afro-Asian
  predecessors 40
Soviet bloc
  Algiers Conference 147
  Colombo Conference 160–161, 184
  Havana Conference 192, 194, 196–197,
  206, 218
  Lusaka Conference 109, 117
Soviet conflict over Berlin, challenges of
  Belgrade Conference 54–55
Soviet direct or proxy interventionism,
  Havana Conference 192–193
Soviet nuclear testing, First Conference at
  Belgrade 59
Soviet policy and Cairo Conference 90
Soviet policy and Havana Conference 212
Soviet 'troika' proposal 47, 57–58
Soviet Union *see* USSR
'Sovietization' 197
Soviet-mediated peace talks, Lusaka
  Conference 103
Soviets on Berlin and nuclear testing,
  Belgrade conference 61
Soviet-Yugoslav relationships of the
  Lusaka Conference 109
Spain, Havana Conference 214–215
'Special Fund for Financing Buffer Stocks'
  183
'Special Fund for Financing Buffer Stocks
  of Raw Materials' 174

Sri Lanka 138
    Algiers Conference 137, 139–140, 142, 150
    Havana Conference 200–201, 208, 211–215, 217
    see also Colombo
Stalin, J. 42
Standing Committee 116–117, 134–135, 136–137, 141, 149–150
State Department 54–55, 176
'Statement on the Danger of War and the Appeal for Peace' 60–61
'Statement on the International Security and Disarmament' 138–139
Subandrio (Indonesian politician) 82–83
Sudan
    Belgrade Conference 54, 57
    Cairo Conference 78, 91
    Colombo Conference 180
    Lusaka Conference 114
Suez Canal 45–46, 101–102, 162
Sukarno (Indonesian president)
    aftermath of Belgrade Conference 62–63
    Cairo Conference 72, 74, 75, 76, 84–85, 86, 87, 88, 91–92
    challenges of Belgrade Conference 54
    First Conference at Belgrade 57–58, 59, 61
    further boost to Belgrade 50
    Havana Conference 203
    initiative of the five 47, 48
    neutralism 19
    non-aligned impetus of Belgrade Conference 46, 47
Supeni, Mrs (Chinese Ambassador talks) 75, 81
superpowers
    détente 100–102
    and the Third World/Cairo Conference 72–75
    see also Britain; China; Europe; India; United States; USSR
Surinam 201, 214–215
SWAPO *see* South West Africa People's Organisation
Sweden, Colombo Conference 161
Syria
    Algiers Conference 150

Colombo Conference 162, 166, 171, 178, 180
Havana Conference 193, 194, 211
Lusaka Conference 101, 116
NAM's Afro-Asian predecessors 42
non-aligned impetus of Belgrade Conference 46

Tanzania
    Algiers Conference 135, 143, 150
    Cairo Conference 91
    Colombo Conference 177, 180
    Havana Conference 202–203, 208, 219–220
    Lusaka Conference 102, 113, 114, 115
Tanzania–Uganda conflict, Havana Conference 193
Tashkent peace talks 103
Tepavac, M. 121
Thailand, Colombo Conference 177
third bloc non-alignment 29–32
    Cairo Conference 89
    Lusaka Conference 119–120
    non-aligned impetus of Belgrade Conference 46
Third World
    aftermath of Belgrade Conference 62
    Algiers Conference 129–157
    Cairo Conference 72–75, 83–84, 90, 723
    Colombo Conference 163, 164–165, 168, 176–177, 180–181, 182
    Havana Conference 193, 198–199
    initiative of the five 47
    Lusaka Conference 101, 103, 118
    non-aligned impetus of Belgrade Conference 45–46
    pillars of non-alignment 29
    regionalism and non-alignment 24, 26
'The Three No's' 101–102
Tibet
    NAM's Afro-Asian predecessors 40–41
    non-aligned impetus of Belgrade Conference 46
Tito, J. B.
    Algiers Conference 135, 149–150
    Belgrade Conference 62–63
    Cairo Conference 76–77, 81, 83, 84–85, 86, 87, 90

challenges of Belgrade Conference 54–55
Cold War framework of non-alignment 21
Colombo Conference 164–165, 182
First Conference at Belgrade 56–57, 59, 60
further boost to Belgrade 49, 50, 51
Havana Conference 198, 201–205, 211–216, 218, 220–222
initiative of the five 47–48
Lusaka Conference 103–105, 107, 109, 111, 116–120
neutralism 19
non-aligned impetus of Belgrade Conference 45–46
as pillar of non-alignment 27, 28, 29
Third Bloc non-alignment 30
Tobago, Lusaka Conference 117
Togo
　Algiers Conference 138–139
　further boost to Belgrade 49
Toure, S. 79, 81, 86
'troika' proposal 47, 57–58
Tunis, Havana Conference 195
Tunisia
　Cairo Conference 78–79, 84–85
　Colombo Conference 179
　further boost to Belgrade 49, 51
　Lusaka Conference 109, 113
　non-aligned impetus of Belgrade Conference 46–47
　see also Bourgiba, H.
Turkey, Colombo Conference 161

U2 incident 47
UAE, Algiers Conference 138–139
UAR see United Arab Republic
Uganda
　Cairo Conference 91
　Lusaka Conference 114
'Ujamaa' socialism 115–116
UN General Assembly (UNGA)
　Algiers Conference 134, 135, 136, 139, 145–151
　Belgrade Conference 49, 63
　Cairo Conference 77, 86, 89
　Colombo Conference 166, 167–172, 174–175, 176–177, 182

further boost to Belgrade 50
Havana Conference 204, 218–219
initiative of the five 48–49
Lusaka Conference 106, 107–108, 114, 116–117, 120
Resolution 3212 161
UN General Secretaries 47
unemployment 163–164
unilateralism, Colombo Conference 160–163, 166–167, 174–175
UNITA see National Union for the Total Independence of Angola
United Arab Republic (UAR)
　aftermath of Belgrade Conference 62, 63
　Algiers Conference 132
　Cairo Conference 71–72, 74–75, 77, 79–85, 88–90
　challenges of Belgrade Conference 54
　further boost to Belgrade 49
　initiative of the five 47–48
　Lusaka Conference 101–106, 108–109, 110, 111, 114, 117
　non-aligned impetus of Belgrade Conference 46
　Preparatory Meeting for Belgrade Conference 52–53
United Nations Conference on Trade and Development (UNCTAD) 63
　aftermath of Belgrade Conference 63
　Algiers Conference 129, 135, 136–137, 143, 148
　Cairo Conference 80, 86
　Colombo Conference 183
　Lusaka Conference 106, 107–108
United Nations Security Council (UNSC) 106, 120, 131, 136, 162
United Nations (UN)
　18 Nations Disarmament Committee 1962 63
　aftermath of Belgrade Conference 63
　Algiers Conference 120, 131, 135, 138–141, 146–147, 151
　Cairo Conference 86, 87–88, 91
　Charter 44
　Colombo Conference 161, 165–167, 168, 171, 172, 176, 182
　First Conference at Belgrade 57–58, 59
　further boost to Belgrade 49–50

Havana Conference 208–209
initiative of the five 47–48
Lusaka Conference 100, 101, 107–108, 111–121
NAM's Afro-Asian predecessors 40, 41, 42–43
non-aligned impetus of Belgrade Conference 45–46
Third Bloc non-alignment 30, 32
United States
aftermath of Belgrade Conference 61–62, 63
Algiers Conference 131, 132–133, 138, 144–146, 147, 151
Bay of Pigs 51
Cairo Conference 73–74, 75, 83–84, 91–92
Camp David Accords 195, 208–209, 211
challenges of Belgrade Conference 54–56
Colombo Conference 159–166, 172–176, 178, 179
Congress 61, 160, 192
coup against Sihanouk 115
Cuban independence 197–198
Cuban Missile Crisis 71, 72
First Conference at Belgrade 59, 61
further boost to Belgrade 51
'Georgetown Declaration' 136–141, 143, 167–168
Havana Conference 193–194, 197–198, 203, 213, 214–215, 216
initiative of the five 47
Kennedy administration 55, 61, 63
Lusaka Conference 100–101, 102, 104, 105, 106, 115
NAM's Afro-Asian predecessors 43, 44
Preparatory Meeting at Belgrade 52
SEATO 43, 177
U2 incident 47
US-Soviet rapprochement/ reconciliation 132–133, 138
see also New York; Washington
UNSC see United Nations Security Council
uranium 171–172
USSR
aftermath of Belgrade Conference 61–62

Algiers Conference 130–131, 133–134, 140–141, 147
Cairo Conference 72–73, 90
challenges of Belgrade Conference 55–56
Colombo Conference 160–163, 179, 184
Cuban Missile Crisis 71, 72
Havana Conference 192–194, 195–196, 197–198, 200, 202–203, 204–205, 207–208, 215–216
Lusaka Conference 100–101, 103–104, 105, 107, 109, 110–112
NAM's Afro-Asian predecessors 42–43
non-aligned impetus of Belgrade Conference 46
Preparatory Meeting at Belgrade 52
'troika' proposal 47, 57–58
U2 incident 47
US-Soviet rapprochement/ reconciliation 132–133, 138
see also Moscow

Vienna, Carter-Brezhnev summit 192
Vientiane, Colombo Conference 163
Vietnam
Algiers Conference 130
Cairo Conference 91–92
Colombo Conference 163, 173, 177, 180–181
Havana Conference 193, 195–196, 201–202, 208, 211, 214–215
Lusaka Conference 105
NAM's Afro-Asian predecessors 43
regionalism and non-alignment 25
see also Hanoi; Provisional Revolutionary Government of South Vietnam
Vietnam War
Algiers Conference 131, 132, 133
Cairo Conference 91
Lusaka Conference 100–101, 102, 104
Vrhovec, J. 204, 214–215

War of Attrition 1969 101–102
Warsaw Pact 109
Washington
aftermath of Belgrade Conference 63
Algiers Conference 130, 143, 147, 151

Cairo Conference 72
Colombo Conference 163, 170, 172
'Georgetown Declaration' 136–141, 143, 167–168
Havana Conference 198–199
Lusaka Conference 104
Preparatory Meeting at Belgrade 52
Watergate 163
West Africa
  Cairo Conference 79
  Havana Conference 214–215
  Lusaka Conference 102, 108
West Bank 101
West German-Soviet Treaty 1970 130
West Germany
  Algiers Conference 130
  Belgrade Conference 54–55, 59
  Colombo Conference 160–161
West Iran, further boost to Belgrade 50
Western bloc
  NAM's Afro-Asian predecessors 42–43
  non-aligned impetus of Belgrade Conference 46
Western Europe
  Algiers Conference 144
  Colombo Conference 164, 176
White House 120–121
  Algiers Conference 151
  Colombo Conference 163, 169
  see also Washington
World Bank 148

Yemen
  Havana Conference 192–193, 194
  Lusaka Conference 112, 113
Yom Kippur War 162, 163–164
Yugoslavia
  aftermath of Belgrade Conference 61–62, 63
  Algiers Conference 134, 135, 137–146, 150, 151

Cairo Conference 71–91
challenges of Belgrade Conference 54–56
Cold War framework 21
Colombo Conference 161, 164–165, 171–174, 177–183
essence of NAM 17
First Conference at Belgrade 59, 60–61
further boost to Belgrade 49, 50
Havana Conference 200–221
initiative of the five 47–48
Lusaka Conference 103–118, 121
NAM's Afro-Asian predecessors 41, 42
non-aligned impetus of Belgrade Conference 45–46
as pillar of non-alignment 26–29
Preparatory Meeting at Belgrade 52, 53–54
Third Bloc non-alignment 30
see also Tito, J. B.

Zaire
  Algiers Conference 150
  Colombo Conference 171, 180
  Havana Conference 205
Zambia
  Algiers Conference 134–135, 137–138, 142, 143
  Colombo Conference 180
  Havana Conference 208, 217, 219–220
  see also Lusaka Conference
Zhou, E. 77, 78–80, 81, 82–83
Zimbabwe
  Colombo Conference 171
  Havana Conference 214–215
  Lusaka Conference 102
Zionism
  Colombo Conference 173–174, 176–177
  pillars of non-alignment 28

www.ingramcontent.com/pod-product-compliance
Lightning Source LLC
Chambersburg PA
CBHW052151300426
44115CB00011B/1620